POWER DOS!

How to Run Your PC Like a Master

ALFRED GLOSSBRENNER

RANDOM HOUSE
ELECTRONIC PUBLISHING

New York

Power DOS!

Published in the United States by Random House, Inc., New York, and simultaneously in Canada by Random House of Canada, Limited.

Manufactured in the United States of America.

Revised Edition

   ISBN 0-679-73924-6

New York   Toronto   London   Sydney   Auckland

CONTENTS

INTRODUCTION

ON BECOMING A POWER USER

———————————————

Have you ever wanted to sit down at your computer and feel at home? Have you ever wanted to feel as comfortable at your PC as you do standing at your basement workbench or kitchen counter—or potter's wheel, painter's easel, or any place else where you not only know your tools but know how to use them with skill and with confidence?

If so, then you're ready to become a *power user!* I'm not kidding. You don't have to spend hours bathed in the glow of a cathode ray tube. You don't have to turn your spouse into a computer widow or widower. You don't even have to be a spreadsheet jockey, WordPerfect wizard, or a master of DEBUG and batch files. And you certainly don't have to think of yourself as a "DOS dummy" or in need of some magic or "voodoo."

All you need is the simple conviction that your computer should operate the way *you* want it to and not the other way around. Personal computers should be *personal.* Your machine should fit you like a pair of hand-made shoes. That's what personal computing in the IBM-compatible/MS-DOS world is all about. That's the essence of being a power user. And the heck of it is, it's easy! So easy that, if most computer users were aware of the information contained in this book, sales of Microsoft Windows, that much vaunted, resource-gobbling, "easy" PC interface would fall through the floor.

In point of fact, only three things are needed to attain power userdom:

1. The right equipment
2. The right understanding of PC basics
3. The right information

The Right Equipment

By the "right equipment," I mean a machine that isn't hobbled by an out-of-date design or doesn't gasp when confronted with modern software. The PC, the XT, and the AT were fine in their day, and the ingenuity the industry has shown in producing add-on boards and other products to keep them going is remarkable. But one can't help thinking of the 1950s era Chevys, Fords, and Chryslers that rumble through the streets in Castro's Havana. They still run, thanks to innumerable patches and repairs, but they would have been melted down for scrap decades ago if there had been any other alternative.

Computer users today, in contrast, have lots of alternatives, all of them affordable. If you've got a PC, XT, or AT, and it's doing the job you want, by all means hold onto it. Run it until it drops—but don't put another dime into it. And, unless you're extremely patient and willing to put up with a lot of aggravation, do not make a machine of that era the focus of your optimization efforts.

Instead, turn your sights on machines built around some version of the Intel 386, 486, or Pentium ("586") processor. Systems based on these CPU chips are incredibly cheap, and they're getting cheaper every day. You can always use your vintage machine as a backup or secondary PC. Or, if your current system is in good shape, you can simply replace its motherboard and continue to use all the other components.

For example, at this writing, you can get a motherboard with an Intel 386 chip operating at 33 megahertz for $150, and you can equip it with memory at a cost of $40 per megabyte. If you don't want to install the board yourself, a technician at your local computer store will do the job for about $35. That means you can turn your current machine into a 386DX 33-MHz computer, equipped with 4 megabytes of RAM, for about $345—or less, if prices continue to fall!

This is crucial, because the computer world made a quantum leap forward with the 386. Succeeding chips have followed its lead. The leap is so great in terms of speed and power and the ease with which 386 and better chips handle memory, that it is simply pointless to spend time and money fooling around with 286-based equipment like AT-level machines or the even less capable XT- and PC-level computers still on the market.

Therefore, the right equipment includes a 386-based or better computer. It also includes at least a megabyte, and preferably at least 4 megabytes, of memory. It includes a VGA or Super VGA video card and monitor, at least a 100-megabyte hard drive, and one 5.25-inch and one 3.5-inch floppy drive, both high-density. Finally, it includes at least DOS 5 or DOS 6 and, optionally, Windows 3.1 and a mouse.

As it happens, these criteria accurately describe today's entry-level systems—the ones you see advertised in *PC Magazine* and *Computer Shopper* for around $1,400, complete. Such packages typically include 24-hour toll-free technical support, a one-year parts and labor warranty, and free on-site service. Add $200 for a 24-pin dot-matrix printer, and the cost of admission to the wonderful world of personal computing is about $1,600. Today. Tomorrow, it is almost guaranteed to be less. Either that, or you will be able to get an even more powerful system for the same $1,600.

From the perspective of someone who bought a stripped-down, October 1981, IBM Personal Computer and paid thousands for the privilege, the price/value relationship in the industry today is mind-boggling. Certainly $1,600 is not a sum to be sneezed at. But with all kindness, I will tell you that if you cannot see your way clear to invest at least $1,600 in the equipment that will be central to your business, to your profession, and possibly to your life, then you don't belong in this game. Besides, most mail-order firms take MasterCard and Visa.

Understanding PC Basics

The point so many people consistently miss about personal computing is where the real cost lies. The most expensive thing about computing is not the hardware. Nor is it the software you run to convert your hardware from an expensive dust collector into something useful. The most expensive thing about personal computing is your *time.*

Regardless of your job or profession, regardless of whether you are self-employed or between jobs, your time has value. The more of it you spend wrestling with a computer or a program, trying to get it to do what you want it to do—or even just what it is *supposed* to do—the more expensive that machine becomes. (Not for nothing have some economists reported that the billions invested in computer hardware and software over the years has had virtually *no impact* on white-collar productivity.)

The way to break this cycle is to start with good equipment. It doesn't have to be the hottest, most powerful machine on the market. But it does have to be at least a 386, as discussed above. Next, you've got to invest your time in the things that really matter. You've got to know the basics.

It is far better in the long run to learn a few simple skills—like how to copy a file or format a floppy disk—than it is to start by trying to master Lotus, Excel, or WordPerfect. Focusing on applications first is like putting the U-Haul trailer before the car. For example, I know any number of people who, after a long struggle, have become quite competent at Word-Perfect. But if something goes wrong with the AUTOEXEC.BAT file their computer dealer created to automatically put them into the program each time they turn on the machine, they are absolutely helpless.

Someone who has taken the time to learn just the basics of hard disk directories and DOS files, in contrast, can more easily learn *any* program. Such a person will not have to call Customer Support when the C> prompt appears unexpectedly on the computer screen. So invest your time wisely by starting from the ground up instead of from the top down. And don't be fooled into thinking that using Microsoft's Windows lets you off the hook. In many instances, Windows merely adds another layer of complexity with no compensating benefits in ease of use. If you plan to run Windows, you've got to know not only Windows itself, but DOS as well, since Windows 3.x rides *on top* of DOS.

The secret to confidently and comfortably running a personal computer is to step back to a point where you can glimpse the larger picture. Neither WordPerfect nor Lotus nor dBASE nor Windows nor any other program you can name exists independently. They all plug into the same underlying matrix that controls and defines every IBM-compatible system. If you understand the matrix, you automatically understand the basics of every program in the PC world.

The matrix, for lack of a more comprehensive term, is DOS—the *Disk Operating System* software produced by Microsoft and cloned by Digital Research/Novell as DR DOS. Everything eventually plugs into DOS. Even Windows 3.1, the current version of Microsoft's heavily promoted operating environment, rides on top of DOS. (Windows NT may be available as you read this.)

For better or for worse—and OS/2 and Windows NT notwithstanding—DOS defines the computers some 100 million of us use today. It thus simply makes good, common sense to spend some time learning how DOS does things and how to do things with DOS.

This is much easier than you might imagine. You do *not* have to learn how to use DEBUG or memorize interminable lines of obscure DOS commands and switches. You do *not* have to master the power of batch files. All you need are the basics. And the basics are summarized in Part 2 of this book, in the section called *Daily DOS: The Ten Essential DOS Commands.*

The Right Information

The third essential for anyone who would become a power user is the right information. I can't give you the hardware; I can only point you in the right direction. Nor do I have space to completely cover basic PC operations. For that, you'll have to see the Random House/Glossbrenner DOS books, *DOS 5* and *DOS 6.* But I can definitely give you the right information, that all-important third ingredient. Indeed, that's what *Power DOS!* is all about.

Gaseous by Design

Let me begin by telling you a secret. Computer magazines, like most magazines, make their money by selling advertising. The subscription fees you and I pay are only a small part of the equation. This is not likely to come as news to anyone who has struggled with the innumerable reader response cards, the multipage fold-outs, and the special heavy-stock ads that make most computer magazines all but unreadable today. What may surprise you is that this wad of slick, four-color paper is delivered to you at a discount nearly as hefty as the magazines themselves, courtesy of the U.S. Postal Service.

To qualify for that discount, the magazines must maintain a certain ratio of advertising to *editorial* (the trade term for articles, features, letters to the editor, and any other non-advertising material). As the number and thickness of computer magazines demonstrates, the demand for advertising space is prodigious. As a consequence, there is a corresponding demand for editorial matter to maintain the ratio the Post Office requires.

In the writing business there's an old saw that goes, "We don't want it good, we want it Tuesday." A cynic might conclude that the 1990s computer magazine version would read, "We don't want it good, we want 3,000 words." In fairness, that's much too critical of the vast majority of today's computer magazines, most of which publish excellent work. But it does contain a grain of truth.

My point is simply that there is a built-in, systemic demand for editorial matter, any editorial matter. And, while there are definitely nuggets to be found within this torrent of words, there is also a lot of dross. I can't tell you how many times I've read an article in a leading magazine that went on for pages as it solemnly described the most backward, convoluted, and complex way of performing a simple DOS task.

The authors of such articles revel in lengthy DOS commands. They love loading up the command line with slashes and backslashes, switches, and other obscure symbols. At the drop of a disk, they'll present some impenetrable block of characters you are supposed to key in using DEBUG. And should they discover some obscure quirk to a DOS command that you might use once in your lifetime, provided the outside temperature was 68 degrees and the moon was at just the right elevation in the night sky, well, it's "Katie, bar the door!"—and two more pages of gaseous prose.

All of which causes one to reply, "C'mon guys, get real!" I'm sorry, but knowing what I do about readily available DOS utility programs that quickly and easily do the same things so laboriously described in such articles, I feel like Indiana Jones. Pistol on his hip, Indy confronts a sword-wielding fanatic in *Raiders of the Lost Ark*. There's a brief look of puzzlement and annoyance, then *Bang!*, next case.

The reason all of these articles and columns can be churned out each month is that personal computers and DOS are very, very flexible. Most of the time, there are many different ways to accomplish the same thing. Not all approaches are necessarily equally good or equally cost-effective in terms of your time and effort. But all are equally valid.

The problem is that computer users are not always aware of this fact. A reputable magazine isn't going to knowingly present bad information. If an article says that a certain technique can be used to accomplish a particular task, you can be pretty sure it will work on your system. But you cannot depend on most magazines to tell you the *best* way to perform a task.

A Quick Example

Let me illustrate this with a simple example. Imagine you have a file on your disk called MAIL.TXT. Imagine that you want to look at the file on your screen. A magazine might advise you to "pipe the file through the DOS MORE filter" by entering a command like `type mail.txt¦more`. Then it might go on about how you could also use the command `more < mail.txt`.

Both commands do indeed work. Both will display the contents of MAIL.TXT one screen at a time. When you are finished reading the first screen, you can hit a key to make the next screen appear, and so on to the end of the file.

What the magazine won't say is that, while you might use this technique in a pinch, it is far too cumbersome and inflexible to use on a regular basis. The *best* way to look at a file is to get a copy of Vernon Buerg's shareware program, LIST.COM, which is readily available from hundreds of sources. Put it into a directory called UTILS or LIST, and add that directory to your path. Then key in `list mail.txt`. You will be able to scroll or page up and down the file, zip from top to bottom, mark and clip out sections of text, and do lots of other useful things—including *searching* the file for specified words or phrases—all with a few intuitive keystrokes.

That's what I mean by "the right information." Vernon Buerg produced the first version of LIST.COM in 1983. (The current version is 7.x.) It is the file lister of choice among power users and has been for years. Buerg's LIST.COM is quite simply the last word in file display programs. But the only time you will find it mentioned is in articles about shareware. (In its January, 1992 issue, *PC Sources* called it "Perhaps the single most indispensable computer utility ever written.") Rarely, if ever, will you find it cited in a tips column or in articles about how to use your computer.

A Philosophy of Computing

Personal computing is so incredibly *easy*—once you know what to do. Once you have the right information. The right information is truly the essence of *Power DOS!*. Within these pages you will find hundreds of tips, tricks, and techniques for making your system do what you want it to do.

But these are not just any techniques. They are, in my opinion, the *best* techniques—tested, developed, and hammered into shape through more than a decade of using personal computers and augmented by an intimate familiarity with public domain and shareware software.

You can't spend nearly every day, year after year, using and interacting with a PC—running programs, working with DOS, optimizing peripherals, and exploring possibilities—without developing a set of strong convictions about the easiest way to do things. What emerges, quite unbidden, is really a philosophy of computing. It is a philosophy based on four major points:

1. Keep it simple.
2. Take the easy way out.
3. Use good equipment.
4. Be ruthless in making the PC conform to your wishes.

Simplicity, Simplicity, Simplicity

The computer industry revels in complexity. In so many instances what appears to matter most is not the task but the technology. Ask a hardware designer to create a machine for swatting flies, and she's likely to come up with a self-propelled unit the size of a vacuum cleaner, equipped with infrared sensors and a fully articulated arm with a fly swatter for a hand. Should a software engineer get hold of this miracle of rare device, he'd probably recommend replacing the swatter with a paint brush and reprogramming the thing to do touch-up painting.

I have no doubt that the hardware would be clever, and that the code (computer programming) would be elegant. Nor have I any doubt that the machine would be expensive—and totally unnecessary. A sprightly middle-aged man with a rolled up newspaper or a paint brush would perform both tasks faster, more efficiently, and at infinitely less expense.

The lesson is this: Just because something *can* be done doesn't necessarily mean that it *should* be done.

In the early days of personal computing, for example, salesmen, trade show booth representatives, and magazines used to seriously suggest that keeping track of your recipes would be a really good reason to invest several thousand dollars in a computer. A computer can indeed do that job and do it quite well. But unless you're a professional chef or run a large catering business, the time and effort required to key in all of your recipes is hardly worthwhile. You will be much better off with the traditional box of 4-by-6 file cards. That's what I mean by keeping it simple.

Unnecessary complexity and the inappropriate, inefficient use of technology crops up again and again in personal computing, in both hardware and software. You can't blame the hardware and software companies for trying. Indeed, you can stand up and cheer for their innovative thinking. But you don't have to blindly follow their suggestions.

The simpler you keep things, the less you will have to remember and the easier your PC will be to use. Indeed, it is not a bad goal to strive to use as *few* commands as possible to make the PC do what you want it to do. It is far better to thoroughly master a few really good programs and utilities than it is to develop a passing acquaintance with scores of lesser programs.

Taking the Easy Way Out

In the best of all possible worlds, we would all be able to instantly diagnose any problem that occurs when working with our hardware or software. We would enter a few well-chosen commands to fix the problem and continue on our way. After all, there's at least one thing you can count on: There is always a reason for a problem.

Your printer doesn't suddenly begin printing strange characters because it doesn't approve of the font you've selected. Your modem doesn't refuse to dial because it thinks you should have been more polite in your last electronic mail message. And your pop-up spelling checker doesn't blank your screen because it's miffed that you haven't been spending more time with it lately. There is always a real, legitimate reason for a hardware or software malfunction.

But most of the time, the cause of a problem is not worth tracking down. Most of the time it is best to take the easy way out. Turn off the printer or the modem to clear its memory. Reboot your system to clear out whatever gremlins have crept in to screw up your TSRs. Only a recurring problem is worth worrying about.

The same thing applies to programming. Programming, whether in DOS's batch language, BASIC, or some other language, can be very satisfying. It is instructive. It is great mental discipline. And it is very time-consuming. It has all the qualifications, in short, of an excellent hobby. Producing a great program, however, requires more time, study, and raw talent than most of us have. That's why it is best to leave the real programming to those who have been blessed with such gifts.

Public domain and shareware libraries are filled with their work. Much of it is free or offered with a request for a small registration fee. Leave the code-writing to others and concentrate instead on locating and learning to use the tools and applications they have created. That's taking the easy way out.

Using Good Equipment

As any professional will tell you, one of the secrets of success is using quality tools with plenty of power. You can cut a 2 by 4 with a hand saw or a power saw. If you only need to perform that task a few times a year, the hand saw is probably your best choice, even though it requires more time and effort. But if you cut 2 by 4s several times a month, you'd be stupid not to invest in an electric saw. And not some inexpensive, underpowered sabre or scroller saw. You want the real thing—a 2.5-horsepower circular saw with a 7.25-inch blade and a plastic housing so your arm doesn't get tired after the first few cuts.

The same is true in computing. If you do a lot of downloading from bulletin boards and online systems, you owe it to yourself and to your family to get a 9,600-bps (or 14.4-Kbps) modem instead of sticking with the 2,400-bps units that are the current industry standard. They're cheap, but a download takes four times longer with a 2,400-bps modem than with a 9,600-bps model.

If you find you are doing more and more desktop publishing or using graphics-intensive paint programs, it makes no sense to put up with the delays caused by an AT-class 286 computer or an 8-bit video card. That's like cutting a 2 by 4 with a cheese saw. It'll get the job done, eventually, but you'll be exhausted by the effort. At the very least, you need a 16-bit video card and a fast 386 or 486 machine with plenty of RAM that your desktop publishing program can use to temporarily store its images.

Dozens of other examples come readily to mind, examples of people putting up with inadequate, underpowered, cranky hardware just to save a few bucks. I've been guilty of it myself. So I know that doing it just makes a PC harder, or at least less satisfying, to use. As I have said, the real cost of computing is your *time*.

Under no circumstances should you feel that you've got to have the latest, leading-edge equipment. In fact, I advise against buying the absolute latest technology. Let some other customer pay for the honor of beta-testing and debugging a company's hardware or software product. Not for nothing do pundits often refer to the leading edge of the technology curve as the "bleeding edge." Wait for the revisions, corrections, and modifications to appear before you consider buying.

But by the same token, it is simply stupid to allow yourself to be hobbled by old, inadequate technology. If you're satisfied with the way your current system is performing, hold onto it. Don't touch a thing. But if you find yourself growing impatient at how long your database program takes to sort your customer records or at the delays involved in repainting a graphics or desktop publishing screen—if you like Windows 3.1 but find its sluggishness on your system intolerable—for heaven's sake *do* something.

It may be a larger, faster hard disk drive; it may be a 16-bit video card; additional RAM might help; possibly a laser printer or font cartridges to expand the range of typestyles you can use; a new motherboard with a faster, more powerful processor (or simply a new processor) may be the solution.

Each of us has different needs, so there can be no definitive answer. The point is to avoid falling into a rut where you somehow convince yourself that you must accept the hardware you have and work within its bounds. If the hardware you have is causing intolerable delays, if it is making it more difficult or less pleasurable to do what you want with your machine, *replace* or *upgrade* it.

Don't be misled by false economies. You may tell yourself that you can't afford to replace or upgrade your system. But, if your time has value, the truth may be that you can't afford *not* to do so. That's what I mean when I say "Use good equipment." You don't want to spend all of your effort and energy sawing the boards. You want to concentrate on building the house. So get a power saw that can perform the boring, mundane tasks with ease.

Being Ruthless in Imposing Your Wishes

I well remember my first computer and the complete bewilderment I felt as I gazed at the buff-colored equipment, the cables, and the styrofoam packing material littering the living room floor. I had used a 1970s-era word processor, with 8-inch floppy disks, for years. But I would have believed anything anyone told me about the proper way to use my new IBM/PC.

What I didn't know then—and what most new PC users today do not know—is that an IBM-compatible or "DOS machine" is infinitely adaptable. With the right software and the right information, you can easily mold, customize, and otherwise modify things to suit your own personal preferences. This is a luxury our Macintosh-using friends do not have. It is the tradeoff they have made for the Mac's so-called "ease of use." In the Macintosh world, to a very large extent, you do things Apple's way or you do not do them.

I would be the last to say that this is the wrong approach. Indeed, there is no "right" and "wrong" way to most things in personal computing. There is simply what works and what doesn't. For about ten percent of the computing world, the Macintosh approach works and works very well. For better or for worse, those of us in the other 90 percent of the computing world are confronted with a machine that can be shaped into anything we want.

We have the freedom. But freedom can be both a blessing and a curse. If we don't like the default way of doing things, most of the time, we can change things. Yet we must also take responsibility and make decisions.

Fortunately, the changes are often easy to make and the burden is light. All that is required is the knowledge that change is possible, the will to make the changes, and the right information. Let me offer a quick example.

Some years ago I wanted to edit a file that was larger than my word processing software could handle. It was a frustrating roadblock, but I wasn't about to give up. I knew enough about computing to be convinced that somewhere there had to be a utility program designed to cut a large text file into smaller pieces. It took me all of five minutes to find such a program on CompuServe, download it to my machine, and set the program to work cutting the big text file down to size. (The program was called CHOP .EXE.) A minute or two later, I was happily editing one of the three subfiles the program had created from my over-large text file.

Not all solutions are that easy. At other times I have spent hours searching for an answer and come up empty. Perhaps it all evens out. But that isn't really the issue. The point is that much of the time, with a DOS machine, you *can* have things the way you want them. You don't have to put up with something you don't like. You can take control!

It is this realization that is fundamental to becoming a power user. It is this goal that is worth pursuing—ruthlessly, if you have to. The benefits are legion.

Why Become a Power User?

The information presented in this book has been selected on the basis of the philosophy of computing outlined above. It represents a distillation of the best tips, tricks, and techniques for using a personal computer the way it ought to be used. If you incorporate this information, seasoned with your own experience and adapted to your own situation, into your own style of using a machine, you will indeed become a power user. But it is perfectly legitimate at this point to ask why one should bother.

Maybe you shouldn't. If you sit down at your machine, turn it on, and a few moments later find yourself automatically placed in Lotus or WordPerfect or dBASE with no idea how you got there—and if this fact does not *bother* you—then you should put this book back on the shelf for someone else to find.

Millions of people use their computers this way. They work with one and only one program all day. When quitting time arrives, they save their work to disk, shut off the machine, and go home. They know nothing about DOS, and when an apparent problem occurs, they call the company's micro manager, information center, or other in-house computer support group and wait for help to arrive.

There is nothing inherently wrong with this. If the company wanted a computer whiz, they should have said so in their job description, right? Yet who can deny that if you had a little more knowledge and understanding, you wouldn't find your work schedule disrupted as you wait a half an hour or more for some computer support person to come straighten things out? You'd get more done, and you wouldn't feel so helpless when things don't go according to plan.

If you're a small-business owner, you can't afford the luxury of using one computer for each program you want to run. Your computer is an asset, and you've got to make it pay. That means running several programs—a spreadsheet to crunch the numbers, a word processor to prepare memos and reports, a communications package to send and receive electronic mail, and so on. It's a tall order, even if you are running Windows or a menuing program to simplify things a bit.

But you, too, can benefit from taking control and becoming a power user. Imagine that you're working late, finishing up a sales presentation for a big meeting tomorrow morning. You complete the writing and exit the program. Then you change your mind and decide that you'd really like a printout to take home. So you reload your word processor and tell it to bring in the file. But the program reports that it cannot find the file you have requested.

Your stomach does a flip-flop and beads of sweat appear on your brow. Could you have supplied an incorrect filename? You try a variant. Still no joy. Where the heck is the thing? It has to be there somewhere—you are certain you saved it to disk.

A power user would be irritated but not overly concerned. The file is on the disk someplace, and we know at least part of its name. The thing to do is to exit the word processing program and return to DOS. Then run a public domain utility called WHEREIS with a command like `whereis report.*`. The program will search the disk and give you the location of every filename starting with "REPORT."

DOS does not include a program like this. But there are scores of public domain utilities of this sort, most of which are called "WHEREIS." A magazine would probably tell you to use a variant of the DOS TREE command, redirect its output to a disk file, and then search that file with your word processor. Both techniques produce the desired results, but using a WHEREIS-style program is much faster. Besides, such programs are typically free.

Power User Benefits

There are, then, at least three benefits to becoming a power user. The first is increased productivity with your current software. Once you've resolved to take control, you will be able to solve many problems on your own, without waiting for outside assistance. Second, you will be able to use your PC for more things and apply its power to more tasks. If you are currently using just a word processing program, for example, you will find it relatively easy to branch out into database or communications or spreadsheet software. Again, once you've taken control, you will be able to more fully tap the power of the PC. You will get much more of what you have paid for.

Finally, there is the most important benefit of all. There is no satisfaction to compare with feeling that you are finally in complete control of the beast, instead of the other way around. As a power user, you can make the computer do your bidding. The confidence this feeling breeds is immeasurable. You will feel like you're flying—soaring—instead of barely keeping your head above water.

As with the game of chess, you can never hope to master all the intricacies of personal computing. But you can reach the point where you enjoy playing and love to learn new moves. This book is designed to help you quickly reach that level with your personal computer.

How to Use This Book

Power DOS! is not a book for all computer users. If you have a PC-, XT-, or AT-class machine, you are welcome to join. You will find much that you can put to good use. But, as noted earlier, personal computing took a quantum leap with the introduction of the Intel 80386 microprocessor, and 386-based equipment is cheap. If you are serious about computing, you simply cannot operate today without a 386-, 486-, or even, Pentium-based system. This book assumes that you are serious about computing. (Intel's so-called 586 chip is officially called the Pentium because, unlike numbers, names can be trademarked to frustrate chip cloners.)

It thus also assumes that you have at least a megabyte of RAM, a VGA card and monitor, an 80-megabyte hard drive complemented by 3.5-inch and 5.25-inch floppy drives, and you are using either MS-DOS 5 or MS-DOS 6. It is essential to be using at least DOS 5 since that product represents a quantum leap in operating system software. But if you are a contented DOS 5 user, there may be no need to spend money upgrading to DOS 6. As this book reveals, much of what DOS 6 offers can be added to DOS 5 through public domain and shareware programs.

This book also assumes that you have at least used a personal computer at some time in the past. We have no desire to leave inexperienced users behind. Indeed, I have been known to throw books like that against the wall in disgust. At the same time, we've all got to acknowledge that no single book can explain everything at a level suitable for the complete novice.

This book offers short explanations to refresh your memory. But if you *are* a complete novice, read one of the Random House/Glossbrenner DOS books first. Those books are designed to take you from Ground Zero to DOS Master in about 868 pages.

Power DOS! is divided into nine parts, each of which covers a major PC activity or topic. Topics include:

- Setting up your system
- Making the most of DOS
- Turbocharged DOS
- Maximizing memory
- Optimizing hard and floppy drives
- Video and keyboard considerations
- Printing
- Communicating
- The Power DOS Toolkit (crucial PD and shareware programs)

Within each part of the book, you will find *sections*. Each section is more or less freestanding and thus not entwined with the other sections in the part, or the other parts in the book. The sections set forth a topic and meet it head on. Each is as long or as short as necessary to cover the subject.

Within each section, as appropriate, you will find boxed PowerPoints. You can think of these as parenthetical asides relevant to the issue at hand. They contain useful but not necessarily essential information. If a Power-Point ever puzzles you, simply skip it. You can always return later, after you've had a bit more experience. You will also find a few DOS 6 Points, each of which is designed to direct your attention to some special feature of Microsoft's DOS 6.

The quick take on *Power DOS!* is this: The book presents a distillation of information about the best way to use a personal computer, and it is organized to make this information as easy to access as possible. If you can't find what you want in the Table of Contents, check the Index. And if you don't know precisely what you want, simply plunge in anywhere and start reading. You are bound to find something you can use.

Public Domain and Shareware Software

As you may have guessed, public domain and shareware software plays a pivotal role in power userdom. *Public Domain* (PD) software consists of programs someone has written and placed in the public domain for all to use free of charge. PD authors, in effect, voluntarily give up their copyright on their output. *Shareware* is software that is offered in much the same way. The difference is that shareware programmers maintain their copy-rights and typically ask you to send them a small registration fee—usually $5 to $35—if you like and regularly use their products.

PD and shareware programs are fully functional. They are not demos. Most include ready-to-print, on-disk manuals. And, when you register a shareware program, you are often entitled to call the programmer directly with your questions or requests for additional features. Both types of soft-ware are widely available from computer user groups, mail-order houses, bulletin boards, and commercial online systems like CompuServe, GEnie, and even Prodigy.

Your only cost in obtaining the software is a small charge for the disk and postage or whatever long-distance or connect-time costs may be in-volved in downloading a program from an online system. Registration of shareware software is completely voluntary.

This is an extraordinary phenomenon. It is based on the simple fact that in the Information Age, you do not have to invest large sums in capital equipment to create popular, money-making products. All you need is tal-ent, a good idea, and a personal computer. Indeed, the best shareware is on a par with the best commercial software. All that's missing is the shrink wrap, the advertising, the middlemen, and the correspondingly high prices needed to pay for all of these "extras."

The Power User Connection

The public domain and shareware realm is so vast and so varied that you could run your PC with nothing but DOS and several carefully chosen PD and shareware utilities and applications programs. That could save you thousands of dollars. You might never need to buy commercial software again. The forthcoming Random House/Glossbrenner book on shareware explains this approach in detail.

What's of greatest interest here, however, is the way public domain and shareware software intersect with power userdom. Why is this kind of software so important to someone who wants to make a PC conform to his or her wishes? The answer goes to the very heart of the phenomenon.

PD and shareware software began when someone refused to accept the defaults and said, "There's got to be a better way!" Fortunately, that someone knew how to write code. So he was able to create a program that would make his PC do what he wanted it to do. But rather than keep the program to himself, he took it to his computer user group and passed out copies to all who were interested.

Tens of thousands of others have followed suit. Without question, some shareware programs today are written as money-making ventures. But the vast majority of PD and shareware programs were created by people who felt a need that wasn't being adequately addressed by DOS. DOS lets you TYPE a file to the screen, but it offers nothing like Vernon Buerg's LIST .COM. DOS offers the DIR command to display all the filenames at a given location, but it has nothing to compare with a WHEREIS-type program. And so on.

Most public domain and shareware utility programs, in short, were created specifically to make a PC do what the programmer wanted it to do. And since most are small, single-purpose programs, they typically have no commercial equivalent. The realities of the marketplace are such that a product must have a certain size, weight, and complexity to be offered as a commercial product. Otherwise a company cannot charge enough for it to make a profit.

That's why PD and shareware programs are so important to any power user. These essential customizing, empowering tools don't exist anyplace else. To take advantage of them, you've either got to know somebody or spend a great deal of time combing through disks of PD and shareware software searching for the real gems. Or, of course, you can read a book like this.

Where to Get the Programs

Throughout these pages you will find many references to specific PD and shareware programs. As I said a moment ago, all of this software is widely available. You can get it from the disk vendors that advertise in nearly every computer magazine, or from the software librarian of your local computer user group. (Ask a nearby computer dealer about user groups in your area.) Most of the programs are also available online.

If you're a CompuServe subscriber, for example, key in `go ibmff` to get to the File Finder feature of the IBM forums. Follow the menus to search for the file you want. Then go to the designated forum and data library and key in `dow` followed by the filename. Pick a download protocol from the menu that appears, and the file transfer starts. Within a few minutes, you'll have the program on your disk.

GEnie, Prodigy, America Online, Delphi, and many other systems also offer PD and shareware software. Consult your system manual or call customer service for instructions. And, of course, there are thousands of bulletin board systems (BBSs) to call. See Part 8 of this book for tips on finding current, nationwide lists of BBS numbers. If you're new to online communications, Part 8 will help you get up and running—and downloading—quickly.

As a convenience, all of the PD and shareware software cited in this book is also available from Glossbrenner's Choice, as discussed in Part 9. This is a small mail-order firm that grew out of reader requests for an easy way to get recommended programs. Glossbrenner's Choice (GBC) offers only the shareware and PD programs that I personally feel are the best in their class: the best word processor, the best spreadsheet, the best database, and the best utility programs.

The 5.25-inch disks are $5, and 3.5-inch disks are $6. For the purposes of this book, however, I've put together a collection of disks called the Power DOS Toolkit. These disks contain the utility programs that are crucial to any power user. I personally refuse to use a computer without them, even going so far as to bring them with me when calling on a client or visiting a friend's machine. The Power DOS Toolkit is available as a ten-disk package for $25.

Every PD or shareware program cited in this book, whether it is part of the Toolkit or available on a non-Toolkit disk, is summarized in Part 9. But it is important to point out that not all of the software recommended in these pages is public domain or shareware. We all want to save money, but the key thing is to get the job done—to get that 2 by 4 cut—as quickly and effortlessly as possible. A number of commercial utility packages are simply superb. The Norton Utilities comes immediately to mind, for example, as does PrintCache, the incredible print spooler from Laser Tools, Inc.

My guiding light is always "What's the best way to accomplish this task? What makes sense? What's the best tool or technique for the job?" Sometimes the answer is a shareware utility, sometimes it's a commercial program, and sometimes it's plain old DOS.

A Power User Paradigm

For example, a power user walks into a bar. . . no, wait a minute, wrong story. . . A power user sitting down at his machine is like a wood carver sitting down at his workbench. Both have a job to do, and both have their tools near at hand. The difference is that the wood carver's chisels and gouges are neatly laid out before him, while the power user's tools are on his disk.

The machine boots up and the C> prompt appears, welcoming the user to the neighborhood, for that's really what a hard disk is. With a few keystrokes, the user can zoom in on any block (subdirectory) in the neighborhood, and with the DIR command, he can see every building (file).

But wait a minute. The list of files produced by the DIR command occupies several screens, most of which have scrolled off into space. No problem. The power user reaches for the first non-DOS tool of the day, the shareware program FANSI Console. Tapping the Pause key once tells FANSI to put everything on hold. A highlight bar appears at the top of the screen, and the user can now scroll *back* through the screens that had apparently disappeared.

FANSI turns the screen into a player piano roll that you can rewind at will. It is available at any time, whether you are at the DOS command line, using a word processor, communicating with a bulletin board or online system, or running some other program. You can clip out portions of previously displayed screens and write them to disk. Or you can simply return to the command line and key in `dejavu` followed by a filename to tell FANSI to dump all saved screens to the filename you have selected.

As an inspection of the list of files in the directory reveals, there are lots of files that can be deleted and several that should be moved to floppy disk for storage. So the power user reaches for the next tool, the shareware program QFILER. He keys in `qfiler`, and the files in the directory appear in sorted order in a window occupying the left half of the screen.

The power user starts at the top, tagging the files he wants to delete by pressing a key or using a mouse. If he is not sure what the file contains, he can view it on the screen with a simple command. Or, if it is a program, he can run it. Or if it is a compressed file (.ZIP, .ARC, .LHA, etc.), he can examine its contents in detail. When all the appropriate files have been tagged, a simple command tells QFILER to delete them. A similar approach is used for copying or moving groups of files.

The power user can apply QFILER to any directory or any disk at any time, thanks to DOS's PATH command. The PATH command tells DOS to automatically look in a series of subdirectories if it can't find a program called QFILER at the power user's current location.

Now our friend leaves QFILER by hitting the Esc key and loads his word processor to edit a file. The editing done, he decides to print it and issues the necessary command. It's a long file, and most users would simply have to wait until it is printed before they could continue with the day's work. But our guy has a better way. His AUTOEXEC.BAT file automatically loaded PrintCache, a commercial print spooler program from Laser-Tools Corporation.

As a result, he can get back to work almost immediately. PrintCache fools the word processing program into thinking that it is the printer. It takes the printer-bound output and stores it temporarily in memory, to be paid out to the printer as time permits.

So as far as the word processing program is concerned, the print job is completed and it's ready to go back to work. So our power user begins working on the next file, while the first file is printed in the "background."

You Can Do It!

Clearly, this isn't brain surgery. It doesn't look complicated. What it looks like is someone who has a simple, basic understanding of files and hard disk subdirectories, a few crucial DOS commands, and the right information about the best utilities and techniques for managing a personal computer.

That's a power user! And there is no reason why you can't become one yourself. This book will show you what to do.

PART I

SETTING UP THE SYSTEM

What You Will Learn

Personal computers are infinitely adaptable. Their software and hardware can be configured in thousands of ways. But flexibility of this sort is a double-edged sword. On the one hand, it means you can customize your machine until it fits you like a Savile Row suit. On the other, it means that you have to have the knowledge and skills to do your own alterations.

Clearly, no single configuration is right for everyone. Yet mail-order firms and computer dealers usually have no choice but adopt a "one-size-fits-all" approach. Most use a configuration designed to give you good speed and performance. After all, it is in their best interests to do so. But it is simply not possible for them to cover everything. Since they have no idea how you plan to set up and use your machine, they can only sketch in the broad outline.

Often that isn't enough. And since equipment vendors rarely provide you with much more than a set of nearly incomprehensible manuals, you're stuck. The manuals lay out your configuration options, but you have no way of knowing which options are really important or what values to use when setting them. As a result, literally millions of computer owners are using systems that are not delivering the level of performance they were designed to provide. All because they are not configured properly.

This part of *Power DOS!* will remedy that situation. It begins with a brief overview of the components of any personal computer and how they work together, including a discussion of CPUs ranging from the 8088 through Intel's Pentium CPU and beyond. Then it presents a section on each of the major configuration points of a system: the CMOS setup, CONFIG.SYS, and AUTOEXEC.BAT. These sections identify the really important setup options, offer strong suggestions on the settings to use, and provide you with the information you need to adapt a performance-oriented setup to your own system, whether you are using DOS 5 or DOS 6.

The final section focuses on the setup-related programs in the Power DOS Toolkit discussed in Part 9. In my opinion, these programs are essential, though most have no commercial software equivalent. Fortunately, they are widely available from user groups and shareware sources.

It seems logical to assume that you are already familiar with at least some of the material in the sections that follow. That's all to the good. But the emphasis here is on presenting a truly comprehensive approach to configuring your system for maximum performance, and it is important to touch all the bases in the process. If you follow these guidelines, and if you incorporate the Power DOS Toolkit programs into your daily routine, you will have a system that not only gives you all the performance you've paid for, but is also as easy to use as anything on the market—including the Macintosh and an expensive, fully-equipped "Windows machine."

SECTION
1-1

BASICS: THE
ESSENTIAL PC

Personal computers consist of five main components: the system unit, the monitor, the keyboard, and the printer. You put information and instructions into the system unit with the keyboard. The system unit processes what you give it, and the monitor displays the results on a screen. The printer produces a paper copy of the results, when desired. If you want to record the results so that you can view or work with them some other time, the system unit can handle the job.

As simplistic as it may seem, that's really all there is to personal computing. But the devil is in the details. There are many different kinds of printers, keyboards, and monitors—each with its own capabilities and specifications. And the system unit is in itself a combination of individual components, each with its own capabilities and specifications. The same goes for the host of other peripherals one can cable to or incorporate within a system. Peripherals like modems, plotters, scanners, tape drives, CD-ROM drives, and sound boards.

The challenge to any computer user, regardless of level of experience, is to make the components of his or her particular system work together in the fastest, most efficient way. Fortunately, tools are available. And I'm not talking about nut drivers, Phillips head screw drivers, tweezers, or similar implements one might use to attack the DIP switches and jumpers found inside most system units.

I'm talking about software. Software in silicon. Software on disk. And software of the gray matter kind. Of these, the last is the most important. For once you understand "the system" and how it works, you will be able to use the other tools with authority and confidence.

Other sections of this book address the inner workings of memory, hard and floppy drives, printers, monitors, and the like. Here, we'll concentrate primarily on the mysteries of the system unit. The goal is to establish a common reference point so that we can be certain that we are all playing with the same deck of cards.

If you are a brand-new user, for example, you may have heard of most system unit components individually but have never been told how everything works together. If you are an experienced user, you may have a general idea of where everything fits, but there may be a gap or two in your knowledge.

Input, Output, and Storage

The heart of every computer is a chip called a *microprocessor*. This chip is usually referred to as the Central Processing Unit or CPU, and although the package it is supplied in may be about the size of a small cocktail cracker, the chip itself is not much bigger than your thumbnail. The chip is a tiny sliver of silicon that has been packed with anywhere from 300,000 to a million or more transistors. In every sense of the word, it *is* the computer. Very little goes on in most PCs without first passing through the CPU.

Like the vacuum tubes that preceded them, on-chip transistors control the flow of electricity. "Hard-wired" into all microprocessors are certain configurations of transistors that are designed to produce certain results when activated. The chips also have many transistors that can be turned on or off, depending on the state of other transistors.

A microprocessor, then, is essentially a collection of switches, some sequences of which are hard-wired into a particular pattern and some of which can be opened or closed at will to produce different results. In the most basic sense, what a microprocessor "processes" is electricity. You pour in one pattern of electrical on/off pulses, turn the processor's crank, and out flows a different pattern.

The pulses themselves are two different voltage levels, each of which exists for a set amount of time determined by a clock of some sort. The amount of time a pulse exists is measured in nanoseconds (billionths of a second), and the microprocessor's clock rate is measured in megahertz (millions of cycles per second), abbreviated MHz. As most people know, these pulses are usually referred to as *bits*, short for "binary digits."

Though it sounds boring and technical, it can be extremely helpful to view all the other components of a personal computer in terms of input, output, and storage. Keyboards, mice, floppy and hard drives, and CD-ROM drives are all designed to get information and instructions into the CPU. Monitors, printers, plotters and other output devices are designed to present the data the CPU has processed. Disk drives and *RAM* (Random Access Memory) are designed to store data and CPU instructions (programs).

Thus, when you want to run a program, you must first load it from disk into RAM. Then you must set the CPU to work on it. The CPU processes the information you feed it, according to the instructions in the program. It then displays the processed information on the screen, sends it to the printer, or stores it on a disk, depending on your commands. All of these input, output, and storage devices "plug into" the CPU through connections located on the *motherboard*—the main circuit board of the computer.

At the Center of the Web

Conceptually, the CPU is at the center of the motherboard, and, like a spider at the center of its web, it is connected to the outside world through a network of filaments. The filaments are actually traces on a printed circuit board, and they run in straight lines and turn at right angles. But in their own way, their design is nearly as beautiful as a spider's web.

The connecting pathways inside a computer are called *buses*. There are several of them, and each carries voltage pulses to and fro. The main and most significant bus is the *data bus*. The data bus connects the CPU with the expansion slots found on every motherboard. Expansion slots are designed to accept the add-on circuit boards needed to connect disk drives, modems, printers, and the like. They can also be used to add more random access memory to a system.

PowerPoint

All about Data Buses

Data buses differ in their width—in the number of "lanes" in the highway—and thus in the number of bits they can accommodate at one time. Most computers today have 32-bit data buses extending to one or two expansion slots (typically used for add-on memory boards), with 16- and 8-bit buses extending to the other slots.

Three bus designs are used: ISA, MCA, and EISA. The ISA (Industry Standard Architecture) bus is the one introduced by the IBM/AT personal computer. It is far and away the most common, even though it is the least capable. It is plain, inexpensive, and nearly everything works with it. ISA is, quite simply, the current standard.

Next is IBM's Micro Channel Architecture (MCA) bus, introduced with the PS/2 series of computers. This was an IBM attempt to regain control of the market after losing out to the clone makers. MCA is technically superior to the ISA bus. It has the ability to automatically detect a given card and configure itself and the card accordingly. Unfortunately for IBM, MCA add-on cards cost more than corresponding ISA cards and are not as widely available. MCA bus slots don't accept ISA cards, so if you switch to a PS/2 with MCA architecture, you will not be able to use your old cards. You will have to buy new MCA-compatible replacements.

The Extended Industry Standard Architecture (EISA) bus is the clone maker's answer to MCA. Developed by Compaq, Zenith, and the seven other computer manufacturers who constituted the "Gang of 9," the EISA bus offers all the advantages of MCA but also accepts ISA cards. EISA cards have longer connectors to reach deeper into expansion slots than the ISA cards. Unfortunately for the Gang of 9, EISA system units cost between $500 and $1,000 more than ISA systems, and EISA cards are not widely available. EISA-based systems are most frequently used in machines designed to act as servers for local area networks and in other truly demanding situations.

Part of the Bus

Once an add-on board is plugged into a socket, it becomes, in effect, an extension of the motherboard and the data bus. The important thing to realize is that add-on cards do more than merely provide a connection between a peripheral device and the data bus. Like the motherboard itself, add-on cards often contain special-purpose microprocessors and control programming frozen in the silicon of Read-Only Memory (ROM) chips.

The actions of this ROM-based programming can sometimes be controlled by setting one or more jumpers or DIP switches on the board. Jumpers are tiny sleeves used to connect two protruding pins. DIP (Dual In-line Package) switches are rectangular arrays of small rocker or slider switches that are best moved with the tip of a ballpoint pen. It may also be possible to configure an add-on board from the keyboard, using special software provided by the vendor.

Making It All Work Together

Now take just a moment to visualize what goes on inside your system unit when you want to edit a file with your word processing program. By typing at your keyboard you issue a command to load the program. The pulses representing that command whiz down the data bus. The read/write heads of your disk drive dart in and out, copying into RAM the magnetic domains on the disk that represent the program. The program begins to run, and the main screen appears on your monitor. And so on.

There is a lot of activity, and the CPU plays a role in almost all of it, aided by subsidiary microprocessors and controllers and add-on card, ROM-based programs. Many different pieces of hardware are involved. Each doing its job. Each working together to put your program on the screen in a matter of seconds. Yet there's something wrong with this picture.

Something is missing. And that is some kind of device or mechanism for controlling things. Microprocessors in and of themselves are actually little more than powerful engines. Something has to steer them in the right direction. Something has to supervise and coordinate the various pieces of hardware so that they work with your word processing or other program.

That something is DOS, the disk operating system from Microsoft used to control all IBM-compatible computers. DOS is explored in every detail in the Random House books on the subject by Alfred Glossbrenner. At this point we will simply note that DOS is a collection of programs, some of them in ROM chips, that lets you configure and control your system and that makes its resources available to your applications programs.

POST Time and Bootup

The portion of DOS frozen in silicon is called the ROM BIOS. You already know what ROM means. BIOS stands for Basic Input-Output System.

Among other things, the BIOS contains the little programs the computer needs to get itself going—to literally pull itself up by its bootstraps. Because these programs are on a chip, they are available for use the moment the power is turned on.

The first task they perform is called the Power-On Self-Test or POST. This is basically a matter of looking around to make sure everything is connected properly, verifying or acting on the configuration information stored in a special section of battery-powered memory called the CMOS, and testing the system's RAM for errors. You can normally stop the memory test by hitting your Esc key. Next, the BIOS looks for two DOS system files on the disk and turns control over to them. These programs load into memory and begin looking for a file called CONFIG.SYS.

If they find that file, they act on the configuration information it contains. Then the search begins for a file called AUTOEXEC.BAT. This file contains a batch of additional configuration commands. Once each command has been executed in sequence, you will see a DOS prompt (usually *C*>) on the screen, unless you have arranged for AUTOEXEC.BAT to load and run a program. (Many mail-order systems arrive with an AUTOEXEC .BAT file set to load and run Microsoft Windows, for example.)

In Sections 1-3, 1-4, and 1-5, we will present techniques and procedures for setting your CMOS configuration and for preparing performance-oriented CONFIG.SYS and AUTOEXEC.BAT files. The next section offers more detail on the CPU and different models now available.

ALL ABOUT CPUs

The CPU *is* the computer. There is thus no more potent performance enhancement option than switching to a system built around a more powerful CPU than the one you are currently using. At the very least, you'll get more speed, possibly a *lot* more. But you will have access to other capabilities as well.

Buying a newer, more powerful system, of course, has always been an option. This is so self-evident that it would barely be worth a mention were it not for the changes that have been roiling the microprocessor marketplace in recent years. Today, there are far more processor models to choose from and far more upgrade options than at any time in the past.

Chips as Products

There are a number of leading chip makers in the world, and, like automobile manufacturers, each offers a selection of models. The models within each chip maker's line are typically built around the same basic design. But each model differs in terms of speed, power, and overall capability. No matter how powerful and feature-filled the chip, however, care is always taken to make sure that software written for earlier models will run on the latest model as well.

Given the pivotal nature of the CPU, the most important decision one can make when buying an IBM-compatible personal computer is the model of microprocessor the computer has been built around. Microprocessor chips, in other words, are *products*. And just like any other product, each has certain features, benefits, and costs. We will not detail the current product lines here. However, whether you are using a hot 486DX-based machine, a 386, an AT-class unit, or even an original IBM/PC or clone, there are a number of key points you need to know.

First, the two most important makers of personal computer CPUs are and always have been Intel and Motorola. Apple computers, from the original Apple I through the Lisa through the latest Macintosh, have always been built around Motorola chips. IBM and compatible computers have always been built around chips from Intel.

Both Intel and Motorola have traditionally held a de facto monopoly in their respective CPU markets. However, in 1991, Advanced Micro Devices (AMD) cloned Intel's 80386 model and offered a version that, at 40 MHz, was twenty percent faster than Intel's top-of-the-line model. Chips and Technologies (C&T), NexGen, Cyrix, and, according to some reports, a host of Asian firms, are joining the clone carnival as well. The result has been plummeting prices for 386-based equipment.

Intel has retaliated by aggressively cutting prices on its 80486 line, accelerating the introduction of the Pentium chip, its next processor, and spending millions in advertising. There is little doubt that Intel is using its muscle to move the market to the 486 which, at this writing, has only one clone competitor—Cyrix's 40 MHz 486DLC, a chip introduced in September, 1992. Nor is there any doubt that Intel will use its enormous power and resources to move the market to the Pentium when the firm feels it is in its best interests to do so. As Intel picks up the pace, chip cloners may find it increasingly difficult to keep up.

The Intel 80x86 Family

The original IBM/PC was built around the Intel 8088, a member of the Intel family founded by the 8086 processor. Succeeding generations included the 80286 (AT-class machines), the 80386, and the 80486. The next member of the family will probably be available as you read this. It is called the *Pentium*, though prior to its official release it was informally known as the 80586 or P5.

Intel ended its practice of using numbers for names after the courts ruled that terms like 386 and 486 were simply part numbers. Thus, if Cyrix or AMD or some other chip cloning company wants to use those numbers in naming its products, it is free to do so. A name like Pentium, on the other hand, can be trademarked, preventing Intel's competitors from using it.

Consequently, at this writing it is impossible to know what the chips that follow the Pentium will be called. But those chips are definitely in the pipeline. The "80686" will probably appear in 1994, and the "80786" may be unveiled as early as 1995. Much depends on market conditions—Intel actually delayed the introduction of the Pentium after it saw how well the 486 line was selling.

The family as a whole is referred to as the "80x86 architecture." The x here stands for anything from nothing (8086) to 2, 3, 4, or some other single digit. Often, the family is referred to as X86 as well.

It is a small point, but 8088 and 8086 are pronounced "eighty eighty-eight" and "eighty eighty-six," respectively. However, in the model numbers that followed, the "80" is pronounced "eight-oh," as in "eight-oh-three-eighty-six." Typically, though, computer users drop the "80" and refer to chips as a 286, 386, 486, and so on. You'll find a quick summary of the leading members of the 80x86 family in Figure 1-2-1 at the end of this section.

The Crucial 386/486 Design

Regardless of the machine you have or are thinking of buying, it is essential to be aware of the corner that was turned with the Intel 80386. The IBM/PC was followed by the XT, which was followed by the AT. But from the user's perspective, very little changed except for processing speed. The 286 at the heart of the AT could address sixteen times more memory than the 8088s and 8086s in the PC and XT, but it did so in such a clumsy way that the capability was next to useless. Besides, memory was many times more expensive than it is today. As a result, for most users, PCs, XTs, and ATs were and are pretty much the same.

Then Intel introduced the 80386, and everything changed. Because the 386 design has been incorporated into Intel's 486, we can refer to it as the 386/486 architecture. These chips handle 32 bits at a time, compared to the 16-bit capabilities of the PC/XT/AT processors. They can directly address up to 4 gigabytes of memory, compared to the one-megabyte maximum of PCs and XTs and the 16-megabyte maximum of ATs. And they do so with the greatest of ease, thanks to built-in memory management circuitry.

The 386/486 architecture also offers three modes of operation: real, protected, and virtual 8086 (V86). The technical details are not important here. In real mode the chip acts like a single 8088/8086 processor, with all the limitations that implies. In protected mode, it offers the ability to run several programs at the same time (multitasking) with each being "protected" from colliding into one another in memory. In V86 mode, it emulates several separate PCs or XTs operating at once as "virtual machines." DOS operates strictly in real mode, but Microsoft Windows and IBM OS/2 take advantage of protected mode.

There is also the matter of speed. Because they are more efficient, 386/486 chips accomplish more during each clock cycle. And because they represent newer technology, they are available in versions that operate at higher speeds. Most 286 systems, for example, operate at 8 or 12 MHz, while 386 chips are available with speeds as high as 40 MHz. Before long, there will be 486 chips operating internally at 100 MHz.

Qualitatively, you will really notice the extra speed and better performance of 386/486 chips when using graphics and paint programs, desktop publishing software, Microsoft Windows, and any other application that puts complex images on your screen. But you will undoubtedly find that the extra speed is important even when you are using a word processing or database program, whether run under DOS or Windows.

Line Extensions

Anyone who doubts that microprocessors are products—like laundry soap, plastic bags, or spaghetti sauce—has only to look at the dozens of models of 386 and especially 486 processors Intel has brought to market. The company's motto seems to be "A processor for every price point!" although "Confusion to competitors and customers alike!" would be equally apt.

Let's see if we can sort things out, starting with the two main 386 models (SX and DX) and then moving on to the plethora of 486 possibilities. There are three primary differences between the 386SX and 386DX designs. The first has to do with the total amount of memory each chip can address. The SX has the ability to address a total of 16 megabytes of memory; the DX can address 4 gigabytes of memory.

The second difference concerns the width of the bus—the highway of circuits—the chips use to access that memory. Internally, both are 32-bit processors. But the SX plugs into a bus that is 16 bits wide. It must thus make two calls to memory to get its 32 bits. The memory bus on 386DX-based machines, in contrast, is 32 bits wide, allowing the chip to fetch 32 bits of information in a single pass.

Qualitatively, the difference is effective speed of operation. There are many ways to stack the deck in one direction or the other. But, all things being equal, given an SX and a DX operating at 25 MHz, the DX will finish a task faster because it can get more done during each cycle of the system's clock. It's reaching for memory with two arms each time, instead of just one.

The third difference between the two chip designs is in processor speed. The top speed available in 386SX chips is 25 MHz. The top speed of an Intel 386DX is 33 MHz. This is more of a marketing decision than anything else. The current AMD clone of the 386DX runs at 40 MHz.

At this writing, there is virtually no difference in price between 386SX and 386DX desktop systems. However, because its narrower 16-bit bus takes up less space, 386SX chips tend to be quite popular among makers of laptop computers. Yet another version, the 386SL, may take the place of the 386SX in the laptop market because it is designed to consume less power.

486 Models: Pick Your Speed

Now let's turn to the 486 in all its many guises. As noted, the chip is based on the 386 design. However, it includes some potentially significant enhancements. For one thing, its internal design is more efficient. That means it can do even more with each tick of the clock than can a 386. It should be noted, though, that most of the software available today—so-called 16-bit software—cannot take full advantage of this feature. Everyone is waiting for true 32-bit operating system software to appear.

The 486 also includes a built-in math coprocessor, also known as a Floating Point Unit (FPU). There has been a math coprocessor available for all Intel chips from the 8088 on. The difference is that in the past, the coprocessor has been packaged as a separate chip that plugged into a special socket on the motherboard, the main circuit board in a computer. By incorporating the coprocessor circuitry on the main chip, Intel says that the 486 can perform 40 percent more efficiently than the 80386 and its math coprocessor mate, the 80387.

The catch is that, regardless of the chip or chips you use, the software you run must be designed to take advantage of a coprocessor. Otherwise it does you no good. Lotus and other spreadsheet programs, desktop publishing, and Computer-Aided Design (CAD) programs typically have this power. But a math coprocessor is not likely to be of much use for word processing, database, or communications applications.

Built-in Cache

The 486 also includes a built-in 8K cache and a cache controller. The cache is a chunk of high-speed memory that has been set aside to serve as a temporary holding tank for information. The idea is that information can be delivered to the CPU faster from the cache than from its "home" location, whether that home location happens to be on a hard disk or in a bank of Dynamic RAM chips (DRAM).

In the old days, the speed of the CPU and the speed of RAM chips more or less matched. There was no need for memory caches to smooth out inequalities. The problem today is that memory chip technology and pricing have not kept up with CPU advances. Memory chips come in two flavors: static RAM (SRAM, pronounced "Es-RAM") and dynamic RAM (DRAM, pronounced "Dee-RAM"). SRAM is much faster, but DRAM is much cheaper.

Ideally, a system built around, say, a 33MHz CPU would have nothing but SRAM matched to the speed of that CPU. But such a system would be horrendously expensive, since SRAM is so costly. As a compromise, computer makers originally introduced the idea of CPU *wait states* to slow down the chip's performance to the point where it more closely matched the speed of the system's DRAM. A wait state is basically an idle period during which the CPU is doing nothing.

Today's solution involves CPU caching. Instead of inserting wait states into the CPU's operation or offering an expensive all-SRAM system, computer makers offer motherboards with fast CPUs, fast DRAM, and a small cache of super-fast SRAM. Most 386DX/33MHz chips, for example, are supplied in systems with external caches consisting of a collection of SRAM chips and a special cache-controller chip. With the 486, in contrast, a CPU cache and controller circuitry are built in. (External caches for 486s are also available and are used primarily in machines designed to serve as the hub of a local area network.)

PowerPoint

Cache Savings

The concept of caching data has long been used in PCs to speed up performance. In its simplest form, it is nothing more than a memory buffer into which a sequence of data is read on the assumption that if the CPU wants Item A from the disk, it will probably also want Item B. Real caching, however, is considerably more complicated, involving the kind of "intelligence" provided by microprocessor controller chips or special software.   *(continued)*

(Cache Savings continued)

Many techniques and approaches exist. They differ in the size of the cache used and, most importantly, in the algorithms used to try to second-guess the processor. When the cache contains the information the CPU requests, the phenomenon is called a *hit*. When it is necessary to go to the source (disk or RAM) for the information instead, the phenomenon is called a *miss*. Due to the need to check the cache first, a miss usually ends up costing more time than simply accessing the source. Consequently, a cache is only effective when it delivers far more hits than misses, and that often depends on the kind of work you are doing.

CPUs spend their time reading, processing, and writing data to memory. All CPU cache designs attempt to speed a CPU's throughput by reading in the data they thing the processor will need next. But typically no attempt is made to reduce the time consumed in writing out the processed data. In other words, most are "write-through" caches.

In recent years, however, "write-back" CPU caches have been introduced. With a write-back cache, data that the CPU writes to memory goes initially to fast cache memory, not to RAM. The cache controller stores that data to slower main memory only if the information is about to overwritten by some other memory operation. In general, you won't see much benefit to a write-back cache unless you are on a network or in a multiuser environment.

Tests have shown that a "post-write" cache—a version of a write-through cache that can delay memory writes using a small write buffer—is nearly as efficient. This kind of cache performs the memory write during CPU idle states or when the CPU moves on to non-memory operations.

Finally, as noted in the text, external CPU caches are available for 386- and 486-based systems. But you should know that Intel's own performance data indicates that for a single-processor system, a cache larger than 128K is difficult to justify. That's something to keep in mind the next time you're shopping for a system.

The 486SX and 486DX

As with the 386, there are two basic versions of the 486 chip: the 486DX and the 486SX. The difference between them, however, has nothing to do with the width of their memory addressing path. Both the SX and DX versions of the 486 use a 32-bit memory bus. The difference is that the math coprocessor on 486SX chips has been either disabled or removed. If the software you run doesn't need or doesn't recognize an FPU, then you will never notice the difference.

Naturally, there are also differences in speed. The chips are available in models that run externally at 20 to 50 megahertz or more. According to Intel, a 486SX running at 20 MHz offers higher performance than a 386 DX running at 33 MHz. And a 486SX running at 25 MHz easily outperforms a 386DX running at 40 MHz.

Clock-Doublers and OverDrive

That sounds confusing, to be sure. But there is one other turn of the screw: clock-doubling. In addition to the 486SX and the 486DX, there is also a line of clock-doubling 486 models. These chips operate twice as fast internally as they do externally. This means computer makers can boost the effective speed of the processor without using high-speed support circuitry, memory buses, and DRAM. The result, according to Intel, is an effective speed increase of as much as 70 percent in some cases, ten to 30 percent in others, depending on the rest of the system hardware and the kind of program being run.

Equally important, it means that you yourself may be able to boost your system's overall speed by removing your original processor and inserting a clock doubler. Indeed, making it possible for users to upgrade their own CPUs is part of Intel's overall plan for the 486 and the chips to come. You've got to have a system that is designed for this, but more and more computer makers are offering them. Look for systems that are designed to make it easy to remove the main processor chip or for systems that include an empty socket next to the main chip. This is the so-called performance enhancement socket, though some people mistakenly believe that it is intended for an optional math coprocessor chip.

At this writing, clock doubler chips are available under two separate Intel brand names: the 486DX2 and the 486 OverDrive. The 486DX2 is the name used for the chips sold to computer makers. The 486 OverDrive is the name used for the chips sold directly to computer users through retail outlets. Both chips include a fully functional math coprocessor (FPU) and an 8K internal cache. The OverDrive is designed as a replacement CPU or for computers equipped with a performance enhancement socket.

PowerPoint

RISC Chips: Reduced Instruction Set Computing

Though it has little current relevance to most personal computer users, it is important to at least be aware of what are called RISC microprocessors. RISC stands for Reduced Instruction Set Computing. The design is based on the idea that it is more efficient for a processor to be built with a handful of hard-wired instructions that it can execute very rapidly than to be built with lots of prepackaged instructions and procedures that must be decoded before they can be executed. The later approach is called CISC, for Complex Instruction Set Computing.

The best known RISC chip is undoubtedly the SPARC (Scaled Performance ARChitecture) chip from Sun Microsystems, Inc. Sun makes workstations—fast, powerful computers that are optimized for CAD (Computer-Aided Design) and other engineering applications.

Two important points stand out about the RISC approach. First, there is no free lunch. RISC chips are less expensive to produce, but they make greater demands on the people and the software used to program them. With a RISC chip it is necessary to include in your program instructions that a CISC chip contains in hardware.

Second, given the speed increases made possible by internal caches and clock-doubling technology, some CISC chips actually outperform their RISC counterparts. When it was introduced, for example, Intel's 50MHz 486 was shown to be 34 percent faster than Sun's then top-of-the line 40MHz SPARC chip. But, of course, the beat goes on.

In general, RISC chips represent a direct challenge to Intel, and they are one of the reasons why Intel has accelerated its chip design and production cycle. In the past, Intel introduced a major new microprocessor every three or four years. Due to the RISC challenge and processor clone makers like AMD and Cyrix, Intel has vowed to cut that time in half.

Figure 1-2-1 All in the Intel 80x86 Family

The following table will help you make sense of Intel processor model numbers. The table includes the leading members of the 80x86 family, past, present, and predicted. The chip's birth year is important because it shows you how old some of the "latest technology" being pushed today really is. In the computer field, a year is like a decade to other industries.

With the introduction of its Pentium chip, Intel has signaled its intention to depart from its long-standing practice of using numbers as product names. It is thus impossible to know what succeeding processors will actually be called.

Official Name	*Nickname*	*Birth year*	*Comments*
8086	none	1978	The founding member of the 16-bit branch of the family. Used in some clone XTs; PS/2 Models 25 and 30. A 16-bit wide data path makes it somewhat faster than the 8088 chip that followed it.
8088	none	1979	The original IBM/PC chip. Identical to the 8086 internally, but designed with an 8-bit data path to be able to take advantage of all the 8-bit hardware that existed at the time. Like the 8086, it can address only one megabyte of memory. Top speed: 4.77MHz.
80286	286	1982	IBM/AT and AT clones; PS/2 Models 50 and 60; a stopgap chip that experts have called "brain dead." Avoid it. Has 130,000 transistors and processes 1 Million Instructions Per Second (MIPS). *(continued)*

(Figure 1-2-1 continued)

Official Name	Nickname	Birth year	Comments
80386DX	386DX	1985	The minimum business standard. A major step forward. PS/2 Models 70 and 80, and lots of clones. Can use 4 gigabytes of memory. Current top speed (Intel version): 33MHz. Clone version from AMD: 40MHz. Boasts 500,000 transistors and processes 5 Million Instructions Per Second (MIPS).
80386SX	386SX	1988	Current "entry level" chip. Limited to 16 megabytes of memory but not really much cheaper than the 386DX. Will probably disappear soon, except for use in laptops.
80486DX	i486, 486DX	1989	The business standard. Generally considered essential to effectively run Microsoft Windows. Irresistible when cheap enough. The *i* in the nickname simply stands for Intel. Has 1.2 million transistors and processes 20 Million Instructions Per Second (MIPS).

(continued)

(Figure 1-2-1 continued)

Official Name	Nickname	Birth year	Comments
80486SX	486SX	1991	A 486DX chip with the math section disabled or removed. This is a good chip to start with if you are on a budget and do not make extensive use of graphics programs, spreadsheets, and other software that would benefit from an on-chip math section.
80486DX2	486DX2 OverDrive	1992	Clock-doubled versions of the 486. Operate at twice the speed internally as they do externally. OEM version is 486DX2; OverDrive is the retail version.
Pentium	586 P5	1993	A 64-bit, 240-pin processor. Will probably be supplied in a 169-pin version with a 32-bit interface so it can be used to upgrade many 486 systems. Expected to have 3 million transistors and, at 100 Million Instructions Per Second, to operate at twice the speed of the fastest 486 chip. Uses superscalar design to execute two instructions at once. Expected to be competitive with RISC chips.

(continued)

(Figure 1-2-1 continued)

Official Name	Nickname	Birth year	Comments
"80686"	—	1994?	Estimated to have 7 million transistors and be able to process 175 Million Instructions Per Second (MIPS).
"80786"	—	1995?	Estimated to have 20 million transistors and process 250 Million Instructions Per Second (MIPS).
"80886"	—	2000?	May have as many as 100 million transistors and be capable of parallel processing. May be able to process 2 *billion* instructions per second. In effect, a 1990s-era supercomputer —on your desktop.

SECTION

1-3

STEPPING THROUGH
THE CMOS SETUP

If DOS is going to manage all the hardware, it's important for it to know exactly what it's dealing with. What kind of monitor is attached? How much memory is there? What's the capacity of the hard disk drive? And so on. Unfortunately, unless you're using an MCA or EISA bus, simply plugging in a card or a bank of memory chips won't do the trick. An ISA system and the hardware it contains cannot configure itself.

Human intervention is needed. In the original IBM/PC and IBM/XT, this took the form of DIP switches on the motherboard. If you were using an IBM monochrome display, you set the switches one way. If you were using a color graphics card, you set them another way. There was a setting to tell DOS the amount of memory installed as well. Needless to say, setting motherboard DIP switches involves opening up the computer and approaching the motherboard with a small screwdriver or ballpoint pen in one hand and your system manual in another.

With the introduction of the IBM/AT, motherboard DIP switches became a thing of the past. The AT design incorporated a CMOS setup feature that let you handle things from the keyboard. CMOS stands for Complementary Metal Oxide Semiconductor. This is in contrast to NMOS (N-channel Metal Oxide Semiconductor), the technology used to produce most microprocessors and DRAM. The technical details are not important. What matters is that CMOS chips consume far less power than those of the NMOS variety. Most are quite happy running off a battery.

This means that you can record your system setup information in CMOS memory and, as long as your system is equipped with a battery, the information will be preserved, even when the system has been shut off. Virtually all personal computers available today follow this approach. Thus, even though CMOS processors and memory chips are frequently used in laptop and notebook computers, when someone says, "Have you checked your system CMOS?," it is understood that the person is referring to the computer's setup information.

What Information Is Recorded?

The CMOS setup procedure is built into the system's ROM BIOS. Since BIOS chips are supplied by different manufacturers—Phoenix, Award, and American Megatrends, Inc. (AMI) are among the leaders—specific procedures will vary. The information requested may vary as well, depending on the speed of your CPU and memory and other design considerations.

In general, however, the CMOS setup will keep track of the date and time, the capacity of your floppy drives (Drives A and B), specifications for your hard disk, the type of video display you are using, whether you want to enable *shadow RAM*, the amount of memory you have installed, and whether or not you have installed a math coprocessor. In some systems, that is all that is required. In others, an extended CMOS (XCMOS) setup option may be available for use in setting things like advanced memory options.

Save the CMOS!

Most new users—and not a few old hands—have never even looked at their CMOS setup. That's perfectly understandable. As supplied by your computer vendor, your CMOS setup should indeed be set up and ready to go. There are only two occasions when most users need to worry about their CMOS: when the backup battery starts to die and when adding more memory or new hardware.

There is a third occasion, however, and that is *right now*! The most important thing you can do regarding your CMOS setup is to make a copy of its contents. Should disaster strike in the form of a defective backup battery, an electrical power surge, a stray bolt of static electricity, or some other unforeseen event, the CMOS settings could be lost. If that happens, you will be unable to fully use your system until they are restored. If you don't have a record of how they were set in the first place, you could be in for some time and trouble and possibly a computer repair bill.

Here's what to do:

1. Most BIOS software gives you access to the CMOS setup when you do a system reset or when you turn the computer on. So, either press the reset button on the front of your computer or turn the machine off, wait a minute, and turn it back on again.

2. The system starts clicking through its memory test. While it is doing this, notice the long, multi-digit number that appears somewhere on your screen, often near the bottom. This is a number like EOX3-1379-083090-KF. This number is used by the BIOS manufacturer to determine the maker of your motherboard and the revision level of the BIOS software. It is a good idea to copy it down, since it is essential should you ever need to contact your BIOS maker.

3. After the memory test is complete, you will probably see a message reading something like *Press <Del> if you want to run Setup.* Do so.

4. You will next see a menu offering you options like Exit for Boot, Run CMOS Setup, and Run Extended Setup or Run XCMOS Setup. (The *X* stands for "extended.")

5. Select *Run CMOS Setup.* Your screen displays information of the sort found in Figure 1-3-1. Make sure your printer is on and ready to go. Then hit your PrintScreen key. Push the button on the printer that takes it off line and then push the button reading "FF" or "Form Feed" to advance the paper to the top of the next page.

6. Return to the main CMOS setup menu by hitting your Esc key (on most systems). Select *Run Extended Setup* or the equivalent menu item.

7. Repeat the process outlined above for producing a printout of each available screen in the extended CMOS setup.

8. Do not change anything at this time. Your goal is merely to make a hardcopy record of your current settings. If you think you have changed something accidentally, turn the system off or hit the reset button again. Nothing is actually written to CMOS memory until you authorize the setup program to do so. Some setup programs even have an option reading something like *Do Not Write CMOS Registers and Exit.*

```
┌──────────────────────────────────────────────────────────────────┐
│            CMOS SETUP (C) 1985-1990, American Megatrends, Inc.      │
├────────────────────────────────────┬───────────────────────────────┤
│ Date (mn/date/yr)   :  Mon, June 29 1992  │ Base memory size : 640 KB     │
│ Time (hour/min/sec):  10 : 36 : 45        │ Ext. memory size : 3328 KB    │
│ Floppy drive A:     :  1.2 MB, 5n"        │ Numeric processor: Not Installed │
│ Floppy drive B:     :  Not Installed      │                               │
│                              Cyln   Head   WPcom  LZone Sect  Size  │
│ Hard disk C: type   :  47 = USER TYPE 987  12     0      0    35    202 MB│
│ Hard disk D: type   :  Not Installed      ├───────────────────────────────┤
│ Primary display     :  VGA or EGA         │            Calendar           │
│ Keyboard            :  Installed          ├──┬──┬──┬──┬──┬──┬──┬──┤
│ Video BIOS shadow   :  Enabled            │1 │2 │3 │4 │5 │6 │7 │8 │
│ Scratch RAM option  :  1                  ├──┼──┼──┼──┼──┼──┼──┼──┤
│ Main BIOS shadow    :  Enabled            │9 │10│11│12│13│14│15│16│
│ Relocate option     :  Enabled            ├──┼──┼──┼──┼──┼──┼──┼──┤
│ AT Clock            :  Enabled            │17│18│19│20│21│22│23│24│
├────────────────────────────────────┼──┼──┼──┼──┼──┼──┼──┼──┤
│ Options:                                  │25│26│27│28│29│30│31│  │
│ Enabled    : AT Clock Enabled             └──┴──┴──┴──┴──┴──┴──┴──┘
│ Disabled   : AT Clock Disabled                                     │
├────────────────────────────────────────────────────────────────────┤
│ ESC = Exit,       = Select,  PgUp/PGDN = Modify                     │
└────────────────────────────────────────────────────────────────────┘
```

Figure 1-3-1 A Typical CMOS Setup Screen

PowerPoint

A Filing System, not a "Piling" System

Whether you are the proud owner of a new system, an old hand, or a prospective computer user, there's one sure way to keep track of many of the details about your hardware. Get a set of manila folders and label each one to correspond with a major component of your system. Your labels might include things like your hard disk drive, monitor, modem, printer, and, of course, your motherboard or system unit.

If you bought your system as a complete package, take the time some Saturday afternoon to round up the specifications and settings for each component, write them down, and place your notes in the appropriate folder. Don't forget to make a hardcopy printout of your CMOS settings, too.

Then put the folders in a file drawer near your computer. While you're at it, collect your system and software manuals, sales receipts, and master program and DOS disks. Take the time to make backup copies of those disks. Put the backups in a disk box near your machine and store the masters in a safe place.   *(continued)*

(A Filing System, not a "Piling" System continued)

In short, get organized! The time and effort you spend now will pay off down the road. Should a problem occur with a component in the future, you will not have to waste time hunting up your sales receipt, vendor phone number, or specifications and settings. You will be able to reach into your file drawer and pull out the appropriate folder.

The effort required is minimal, compared to the time and anxiety it will save in the future. And, once you get such a system set up, it will serve you well for years to come as you add or swap in new components.

Extended CMOS Setup and CMOS Manuals

The main CMOS setup of the sort shown in Figure 1-3-1 is the only setup screen most users ever need to deal with, usually when adding or changing hard disks. The extended or XCMOS setup, in contrast, concerns things like the wait-state setting of your DRAM (if any), the bus clock, the enabling/disabling of a fast A20 gate, and other arcana.

In general, there should never be a need for you to change any XCMOS setting. If, for whatever reason, you are inclined to do so, do not attempt it without a manual. Since many systems do not include BIOS and motherboard manuals, obtaining the information you need may take some doing. (If you have inadvertently messed up your settings, you may be able to return your system to its defaults by turning it off and then holding down the Ins [Insert] key as you turn it on again.)

Your motherboard manufacturer may be able to help, but it might be necessary for you to know how to speak Chinese. Your best bet is to contact either the BIOS manufacturer or a third party company that specializes in providing BIOS chips and BIOS upgrades.

You'll find ads for such companies in *Computer Shopper*. But one firm we can recommend is Upgrades, Etc., 2432-A Palma Drive, Ventura, CA 93003; phone: (800) 955-3527. Upgrades, Etc. sells virtually every leading brand of BIOS at prices ranging from about $60 to $164. As a phone conversation confirmed, they will sell you the BIOS manual you may need for your current system. When you call, be sure to have ready the name of your BIOS maker and the number that appears on your screen during the memory test.

Here are the names, numbers, and addresses of the three leading BIOS manufacturers, in case you would like to contact them directly:

American Megatrends, Inc.
1346 Oakbrook Dr., Ste. 120
Norcross, GA 30093
(800) 828-9264
(404) 263-8181

Award Software, Inc.
130 Knowles Drive
Los Gatos, CA 95030
(408) 370-7979

Phoenix Technologies, Ltd.
846 University Ave.
Norwood, MA 02062-3950
(800) 344-7200
(617) 551-4000

Three Important Settings

The BIOS in your computer represents a cooperative effort between the BIOS manufacturer and the company that makes your motherboard. In almost every case, motherboard manufacturers customize a brand-name BIOS in some way to adapt it to their design. There are thus so many variations that it is impossible to cover every aspect of every BIOS in creation. For specific information, you will simply have to rely on the companies that made your equipment.

However, there are three common CMOS settings you will want to know about. These are the hard disk drive type, video shadow RAM, and main BIOS shadow RAM. As explained in Part 5 of this book, a hard disk drive consists of a stack of coated platters and a comb-like arrangement of read/write heads that dart in and out of the stack reading or writing data. Data is recorded in numbered concentric circles called tracks. If you were to draw vertical lines connecting all of the tracks of the same number on all of the platters, you would have a cylinder.

Setting the Drive Type

If DOS and the BIOS are to be able to use your hard disk drive, they have to know how many cylinders and read/write heads it has. They also have to know how many sectors each track has been subdivided into. (The most common number of sectors per track is 35.)

Since the software knows how many bytes are recorded in each sector, with this information it can calculate the number of megabytes your disk can hold. DOS and the BIOS may also have to be told whether the drive uses a technique called *write precompensation* when writing to the smaller sectors nearest the center of the stack. And they may need to know if the drive uses a particular track as a landing zone to park its heads when they are not in use. All of this information combined represents your hard disk's set of parameters or *drive geometry*.

For technical reasons, there are a large number of commonly used disk geometries. Thus, there are a number of common drive "types." Almost every BIOS since the introduction of the IBM/XT in the early '80s has contained a table of drive types, each with a different cylinder, head, and sector configuration. If the drive in your system matches one of these types, telling the CMOS about it is a simple matter of scrolling through the various types and selecting the appropriate drive type number. If you do not know your hard drive's parameters, check the documentation supplied with the unit. Or check the unit itself for a sticker that contains the necessary information.

Technology marches ever onward, however. When different drive geometries began to appear, the BIOS makers had to adapt. That's why most systems today include a "user type" that lets you key in the cylinder, head, sector, and other information that matches your particular equipment. The drive type information shown in Figure 1-3-1, for example, was entered by the user.

If you upgrade your current hard disk drive or if you add a second hard drive, you have to record its parameters in your system's CMOS. Otherwise, DOS will not be able to use it correctly.

ROM/RAM Shadowing

Setting your hard drive type is a necessity. Enabling or disabling shadow RAM is a performance decision. As you can see, the CMOS setup shown in Figure 1-3-1 lets you opt for *Video BIOS shadow* and *Main BIOS shadow*. These options sound mysterious, but they are easily understood.

Both your video card and your motherboard have BIOS programming frozen in ROM chips. This programming is absolutely essential and is used frequently during any computing session. However, to save money, motherboard designers often arrange for the main and the video BIOS to be connected to the CPU via a 16-bit bus.

As you may recall, however, 386 and better processors can access random access memory via a 32-bit data path, 32 bits at a time. So, to improve performance, most makers of 386 and better systems give you the option of copying video and main ROM BIOS programming into 32-bit memory. The built-in memory-mapping capabilities of the 386/486 design are then used to *redirect* main and video ROM BIOS calls to the appropriate 32-bit memory location. The result can be a boost in overall performance by a factor of four or more.

Shadow RAM, as this 32-bit memory is often called, is typically located between the 640K mark and the 1M mark on the PC memory column. That means you will need a system with at least one megabyte of memory to take advantage of this feature, though these days such systems are common.

When the Battery Starts to Fail. . .

There's one final point to be made regarding your system's CMOS, and that concerns the battery that preserves the settings in CMOS memory. Virtually all motherboards today come equipped with a lithium battery. The battery recharges while your system is running and maintains the CMOS when it is off. These batteries typically last anywhere from three to five years. Eventually, however, they do begin to fail. And here is where quick action can save you a great deal of time and trouble.

The first day you turn on your system, wait until the DOS prompt appears and key in `date` and then `time`. If the date and time reported by the system are accurate, there is no need to do anything. If there is a discrepancy, correct it by answering the prompts that appear when you key in these commands. Then do a system reset and review the CMOS settings. Make any corrections that may be necessary, tell the computer to write the new settings to disk, and go on about your business.

In almost every case, the CMOS keeps track of the date and time, and passes this information to DOS each time you boot up. DOS uses the information to time- and date-stamp the files you create or edit.

Ideally, years will go by with no need to reset the date and time, other than twice a year when you switch to and from daylight savings time. Some of the newer BIOSes even include a daylight savings time option to eliminate even this minor chore.

However, should you discover that your files are no longer being correctly date- and time-stamped, it is a pretty good sign that your battery is failing. It may have enough juice to carry you from one weekday to another. And you can temporarily correct the situation by keying in `time` and `date` and setting the system clock/calendar each time you boot up.

But when the system has been turned off for two consecutive days over the weekend, you may come in on Monday and find that you can no longer use your hard disk drive because all of your CMOS settings have disappeared. If you have followed our advice and made a hardcopy printout of your CMOS setup, this amounts to a minor inconvenience. But it is not an acceptable long-term solution.

Indeed, the only acceptable solution in most cases is to buy an add-on battery to replace the one on the motherboard. True, it may be possible to de-solder the motherboard battery, buy a replacement, and solder it into place. But that's not the best use of your time. It is far easier and cheaper to simply buy an add-on battery and plug it into the pin header most mother-boards provide for this purpose.

Expect to pay between $15 and $30 for the replacement. If you don't know where to plug it in, ask your computer vendor for help. If that is not possible, check your motherboard manual. And if you do not have such a manual, open your system and look for a four-pin connection on the motherboard somewhere near the location of the multicolored cables of the power supply/fan unit. The pin header may even be labeled on the motherboard with "External Battery" or words to that effect.

There are two final points you need to know. First, you need to get a battery that supplies the correct voltage. The two most common voltage ratings are three volts and six volts. If you do not know which your system requires, contact your system vendor. Second, it may or may not be possible to plug in the cable attached to the battery in two different ways. The plug may or may not be keyed.

If the battery plug is not keyed, plug it in one way. Boot up your system and set the date and time with the DATE and TIME DOS commands. Turn the system off for five minutes; then turn it on again and reboot. Key in time and see if the CMOS has kept track. If it hasn't, turn the computer off. Wait a minute or so for all the power to drain away. Then reverse the battery plug and repeat the procedure.

PowerPoint

If It Doesn't Fit. . .

One of the recurring themes in the Lawrence Kasdan movie *Silverado* is, "If the world doesn't fit your needs, make adjustments." When adding a backup battery to one of my systems recently, I had to do just that. The pin header connection on the motherboard offered four pins. The battery connection had space to accommodate them, but one of the four receptacles was filled with plastic.   *(continued)*

Neither CONFIG.SYS nor AUTOEXEC.BAT is required. All DOS needs are those two invisible system files and COMMAND.COM, the DOS program that interprets and translates your keyboard commands into a form DOS can understand. If CONFIG.SYS and/or AUTOEXEC .BAT *are* found, however, DOS will read them and process each line they contain in sequence.

DOS can only read plain ASCII text. Therefore, when preparing or editing your CONFIG.SYS and AUTOEXEC.BAT files, make certain that you use a word processing program or editor capable of producing plain text. If you have any doubts, create a text file with your software; write it to disk; then exit the program and key in type followed by the name of the file. If any non-text characters or symbols appear on your screen, consult your software's documentation for information on using it to create a DOS, ASCII, or non-document mode file.

Available Commands

As you know, it is the job of the operating system to coordinate the various pieces of hardware and software that make up a personal computer. Every piece of hardware requires software of some sort to integrate it into the system. Since neither Microsoft nor anyone else could possibly produce an operating system that took into account the requirements of all the many different kinds of hardware components, the CONFIG.SYS concept was developed to allow users to add the software needed for their particular hardware.

This software takes the form of a *device driver*, usually a small file that mates with DOS and gives it the information it needs to control a particular component. CONFIG.SYS is the mechanism used to tell DOS to load specific device drivers. The commands used are DEVICE= or DEVICE HIGH=, followed by the location and name of the target driver file. The device drivers you need should be supplied by the company that makes whatever hardware you are adding. But DOS itself includes a number of drivers you can use to customize the way your hardware behaves.

CONFIG.SYS also lets you use commands to customize certain aspects of DOS to your liking. You can make DOS more sensitive to a Ctrl+Break command (used to tell DOS to stop what it's doing), for example. You can improve the performance of your disk drives by specifying the number of memory "buffers" DOS sets aside for disk operations. You can control how DOS treats your system's available RAM and what it uses it for.

A complete list of all available CONFIG.SYS commands is presented in Figure 1-4-1. You may want to consult your DOS manual or the Glossbrenner/Random House DOS books for more detailed information on each of them. Here, however, we will zero in on the commands that can improve system speed and user convenience. Commands related to memory management are discussed in greater detail in Part 4 of this book.

Figure 1-4-1 Available DOS 5 and DOS 6 CONFIG.SYS Commands

The following list includes all the commands one may include in a CONFIG.SYS file when using DOS 5 or DOS 6:

BREAK=   Causes DOS to check more frequently for a Ctrl+C or Ctrl+Break keypress. Can also be used in AUTOEXEC.BAT as BREAK ON or BREAK OFF (no equals sign needed).

BUFFERS=   Determines the amount of RAM DOS sets aside to store information read in or written to a disk. Can speed up performance of both floppy and hard disks.

COUNTRY=   Used to set your system for different language conventions: date, time, currency, case conversions, and decimal separators.

DEVICE=   Used to load a device driver like ANSI.SYS, RAM DRIVE.SYS, or some third-party driver supplied by the maker of a piece of hardware.

DEVICEHIGH=   Loads a device driver into the Upper Memory Area (UMA), the memory that lies between the 640K mark and the 1M mark. This has the effect of leaving more conventional (640K) memory free for use by applications programs. Not all device drivers work from this location, but it doesn't hurt to try.

DOS=   Used in the form *DOS=HIGH* to load the DOS kernel into the High Memory Area (HMA). Also used to connect the Upper Memory Blocks (DOS=UMB) to DOS so you can use the LOAD HIGH and DEVICEHIGH commands. Most typical usage is DOS=HIGH,UMB.

DRIVPARM=   Lets you "attach" a nonstandard disk drive and tell DOS what to expect by specifying drive parameters.   *(continued)*

(Figure 1-4-1 continued)

FCBS= Determines the number of File Control Blocks DOS can open concurrently. May be needed on some networks but probably not on single-user systems.

FILES= Determines the number of files DOS can have open at one time, systemwide.

INSTALL= Loads memory-resident programs like FASTOPEN, KEYB, NLSFUNC, and SHARE into conventional memory. Most useful on a system that does not have extended or expanded memory, since INSTALL= does not create an environment for the programs it loads, thus preserving conventional memory. If you have extended or expanded memory, use DEVICEHIGH= to load drivers or the AUTOEXEC.BAT command LOADHIGH to load drivers and TSRs into the Upper Memory Area.

LASTDRIVE= Sets the number of valid drive letters. Intended mainly for those making extensive use of the SUBST command. Generally, there is no need to use this command unless you have added a device, like a CD-ROM drive, with documentation telling you to do so.

REM Negates a command line in CONFIG.SYS or AUTOEXEC .BAT. A handy way to test different configurations without actually removing former configuration lines. Simply edit the file to place REM in front of any command line you want DOS to ignore.

SHELL= Tells DOS which command interpreter to use, should you opt for something other than COMMAND.COM. But most useful in setting the size of the environment, DOS's internal scratchpad. For technical reasons, SHELL= should be the last command in your CONFIG.SYS.

STACKS= Tells DOS how much memory to allocate for processing hardware interrupts. Rarely needed. Use with a value higher than 0 only if you get an Internal Stack Failure message.

SWITCHES Tells DOS to treat your enhanced keyboard as a conventional keyboard. *(continued)*

(Figure 1-4-1 continued)

In addition to all of the above commands, DOS 6 makes the following commands available for use in your CONFIG.SYS file:

INCLUDE   Used with DOS 6's optional startup menu feature to add the contents of a configuration block to a menu block. The INCLUDE command lets you include the configuration settings you have already specified for one menu item in some other menu item. This saves you from having to key in all the configuration settings for each and every alternate configuration menu item.

MENUCOLOR   Sets the text and background colors for the optional DOS 6 startup menu feature.

MENUDEFAULT   Specifies the default menu item (available configuration) on the startup menu and sets an optional timeout value after which the menu will disappear and the default selection (available configuration) will go into effect as the system continues the boot up process.

MENUITEM   Defines up to nine items on the optional startup menu. This is how you tell DOS the name of each selection and whether you want each selection name to be followed by explanatory text.

NUMLOCK   Lets you specify whether the NUMLOCK key should initially be set to ON or OFF.

SET   Displays, sets, or removes environment variables. In DOS 6, the SET command may be used in both CONFIG.SYS and AUTOEXEC.BAT. It may also be used from the command line as in previous versions of DOS.

SUBMENU   Defines an item on the startup menu that displays another set of choices (a submenu) when selected.

VERIFY   Tells DOS whether to verify that your files are correctly written to disk each time you copy or otherwise record a file on disk. In DOS 6, the command may be used in CONFIG.SYS as well as from the command line or AUTOEXEC.BAT.

PowerPoint

Create an "Escape Hatch" Disk

It is crucial to make a backup copy of your CONFIG.SYS before even thinking about modifying the file. Better still, take the time right now to create an "escape hatch" disk for yourself. Put a disk into Drive A and use DOS's FORMAT command with the /S switch to create a system or boot disk. (See your DOS manual for details.) Then copy your current CONFIG.SYS and AUTOEXEC.BAT files onto this disk and put it in a safe place.

You can use this disk to get your system started properly at any time in the future. Or, should you create a CONFIG.SYS or AUTO-EXEC.BAT file on your hard drive that causes the system to "hang," you can use your floppy to both boot the system and restore your original files.

A Baseline CONFIG.SYS

As noted at the beginning of this book, we are going to assume that you have a system based on a 386 or better CPU, that you have one to 4 megabytes of memory, and that you are using Microsoft's MS-DOS, version 5.0 or higher. Here is the CONFIG.SYS file you might want to use as your base point, customizing it as necessary for your specific hardware. If you are running MS-DOS 6, you may want to create a baseline CONFIG.SYS file like this, boot your system, and then run the DOS 6 MemMaker program to optimize your memory usage as discussed in Part 4 of this book:

```
DEVICE=c:\dev\setver.exe
DEVICE=c:\dev\himem.sys /machine:1
DOS=high,umb
DEVICE=c:\dos\emm386.exe i=e000-efff noems
STACKS=0,0
REM The four lines above deal with memory and
REM are considered in Part 4 of this book.
DEVICEHIGH=c:\dev\ansi.sys
DEVICEHIGH=c:\dev\smartdrv.sys 2048 512
REM If you use MS-DOS 6, do not include the above
   SMARTdrive line.
DEVICEHIGH=c:\dev\ramdrive.sys /e
BREAK=ON
```

```
BUFFERS=32
FILES=30
SHELL=c:\dos\command.com c:\dos /e:512 /p
```

We're going to step through this sample baseline file in sequence, explaining the whys and wherefores of each line. Before we do, however, there are two things you should know. First, this baseline file assumes that you have created two directories on your hard disk: C:\DOS and C:\DEV. If you have not done so, now would be a good time to remedy the situation.

Get to your root directory on Drive C by keying in cd\. Then create the two directories by keying in md dos and md dev. Copy all of your DOS files into C:\DOS. Then copy your DOS and other device drivers (many of which end in .SYS) into C:\DEV.

Hard disk subdirectories are your filing system. So, while you *could* have all of your DOS and driver files in the root directory, along with everything else, you will find that the computer is much easier to use if you simply put appropriate files in appropriate subdirectories. It is not a bad goal to try to arrange things so that your root directory contains only CONFIG.SYS, AUTOEXEC.BAT, and possibly COMMAND.COM, and entries for each subdirectory.

Stepping through the File

We can dispose of the first six lines of the baseline CONFIG.SYS file rather quickly. The first line loads the device driver SETVER.EXE. Many applications programs are designed to look at the version of DOS you are running. If they don't like what they see, they may refuse to run. SETVER .EXE is designed to fool specific programs into thinking that they are running under an older version of DOS than the one you are actually running. Your manual will explain how to add to or modify the list of programs SETVER.EXE covers.

Remember that DOS processes each line in CONFIG.SYS in sequence. By installing SETVER.EXE first, you can make sure that it is loaded and running before any drivers or programs that may be DOS version-incompatible are installed.

The next four lines include HIMEM.SYS, the DOS= command, a command that loads the EMM386.EXE driver, and the STACKS= command. All four lines are related to DOS memory management and maximization, a topic addressed in Part 4. These lines are followed by two beginning with REM, which is short for remark. DOS ignores any line beginning with REM in either CONFIG.SYS or AUTOEXEC.BAT. The REM command thus lets you add explanatory comments to these two files.

The REM command also lets you deactivate a particular line without completely removing it. This is called "commenting out" or "remarking out" a line, a technique that can be handy when you want to be able to remove a device from your configuration and reboot. Later, you can edit the REMs out of the file and reboot to activate your original configuration.

The next line loads the DOS device driver ANSI.SYS. ANSI (pronounced "an-see") stands for American National Standards Institute. This driver extends DOS's normal screen and keyboard handling powers in a way that conforms with a standard laid down by that organization. Once ANSI.SYS has been loaded, you will be able to reassign keys, control the colors of your screen or the number of lines it displays, and set up a DOS prompt that will always include the name and path of your current location on the system, the day and time, or other information. Instead of a prompt like *C>*, you can cause DOS to give you *C:\DEV\ORIG*, if you happen to be logged to that location or *D:\WP\ARCHIVE* if you happen to be there. We'll look at the PROMPT command in the next part of this book.

SMARTDRV and RAMDRIVE Performance Boosters

The next two lines are probably the most important of all from a performance standpoint. But as we will see later, you may not want to make them a permanent part of your own CONFIG.SYS file. If you are a DOS 5 user, the following two lines load your DOS *disk cache* and electronic disk or *RAM drive*:

```
DEVICEHIGH=c:\dev\smartdrv.sys 2048 512
DEVICEHIGH=c:\dev\ramdrive.sys /e
```

If you are a DOS 6 user, you will find that your RAMDRIVE.SYS driver can be loaded as shown above. However, with DOS 6 Microsoft includes SMARTDrive 4.0, a version that represents a substantial improvement over SMARTDrive 3.13, the version supplied with DOS 5. (SMARTDrive 4.0 was first introduced with Windows 3.1.)

The most significant change is that the driver is now an .EXE program file. That means that it can be loaded as a TSR directly from the command line and that caching can be turned on or off at will. Prior to DOS 6, the only way to deactivate SMARTDrive was to edit your CONFIG.SYS file and reboot.

The SMARTDRV.EXE program supplied with DOS 6 can also be loaded via CONFIG.SYS when it is necessary to activate its *double-buffering* feature. Double-buffering makes SMARTDrive compatible with hard disk controllers that cannot work with the memory provided by DOS's

EMM386.EXE program or with Windows when running in 386 enhanced mode. It is most often required if you are using an older SCSI hard
disk or other device, though it may be needed with ESDI or MCA equipment as well.

Check to see whether your SCSI drive, device, or special SCSI software
driver supports the Virtual DMA Services (VDS) specification. If it does,
then you probably will not need double-buffering with SMARTDrive.
(Older equipment does not support the VDS standard.) Double-buffering
is also available to users of DOS 5's SMARTDRV.SYS via the undocumented /B+ switch (device=c:\dos\smartdrv.sys /b+).

Cache Considerations

If you are getting the feeling that there is more to running a disk cache than
you thought, you are absolutely right. We will explore the options in more
detail when we look at how to maximize hard disk performance in Part 5 of
this book. (We will also discuss the DOS 6 DoubleSpace disk compression
driver, DBLSPACE.SYS, at that time.) For now, you need only know that
a cache boosts performance by reading more data into memory than has
been requested by you or the program you are using.

The theory is that the extra data is likely to be requested next, so when
the request comes in, the data can be supplied from the cache at RAM-chip
speed instead of at hard disk speed. Similarly, some caches delay writing to
disk until you have given them enough data to make it worthwhile to activate the hard disk read/write heads. Indeed, the whole idea behind disk
caching is to minimize hard disk head movement and make reads and
writes as efficiently as possible.

Disk caches vary in their efficiency and speed. And, of course, they can
be fine-tuned and adjusted. The CONFIG.SYS line shown above, for example, sets the DOS 5 version of SMARTDrive for a maximum cache of
two megabytes (2,048K) and a minimum cache size of 512K. The minimum setting is needed because other programs, including Windows, have
the ability to reduce the size of the SMARTDrive cache and use the memory thus freed for themselves. To set the DOS 6 version (SMARTDRV
.EXE) the same way, you would key in `smartdrv 2048 512` at the DOS
command line.

You may wish to try SMARTDrive at this time, or you may prefer to
wait until you have read the information presented in Part 5. If you do
choose to try SMARTDrive right now, be sure to read your manual and to
take advantage of DOS's built-in help function to get more information
on this feature. As noted, you may need to set the program for double-buffering if you are using an older SCSI hard disk drive or device.

If your hard disk was partitioned by anything other than DOS's own FDISK (for example, Ontrack's Disk Manager or Storage Dimensions's SpeedStor), you may have a compatibility problem when running SMART-Drive 3.13 (the DOS 5 version). Be sure to check first with your computer dealer or the maker of your partitioning software. Alternatively, you might try the undocumented /P switch (device=c:\dos\smartdrv.sys /p) to tell SMARTDrive 3.13 to load even if there is an incompatible partition.

It is important to be aware that SMARTDrive (both 3.13 and 4.0) requires a system with either extended or LIM EMS-compatible expanded memory. If you have a 386-based system with DOS 5 or better and a meg or more of memory, this is not a problem. SMARTDrive does *not* use conventional 640K memory for its cache storage. You should also know that, to avoid losing data, SMARTDrive should *not* be loaded or should be deactivated when you are using a program to defragment your hard disk.

Finally, because the DOS 6 version of SMARTDrive delays writing to disk, you could lose data if you shut your computer off or hit the reset button before flushing the cache to disk. To flush the DOS 6 SMARTDrive cache, key in `smartdrv /c`. Fortunately, the program is designed to automatically write the cache to disk if you reboot with the Ctrl+Alt+Del combination. In addition, the DOS 6 version of SMARTDrive is designed to write cache contents to disk as soon as any data it contains is older than five seconds. So you're not likely to lose very much data should the worst case occur.

PowerPoint

A Memory Refresher: Conventional, EMS, and XMS

If you are an experienced PC user, feel free to skip this PowerPoint. However, if you are a new user, you may want to know just a bit about the three main kinds of memory you probably have in your system. These are conventional, expanded (EMS), and extended (XMS) memory.

You'll find more details in Part 4 of this book. But for the time being—while you are preparing your CONFIG.SYS and AUTOEXEC .BAT files—here is what you need to know. The chip used in the original IBM/PC could address one megabyte (1,000 kilobytes) of RAM. Microsoft and IBM designed DOS to use 640K of this memory for programs. The memory addresses of the remaining 360K were reserved for use by add-on boards, like your video card or your internal modem.   *(continued)*

(A Memory Refresher: Conventional, EMS, and XMS continued)

DOS's original 640K is called conventional memory. The remaining 360K is called the Upper Memory Area, and it is divided up into Upper Memory Blocks or UMBs. The memory that stands behind the addresses in the Upper Memory Area is physically located someplace else, but it is mapped to those locations by the CPU (386 and better chips).

Those locations or UMBs that are occupied by add-on cards are not available. But almost every system has some free UMB addresses that can be used by the DEVICEHIGH or the LOADHIGH command. The goal is to free up as much conventional memory as possible by loading things that don't need to be in the first 640K into some other location.

The very first 64K block of upper memory is called the HMA or High Memory Area. For technical reasons, as long as your CPU can map physical memory chips to this spot, you can load most of DOS 5 into it, thus freeing some 48K of conventional memory for use by your programs.

Extended memory is memory that extends beyond the one megabyte mark. Expanded memory is memory that can be accessed through a "window" located within the first megabyte of address space. With DOS's EMM386.EXE and a 386, 486, or better CPU, you can not only remap memory to different locations, you can configure it as either extended or expanded memory—whatever the programs you run need.

Setting Up a RAM Drive

The second performance-oriented CONFIG.SYS line cited above is: DEVICEHIGH=C:\DEV\RAMDRIVE.SYS /E. This loads a DOS driver designed to carve an "electronic disk" out of some of your RAM. Once this driver has been loaded, that memory appears to DOS as if it were a disk drive. You can copy files into it, run programs from it, and do anything else you would do with a standard floppy or hard drive.

The /E switch tells the driver to use extended memory. If you enter the /A switch instead, expanded memory is used. If neither switch is included, RAMDRIVE.SYS uses conventional 640K memory, which is not a very good idea, since your applications programs will want most of it. RAM

DRIVE.SYS defaults to creating a disk of 64K, but you can specify anything from 16K through 4 megabytes. A line like this would set up a 360K RAM disk in expanded memory, for example: RAMDRIVE.SYS 360 /A. (See your DOS manual for more details.)

The advantage of using a RAM drive is pure speed. A program loaded from a RAM drive, for instance, comes up immediately—almost as if it were already in memory, which, in a sense, it is. If you are editing a large text file or large graphic image stored in a RAM drive, you will find that you can scroll through it much faster, since there is no delay imposed by the need for your program to pull in pieces of the file from a real disk.

There are certain disadvantages, however. You can tell RAMDRIVE .SYS to use any kind of memory (conventional, extended, or expanded), and you can set its size anywhere from 16K to 4 megabytes. But one way or another, you will have to give up some of your memory. In addition, before you can run a program out of a RAM drive, you must first copy that program into it.

Most important of all, whatever you have stored in your RAMDRIVE disappears the moment you reboot or turn off the computer. Imagine that, operating out of your RAM drive, you've worked all day on a major proposal. You decide to put the finishing touches on it tomorrow. So you switch off your computer, and your proposal disappears! If you neglect to copy your data files out of your RAM disk and onto a real disk, there isn't an unerase program in the world that can bring them back after you turn off the system.

RAM Disk Misgivings

RAM disks are a clever idea that is nearly as old as personal computing. Even before Microsoft gave the concept its blessing by including the necessary driver with DOS, RAM drive utilities were available. A decade ago, when 20MB hard drives sold for over $2,000, a RAM drive made a great deal of sense. It was the only affordable way for most users to get hard drive-like performance. When your only alternative is a clunky, full-height 5.25-inch floppy drive, a RAM drive seems like a dream come true. Today, with a speedy, reasonably priced hard drive in nearly every computer, this is no longer the case.

In my opinion, most users today should *not* use a RAM drive, at least not as a substitute disk drive. The penalties it imposes are simply too great, starting with the time required to copy files into the drive and ending with the need to record your data files onto a real disk before cutting the power.

Add to this the risk of a power failure, an errant voltage spike, or some well-meaning associate turning off your system while you are out of the room, and you'll conclude that it just isn't worth it.

The *Right* Way to Use a RAM Disk

That's not to say that you shouldn't try a RAM disk on an experimental basis. Indeed, there are times when a RAM drive can speed up your system with no risk to your freshly created data files. For example, a RAM drive can be a good place to store frequently used batch files. Include a command in your AUTOEXEC.BAT file to copy those files into the RAM drive, and add the RAM drive's drive letter to your PATH statement.

You might also want to experiment with storing COMMAND.COM in a RAM drive. DOS loads COMMAND.COM when it first boots up, but COMMAND.COM allows itself to be overwritten by some other program that needs more memory. When that other program ends, DOS must reload COMMAND.COM before it can continue. Often this involves a brief pause as DOS locates the file on disk and loads it back into memory. That pause can be eliminated if you load COMMAND.COM into a RAM drive and tell DOS to look for it there.

Start by adding the RAM drive enabling line to your CONFIG.SYS file. Then reboot the computer. The drive letter of your RAM disk will always be the letter after that of your last physical drive. If you have two floppies (A and B) and two hard drive volumes (C and D), your RAM drive will be Drive E. COMMAND.COM occupies about 48K of space, so the RAM-DRIVE.SYS default disk size of 64K will be fine.

Now do a test. Load and then shut down one of your favorite programs. Try to get a sense of how long DOS takes to present you with its command line prompt after you close down the program. Now key in `copy command.com e:\`. Then tell DOS to look for COMMAND.COM in that location by keying in `set comspec=e:\command.com`. Load and exit the same program again.

Did the DOS command line prompt appear any faster this time? If it did, then you may want to make this part of your regular way of using the system. Leave the RAM disk line in CONFIG.SYS and add the commands COPY COMMAND.COM E: and SET COMSPEC=E:\COMMAND .COM to your AUTOEXEC.BAT file so that they will be executed automatically each time you boot up the system.

Another safe and effective way to use a RAM drive is to tell DOS to use it as a temporary storage area. DOS and other programs create and then delete temporary files on disk when performing certain operations. Often, you can speed things up by telling DOS or the other programs to use a RAM drive instead of your hard disk for this purpose. (If you want to use a RAM drive to hold temporary files created by Windows, Microsoft recommends that you set up a drive of at least 2MB for Windows standard mode and 1MB for enhanced mode due to the large size of the temporary files Windows creates.)

The technique involves *environmental variables*. We will have more to say about the environment in a moment. What you need to know right now is that if you want to get DOS and many other programs to use your RAM disk (Drive E, let's say), you must enter a series of commands like the following:

```
set ramdisk=e:\
set temp=%ramdisk%
set tmp=%ramdisk%
path %ramdisk%; c:\dos
```

This creates an environmental variable called RAMDISK and defines it as E:\. Then it creates variables called TEMP and TMP and defines each of them as %RAMDISK%. (Many programs that create temporary files look for one of these variables in your environment.)

The paired percentage signs may throw you, until you know that this is simply a DOS convention. They identify the expression as an environmental variable, so DOS knows where to look to find its value. The same convention is followed when using environmental variables in a batch file.

The last line incorporates the environmental variable %RAMDISK% in the PATH, the collection of places DOS searches to find the program you or some other program want to run. Your own PATH statement may be much longer than the one shown here. All of these commands can be incorporated in your AUTOEXEC.BAT, of course.

Finally, it may make good sense to use a RAM disk if you are about to settle into a long desktop publishing session with Ventura or PageMaker, or if you are about to do some serious graphics editing with PC Paintbrush, Corel Draw, or some similar program. You can load all your data files into the RAM disk and begin. You will be very pleased with how quickly graphic images can be called up and onto the screen from a RAM drive.

Just remember to copy them to your hard disk before you reboot or power down. Indeed, it is a good idea to periodically save your work to a hard or floppy disk location, even before you are finished. Without wishing to seem a Nervous Nelly, I must point out again that any data in a RAM disk that hasn't been saved to a real disk is fair game for Murphy's Law. So don't leave anything unsaved that you can't afford to lose.

BREAK, BUFFERS, and FILES

Now let's move on to the next three lines, the ones dealing with BREAK, BUFFERS, and FILES. While their impact may not be dramatic, all three commands can affect your system's performance and ease of use.

Give Yourself a BREAK=ON

The BREAK command can be used in CONFIG.SYS and from the command line. The status can be either ON or OFF. When used in CONFIG .SYS, you must use an equals sign (BREAK=ON). When used from the command line, you do not need the equals sign (BREAK OFF). By turning the BREAK setting on, you tell DOS to check the keyboard more frequently than it ordinarily would for a Ctrl+Break or Ctrl+C keypress. Note that your Pause and Scroll Lock keys may carry an additional label reading "Break." That is your Break key, but it is only effective when you hold down the Ctrl (Control) key at the same time.

If you do not turn BREAK on, then DOS checks for a BREAK signal only while it is processing input from the keyboard or writing to the screen. It does not listen to you when it is reading or copying a file to and from disk. By turning BREAK on, you cause DOS to respond to a BREAK signal during disk operations as well as screen and keyboard operations. DOS's default setting is BREAK=OFF.

Optimal BUFFERS Settings

The BUFFERS command tells DOS how much RAM to set aside as a storage area for the sectors it has read off your hard or floppy disk. Once you have sent a disk's read/write heads to a particular track and sector to start reading a file, it makes much more sense to have the read/write heads continue to read the disk, even if the CPU isn't quite ready to process all the information they pick up. The alternative of reading a sector only when the CPU is ready for it would slow things down.

Conversely, increasing the number of buffers the system allocates can speed things up. In effect, a disk buffer is a very basic cache. The trick is to find the BUFFERS= setting that maximizes disk performance while minimizing the amount of memory required to buffer the data. You can use a value of anywhere from 1 through 99, but after about 50 you will experience diminishing returns. Each buffer occupies about 532 bytes of RAM.

The BUFFERS setting speeds up the performance of both hard and floppy disks. SMARTDrive, in contrast, affects only hard disk performance. Also, you should know that if you have loaded DOS into the High Memory Area (HMA) with the DOS=HIGH command, the memory for your disk buffers will come from the HMA as well, instead of from conventional memory. Once the bulk of DOS has been loaded into this 64K of memory immediately above the 640K mark, that memory can be used for nothing else but disk buffers. The amount of memory left can accommodate 32 disk buffers, so a setting of BUFFERS=32 is often ideal.

This is well below the point of diminishing returns, it costs you nothing in terms of memory, and it happens to be close to the recommended setting of 30 buffers for systems with hard drives of between 40M and 80M. If your drive is smaller than 40M, set your buffers to 20. If your disk is larger than 80M, set your buffers equal to 40, and if it is larger than 120M, set your buffers to 50.

These are good starting points for your BUFFERS= settings. If you need to refine the settings further, based on your own system and the programs you use, you may be able to free up a few additional kilobytes of memory by reducing the number of buffers. All we can advise is to experiment with the software you use every day. In the meantime, you can't go far wrong with the settings suggested above.

The FILES= Command

The FILES= command tells DOS how much space to set aside for its file handles. There are two limitations. The first is the number of files that can be open simultaneously in your entire system. The second is the number of files any single program can have open at one time.

The default value for FILES= is 8, but you can go as high as 255. Each notch above 8 will cost you about 40 bytes of RAM. The FILES= setting has nothing to do with speed and performance, so setting a larger number than necessary will not have a beneficial effect. Too large a FILES= setting merely wastes memory.

The trick is to use the smallest number you can while still being able to run all of your favorite programs. In some cases, settings of 60 files or more may be necessary, as when you are trying to run some programs on different local area networks. But in most cases, you can start with FILES=30 and increase that number only if you get a *No free file handles* message when trying to run a program. The memory cost for FILES=30 is about 800 bytes.

The SHELL= Command

As you may know, the DOS command interpreter, COMMAND.COM, is responsible for translating your commands (like DIR, TYPE, COPY, etc.) into a form that the operating system can understand and act upon.

COMMAND.COM thus serves quite literally as a "shell" around the guts of the operating system—those two hidden system files that load in upon bootup. It is the shell that gives the system its English-language face.

Interestingly, starting with DOS Version 2.0 years ago, Microsoft made it possible for users to load a different command processor that would supply a different user interface. It is not exactly clear what the company was thinking. Or perhaps it was not thinking, since it is hard to imagine anything worse than a world in which everyone used completely different commands to operate his or her computer.

The only COMMAND.COM replacement we know of is the shareware program 4DOS. The same program is available commercially as NDOS from Peter Norton Computing. Both versions do everything that COMMAND.COM does, but they do many other things as well. They are certainly worth testing.

In any case, it is the replacement of the user interface or shell that is the reason for the SHELL command. But that's not really how most people use it. In the real world, the SHELL= command is used for two purposes. It is used to do the same thing done by the SET COMSPEC= command— which is to say, it tells DOS where to look for COMMAND.COM when that file must be reloaded. Second, it is used to set the size of the environment, and thereby hangs a tale.

The Environment Is DOS's Scratchpad

This requires a little explanation, though the concept of the environment can be summed up in a single word: scratchpad. The environment is the place in memory where your PATH command string is stored. It is where any ANSI escape sequences or other characters used to define your PROMPT are stored. And it is where your current COMSPEC setting can be found. To see the contents of your current environment, get to the DOS prompt and key in `set`.

The environment is thus a place of character strings associated with variable names. Indeed, all entries in the environment begin with *variable=* followed by a text string of some sort, where *variable* can be any word or series of characters. Some programs take advantage of this feature by telling you to place a specific variable in the environment, followed by the path where their essential files can be found. For example, you might be told to key in the command `set progdata=c:\prog`. When the program needs specific files, it will search the environment for the variable "progdata" and follow the path it finds there. Normally, you would include the SET command in your AUTOEXEC.BAT file, as we shall see later.

Different versions of DOS default to different environment sizes. The default size in DOS 5, for example, 256 bytes. But that may not be enough, considering how much the environment gets used these days. A value of 512 bytes is more realistic.

Using the SHELL= Command

And this is where the SHELL= command comes in. Using SHELL= to load COMMAND.COM as the *secondary command processor* (as the DOS manual puts it) with several key switches is the preferred way to increase the size of your system's environment. Here is the kind of command you should use:

SHELL=c:\dos\command.com c:\dos /e:512 /p

What makes this line a bit confusing is that it is actually two commands in one. The first command is the SHELL= command and reads: SHELL= C:\DOS\COMMAND.COM. That says to DOS "Load a different command processor located along this path, instead of what you would normally load."

Now, we all know that the alternative command processor here is good old COMMAND.COM. But that doesn't matter. As far as DOS is concerned, when it sees the SHELL= command, it loads whatever command processor SHELL specifies. DOS is not aware that we are telling it to load the same file it would normally load, but from a different location.

The second part of the command is this: COMMAND.COM C:\DOS /E:512 /P. Nothing that follows the filename COMMAND.COM has *anything* at all to do with SHELL=. These parameters are intended only for COMMAND.COM. The first parameter (C:\DOS) tells COMMAND .COM where to find itself. This is necessary because of a neat memory-conserving trick Microsoft introduced with COMMAND.COM long ago. When COMMAND.COM loads into memory, it splits itself in two. It puts the resident portion of itself into low conventional memory and its transient portion into high conventional memory (near the 640K mark).

If one of your applications programs needs the memory space occupied by the transient portion, COMMAND.COM allows itself to be overwritten. It yields to the program the memory its transient half was occupying. When you are finished with the program, however, COMMAND.COM must be able to reload its transient portion. To do so, it needs to go out to disk and find a copy of itself to load in again.

The problem is that there is not enough of COMMAND.COM left in memory to remember where it came from. That's why you've got to tell

COMMAND.COM that, in this case, it is located on C:\DOS. This parameter sets the COMSPEC variable in your environment. So, unless you are loading COMMAND.COM into a RAM disk as discussed earlier, you can eliminate the line SET COMSPEC= from your AUTOEXEC.BAT file.

The next parameter (/e:512) sets the size of the environment to 512 bytes. This value must be in a range between 160 and 32,768 bytes ("32K"). DOS will round whatever you specify up to the next multiple of sixteen.

Finally the /P switch tells DOS to make COMMAND.COM "permanent." It also causes DOS to run AUTOEXEC.BAT automatically. That might not come as a big surprise. But remember that as far as DOS is concerned, COMMAND.COM as specified here is an *alternative* command processor. Once it is loaded by the SHELL command, DOS's normal procedures are not in effect. Thus if you do not specify the /P switch, AUTOEXEC.BAT will not run automatically.

Multiple Shells and EXIT

It is important for you to know that multiple *shells* (command interpreters) can be loaded one on top of the other. Indeed, that's what happens when you *shell out* to DOS from an application program. You might, for example, want to be able to leave your word processor or communications program to go check on a file, possibly on a different drive. If the program supports shelling out, you could return to DOS, check the file you were interested in, and then key in exit to be returned instantly to your word processor or comm program at the exact point you departed from.

To you, it looks as if you have returned to DOS, performed a task, and then come back again. But that's not quite accurate. In reality, your comm program or word processor loads a *second copy* of COMMAND.COM. It is this second copy that you talk to when you are out and about checking on that file, and it is the second copy that you EXIT from to return to your original program.

To see this more clearly, get to the DOS command line and key in command three or four times. The Microsoft name and copyright will appear as each copy of COMMAND.COM is loaded. Then get to your DOS directory and key in mem /c ¦ more. Notice the multiple copies of COMMAND.COM loaded into memory, one after another. To remove them, key in exit the same number of times you keyed in command. Or simply reboot the system.

PowerPoint

Use PopDOS to Shell Out of Any Program

Many programs today include an option to shell to DOS. But some do not, and many older programs do not include this feature. If you would like to *add* this capability, however, you can do so with a program called PopDOS. At your command, the program will use either expanded memory, extended memory, or disk space as its swapping medium. Once loaded into memory, PopDOS will let you shell out of almost any program. All you have to do is press its user-definable hot key.

And PopDOS is free! Author Kim Kokkonen asks no contribution or registration fee. It is yours to use, enjoy, and pass on to others. You'll find a copy in most shareware collections, and of course, it is among the programs in the Power DOS Toolkit.

A Word about INSTALL=

If you have a 386 or better system with a megabyte or more of memory, you will probably never need to use the INSTALL= command in your CONFIG.SYS. But since the command exists, and since it can prove confusing, it is worth considering for a moment. The bottom line is this: INSTALL= is designed to help users who do not have extended or expanded memory conserve their conventional 640K memory. If you have a megabyte or more of memory, you will be much better off using the LOADHIGH command from the command line or in your AUTOEXEC .BAT instead.

The INSTALL= command does not load device drivers. It loads Terminate-and-Stay-Resident (TSR) programs. These are the kinds of memory-resident programs that are typically loaded from the command line or via the AUTOEXEC.BAT file.

Second, INSTALL= loads TSRs into conventional memory. Every TSR you load this way will nibble away at the 640K of memory your applications programs have to work with. Third, and most important, INSTALL= loads a program without creating an environmental scratchpad for it. This is its main reason for being.

Each TSR normally takes a copy of the DOS environment with it into memory. Thus, if the DOS environment is 512 bytes after CONFIG.SYS has been processed and you key in the command to load a TSR, 512 bytes of your conventional memory is set aside for use by that TSR. If you load a second TSR, another 512 bytes is allocated for its environment. And so on.

The INSTALL= command offers a better alternative to users with only 640K of memory. It lets them use CONFIG.SYS to install TSR programs *before* the environment size has been set by the SHELL= command or DOS. It lets them load TSRs into conventional memory in such a way that those programs occupy the smallest amount of space. If you have a megabyte or more of memory and a processor that can use it, however, it simply does not make sense in most cases to use INSTALL=. You are far better off with the LOADHIGH command, entered from the command line or via AUTOEXEC.BAT.

DOS 6 Point

Bypassing CONFIG.SYS Commands on Boot-up

MS-DOS 6 offers a number of interesting new CONFIG.SYS-related features and commands designed to make the boot-up process more flexible.

With DOS 6, for example, you can include a line reading `numlock= off` to tell the system to toggle off the NumLock key each time you start your computer. This will let you use the arrows on the numeric keypad. You may also use the SET command in the CONFIG.SYS file to set the prompt and environmental variables. In previous versions of DOS the SET command could be used only from the command line or via the AUTOEXEC.BAT file.

There is even a group of commands for creating an opening menu offering a selection of configurations each time you boot up. (We'll look at these commands a bit later in this part of the book.)

In addition, with DOS 6, it is possible to dynamically control which CONFIG.SYS lines are acted upon and whether or not the system ignores CONFIG.SYS and AUTOEXEC.BAT on boot-up:

- To bypass all commands in CONFIG.SYS and AUTOEXEC .BAT, wait for the text *Starting MS-DOS. . .* to appear on boot-up and then press your F5 key or press and hold down your Shift key. *(continued)*

(Bypassing CONFIG.SYS Commands on Boot-up continued)

- To cause DOS to prompt you before implementing each line in CONFIG.SYS, press your F8 key after the *Starting MS-DOS...* text has appeared. The system will display each line in turn and prompt you for a *Y* or *N*. You will also be asked whether you want to run your AUTOEXEC.BAT file or go directly to the command prompt.

- If you would like to have the system prompt you automatically before acting on a particular CONFIG.SYS line, edit the file to insert a question mark (?) after the command name but before the equals sign (=). For example, the line `device?=c:\dev\ramdrive.sys` will cause DOS 6 to automatically prompt you before loading the RAM disk software each time you boot up. No need to press your F8 key each time.

A GOOD START: AUTOEXEC.BAT

The concept of an automatically executing batch file is a wonderful invention. It insures that your system automatically comes up configured just the way you want it and even begins to run a program automatically, if you like. If this feature did not exist, you might have to laboriously key in many lines of information each and every time you turned on your computer or rebooted. At the very least, you would have to key in a command to run a batch file that would serve the same purpose as AUTOEXEC.BAT.

As it is, you can include anything in AUTOEXEC.BAT that you can type from the command line. The only feature that distinguishes the file from any other batch file is its special name and the fact that DOS always looks for it on bootup. Incidentally, when DOS runs AUTOEXEC.BAT, it does not prompt you for the date and time as it otherwise would. You can make it do so by including the DATE and the TIME commands in your AUTOEXEC.BAT file.

AUTOEXEC.BAT: Have It Your Way

Your AUTOEXEC.BAT file is your first opportunity to really work your will on the computer. CONFIG.SYS is crucial, but the settings you enter there are largely invisible. With AUTOEXEC.BAT, you can make things *happen!* You can almost completely control the way the computer looks and feels to you. Each time AUTOEXEC.BAT runs, it is as if a cloud of functionaries, minions, and hangers-on had been sent ahead to prepare the castle for your royal visit.

Which tapestries would you like on the walls, M'Lord? What toys and baubles do you want placed at your fingertips? So please Your Majesty, should the Count of Lotus be on hand to greet Your Highness? Or would you prefer to look through Windows when you arrive? Your wish is our command.

Damn right. And if your wishes are not obeyed, or if your whims and desires change, you can make a few adjustments. Often by commenting out a command in AUTOEXEC.BAT with REM, just as you did with CONFIG.SYS. Not for nothing do most experienced users assume a proprietary and protective air about their AUTOEXEC.BAT files. It is truly *the* file that lets you "have it your way." Once you get the system set up the way you want it, you will not look kindly on any program with the effrontery to change or alter either CONFIG.SYS or AUTOEXEC.BAT without your express permission.

PowerPoint

Save the Root!

You should always back up your system by copying at least your data files to floppy disk or to tape. But it is also a good idea to make copies of CONFIG.SYS and AUTOEXEC.BAT as well as any device drivers and programs they load. This way you can get to these essential files quickly, without the need to load your backup software and go through the restoration process.

Make a directory for the purpose by logging onto Drive C and keying in cd\ to get to your root directory. Then key in md saveroot to create a directory by that name. Finally, key in copy *.* c:\save root to copy AUTOEXEC.BAT, CONFIG.SYS, and every other file in your root directory into C:\SAVEROOT. You might even create a batch file called SAVE.BAT to automate the process of copying the files. *(continued)*

(Save the Root! continued)

One caveat applies if you are a brand-new user. If you have just gotten your computer, the chances are that you have not yet organized
your hard disk. You may thus have files in your root directory that
you do not want to copy to C:\SAVEROOT. If that is the case, use
these two COPY commands instead: `copy config.sys c:\save`
`root` and `copy autoexec.bat c:\saveroot`.

Everyone's AUTOEXEC.BAT is different. The settings you include
depend on your specific hardware, software, and personal preferences.
However, there are several settings that everyone should consider, if only
because they make the computer so much easier and more enjoyable to use.
These are summarized in Figure 1-5-1 and discussed below.

The Screen

We can use the system's hardware as a framework, starting with the screen.
If you have followed our advice and loaded the ANSI.SYS driver via
CONFIG.SYS, you can use the PROMPT command in AUTOEXEC
.BAT to set the screen to your preferred color combination. For example, if
you have a color monitor and include the line `prompt $e[40;32m` in
AUTOEXEC.BAT, the screen's background will be black, while the text
displayed will be green.

This looks like a lot of computer nonsense. But it is simple enough
when you realize that the *$e[* and the final *m* are just characters needed to
get the ANSI driver's attention, and that *40* and *32* select certain pre-
specified colors. If you were to use *47* instead of *40*, you would see a white
background, for example, while *34* (instead of *32*) would bring you a blue
foreground.

The PROMPT command can also be used to present you with the time
and date and your currently logged path location, if you like. A lot of users
do indeed like some variation of this elaborate prompt, though personally,
I find that it clutters the screen. If I've forgotten where I am, I simply use
the CD command to "check directory," and I really don't need to be constantly reminded of the time or the date.

The Keyboard

Baseball players are very particular about their bats. As the author, in a previous life, of a number of books on the sport, I can affirm that every player

has his own way of taping, pine-tarring, sanding, or otherwise customizing his bat's handle to his liking. And why not? A baseball bat is a player's "interface" to the game. Why shouldn't he do everything he can to make it fit him like a glove?

The keyboard, of course, is *your* interface. Don't put up with anything less than perfection. Sometimes the right keyboard interface is a hardware matter, as we will see in Part 6. But you should certainly do everything you can in software to mold it to your personal needs and requirements.

For example, like many longtime computer users, I have the habit of using the numeric keypad at the far right of the keyboard for cursor control (Page Up, Home, Right Arrow, etc.). It simply feels better to me than using the dedicated cursor keys on an extended keyboard.

The fact that DOS toggles on the NumLock key each time it boots up is thus extremely annoying. That's why one of the lines in *my* AUTOEXEC .BAT file runs a little program called NUMOFF.COM that toggles NumLock off. I also use ANSI.SYS commands to reassign a few keys so that the keyboard more closely matches my particular style of typing (and a few of the bad habits I have developed over the years).

We'll look at how to reassign keys in Part 6. The point here is not that everyone should follow the same procedure. But it is important to be aware that your keyboard is as important to you as a bat is to a ballplayer. With the tools DOS places at your command, there is no need to accept the stock, run-of-the-mill way of doing things. Make the keyboard conform to *you*, and do so with AUTOEXEC.BAT.

Finally, every computer user should use AUTOEXEC.BAT to load the DOSKEY program supplied with Microsoft's DOS (version 5 and above). Or better still, Chris Dunford's shareware CED (Command EDitor) program. Both of these programs "remember" the commands you have issued since your last system boot.

This means that if you issue a command and get an error message like, say, *File not found*, you can simply hit your up arrow key to bring the command back. Then you can edit it as you would edit a line of text with your word processor, making full use of the Ins, Del, and arrow keys to insert, delete, and move along the command line. With the error fixed, you can hit Enter to issue the command again. Both programs have other impressive powers as well, as we will see. But the bottom line is that once you've tried either DOSKEY or CED, you will not want to use a computer without it.

Printer Configuration

In most cases, the main thing you will want to do as far as your printer is concerned is to include the GRAPHICS command so you will be able to do bitmapped screen dumps with the PrintScreen key. If you have an HP LaserJet II or compatible, for example, include this line in your AUTO EXEC.BAT:

```
graphics c:\dos\laserjetii
```

Make sure that the GRAPHICS program knows where to find the file GRAPHICS.PRO. Here we are assuming that GRAPHICS.PRO is in C:\DOS.

The All-Important PATH Command

With the hardware components more or less under control, let's move on to configuring DOS itself. If I were limited to recommending one and only one command that would make any PC easier to use, it would be the PATH command. The PATH command can be entered from the command line, of course, but it is most often used in AUTOEXEC.BAT.

PATH simply tells DOS where to look for a program you want to run. For example, suppose you are at this very moment logged onto a directory called \WP on Drive C. The DOS command prompt is on the screen, and your next task is to format a floppy disk in Drive A so you can store the latest chapter of your great American novel.

If you were to key in format a:, DOS would search through your \WP directory looking for a program by that name (FORMAT.COM). But of course, it would not find it. DOS would then do one of two things. If you had not used the PATH command, it would say *Bad command or filename* and present you with its prompt again. If, however, you had previously entered a command like path c:\dos, it would look in *that* path to see if it could find the FORMAT.COM program. If it then found the program, it would run it, just as if you were currently logged onto C:\DOS and had issued the command from there.

In a very real sense, the PATH command gives you the best of both worlds. Ideally, for example, all of your files and programs would be organized in a way that made them easy to find (subdirectories). But, ideally, you would also be able to run any program from any location in the system, regardless of the subdirectory that contained it.

The PATH command makes this ideal a reality. You can use PATH to tell DOS to look in as many subdirectories on as many disks as you want— as long as the total PATH specification does not exceed 127 characters. (As explained in Section 1-6, Tom Walker's shareware XPATH program offers a way around this limitation, if necessary.)

This makes a computer infinitely easier to use, since you can, in effect, enter any command to run any program from any location. You can set things up easily, with just a small amount of effort. For example, you should make a directory called DOS for all of your DOS programs and one called BATS for your batch files. You might also want to make a directory called UTILS to hold all of your utility programs. Then enter a line like the following in your AUTOEXEC.BAT: PATH C:\DOS;C:\BATS;C:\UTILS.

Notice that a semicolon (;) is used to separate the individual paths. Whenever you enter a command that cannot be executed using a file in your current location, DOS will search each PATH entry in turn for the file you need.

Loading High

Finally, it is important to think about the TSRs you may want to load. TSRs are terminate-and-stay-resident programs that load into memory and then can be popped up at the press of a "hotkey" key combination. Borland's SideKick, for example, can be popped up to give you instant access to a notepad, a calendar, a calculator that uses the numeric keypad, and many other convenient tools. Other TSRs are not as elaborate. DOS KEY and CED, for example, are TSRs. Keyboard macroing programs like ProKey or its shareware equivalent, NewKey, are TSRs that let you load elaborate series of commands and characters into a single key combination.

Most users today take advantage of one or more TSR programs. And most of this software is, understandably, loaded via AUTOEXEC.BAT. There are two main points to be concerned with: the load order and memory maximization. Though things have gotten much better in recent years, not all TSRs get along. Often compatibility problems can be solved by changing the order in which the programs are loaded. So if you have a load order that works on your system, don't change it. Or if you plan to fiddle with it, be sure you have a hardcopy printout of your AUTOEXEC .BAT file, as well as an extra copy on disk.

With a 386 or better machine and at least one megabyte of memory, you can probably load many of your TSRs into the Upper Memory Area that lies between the 640K mark and the one megabyte mark. You will want to see Part 4 for more details on this and on the DOS 6 MemMaker program, but if this memory is available, all you have to do is precede the program's command with LH or LOADHIGH in your AUTOEXEC .BAT file, like this: LH C:\DOS\DOSKEY.

DOS loads the largest UMB first, and because CONFIG.SYS is processed first, any driver loaded with the DEVICEHIGH= command will already be in a UMB by the time AUTOEXEC.BAT begins to run. From the standpoint of efficient memory usage, it is usually best to try to load your largest TSRs and utilities first. But that may change your current load order, leading to possible TSR conflicts.

You should also be aware that just because a program is successfully loaded high does not necessarily mean that it will work from its new location. Finally, you should know that when DOS cannot fit a program into a UMB, it simply loads it into conventional memory as usual. But DOS won't inform you of this fact, so you will have to use the DOS MEM command to look at your memory and at what's loaded where.

Everyone's hardware and software configurations are so different that the only way to see if something will work is to try it. Therefore, begin by placing LH in front of all your TSRs and utility programs in AUTOEXEC .BAT. Reboot and see what happens. (Don't forget to have an "escape hatch" system disk handy to reboot from your floppy drive in case the computer locks up.)

Use the command `mem /c | more` to check on the results and on which programs were loaded where. Then test all of those that were loaded into UMBs to make sure they work.

Figure 1-5-1 A Basic AUTOEXEC.BAT File

Here is an AUTOEXEC.BAT file incorporating the lines discussed in the main text. The first command sets the screen background and border to black with a green foreground for text. The PROMPT command shown here assumes you have loaded ANSI.SYS via CONFIG.SYS. The next line runs the public domain program NUMOFF .COM (located in the UTILS directory of Drive D), to turn off the NumLock function of the numeric keypad. Then DOSKEY.COM and GRAPHICS.COM are loaded high with the LH command. The PATH is set, and an environmental variable called CDPATH, used by software that accesses the CD-ROM in my system, is set. Finally, the screen is cleared with the DOS command CLS:

```
prompt $e[40;32m$p$g
d:\utils\numoff
lh c:\dos\doskey
lh c:\dos\graphics laserjetii
path c:\dos;d:\utils;c:\bats;e:\ed;c:\procomm
set cdpath=d:\books;e:\software;e:\book
cls
```

DOS 5 and DOS 6 Hard Disk Drive Settings

One recommended line has been left out of the baseline AUTOEXEC .BAT file presented in Figure 1-5-1. It is a line that has the same purpose but differs depending on whether you are using DOS 5 or DOS 6. The purpose of the line is to activate DOS's file deletion protection plan. Once this has been done, DOS sets up a safety net that makes it virtually impossible to mistakenly erase and destroy a file.

Several levels of protection are available, and the place to activate the one you choose is in your AUTOEXEC.BAT file. If you are using DOS 5, the line to enter for maximum protection is: `c:\dos\mirror /tc /td`. This assumes that you want to protect drives C and D. The MIRROR command loads a program that automatically preserves the information the DOS UNDELETE command may need to recover an erased file. You can run MIRROR against all of your logical hard drives so that it takes its picture and quits. Or you can load it as a TSR so that it updates its files continuously as you add and delete files. With MIRROR, UNDELETE, and UNFORMAT, DOS 5 gives you everything you need to construct a virtually foolproof safety net.

MS-DOS 6 goes even further. If you are a DOS 6 user who wants the maximum level of file deletion protection, the line to enter in your AUTO EXEC.BAT is: `c:\dos\undelete /sc /sd`. This activates the DOS 6 UNDELETE command's Data Sentry option that automatically moves the files you delete to a hidden directory as you delete them. The files will no longer show up with the DIR command, but they will still be intact on your disk, so complete recovery is assured. The hidden SENTRY directory will occupy a maximum of seven percent of your disk. Should you reach this limit, the program will automatically purge the oldest files until enough space has been cleared to accommodate the latest file you wish to delete. Once a file has been purged, it really is gone from the disk.

Of course there are costs. The DOS-provided safety net imposes an overhead of small delays during disk writes, and reduced disk capacity, not to mention adding yet another layer of complexity to the system. Yet the DOS safety net works well, and new users should probably install it. Personally, though, I think defragmenting or "compacting" your disk on a regular basis offers a better solution.

We'll go into more detail in Part 5. For now you should know that programs like Speed Disk from Symantec/Peter Norton Computing, and the DEFRAG program Symantec licensed to Microsoft for inclusion with DOS 6 do an excellent job of making sure that all of your files are stored in contiguous disk sectors—and are thus easy to unerase with DOS's UN-DELETE or some other program, should the need arise.

I prefer this approach to the full safety net, because it eliminates the delays the safety net imposes and boosts overall hard disk performance while still providing good odds that you will be able to easily recover deleted files. If you have never defragmented your disk, the initial session could take a while. But once you've gotten the disk into good shape, only a minute or two is needed to run a defragmenting program each day—less time than it takes for you to cruise on down to the water cooler to see what's really going on in the company.

SECTION
1-6

CRUCIAL TOOLS

It may well be that familiarity breeds contempt, but it also yields understanding. Certainly Microsoft's DOS—any version—has its faults. Certainly it is not the easiest piece of software to learn to use, particularly if you have no notion of what a computer is and does.

However, many of those who chastise Microsoft for this or that sin of omission clearly have severe cases of "movie critic's disease." Just as it is not fashionable to like Arnold Schwarzenegger movies, regardless of how well they do at the box office, it is not fashionable to approve of DOS or of Microsoft. The causes of the disease need not concern us, though it's a good bet that they've more than a little to do with envy and a bit of resentment at Microsoft's near monopoly on system software.

The point is that DOS is a major achievement. It does an excellent job of offering a reasonable amount of customizability while satisfying the lowest common denominator. There are over 100 million DOS users in the world, and most never feel the need to look elsewhere for additional operating system-style capabilities.

Relevant Power DOS Toolkit Programs

Power users, however, are not among them. Part of being a power user is claiming the promise of personal computing by making your system do what *you* want it to do. If you don't like the way DOS does things, you make some adjustments. With literally tens of thousands of public domain and shareware programs and utilities to choose from, the tools you need are readily available.

Since they tend to be small and highly focused, most of these tools have no commercial equivalent. Commercial software houses would have difficulty marketing this kind of software and charging enough to make the effort worthwhile. That's why such programs are distributed through public domain (PD) and shareware channels. Users pay a small fee to cover mailing and media expenses and in return get a disk filled with programs. Under the shareware "try before you buy" concept, users can try everything and pay only for the programs they like by sending the authors the registration fees they request.

Everyone benefits. The only problem is that there are so *many* shareware and PD programs, it is very difficult for a busy user to know which ones to choose. As discussed in *On Becoming a Power User* at the beginning of this book, the multi-disk Power DOS Toolkit was created to solve that problem. It incorporates what I feel are the very best PD and shareware tools for making your system do what *you* want it to do. I have personally tested and selected every program. They're the ones I myself use every day. Indeed, I would not want to use a computer without them.

The tools presented here deal, as you might imagine, with system setup. From Larry Weaver's AutoCon, which lets you switch among a variety of CONFIG.SYS and AUTOEXEC.BAT configurations with a few keystrokes, to Tom Walker's XPATH, which lets you lengthen your PATH string beyond the 127-character DOS limitation, these programs put you in control from the start.

DOS 6 Startup Menus

Before we begin, however, we must give DOS its due. User-selectable startup configurations was one of the more interesting features introduced with DOS 6. The concept is simple. The actual text describing the selections on the menu that will appear on boot-up is placed under a header line reading [*MENU*] in your CONFIG.SYS file. Then the configuration that is to be implemented by each menu item is entered beneath a line identifying the menu item. This has the effect of creating a CONFIG.SYS file for each item on the opening menu.

DOS 6 even includes a command to implement submenus—menus that will appear whenever a given item on the main menu is selected—and to control menu colors. There is also a command to set the default configuration that will go into effect after a specified amount of time, should no selection be made from the main menu.

For example, here is a simple CONFIG.SYS file designed to offer two menu items, Orange and Black:

```
[Menu]
menuitem=Orange
menuitem=Black

[Orange]
files=40
device=c:\device1.sys

[Black]
files=10
device=c:\device2.sys
```

When a computer with the above CONFIG.SYS file is started, the following menu will automatically appear:

```
MS-DOS 6 Startup Menu
---------------------

1. Orange
2. Black
```

Be sure to consult your DOS 6 manual and the DOS 6 online help function for more information on the menu feature. The main commands to look for are: MENUITEM, MENUCOLOR, MENUDEFAULT, SUBMENU, and INCLUDE. The DOS 6 manual also contains instructions for modifying your AUTOEXEC.BAT file for multiple configurations using the environmental variable CONFIG that DOS 6 creates whenever the startup menu feature is used.

For example, imagine that your AUTOEXEC.BAT file contains two labels *:ORANGE* and *:BLACK*. The batch file commands that follow each label are the commands you want to execute when each configuration has been selected. As soon as you select menu item Black or Orange, DOS sets the environmental variable CONFIG to read *BLACK* or *ORANGE*. Thus, if you include a line in AUTOEXEC.BAT like goto %config%, DOS will read that as either goto orange or goto black, depending on the item you chose from the Startup Menu. For more on using batch files, please see Part 2 of this book.

Changing Configurations with Batch Files

Although DOS 6's alternate configuration and startup menu feature is only about ten years late, Microsoft is clearly onto something. It is probably no accident that these features appear at a time when many users find that they are increasingly running both DOS and Windows programs. For optimal performance, DOS and Windows often require a different configuration of hardware and software resources. Some of your favorite utility programs, for example, may not be compatible with Windows—but you refuse to use DOS without them. You may like the way Windows runs with a particular memory configuration but find that you need something different for your DOS applications.

Even if you never go near Windows, you may need different configurations to run different DOS programs. For example, your "normal" configuration may include a software disk cache and a large print spooler (a program that lets you get back to work immediately after you have issued a print command). Now you want to run a program that is incompatible with the disk cache or a program that needs the memory currently used by your print spooler.

To prepare your system for such a program, you may have to edit your configuration files, inserting REM statements to temporarily nullify the lines that load your caching software or your print spooler. Then you must reboot and run the desired program. When you're finished, you must edit your configuration files again, removing the REM statements, to put things back the way they were. Then reboot.

Over the years, creative computer users have developed a number of solutions to ease this burden. DOS 6's Startup Menu option is only the latest, and possibly not even the best. Techniques vary, but they all hinge on creating a collection of files representing different configurations and then renaming them CONFIG.SYS and AUTOEXEC.BAT as appropriate.

For example, you might make a directory called CONFIG and create three files within it: BARE.SYS, NORMAL.SYS, and WIN.SYS. You could then create a batch file called BARE.BAT that contains the command COPY C:\CONFIG\BARE.SYS C:\CONFIG.SYS, copying your "barebones" configuration file into your root directory under the name CONFIG.SYS.

Batch files called NORMAL.BAT and WIN.BAT would do the same thing for your normal and Windows configurations. You could then reboot by pressing Ctrl+Alt+Del and your system would come up loading the desired configuration. If you needed to run a different AUTOEXEC.BAT file with each configuration, you could follow the same procedure, creating BARE-SYS.BAT, NORM-SYS.BAT, and WIN-SYS.BAT and including in your BARE.BAT file a line like COPY C:\CONFIG\BARE-SYS.BAT C:\AUTOEXEC.BAT. The file BARE.BAT would then contain the following two lines:

```
copy c:\config\bare.sys c:\config.sys
copy c:\config\bare-sys.bat c:\autoexec.bat
```

PowerPoint

How to Create REBOOT.COM

The batch file approach to reconfiguring your system is ideal if you need only a few sets of configuration files. It's clean and simple. But you can automate things even further by eliminating the need to press any keys to reboot your system. All you have to do is make the last line of your BARE.BAT, NORMAL.BAT, WIN.BAT (or whatever) files call a little program that will automatically reboot your system.

The program REBOOT.COM can be found in the Power DOS Toolkit, but here's how you can create it yourself in about a minute. Take a deep breath, and go to your DOS directory or wherever you have stored the DEBUG.EXE program that came with your DOS package. Then key in just the red text shown below. Don't worry if the numerical responses you see on your screen do not match the non-boldface text shown below.

Also, notice that after you have entered `jmp ffff:0` and DEBUG has responded, your next move is to hit your Enter key, as indicated below. When DEBUG has written the file to disk, key in `dir reboot.com` to make sure that it is there. Then key in `reboot` to reboot your computer. Here are the commands to enter:

```
debug reboot.com
File not found
-a 100 284b
2232:0100 mov ax, 40
2232:0103 mov ds, ax
2232:0105 mov ax, 1234
2232:0108 mov [72], ax
2232:010B jmp ffff:0
2232:0110 (Hit your <Enter> key.)
-r cx
CX 0000
:10
-w
Writing 00010 bytes
-q
```

AutoCon for More Complex Configurations

If you regularly need to use more than two or three configurations, Larry Weaver's AutoCon can be a big help. AutoCon is essentially a database manager for your AUTOEXEC.BAT and CONFIG.SYS files. It enables you to create and easily activate up to 50 different configurations.

Each configuration consists of a CONFIG.SYS and an AUTOEXEC .BAT file stored under a name of your choosing. You can create the files using AutoCon's built-in full-screen editor, or you can tell the program to use your favorite word processing software. (As noted repeatedly, your configuration files must be pure, plain, non-document mode ASCII text.)

Once you have used AutoCon to create your configuration files, you have a choice. You can either load AutoCon and select a new configuration from a menu, or you can operate from the command line by keying in something like `autocon win3` to load your Windows 3.1 configuration. AutoCon will take care of the rest.

Once-a-Day with ONBOOT

Some company, somewhere has probably done a study revealing how many times the average computer user reboots his or her system during a typical day. There are probably even statistics distinguishing between *warm reboots* of the sort you effect with the Ctrl+Alt+Del combination and *cold boots* of the sort that take place when you turn your system on or press the reset button.

Probably, most users reboot their systems more frequently than even they realize. All it takes is a program that leaves your cursor in a funny shape or some other program that manages to lock up your system, and you reboot, even if you have no intention of changing your current configuration.

This does not present a significant problem—unless you like to run some time-consuming program or procedure each morning when you turn the machine on. You may want to run a complete memory test, or you may want to perform a thorough optimization of your hard disk drive. You may simply want to have the machine automatically check your electronic mail the first thing each morning.

The point is that, while you may want the machine to do these things while you get your first cup of coffee, you do *not* want it to do them every time you reboot during the day. The solution is easy, thanks to Chris Dunford, the same master programmer who created CED, the DOS command line editor. Mr. Dunford's answer is ONBOOT.EXE.

With ONBOOT, you can arrange for your AUTOEXEC.BAT file to run selected programs only during a warm reboot, only during a cold boot, or only during the first boot of the day. All you need to do is preface the appropriate lines in your AUTOEXEC.BAT file with onboot warm, onboot cold, or onboot daily. The effective lines may contain a plain command, or they may call a subsidiary batch file or the sort you might use to check your electronic mail. The program cleverly keeps track of the date by changing its own date stamp to match the current system date the first time it is run each day.

Breaking the 127-character PATH Barrier

The DOS PATH command is one of the essential secrets of making any IBM-compatible computer a snap to use. The only problem is that the PATH command does not normally accept more than 127 characters. This effectively limits you to about ten directories with eight-character names in your PATH. If you want to include more, you must either shorten your chosen directory names, making them even more difficult to understand, or you must use a utility like XPATH.

With XPATH, you create a file that contains one line for each directory you want in your path. You then simply execute XPATH, specifying the file that contains the directories you want in your path. But that's only part of the story. XPATH also lets you add and delete directories from your PATH on the fly. For example, if you wanted to add the directory C:\ WING to your path right away, you would simply key in xpath -a c:\wing.

The DOS alternative, as experienced users know, is to key in the entire current PATH statement again, plus c:\wing. When you want to delete a directory from your path, you can key in something like xpath -d c:\ bats. Tom Walker's XPATH, in short, gives you complete control over this most valuable and convenient of DOS commands.

Controlling TSRs with Mark/Release

Kim Kokkonen and TurboPower Software, the same folks who brought you PopDOS, give you a similar measure of control over your terminate-and-stay-resident programs with their TSR Utilities package, also known as Mark/Release.

I don't know who invented TSRs, but clearly the concept was first fully developed and wonderfully exploited by Borland International and its SideKick program. It's funny, but the DOS PATH command and the

TSR concept have a great deal in common. Both are designed to give you access to programs, regardless of where you happen to be on your system. You do not have to log onto the drive or directory that contains a program to be able to run it.

The difference is that a TSR is available even when you are running some other program. That's because it is loaded into memory and "popped up" when you hit an activating "hotkey" combination. Once loaded, usually via AUTOEXEC.BAT, a TSR sits in memory, monitoring the keyboard for the specific hotkey combination that will signal it to swing into action.

Unfortunately, once they are loaded, many TSRs cannot be *unloaded* without rebooting, usually with an AUTOEXEC.BAT file that has been modified to prevent them from loading. Thus, if you want to run a program that requires every last kilobyte of conventional memory you can scrape up, you may find that you have to reboot with an AUTOEXEC .BAT edited to comment out the TSRs you normally load.

With the Mark/Release package, however, you can remove TSRs from memory and disable or reactivate them without modifying your AUTO-EXEC.BAT file or rebooting. The latest version of the program is completely compatible with DOS 5 and above and is thus designed to handle not only conventional memory, but expanded and extended memory and upper memory blocks as well.

Having It Your Way

Personal computers are and always will be *personal*, despite the inevitable pressures to link them all into centrally controlled networks that are the 1990s version of a mainframe. You may have to do things in a prescribed way when you're connected to the net, but when you're running the machine on its own, there is usually no reason why you can't customize it to suit your own personal needs and desires.

You don't have to settle for the default configuration. If the system doesn't fit your particular preferences and style of working, make some adjustments. DOS provides many of the necessary tools, and public domain and shareware software provide the rest. All you have to do is take a moment or two to learn to use them.

PART II

MAKING THE MOST OF DOS

What You Will Learn

In this part of the book, we will examine DOS and nothing but DOS. We'll start with a brief discussion of the role of the operating system, calculated to get you thinking about DOS in a new way. Then we'll highlight the commands—the *only* commands—you need to run your system day in and day out. There are just ten of them. Master them thoroughly, and you will never be dependent on the programs or batch files someone *else* has created. You'll have the power to deal with Microsoft's Windows on your own terms—running it or not running it as you please.

Next we will consider those commands you typically use for special occasions. The ASSIGN command, for example, can help you deal with some older programs that insist on being run from a particular disk drive. The PROMPT command can be used to set the colors of your screen. The LOADFIX command provides the answer to the *Packed file corrupt* error message. And so on.

From there it's on to batch files, those infinitely customizable tools that every power user creates to save keystrokes and time. Batch files are too good to pass up, but you can have too much of a good thing, as we will see. You can easily spend more time creating a batch file, getting it just right, than it will ever save you in a month of Sundays. Section 2-4 offers a more sensible approach.

In the final section, we will consider the tools that can make batch files more powerful, yet easier to create. Many of these tools are tiny, single-purpose utility programs. But for serious batch file programmers, there is a rich programming package called Extended Batch Language (EBL) that adds features you would never dream possible to DOS batch files. All of the software cited in Section 2-5 is available through PD and shareware channels.

PowerPoint

DOS Support from Microsoft

Since this part of the book focuses on DOS, it seems appropriate to summarize the various support options that are available. Microsoft offers plenty of help and support for DOS users, though it isn't always free. Here are your options:

- Technical Support   (206) 646-5104. Hours: Mon.–Fri., except holidays, 6 AM–6 PM, Pacific Standard Time. Free for 90 days from the date of your first call. Have your serial number ready when you call. It can be found inside the back cover of your manual.   *(continued)*

(DOS Support from Microsoft continued)

- Microsoft FastTips   (206) 646-5103. Hours: 24 hours a day. Automated system offers answers to most frequently asked questions about DOS. You can opt to listen or request the information be sent by mail or fax. A touch-tone phone is required. There are FastTips numbers supporting Windows, Excel, Word, and Microsoft Project for Windows as well. Call the company's general product support services number, (206) 454-2030, for more information.

- Microsoft OnCall for MS-DOS 6   (900) 555-2000. Hours: Mon.–Fri., except holidays, 6 AM–6 PM, Pacific Standard Time. Cost is $2 per minute. According to Microsoft: "Hold time will be minimal on the 900 phone number."

- Flat-fee Service   (206) 646-5108. Hours: Same as OnCall. Cost is a flat fee of $25 per call.

- International Connections   For information about international versions of Microsoft products or versions localized for a specific country, call the Microsoft office in that country, or phone Microsoft International Customer Service in the U.S. at (206) 936-8661.

BASICS: DOS AND COMPANY

The shortest, most accurate definition of a personal computer is this: A collection of various electronic parts held together by solder and software. The entire contraption exists because someone discovered that you could use electrical pulses to represent letters and numbers. By manipulating the electrical pulses, you manipulate the information they represent. You can display it, erase it, add to it, record it for future use, print it out, or send it over the telephone.

A personal computer, then, is a machine designed to manipulate electrical pulses. That's the purpose behind every component in your system from the CPU to the hard drive to the keyboard and video monitor. It is also the purpose behind every piece of software you run.

It is very helpful to keep this concept in mind when exploring and using DOS, because you will then realize that DOS is not something complex and mysterious. It is simply the control panel you use to convey your wishes to the hardware—to tell it how you want your electrical pulses manipulated. It is also helpful to know that, while DOS effectively defines personal computing today, it is far from being the only way things could be done.

Imagine a wonderful set of Tinker Toys, each component of which is actually a piece of hardware or a piece of software. You could quite literally assemble and connect these components in a nearly infinite number of ways. You could also make your own parts and incorporate them in your design.

You could write a program that would take direct control of the hard drive, the printer, the screen, and the microprocessor, eliminating DOS completely. Of course, you would probably have to produce a separate version of the program for every make and model of computer on the market. Your program would have to know about and be able to deal with the quirks and special requirements of every hard drive, every printer, and every CPU. But it could be done.

There is no physical or scientific reason why things have to be done the way we currently do them. But there are very good practical reasons why things are they way they are. Let the hardware be as varied as its makers want it to be. But let the computer manufacturers take responsibility for making the low-level modifications in DOS needed to make it work with the equipment they've chosen. In other words, let DOS control the hardware. The programs that want to use the hardware can then talk to DOS.

Thus, when a word processing program wants to put a character on the screen, it can tell DOS to do it. When a spreadsheet program wants to record information in a hard disk file, it can simply pass the file to DOS and ask it to take care of the details. This procedure has enormous advantages. When you write your applications program to interface with DOS instead of trying to directly control the hardware, everyone who runs DOS can run your program, regardless of the specific hardware in his or her system.

If this approach is followed, it is clearly beneficial to have a single operating system that everyone agrees on and uses. That's the reality of the marketplace, and it has made Bill Gates, chairman of Microsoft Corporation, a very rich man.

It should be noted, however, that DOS did not become the standard because it was necessarily superior software. The product we now know as Microsoft DOS was chosen because Mr. Gates made sure he was in the right place at the right time with the right product. When he learned that IBM had followed his advice and selected the new Intel 8088 for its original PC and was now looking for operating system software, he found a company that had such a product, licensed it, and hired Tim Patterson, the programmer who created it.

The rest, of course, is history. History largely shaped by Mr. Gates, an extraordinary individual who combines profound technical knowledge with equally deep business acumen. If, as *Business Week* (June 1, 1992) reports, there are 100 million IBM-compatible "DOS machines" in existence, Bill Gates has had a direct impact on a group of people equivalent to 40 percent of the population of the United States or 100 percent of many of the world's countries. All in just over ten years and all well before reaching the age of 40.

Operating System Operations

Operating system (OS) software like DOS literally operates the hardware. And since the microprocessor is the heart of the hardware, it is not surprising that OS software of any kind is closely entwined with the CPU. DOS, of course, is designed to work with the Intel 80x86 family of CPUs. DOS cannot do anything that the CPU cannot do, though CPUs of the 386 class have powers that no version of DOS has yet fully tapped.

That's what Windows, OS/2, and Windows NT are all about. All three products are designed to give you and your programs access to the advanced features of 386 class and better CPUs. All versions of Windows current at this writing load in on top of DOS and thus are in some way constrained by its limitations. (A "lite" desktop version of Windows NT that does away with DOS may be available as you read this.) IBM's OS/2, in contrast, wipes the slate clean. It takes complete control of the machine and lets you run DOS or Windows almost as if they were applications programs. Windows NT (New Technology) will do essentially the same thing when it appears.

Never has there been such turmoil in the operating system arena. Personal computers are really only about a decade old. It seems clear that the battles currently raging among IBM's OS/2, Microsoft's Windows, Digital Research/Novell's DR DOS, and a number of minor players are being fought to determine who will control the all-important operating system market for the second decade of personal computing.

It is also clear that reaching a final decision will take years. And even then, the decision may be irrelevant to the vast majority of personal computer users. Many, many users today find that ATs, XTs, and even PCs offer them all the power they need. Many users are quite satisfied with older versions of DOS and older versions of their favorite applications programs.

These are not aspiring power users. The only thing that will persuade them to upgrade their hardware and install new operating system software is some irresistible "killer" application. It is impossible to predict what that program might be. All one can say with certainty at this writing is that no such application appears anywhere on the horizon.

Of course, DOS must be replaced—eventually. But 100 million DOS users worldwide cannot be switched over to Windows or anything else overnight. Too many people and organizations have too much invested in DOS (applications software, hardware, user skills, etc.) to completely convert to anything else any time soon. The uncertainty about which operating system software will win out in the end, the large amounts of RAM and hard disk space needed to run new OS software and applications, and the simple fact that DOS and DOS applications offer more capability than most people currently use will retard the pace of conversion.

That's why it seems safe to say that for the foreseeable future, DOS and the way DOS does things will define personal computing. And even when DOS is replaced by something else, the basic elements of controlling and managing a computer system will remain the same. Information, whether it is programming, numerical, or textual, will still be stored in *files*. You may be able to give your files longer, more descriptive names. But a file is still a file. There must always be some way to store discrete units of information.

Similarly, there must always be a way to control your printer, your monitor, your modem, and all your other equipment. The operating system concept, as opposed to forcing every applications program to control the hardware itself, has become a central element in personal computing. The operating system you find yourself using ten years from now may do things in a different way, but it will still "operate" the hardware.

How to Look at DOS

It also seems likely that operating system software will continue to consist of a collection of *tools*. The mistake so many people make when approaching DOS for the first time is to see it as a monolith—a single, shiny, seamless whole. Nothing could be further off the mark. DOS is simply a collection of pieces, just as all computer systems are collections of pieces. Like hardware components, all of DOS's pieces are designed to more or less plug in to each other and work together. But at bottom, each really is a discrete entity.

For example, here's a quick rundown of the components of DOS, some of which are visible and some of which you never see. You can start with the BIOS, the Basic Input/Output System that the computer maker customizes to work with the hardware components selected for his or her machine. The BIOS is frozen in silicon chips, and every PC has one.

When you turn your PC on, a little program in the BIOS begins to run, causing the system to look for two invisible files. If you are using Microsoft's DOS, these two files are called IO.SYS and MSDOS.SYS. They are placed on a disk by the DOS SYS command, and they are always put in the same location because the little bootstrap loader program in the BIOS is not smart enough to search the disk for them.

The two system files load into memory and immediately load COMMAND.COM, the program that translates your `dir` and similar commands into instructions the operating system can follow. Once COMMAND.COM has been loaded, DOS is in control. Everything else —*everything*—is optional. That includes CONFIG.SYS and AUTO-EXEC.BAT.

The other components of DOS consist of separate programs that come with the DOS package. Programs like FORMAT.COM, ASSIGN.COM, SORT.EXE, and so on. These programs are simply tools you can use or not use as you see fit. But notice that they can be classified into categories on the basis of their purpose. There are disk preparation tools like FORMAT.COM and FDISK.EXE. There are file-related commands like XCOPY.EXE and UNDELETE.EXE. And so on. The commands made available to you, thanks to COMMAND.COM, also fall into such categories. COPY, DEL, and TYPE deal with files. DIR and LABEL deal with disks. And so on.

Once you realize that DOS is essentially a toolkit, not some monolithic, intimidating entity—once you understand that its role is to control the hardware—personal computers become much easier to understand and use. Something else becomes clear as well, and that is that just because DOS makes a command available doesn't mean you have to use or master it. You can substitute something else, if it is more convenient, more powerful, or more to your liking. Or you can forget about it altogether.

Indeed, most users, power or otherwise, will find that they can get by quite comfortably with just ten DOS commands. These are presented in the next section. Learn them and learn them well. On those rare occasions when you need to accomplish some special task, you can always turn to the DOS manual for instructions on using some specialized tool. Why take the time and trouble to learn something you will only use once a year, if that?

DAILY DOS: THE TEN ESSENTIAL COMMANDS

New users are often terrified by the sight of the DOS command line prompt (C>), but to a power user, it's a welcome friend. Both types of users have the same commands at their disposal. But the power user has two things the new user lacks. The first, obviously, is a knowledge of what commands to enter to accomplish a desired task. But that's not the most important difference.

The main difference between a power user and a beginner is that the power user has a mental concept of the system. To the power user, the various disk drives and subdirectories are part of a *neighborhood* or a small town. When an experienced user moves from one subdirectory to another, it is as if she had walked down the block, turned the corner, and entered the first building on her left.

I don't mean to make too much of this. This concept is not something you must strive to create. It develops naturally in anyone who operates from the DOS command line or who spends much time working with Compu-Serve, DIALOG, or other online systems. As human beings, our brains tend to impose a three-dimensional metaphor to help us manipulate abstract systems. That's why you will often hear a computer user say, "I finished up on C and then went over to Drive A to look for the file." Or, "I went down to the \PEARS subdirectory in my \FRUITS directory to delete a file. Then I went up to the root directory on C and edited my AUTO-EXEC."

Clearly no one really went "over" or "down" or "up" or physically moved anyplace else. The users simply entered commands that caused DOS to focus on some particular location. But it helps enormously to think of yourself as moving around the disk or the system—as you would move around a neighborhood—instead of logging onto this drive or that.

Viewed from this perspective, it is clear that most of us spend most of our time moving from one location to another, looking to see what's there, and running the programs we find at such locations. Every now and then, it is necessary to do a little urban redevelopment by eliminating subdirectories that are no longer necessary, making new ones when we need a spot to keep a discrete collection of files, deleting files we no longer want (or undeleting them if we later find we have acted in haste), and copying files from one location do another.

Every now and then, we have to format a blank floppy disk to use for archival storage. But that's just about it. That's how most power users spend most of their work time every day—moving from place to place and running programs. And only ten commands are needed to do it. These are:

1. CD (CHDIR, "change directory")

2. DIR

3. MD (MKDIR, "make directory")

4. RD (RMDIR, "remove directory")

5. FORMAT

6. COPY

7. DEL

8. UNDELETE

9. TYPE

10. Ctrl+Break (or Ctrl+C)

PowerPoint

Five Steps to Becoming an Instant Power User

Here's a cookbook approach to convincing everyone that you are a power user, even if you have never used a computer before. We assume that you are starting from the DOS command line. If the system automatically comes up in a menu program or Windows, tell your host you'd like to exit to the DOS command line.

You can exit many menu programs by hitting the Esc key. In Windows, look for the word *File* on the menu line, move the arrow to that spot with the mouse, then click to drop down a menu. Look for the word *Exit* on that menu and click on it. That returns you to DOS. Then enter the following commands:

1. Once you are at the command line, key in `cd\` to get to the root directory.

2. Key in `dir /p` to call for a file directory that will pause after each screen has been displayed. This makes for easy reading.

3. Notice any lines containing *<DIR>*. These are subdirectories. Find a subdirectory that sounds interesting, and key in `cd \name`, where *name* is the name of the subdirectory of interest (CD\TEST, CD\WP, CD\LOTUS, etc.).

4. Key in `dir *.exe`. If you don't see one or more lines containing filenames like WP.EXE, 123.EXE, and so on, key in `dir *.bat`. And if that doesn't work, try `dir *.com`.

5. Choose any .EXE, .BAT, or .COM filename, and key in whatever name is to the left of these extensions. To run WP.EXE, for example, simply key in `wp`. No need to worry about the ".EXE."

Your new-user friends will be amazed. Since anything ending in .EXE or .BAT or .COM is a program, that program will now be running on the screen. If it seems appropriate, and if you're feeling lucky, try hitting the F1 key. In many programs this calls up a help screen. To exit and return to DOS, try hitting the Esc key, since this, too, works in many products.

Finally, when you are at the command line again, key in `path`. If the user's path does not include "C:\DOS," suggest creating a DOS directory on Drive C, copy all DOS files into it, and add it to the path statement in AUTOEXEC.BAT. *(continued)*

(Five Steps to Becoming an Instant Power User continued)

You probably won't be able to parlay these skills into a month of dinner invitations. But you will definitely impress your friends, and maybe even yourself.

Practicing the Ten Essential Commands

You do not have to master every aspect of every essential command. You do not have to memorize all the switches and possible settings. But you should take about half an hour to practice with them until you begin to feel comfortable with the commands in their basic state. Sit down at your machine with the DOS manual, or with one of my Random House DOS books, and practice.

Start with the DIR command. Get to your root or top directory with the `cd\` command. Then key in `cd` to check your location. Key in `dir` and look at the list of files that appears. Try to find a line containing a name and *<DIR>*. That's a subdirectory. Change to that subdirectory by keying in `cd\dirname`, where *dirname* is the name of the subdirectory.

Key in `dir` again to see what's there. Move back up to the root with `cd\`. Then make a directory called TEMP with `md temp`. Move down to C:\TEMP to see what's there. (There won't be any files, but you will see a "dot" and "double dot" entry. These are special files DOS itself uses.) From this location, move back to the first directory you checked with a command like `cd\dirname`. Copy all of the files from this directory into C:\TEMP with the command `copy *.* c:\temp`. Then go to C:\TEMP to check your work with the DIR command.

If any text files have been copied, you can look at them with the TYPE command. You should also use DEL to delete one or more files. Enter `dir` to make sure they are really gone. Then immediately key in `undelete` to start the process of bringing them back to life. When you are finished practicing in C:\TEMP, key in `del *.*` to delete all the files. Key in `cd\` to return to the root directory. Then get rid of C:\TEMP by keying in `rd temp`. Complete your practice session by formatting a floppy disk or two.

The PATH Command Again

When you install either the DOS 5 or DOS 6 upgrade using the SETUP command from the first floppy disk in the package, a directory called C:\DOS is created on your hard drive, and all of the DOS files are copied into it. If your machine arrived with DOS 5 or DOS 6 already installed, it's a good bet that you already have a directory called C:\DOS on your disk. (You can check by keying in cd\ and then dir at the C:> prompt.)

As I have emphasized repeatedly, it is essential to include this directory in your PATH statement so that all DOS programs will be available to you at any time. If C:\DOS is not part of your PATH, you will have to change to that directory every time you want to run one of the many utility programs supplied with the package (the so-called external commands).

Fortunately, the DOS 5 and DOS 6 SETUP program automatically adds this directory to your PATH by modifying your AUTOEXEC.BAT file. If there is no PATH statement in that file, SETUP creates one. Still, it doesn't hurt to check. So, before you begin your practice session, key in path to ask the system to report the current PATH setting.

If C:\DOS is not among the directories that have been "pathed," key in path c:\dos to correct the situation. Later, you can use DOS's EDIT command or your favorite word processor to add that PATH statement to your AUTOEXEC.BAT file. AUTOEXEC.BAT must be a pure ASCII, non-document file. The DOS 5 and DOS 6 EDIT program automatically produces such files. If you use a different program, make sure it can produce a plain text file.

Of the Ten Essential Commands, only FORMAT and UNDELETE are provided by separate utility programs. All the rest are built into COMMAND.COM. As we will see in a moment, however, there are other commands you will want to use occasionally for special tasks.

In addition, there is the HELP command. Under DOS 5, when C:\DOS is in your path, you can key in help at any time and be shown a list of all DOS commands and brief explanations of each. This information is supplied by a text file, DOSHELP.HLP, located in C:\DOS. If you need more detailed information on a command, like, say, XCOPY, you may key in help xcopy or xcopy /?, and you will be shown a screenful of text explaining that command. This information is built into the external command utility program (or COMMAND.COM) itself.

With DOS 6, Microsoft takes online help to a new level by adapting the help facility it introduced for use with QuickBASIC to provide help information for DOS. Under DOS 6, when you key in help at the command line, you will be taken to the MS-DOS Help Command Reference screen. There you will see a list of all DOS commands on the screen and be able to select a command by using your cursor or mouse or by keying in the first letter of its name.

Once you click your mouse or hit the Enter key to select a particular command, you will be shown the first of what may be several available screens explaining the command and how it should be used. Examples and notes on commands are often available as well. You can even use the feature to search for specific words in the help database. And, of course, you can opt to print out any information you find. With DOS 6, in short, Microsoft has put most of the DOS manual on disk for easy reference.

If you want to reach the extended information on a command directly, without the need to select a command from the main Command Reference screen, you can simply key in a command like `help xcopy`. If you want only the brief, single-screen help of the sort available in DOS 5, key in `xcopy /?`.

Advanced Techniques

At this point, we are going to assume that you are either an experienced user or that you are a new user who has followed our advice and taken the time to practice the Ten Essential Commands until you have reached a certain comfort level. Here we are going to discuss the most important tips and tricks for using the Ten Essential Commands.

CD, MD, and RD

Let's start with CD, MD, and RD. The main trick is in using these abbreviations instead of the more formal CHDIR, MKDIR, and RMDIR. The DOS manual acknowledges that you may use the two-character abbreviations, but it lists the commands under their longer forms.

Hard disk drives are typically organized into subdirectories. The CD (Change Directory) command lets you move among them. There are just a few things you need to know. If you enter `cd` by itself, the system reports your current location. If you enter `cd\`, you are taken to the root directory —the very top directory—of your current drive. If you enter `cd\fruit`, you are taken to the \FRUIT subdirectory. But if you want to go to the \PEARS directory that branches off of that, you must enter a command like `cd\fruit\pears` to get there. In other words, the CD command always requires you to enter the complete pathname of your target location.

The concepts of "above" and "below" are important for all three of these commands. The main trick for using CD is the command CD ... All subdirectories contain "dot" and "double dot" entries that DOS uses to keep track of things. The "double dot" entry represents the directory *above* your current location. So if you are currently in C:\FRUIT\PEARS and you key in `cd ..`, the system reacts just as it would if you had keyed in `cd c:\fruit`. That is, you are moved to the directory immediately above your current location. The main advantage of the double dot trick is that it saves keystrokes.

Your location is also important when using MD (Make Directory) to make a directory, or RD (Remove Directory) to remove one. These commands are downward looking—they always operate on directories below your current location. Therefore, if you want to remove C:\FRUIT\ PEARS, you must be located in some directory *above* \PEARS to apply the RD command. Similarly, if you are in C:\FRUIT and you key in md apples, the result is C:\FRUIT\APPLES. But if you are in the \PEARS directory and you do the same thing, the result is C:\FRUIT\PEARS\ APPLES.

Now you're ready for the best directory-related trick of all. The official way to remove a subdirectory is to change down to it, delete all of the files, move up above it, and apply the RD command. That's a lot of typing. There are utility programs that can short-circuit the process, but if you are working strictly with DOS, here's what to do.

Move to the directory immediately above the one you want to get rid of. We'll assume you want to get rid of \PEARS, so log onto C:\FRUIT with the command cd\fruit or cd c:\fruit. (Both commands produce the same result if you are logged onto Drive C.). Then key in del pears. DOS responds with a warning that all files (in \PEARS) will be erased and ask if you want to proceed. This is the same warning that appears when you use the command DEL *.*. Respond with y as prompted. Then key in rd pears to remove the directory.

This trick saves hundreds of keystrokes a year. The only times it does not work is when the directory you want to remove contains subdirectories itself or if some program has placed hidden or unerasable files in that location. In such cases, you have to use a variant of DIR—and possibly the DOS ATTRIB command—to make the files erasable.

PowerPoint

Redirection Refresher

Some of the handiest tools DOS offers are its redirection commands. For example, when you key in dir, the command's output is normally sent to the screen. But if you want to redirect that output into a file, all you have to do is key in dir > dir.txt. The filename can be anything you want, in any location. Just add the desired path (DIR > D:\FILES\DIR.TXT). The output can be anything from that of a plain DIR command to the most elaborate collection of DIR command switches (DIR /O:S > D:\FILES\DIR.TXT).

(continued)

(Redirection Refresher continued)

The other redirection symbol you will use frequently is the one that tells a command to *append* its output to a file. The greater-than symbol (>) causes a new file to be created each time. But the double greater-than sign (>>) appends subsequent output to a file instead of overwriting it.

Let's say you want to create a file called FILES in a subdirectory on Drive D. You want the file to contain a directory list for locations C:\ and D:\. To do this, you would go to C:\ and key in `dir > d:\ files\dir.txt`. Then, you would go to D:\ and key in `dir >> d:\files\dir.txt`. (Note that we used a single greater-than symbol to create the file DIR.TXT in the first command, and a double greater-than symbol to append that file in the second command.)

You can also control the input given to a command or a *filter* with the less-than symbol (<). For example, the command SORT < CUST .TXT would run DOS's SORT.EXE program and tell it to take its input from the file CUST.TXT. You can also pass output through a filter like MORE or FIND with the vertical line or pipe symbol (¦). The command DIR ¦ FIND "CUST," for example, displays only those filenames containing the string "CUST." (Uppercase is important here since the DIR command normally produces uppercase text, and FIND looks for names that match the DIR command output.)

The DIR Command and Wildcards

The DIR command produces a directory of all the files and subdirectory names at your current location. It can do a lot of tricks, such as showing you the files sorted in a particular order or in a wide format consisting of five columns across the screen. But I think most people will find that most of these tricks aren't worth mastering.

The two most important things to learn about the DIR command are using it with wildcard characters (? and *) and setting its defaults with the environmental variable DIRCMD. The question mark stands for any character, but one and only one character. The asterisk or star stands for an unlimited number of characters. See your manual for details, and practice pulling a directory containing only those files that meet the criteria you have specified with your wildcards.

It is important to know that the DIR command treats wildcards just a bit differently than most other DOS commands. The DIR command looks at a filename as one continuous string of characters, making no distinction between the name and extension. Thus, TEST.TXT is the same as TEST to the DIR command when you key in `dir t*`—both files fit the bill.

The DEL (delete) command, in contrast, treats the filename as two separate fields. The star wildcard applies only to the end of a field. Thus, while DIR T* would call up both TEST and TEST.TXT, the command DEL T* would delete only the file called TEST. If you wanted to delete both files, you would have to use the command DEL T*.*, supplying the second star to cover the file extension. Most DOS commands respond like DEL. The DIR command is thus the odd woman out.

PowerPoint

Wildcards!

Wildcard characters can be used with the following DOS commands: ATTRIB, BACKUP, COPY, CHKDSK, COMP, DEL, DIR, ERASE, PRINT, RECOVER (a bad idea), REN, REPLACE, RESTORE, UNDELETE, and XCOPY.

This means, for example, that if you have a lot of files ending in .TXT that you would like to make end in .OLD, you can key in `ren *.txt *.old`. (You can do the same thing with the COPY command if you want to copy files instead of renaming them.) Similarly, if you want to hide all .TXT files in a given subdirectory with the ATTRIB command, you may key in `attrib +h *.txt`. If you knew you only wanted to undelete program files, you might key in `undelete *.exe` or `undelete *.com`, and the program would present you with just the deleted .EXE or .COM files.

Also, most people don't know that the command `dir *.` will give you a listing that includes only subdirectory names.

Personally, I like my directories to be sorted alphabetically by filename. The program I use is DIRSORT.EXE from the Norton Utilities. This program is so popular that when Symantec left it out of one version of the Utilities, public demand caused the firm to reinstate it in the next version. DIRSORT physically rearranges the directory entries and records the result on disk. (The DEFRAG program Microsoft licensed from Symantec for DOS 6 can be used to physically sort your directories as well.)

If you don't have the Norton Utilities, you can produce similar results with the command DIR /O:N. This tells the command to present the files ordered (*/O:*) by name (*N*). The DIR command has many other options that may interest you, but all of them involve more typing than a simple `dir`. Therefore, decide which way you would like your files to be presented by DIR and make that your default.

The way to do this is by including a command like SET DIRCMD=/P/ O:N in your AUTOEXEC.BAT file. This particular command tells DIR to present files sorted by name and to pause after each screen has been displayed. The DIR command looks for the environmental variable DIR-CMD each time you run it. So, by defining the variable with the switches you want DIR to use, you can simply key in `dir` and not worry about keying in the switches each time yourself. Whatever switches you *do* use temporarily override the DIRCMD setting whenever you use them. Thus, if you frequently need to see files sorted in a different order, you may want to create a series of batch files, each of which contains a DIR command and the desired set of switches.

If you would like to see a directory of every file on your hard disk, key in `dir c:\ /s /a /w /p`. This presents a list of all files, including system and hidden files, in a wide format, pausing after each screen. If you want to redirect the output to a file that you can print, view, or search, key in `dir c:\ /s /a /w > dir.txt`.

Using the FORMAT Command

The FORMAT command is used to prepare a blank floppy disk to hold files. It sets up a magnetic framework on the disk, mapping everything out and establishing the tracks and sectors DOS will use as pigeonholes for storing pieces of files.

The command used to be quite simple. But today, with two 5.25-inch formats and three 3.5-inch formats, things have gotten a little complicated. In the absence of any instructions to the contrary, FORMAT always tries to format a disk to the highest capacity permitted by the drive. That can cause problems.

You can format a low-density (360K) floppy for high-density (1.2MB) use, but you cannot reliably store data on a disk so formatted. The coating on a high-density 5.25-inch disk is physically different (it's thicker), even though both types of disks look the same. The plastic shells of high-density 3.5-inch disks have a very visible extra hole to distinguish them from the low-density variety. But that does not seem to matter to FORMAT, since it will opt for high-density even though the disk you have inserted is of the low-density, one-hole variety. FORMAT will try, and it will fail, reporting the disk unusable.

The solution is to always use FORMAT with the /F:*size* switch, where *size* is 360, 1.2, 720, 1.44, or even 2.88. Thus, to format a low-density 5.25-inch floppy in a high-density drive, you would key in `format a: / f:360`.

Beginning with DOS 5, an additional layer of complexity was added to the FORMAT command. By default, the command now saves the format-related information it finds on any previously formatted disk. It does this in case you want to use the UNFORMAT command to restore that information. This will make more sense to you once you realize that information does not have to be physically erased to make a disk "blank." It is only necessary to erase the disk's table of contents. By default, FORMAT saves the old table of contents before reformatting the disk.

I suppose this is a good idea, though I can't say that I've ever found it useful. I can't think of a single time when I've ever wished to be able to unformat a floppy disk. Therefore, I recommend using the FORMAT command with the unconditional (/U) switch. It saves time and it saves a bit of floppy disk space. Thus, the command I use to format a low-density 5.25-inch disk in a high-density drive is: FORMAT A: /U /F:360.

But that's far too much typing. The solution is to turn that command into a one-line batch file called F360.BAT. Create that file in pure ASCII text. Place it in a directory called C:\BATS, and make sure that both C:\DOS and C:\BATS are part of your path. Then you can key in `f360` at anytime and format a 360K disk in Drive A. You can create similar one-line batch files for the other floppy formats you deal with.

The FORMAT command automatically prompts you for a disk label, and it automatically adds a randomly generated serial number to the disk. The label and serial number remain on the disk until you format it again. If you do not want to give the disk a label, simply hit your Enter key. If you do give the disk a label and you later want to change it, you can always use the DOS LABEL command to do so. A public domain utility called DISKID, discussed later, lets you alter the serial number of a disk.

The Wonderful COPY Command

The COPY command is easy to use. If you want to copy a file from one location to another, all you have to do is enter the command and tell DOS the name and location of the target file and the place you want to put it: `copy temp.txt a:`. You can also copy a file to a different location and give it a different name in the process: `copy temp.txt a:new.txt`. And, of course, you can use wildcards: `copy *.txt a:`.

PowerPoint

Creating Phantom Drives

The DISKCOPY command can be used in the form *diskcopy a: a:* to create a duplicate disk in the same format as the original. But if you have a *file* on, say, a 5.25-inch disk that you want to copy to another 5.25-inch disk, you cannot use COPY or XCOPY to do the job. These commands will think you are trying to copy a file onto itself. The easiest solution is to use COPY to copy that file onto your hard drive, swap floppies, and then copy it from the hard drive onto the second disk.

If you find that you have to do this frequently, however, you should install the DRIVER.SYS driver that comes with DOS in your CONFIG.SYS file. DRIVER.SYS was designed to attach an actual physical drive to the system, but you can use it to create a second "phantom" drive with a different drive letter for each of your floppy drives. Assume you have floppy Drives A and B, and hard drive volumes C and D. The next available drive letter is *E*, followed by *F*, of course. To create a phantom drive for Drive A, include these two lines in your CONFIG.SYS file and reboot:

```
device=driver.sys /d:0 /f:1
device=driver.sys /d:0 /f:1
```

You are *not* seeing double. These are two identical lines. Note that the lines assume that DRIVER.SYS is located in your root directory in Drive C. If you have moved it elsewhere, possibly to a directory called C:\DEVICE or C:\DOS, be sure to add the correct path location to these lines. Also, if you are using CONFIG.SYS to establish a RAM drive, you will have to adjust your LASTDRIVE statement upward accordingly. (The LASTDRIVE statement is usually required whenever you're fiddling around with drives that aren't really there, like RAM drives and the phantoms we're dealing with here.)

The /D:0 stands for drive number 0 (Drive A). The number of the physical floppy drives in a system can range from 0 through 127. The /F:1 command designates the drive as having *form factor 1*, a 1.2MB floppy. There is a form factor number for every size of floppy drive. See your DOS manual for more information. *(continued)*

> *(Creating Phantom Drives continued)*
>
> The reason you need two *identical* lines is to get DOS to prompt you to remove and insert disks when copying to your phantom drive. After the above two lines have been processed, your A drive will be accessible as Drive A, Drive E, or Drive F. (If you're quick, you may see the message *Loaded External Disk Driver for Drive A* appear twice on your screen.) Don't worry about Drive F. From this point on, you can enter a command like `copy a: *.* e:`, and DOS will prompt you to swap disks in and out of the same physical Drive A.

Most of the time, COPY is used for copying files from one location to another. But it has many other applications. For example, when I want to get a quick printout of a file, I key in `copy filename.ext prn`. This copies the specified file to the DOS "standard device" PRN, or the printer. This is often much quicker than loading a word processor or text editor and printing the file from there.

The only drawback is that you must usually take the printer offline and hit its form feed button to make it disgorge the last part of the file. But if your printer is within arm's reach, this is not much of a problem. If the printer is *not* conveniently located, use the COPY command to create a tiny form feed file called FF.

Key in `copy con:ff`. On the blank line that appears after you hit Enter, place a Control-L. (Hold down your Ctrl key and hit your L key.) The result will look like this: ^L, but make sure that you use the Ctrl+L combination to produce it. Then hit your F6 key to put a Control-Z in the file, and hit Enter. Now key in `copy ff prn`. Your printer will disgorge a single blank page.

If you find that you are copying files to the printer frequently, it may pay you to create a batch file to automate the process. You might call such a file DUMP.BAT and place both it and your FF file in C:\BATS. (Don't call your file PRINT.BAT, since this will conflict with another DOS command.)

Make the first line read: COPY %1 PRN. Make the second line read: COPY C:\BATS\FF PRN. As long as C:\BATS is part of your path, you can key in `dump filename.ext` at any time. The file will be printed and a form feed will be sent to the printer.

As you cannot fail to notice, we've been using the COPY command to actually create files. No word processor. No text editor. Just plain old COPY. There are just a few things you have to know. First, the proper syntax is COPY CON:*filename.ext.* This tells COPY to take its input from the console, computer talk for the keyboard. Second, you may type anything you want, but once you hit Enter, you cannot go back. Third, when you are finished, hit your F6 key or Ctrl+Z, and then hit Enter to write the file to disk.

You can apply the same technique to type directly to the printer, though I don't recommend it unless you are a pretty good typist. If you want to send the text that you type directly to the printer, key in `copy con: prn`, type in your text, then hit F6 and Enter.

The COPY command can also be used to combine files. In computer-speak, this is called *concatenation.* Two approaches are available. If you want to combine all the .TXT files in a directory into one big text file, you can key in `copy *.txt bigfile.txt`. COPY starts with the first .TXT file in your directory and proceeds until it reaches the last one, combining all into the file BIGFILE.TXT.

If you would like more control over the process, you can take the second approach. You can specify the filenames and the order in which they are to be concatenated. Thus, you might enter a command like this: `copy jan.txt+feb.txt+mar.txt qtr-1.txt`. This command would combine the January, February, and March text files into a file covering the first quarter—regardless of the order of those files in your directory.

There's only one other small point to be aware of, and that is that COPY actually looks at your files as it does its work. In one mode, it pays no attention at all to the contents of the files. In another, it looks for a Control-Z character, an ASCII 26. The Control-Z character—it usually appears as a little right-pointing arrow—has traditionally been used to signify the end of a text file. So if COPY happens to be looking for it, the command will assume that it has reached the end of the file and forget about anything that might follow it.

The two modes are called binary and ASCII and are controlled by the /B and /A switches, respectively. By default, most of the time, COPY operates in binary mode, ignoring the contents of the file. This is good, since an ASCII 26 character can easily appear in a spreadsheet or other binary file and not signify "end of file" at all. But when you enter a command that makes COPY think that you are concatenating files, it automatically switches to ASCII (Control-Z-sensitive) mode.

Most of the time, this isn't a problem, since it usually makes no sense to concatenate binary files. But there are a few times when COPY can trip you up. For example, suppose you had a spreadsheet file (binary) called TEST.WK1 that you wanted to copy to Drive A under a different name. To save keystrokes, you might enter `copy t*.wk1 a:save.wk1`.

This *could* result in a truncated file, if COPY happened to encounter a Control-Z. The reason is that COPY assumes that a wildcard in the source filename means you want to copy more than one file. And, when you enter a target filename like SAVE.WK1, it assumes that you want to concatenate all matching files into a new one. COPY therefore defaults to its /A or ASCII mode, making it sensitive to any Control-Zs it happens to find. Thus if your binary file contains a Control-Z character, anything after that character gets cut off.

PowerPoint

Updating a File's Date

As every DOS user knows, a "file cannot be copied to itself." But it can be concatenated to itself, and the benefit of doing so is that the file's date is changed in the process.

When I want to change a file's date and time stamp, I use a utility called FDATE. But if you don't happen to have such a program on your disk, you can use the COPY command instead. Simply key in `copy /b filename.ext+ ,,` (the paired commas are part of the command), and the date and time stamp of FILENAME.EXT will be set to the current system date and time. The /B (binary) switch is used here as a precaution to make sure that any Control-Z characters in the file are ignored.

For more complete control, use the DOS TIME and DATE commands to set your system time and date to the desired values. Then use the COPY command as described here. Finally, use TIME and DATE again to restore the actual current time and date.

I should note here that if you are going to do a lot of file copying, and you are working with DOS alone, you may find that the XCOPY command offers you more speed and flexibility than COPY. COPY operates by loading each file into memory and dumping it to the target location one file at a time. XCOPY, in contrast, reads in as many files as your available memory will allow before dumping them to their target location.

PowerPoint

A Do-It-Yourself MOVE Command

Versions of DOS prior to DOS 6 do not offer you a simple way to *move* a file from one location to another. The best you can do is to COPY a file to a different location and then DEL it from its original location. There are any number of public domain move utilities that fill this gap. But if you are operating with DOS alone, you can create your own MOVE command with a simple batch file.

All you have to do is create a batch file called MOVE.BAT containing the following two lines:

```
copy %1 %2
del %1
```

Place MOVE.BAT in a directory called C:\BATS and make sure that directory is part of your path. To use the command, key in something like this: `move cust.txt c:\storage`. The batch file replaces *%1* with CUST.TXT and *%2* with C:\STORAGE. By copying and then deleting the target file, MOVE.BAT effectively moves it to a different location.

DEL and UNDELETE

To get rid of a file, simply key in the DEL command and tell DOS the location and name of the target file. If you want to delete LETTERS.TXT, key in `del letters.txt`. If you are currently on Drive C and you want to delete a file on Drive A, you may key in `del a:letters.txt`. But I believe it is good practice to actually move to the target location and do your deletions from there. Fewer keystrokes and less mental energy are required, and once you are at the target location, you can easily do a DIR to make sure that you know the exact name of the file you want to delete. (Note that although it is no longer documented, you may also use the ERASE command to do the same thing as DEL or DELETE.)

It is often useful to use wildcards with the DEL command. If you key in `del *.txt`, for example, all files ending in .TXT will be deleted. Before doing a global delete of this sort, however, it is best to verify that only the files you intend to erase will be deleted. The best way to do that is to enter a command like `dir *.txt` first. Check the resulting list of files to make sure that you do indeed want to get rid of all of them. (A public domain utility called NO.COM will let you delete all but one or two files in a group, as discussed below.)

To get rid of all of the files on a disk or in a particular subdirectory, log onto that location and key in del *.*. This is such a drastic step, from DOS's perspective, that you are prompted with an *Are you sure?* message. If you are sure, press the Y key and hit Enter. If you are really confident about the DIR *.* command, you can answer the *Are you sure?* question before it is asked by keying in echo y | del *.*. You might put this command into a batch file called ALL.BAT and use it whenever you are absolutely certain that you do indeed want to delete all files.

Fortunately, even if you make a mistake with DEL, there's a good chance that you can recover the file with the UNDELETE command. The key thing to remember is to stop everything the moment you realize there is a file you want to recover. If you add a file to the disk or subdirectory or change it in any way, there's a chance that UNDELETE will not be able to work its magic.

As long as C:\DOS is "pathed," all you have to do is go to the target location and key in undelete. The program shows you the names of every deleted file, but each filename is missing its first character. If you want to undelete a file, respond y for "yes" when prompted and supply the correct missing first character. Most of the time, UNDELETE is able to recover your file. If it cannot, you may need a program like the Norton Utilities or some other package capable of recovering portions of a file by giving you access to the actual sectors of the target disk.

The switches one can use with UNDELETE are particularly important. Keying in undelete /list, for example, gives you a list of all deleted files that are available for recovery. You can then use the command with wildcards to zero in on a particular file or files. Keying in undelete /all will tell the command to undelete all files without prompting you to supply the first character of the filename. Undelete simply uses the pound sign (#) or the question mark (?) for the first character instead.

Microsoft licensed the UNDELETE program from Central Point Software, Inc., producers of PC-Tools, and included it first with DOS 5 and then with DOS 6. There are some differences between the two versions. DOS 5 included a Central Point Software utility program called MIRROR .COM that was designed to take a snapshot of a disk's table of contents. The snapshot was recorded in a hidden tracking file that UNDELETE knew to look for when necessary. The tracking file preserved location and address information on the deleted file but not the file itself.

DOS 6's UNDELETE

DOS 6 does not include the MIRROR command. Instead, the DOS 6 version of the UNDELETE program has the ability to create the tracking file on its own. But it also has the ability to take things a step further. The

DOS 6 UNDELETE utility can be told to set up a hidden directory called SENTRY on each drive. Once the directory has been created and UNDELETE has been loaded as a TSR, each time you use the DOS DEL command, UNDELETE will intervene to *move* the target file to the hidden SENTRY directory. Since the files in the SENTRY directory remain completely intact, you can always recover them. You don't even have to tell UNDELETE the first character of the filename. This amounts to the ultimate DOS file deletion protection.

Let me summarize the situation. If you use a version of DOS prior to DOS 5, you have no built-in file recovery features to call upon. You must rely on the file recovery facilities of packages like the Norton Utilities, the Mace Utilities, or PC Tools. (This is not necessarily a bad idea in any case, since there are some file recovery tricks you can perform with these third-party utilities not available in either DOS 5 or DOS 6.)

If you have DOS 5, you have two main file recovery options. You can use the MIRROR command to create a deletion tracking file to aid the UNDELETE command and improve its chances of success. This *Delete Tracker* option records the cluster addresses of deleted files. As long as those clusters have not been overwritten by new data, there is an excellent chance of recovery.

Alternatively, you can opt to simply use the UNDELETE command whenever you need it. With no tracking file to rely on, UNDELETE may not always be quite as successful, but you can improve its chances and boost hard drive performance at the same time by keeping your files unfragmented.

DOS 6 users have a third level of protection. Level One is simply using the UNDELETE command. Level Two is using UNDELETE to create a Delete Tracker file that will improve the chances of successful file recovery. Level Three is the *Delete Sentry* option under which files are not deleted but moved to a hidden directory called SENTRY. (The DOS 6 package also includes a Microsoft Windows version of UNDELETE in the file MWUNDEL.EXE. If Windows has been installed on your machine, the DOS 6 setup program will automatically install the program into Windows.)

Which Option for You?

The option that is best for you depends on your level of experience and the size of your hard disk. There isn't a computer user alive who has not at one time or another regretted erasing a file or group of files. Mistaken file erasure is simply a fact of life. Therefore, the ideal option is the one that makes file recovery as easy and as certain as possible.

That option is DOS 6's Delete Sentry. As discussed, Delete Sentry preserves an actual copy of the deleted file. But of course, there's a cost. When loaded as a TSR, UNDELETE occupies 13.5K of memory. More important, the hidden SENTRY directory can occupy up to seven percent of your hard disk space. Thus, if your 120MB hard drive is worth about $320, the SENTRY directory or directories will occupy a maximum of 8.4 megabytes or $22.40 worth of space. On your $540, 200MB drive, the SENTRY directory may occupy a maximum of 14 megabytes, worth about $38.

That's not too bad. Indeed, given the low cost and high capacity of the drives people are buying today, it is a very acceptable solution. If Delete Sentry's assured file recovery saves you just an hour of time in the course of the year, it is well worth the costs it imposes.

DOS 6 Point

Using Delete Sentry

The command to enter to activate Delete Sentry protection on Drive C is `undelete /sc`. To protect Drive D, enter `undelete /sd`, or simply use the single line: `undelete/sc/sd`.

The first time you enter this command, the program will set up a hidden directory C:\SENTRY—and D:\SENTRY, if you are protecting Drive D as well—and load itself as a TSR. Since Delete Sentry must be loaded into memory if it is to do you any good, be sure to include `undelete /load` in your AUTOEXEC.BAT file. UNDELETE may also be loaded high, if you have the memory.

Each SENTRY directory contains a file called CONTROL.FIL. This file has the *system* attribute and thus will not show up when you use the DIR command. Should you wish to remove the SENTRY directory from your hard disk, reboot your system *without* loading UNDELETE as a TSR. (You cannot delete CONTROL.FIL or change its attribute if UNDELETE is in memory.) Key in `cd\ sentry` to log onto the hidden directory. Then key in `attrib -s control.fil` to remove the system attribute. (This assumes that the DOS 5 or DOS 6 utility ATTRIB.EXE is in your path.) Next use the DIR command to reveal the file. *(continued)*

(Using Delete Sentry continued)

You are now free to delete all the files in \SENTRY with the command `del *.*`. The final step is to key in `cd\` to get to your root directory and then key in `rd sentry` to remove the \SENTRY directory.

As you may know, Delete Sentry offers an all-or-nothing PURGE option for cleaning out the SENTRY directory. Should you wish to be more selective, use a program like XTREE or QFILER to go into SENTRY and selectively delete files. Just be sure to reboot *without* UNDELETE loaded as a TSR before you do so.

Still, the main reason for erasing a file in the first place is to preserve disk space. In most cases, if you need to hang on to more than a few megabytes of deleted files in your SENTRY directory, there is probably something wrong with the way you are using your computer. Fortunately, you can use the PURGE option of the DOS 6 UNDELETE command to really delete the contents of the SENTRY directory at any time and keep its space consumption under control.

If hard disk space is scarce, however, I recommend simply keeping your disk in good shape and using the plain UNDELETE command to recover files. You will want to keep your files defragmented (stored in contiguous clusters) in any case, since this boosts hard disk performance. (DOS 6 includes a disk defragmenting program.)

This makes it much easier for either the DOS 5 or DOS 6 UNDELETE program to recover an erased file. Indeed, if you attempt to recover an unfragmented file soon after you have erased it—the most likely scenario—your chances of complete success are excellent. Everything depends on how many other files have been written to disk between the time you erased the file and the time you attempt recovery.

I do not recommend the middle option of Delete Tracking. In the first place, the hidden deletion tracking file does indeed occupy disk space. But more objectionable, in my opinion, is the noticeable delay Delete Tracking imposes each time you erase a file. I simply find it unacceptable.

TYPE and Ctrl+Break

The TYPE command lets you see the contents of a file. Its performance is mostly unsatisfactory, but it will do in a pinch. The best way to look at a file is to use the Toolkit program LIST.COM by Vernon Buerg. If LIST is not available, however, you can get by with a command like this: `type filename.ext | more`. This displays the contents of FILENAME.EXT one screen at a time.

Finally, DOS's "all stop" command is the key combination Ctrl+Break. If, for example, TYPE is merrily displaying a continuous stream of text and you don't want to wait for it to finish, or if you want to stop the COPY command in its tracks, hold down your Ctrl (Control) key and hit your Break key. On most keyboards Break shares a key with Pause. Entering a Ctrl+C has the same effect. Whatever is taking place stops, and you are returned to the DOS prompt.

You can use Ctrl+Break to break out of batch file programs. The system stops the batch file and presents a prompt allowing you to continue the program or return to DOS. You can also use Ctrl+Break to stop many BASIC programs, provided the programmer has not disabled that built-in function. (Once you've broken out of a BASIC program, key in `system` to return to DOS.) By including the line BREAK=ON in your CONFIG .SYS file, you tell DOS to look for a Control-Break more often than it normally would. Still, the command does not always work in all situations. So, if all else fails, do a Ctrl+Alt+Del to reboot the machine, or hit the reset button on the front of the system unit.

SECTION
2-3

COMMANDS FOR
SPECIAL OCCASIONS

The Ten Essential DOS Commands will stand you in good stead, day in and day out. As we'll see in Part 3, you will want to supplement or replace them with more powerful, easier-to-use shareware and PD utilities. But you really can get by quite nicely with the information presented in Section 2-2.

DOS does have other commands, of course. And while you may choose to ignore them in favor of third-party utilities, you should at least be aware that they exist. Many of the other DOS commands are discussed elsewhere in this book. But there are some that I would like to call your attention to here, starting with two commands you *shouldn't* use.

Probably the worst DOS command of all time is RECOVER. This command reads files sector-by-sector from a bad or defective disk and recovers as much data as possible. On the surface, this sounds like a great idea. But it should only be used in the form RECOVER D:*FILENAME* *.EXT*, where *D:* is any drive letter and *FILENAME.EXT* is a specific file. Don't *ever* enter a command like RECOVER C:, since doing so will make a complete mish-mash of your hard disk.

The other command you may not wish to use, at least not on a regular basis, is DOSSHELL. This command loads the DOS Shell program that comes with DOS 5 and DOS 6. The DOS Shell isn't a bad program, but it is unworthy of your time. Play with it as you please. But if you want a mouse-driven graphical user interface, buy Windows or OS/2. Forget the thin broth of the DOS Shell and go for the real thing.

Finally, if you do not have access to Chris Dunford's CED (Command EDitor) program, I strongly urge you to incorporate a line like `c:\dos\doskey` in your AUTOEXEC.BAT. This loads the DOS DOSKEY command buffer that lets you recall previously issued commands using the up and down arrow keys. You can then edit the commands using Ins, Del, and other keys, just as if you were using a word processor.

DOSKEY and CED are particularly helpful when you have made a mistake in a long command line. The system presents you with an error message the first time you enter the command. You can then bring the command back to the command line, correct the mistake, and reissue it. This saves a great deal of typing and mental energy.

Command Highlights

Now let's pay a brief visit to some DOS commands you may want to use every now and then. The commands are presented in alphabetical order, and you will want to consult your manual for more details on how to use them.

ASSIGN

This command is used to route requests for disk operations from one drive to another. You can thus make Drive B appear to be Drive A with a command like ASSIGN B=A. This lets you cope with older programs that insist on being run or installed from a particular drive. (With DOS 6, use SUBST to perform this function.)

ATTRIB

The ATTRIB command changes the attributes of a file or group of files. Every file has a series of unseen bits that signify its attributes. Possible attributes include read-only, hidden, archive, and system. The command ATTRIB +H FILENAME.EXT, for example, sets the hidden attribute for FILENAME.EXT and makes it invisible to the DIR or DEL commands.

The archive bit is reset or cleared by many hard disk backup programs, once the file has been backed up to a floppy disk or to a tape drive. If you make a change to the file afterward, the archive bit is set to indicate that the file has been changed. The next time the backup program is run, it notices that the archive "flag" is up, and it knows to make a copy of the file.

In a pinch, with no special utility to aid you, you can use the ATRRIB command to *exclude* specified files from a COPY or DEL operation. For example, if you wanted to delete everything but files ending in .TXT from a directory, you could first key in `attrib +h *.txt` to hide all .TXT files. Then, key in `del *.*` to erase all the files the DEL command can see. Finally, restore the .TXT files to visibility with `attrib -h *.txt`.

You might use the same approach to create a batch file that would automatically exclude whichever file or group of files you specify. Call the file HIDE.BAT and include the line ATTRIB +H %1. Then create a second file called UNHIDE.BAT with the line ATTRIB -H %1. You can then key in commands like `hide *.txt` or `hide filename.ext` to hide either a group of files or a single file. Execute your COPY or DEL command. Then key in `unhide *.txt` or `unhide filename.ext` to make the designated file or files visible again.

CHKDSK

The "check disk" command is useful when you want to know whether a floppy disk has any bad sectors that will reduce the amount of data it can hold. The FORMAT command automatically senses and blocks out any bad portions of a disk, but that naturally reduces the disk's capacity.

CHKDSK is also used to locate and eliminate lost *allocation units* or *clusters*. These are pieces of files that have somehow gotten detached from the main file body. When you enter the command `chkdsk /f` (the /F stands for "fix"), CHKDSK finds these orphans and writes each to disk as a file with a name like FILE0002.CHK. Those pieces won't do you any good if the parent file is a program, but they can help you recover lost text.

In general, it is a good idea to run CHKDSK with the /F switch once a week or so, if only to keep your hard disk in good condition. Most of the time, you will want to delete the .CHK files after you have looked at them, in order to save disk space.

FOR. . .IN. . .DO

The FOR command, as the FOR. . .IN. . .DO sequence is often called, is extremely powerful. So powerful that, if you have never used it or haven't used it in awhile, you should probably practice with it before directing it at anything you care about. The FOR command repeatedly applies a DOS command to a specified set of files.

When issued from the command line, the format is FOR *%A* IN (*SET*) DO *COMMAND*. You may use *A* or substitute any character you like except the digits 0 through 9. When you use this command in a batch file, however, you must use two percentage signs to prevent confusion with other batch file variables (%%A).

Here's a quick example:

```
for %a in (*.txt) do del %a
```

Translated, *for %a* says, "We are going to use the expression *%a* as our variable. It comes into effect later in the command line." The next phrase, *in (*.txt)*, tells DOS what set to use as criteria when *replacing* that variable as it executes the command. You can include almost any number of file specifications, with or without wildcards, to guide DOS in making its replacements. Just be sure to separate each with a space or a comma inside the parentheses.

The rest is easy. The phrase *do del %a* tells DOS to use the DEL command on whatever filename it has substituted for *%a*. Make sure the variable at the end matches the variable at the beginning exactly. If one is lowercase, the other must be lowercase also; otherwise DOS will see them as two separate variables.

Thus, if you had the files MAY.TXT, JUNE.TXT, and JULY.TXT on your disk and you issued this command, the first time it executed it would do a DEL MAY.TXT. Then DOS would look for more *.TXT files and do a DEL JUNE.TXT. The process would repeat until the DEL command had been executed once for each file DOS found in the specified set.

It is worth noting that the criteria you specify as your set do not have to consist of filenames. You could use DOS commands. Or, if you are using the command in a batch file, you could use an environmental variable like %PATH%. The batch file command FOR %%X IN (%PATH%) DO DIR %%X calls up a directory of every subdirectory in your current path.

The command line example offered above is quite simple and quite unnecessary. After all, if you were going to delete all *.TXT files, you would key in `del *.txt` and have done with it. However, suppose you wanted to delete all *.TXT files and all *.BAK files as well. Then you could enter `for %a in (*.txt, *.bak) do del %a`. That's still a lot of typing for a single command line command. If you needed to issue a command like this frequently, you would probably want to put it into a batch file. And batch files are what we will consider next.

LOADFIX

This command is discussed in the DOS startup guide. Should you ever try to start a program and get the message *Packed file corrupt*, key in `loadfix` followed by the program name to run it again. The error message is due to a bug in the Microsoft compiler that was used to create the program.

As a result, the program expects DOS to occupy the first 64K of memory. When it discovers that the first 64K of memory is not occupied, because, power user that you are, you have loaded DOS into the HMA with the DOS=HIGH command in CONFIG.SYS, the error message appears. LOADFIX fools the offending program into thinking that the first 64K of memory is occupied.

MOVE

Introduced with DOS 6, the MOVE command lets you move one or more files to the location you specify. Equally important, MOVE can be used to rename directories. Simply key in the command followed by the target file and the path of the target destination. Or key in `move` followed by the current name of the directory you want to rename and the new name you wish to use.

PROMPT

The PROMPT command has all kinds of possibilities. The default prompt is simply the letter of the currently logged drive and a greater-than symbol (C>). But you can use the PROMPT command to make the system display things like the current drive and path, the time, the date, and so on. You can even make it include a special text message.

The necessary commands are detailed in your manual, but you will find that many users like the command PROMPT PG, since this presents both the current drive and path ($P) and the greater-than sign ($G). To set the prompt to this, simply include the above line in your AUTOEXEC .BAT.

Personally, even something like C:\GAMES\KEEN> is too cluttered for my tastes. I prefer the bare C> prompt. If I have forgotten which subdirectory I'm in, I just key in `cd`. But this really is a matter of personal preference.

For my money, the most powerful use of the PROMPT command is in setting the screen colors. I despise white text on a black screen, the DOS default on most systems. I much prefer green text on black. So I have placed the following command in my AUTOEXEC.BAT file: PROMPT $e[40;32m$n$g.

I know this looks like hopeless gobbledy-gook. But I can simplify it for you. First, the *$e[* is a signal to DOS's ANSI.SYS screen driver that you loaded via CONFIG.SYS. It gets the driver's attention. The numbers simply specify colors.

The first number is the background color; the second, the foreground color. The *m* tells the ANSI driver that this is the end of the command as far as it is concerned. The *ng* represent the disk drive and the greater-than symbol. Now all you need is the color table, and you can find that in Figure 2-2-1.

REPLACE

The REPLACE command is like a smart COPY command. It replaces files on the destination drive with files on the source drive that have the same name, or have the same name and meet certain criteria. For example, you might have copied a bunch of files from your desktop system's hard drive to a floppy disk used in your laptop. If you work with those files on your laptop, some—but not all—of those files are bound to have been changed.

When you later wish to copy those changed files—and only those changed files—back to your desktop system, you can issue a command like this: `replace b: *.* c:\ /s /u`. This tells the command to compare the files on Drive B with those in all the subdirectories of Drive C (/S) and replace only those files on the Drive C that are older (/U for "update") than the versions on Drive B.

Once you've done that, you must be sure to add to Drive C any *new* files on Drive B with the command `replace b: *.* c: /a`. Note that one cannot use the /S switch with this command, so all new files will be copied into the root directory of Drive C. That means you will have to move them to their proper locations on your desktop system once REPLACE has finished. Alternatively, if you want to put all of the brand-new files on the floppy into a particular directory on Drive C, log onto that location *before* issuing the above command.

Figure 2-2-1 The Color Key for the PROMPT Command

Once ANSI.SYS has been loaded via CONFIG.SYS, it is easy to control the color of your screen's foreground and background and its color or monochrome text attributes, with the PROMPT command.

The PROMPT command format is: PROMPT $e[*X;Y;Z*m, where *X, Y,* and *Z* are replaced by foreground, background, and text attribute numbers from the tables below. The order in which the *X, Y,* and *Z* numbers appear in the command does not matter.

Thus, if you want a black text (foreground) on a black screen (background) you enter `prompt $e[30;47m`. If you want the prompt to display the drive letter and the greater-than sign, you must tell it to do so by adding *ng*, like this: `prompt $e[30;47m$n$g`.

Values for Foreground and Background Colors

30	Black foreground	40	Black background
31	Red foreground	41	Red background
32	Green foreground	42	Green background
33	Yellow foreground	43	Yellow background
34	Blue foreground	44	Blue background
35	Magenta foreground	45	Magenta background
36	Cyan foreground	46	Cyan background
37	White foreground	47	White background

Values for Text Display Attributes

0	Normal (no attributes; white on black)
1	Bold (character colors are high-intensity)
4	Underline (monochrome monitor only)
5	Blink
7	Reverse video
8	No text displayed

TREE and DELTREE

When you have nothing better than DOS to work with, you can use the TREE command to display a list of all subdirectories or all subdirectories and the files they contain. With your C:\DOS directory pathed, simply go to your root directory and key in `tree /f` to watch the command at work.

The best way to actually *use* the command is to redirect its output to a file with a command like TREE /F > TREE.TXT. You can then bring the file into your word processor or look at it with Vernon Buerg's LIST program, or you can print it out. Both LIST and your word processor can be used to search for specific filenames. You can thus use TREE and the file it produces as a crude WHEREIS utility.

Introduced with DOS 6, the DELTREE command is also handy. It lets you instantly prune a directory and any subdirectories branching from it. Simply key in `deltree` followed by the name of the target directory.

XCOPY

It's often difficult to decipher the meaning of an *X* in a program name. Sometimes it stands for "transfer" as in "X-fer;" sometimes it stands for "extended." In the case of XCOPY, the *X* probably stands for "extended," since the command extends the capabilities of the plain COPY command.

XCOPY does this in two main ways. First, it gives you greater control over which files are copied. With COPY you can only specify the filename of the target file or group of files. With XCOPY, you can specify an attribute and a date as well. That means, for example, that you can copy all files created after or before a certain date. XCOPY can also be made to copy entire subdirectories and the files they contain, instead of just one file or group of files in the current directory.

If you want to copy to Drive D the directory TEST, all the files it contains, plus all subdirectories branching off TEST and any files they contain, enter `xcopy c:\test d: /s /e`. This tells XCOPY to copy all the files in C:\TEST, plus any subdirectories (/S) whether or not they are empty (/E).

Second, XCOPY offers a faster way to copy large groups of files. The COPY command operates on one file at at time, reading it into memory in chunks no larger than 64K and dumping it to the specified location. The XCOPY command, in contrast, reads in as many files as your memory will hold before dumping them to a new location. If you have a lot of files to copy, XCOPY thus saves you a little time.

You should also be aware of another difference that distinguishes both XCOPY and COPY from the DISKCOPY command. DOS stores files in pieces located all over the disk on a "space available" basis. As we will see later in this book, this can lead to file fragmentation, and that can cause delays in retrieving a file. DISKCOPY makes an exact copy of a floppy disk, fragmented files and all. XCOPY and COPY, in contrast, read in one file at a time, so the pieces of the files they record are always contiguous.

PowerPoint

When One Disk Is Not Enough

Imagine you have a directory containing over a megabyte of files that you want to copy to 360K floppy disks. If you use COPY, the command simply quits after the disk is full. To continue the process, you will have to pick up where COPY left off and copy the remaining files by entering a COPY command for each one.

The shareware program COPYIT solves this problem. But if you do not happen to have this utility, XCOPY provides a creditable solution. The key is XCOPY's sensitivity to the archive bit. You can enter a command that sets the archive bit of every file you want to copy. Then tell XCOPY to copy the files and to reset that bit as it does so. When the first disk is full, put another disk in the drive and reissue the XCOPY command. Since the files it has already copied have been "marked" with a reset archive bit, XCOPY ignores them and picks up where it left off.

The first command to enter is something like `attrib +a *.*`. This sets the archive bit of every file in the directory. Then enter a command like `xcopy *.* a: /m`. The /M switch tells XCOPY to reset the archive bit of each source file that it copies. When the first disk is full, put a new one in the drive and issue the command `xcopy *.* a: /m` again. Repeat the cycle until all files have been copied. Note that the DOSKEY utility provided with DOS 5 and DOS 6 makes it easy to reissue commands by hitting your up or down arrow keys. Simply key in `doskey` before you begin the copying process.

PowerPoint

Answering Questions Before They Are Asked

We'll close this section with one of the simplest yet niftiest tricks of all. Use the COPY CON:FILENAME.EXT technique to create a little file called Y.TXT. Enter `copy con:y.txt`. On the blank line that appears, enter a `y`. Don't forget to hit your Enter key after pressing your Y key, since this puts a needed carriage return into the file. Finish the file by hitting your F6 key and then Enter to write the file to disk.

You can now use this file, along with the DOS less-than redirection symbol (<) to supply the response needed by a command like DEL. Thus, if you do not want to be prompted when you order DOS to delete all files, you could enter a command like this: `del *.* < y.txt` to supply a *y* to the DEL prompt *Are you sure?*

Similarly, you can record responses to prompts produced by the FORMAT command. You could use the same technique outlined above to create a file called N.TXT. The file should consist of two blank lines and an *n*, so hit your Enter key twice, then press your N key, and then hit Enter again. Finish with your F6 key and Enter.

If you were then to key in `format a: /u /f:360 <n.txt`, everything would happen automatically. You would not have to "press ENTER when ready," and N.TXT would supply an Enter to pass over the prompt for a volume label. Finally, the *n* followed by Enter that constitutes the last line of the file would respond to the FORMAT prompt *Format another (Y/N)?*, and you would be returned to the DOS prompt.

You can use this trick for many commands and programs. Indeed, it can be especially handy in your AUTOEXEC.BAT file, since it can eliminate the need for you to be sitting at your system as it goes through the bootup process. The key thing is to run the command or program by hand, keeping notes on the prompts and responses required. Then create your file to answer the questions before they are asked.

SECTION
2-4

BATCH FILE TECHNIQUE

I have a confession to make: I *love* batch files. Once you've gotten to know DOS and have a comfortable grasp of its main tools, few things are more enjoyable than creating a "batch" of properly sequenced commands, recording them as a file, and running them as a program. Batch files, in short, take you to new heights of pleasure and control, for they let you literally program your computer, even if you don't know a word of BASIC or a line of Pascal.

The handful of special batch file commands DOS provides, combined with every regular DOS command, do indeed constitute a programming language. But you should know that every programming language is seductive, and DOS's batch language is the most seductive of all. It consists of apparently simple, familiar commands, many of which you use every day. Yet this simplicity is deceptive, for once you really get into batch programming, you will find that the language is as demanding and time-consuming as anything this side of assembler.

It's great mental discipline, and it is guaranteed to provide you with hours of enjoyment. The problem is that many people, myself included, don't have hours to spend creating wonderful batch files. That's why I recommend the following approach.

The Power-User Approach to Batch Files

The batch file capabilities offered by DOS are simply too good to ignore. Every user should learn the basics, since this knowledge will save thousands of keystrokes in the course of a year.

If there are several programs you run every week, for example, create a little batch file for each and store it in C:\BATS. Add that directory to your path, and you can key in something like wp to run WordPerfect from any location on the system. No need to key in c: and then cd\wp51 and then wp. By incorporating those commands, a simple batch file called WP.BAT can handle everything for you. (Don't forget that batch files must be plain ASCII text DOS files. See your word processor manual for instructions on saving files in non-document or unformatted mode.) This technique has the added advantage of conserving the memory space DOS allocates for your PATH statement since you need only include C:\BATS in your PATH statement instead of using an entry for each directory containing a major program.

You will want to know about *replaceable parameters* (variables), labels, and a few other tools as well. But by and large, if you find that your batch files tend to grow much beyond five or six lines, you're probably spending too much time creating them. The exception, of course, is AUTOEXEC .BAT, which must be as long as it must be to get your system set up the way you want it.

You will be much better off looking for a batch file someone else has written that you can quickly adapt for your own purposes. Again, to be able to edit and adapt a file, you will have to have a basic knowledge of how batch files work. But that's not too difficult. There are batch files in public domain and shareware collections, both on disk and online, but the best source is often a book/disk package.

Windcrest/McGraw-Hill, for example, publishes an entire series of batch file books written by either Ronny Richardson or Dan Gookin. Titles include *Batch Files to Go: A Programmer's Library*, *MS-DOS Batch File Utilities*, and *Advanced Batch File Programming, 3rd Edition*.

At some point, though, batch files can become so elaborate and complex that you will probably get better results using a PD or shareware utility. A menu system is a good example. With so many powerful, easy-to-use menu programs available, most of which were written in C or Pascal, it simply doesn't make good sense to try to reinvent the wheel with a batch file-based menu system.

For Serious Programmers

Finally, if you are really interested in batch file programming, insist on a really good set of tools. DOS is fine, as far as it goes, but once you get into it, you will be frustrated by its limitations or by the kludgey techniques required to get around those limitations.

At the very least, you'll need a set of small utility programs to respond to user input and handle other little chores. And, if you are interested in becoming a serious batch file programmer, you will want to consider a program like Frank Canova's Extended Batch Language (EBL). As we will see in Section 2-5, registered users of this shareware package even receive a compiler capable of turning EBL batch programs into .EXE files for much faster execution.

Command Refresher and Command Tips

Other Random House/Glossbrenner books devote entire chapters to batch file programming and technique. Here we will simply summarize the special commands DOS makes available for use in batch files, combined with a few tips and tricks for using them most effectively. Then we will show you how to solve two problems that confront most batch file programmers.

Every regular DOS command can be incorporated in batch files. After all, in its simplest form, a batch file is really just a series of DOS commands a user might enter if he or she liked to type and wasn't keen on automation. The special batch file commands DOS gives us are designed to turn batch files into real programs capable of testing for the existence of files, conditional branching, looping, and doing many of the things "real" programs do. You will want to see your DOS manual for more details, but these special commands are:

CALL
CHOICE (MS-DOS 6 only)
ECHO ERRORLEVEL
FOR. . .IN. . .DO
GOTO
IF/IF NOT
PAUSE
REM
%0—%9 (Replaceable Parameters)
%environment-variable%
SHIFT

If you need instant help using most of these commands, simply key in help followed by the command name (HELP CALL, HELP REM, etc.).

This assumes that all DOS files are in C:\DOS and that that directory is in your path. The only commands that have no help available are ERROR-LEVEL (the HELP IF command covers this topic) and %0.

CALL

The CALL command is used to run a second batch program and then return control to the original batch program. This is important, because if you do not use CALL to run a different batch program, that program takes control and you never return to the original. The state of ECHO (ON or OFF) is retained by the "CALLed" batch program.

CHOICE

For years, DOS users and batch file programmers have sought ways to solicit user response and make their programs take actions based on those responses. Small public domain utilities appeared to answer this need, but not until MS-DOS 6 did DOS itself offer a solution. That solution is the CHOICE command.

Basically, the CHOICE command lets you prompt for a Y/N response or give the user a choice of keys. Since a different ERRORLEVEL result code will be generated by DOS for each response, it is easy to cause your program to branch with IF ERRORLEVEL...GOTO statements. All you need do to present your users with a "menu" is to use the ECHO command (ECHO A Press A to run EDIT; ECHO B Press B to run DEFRAG; etc.).

ECHO

The commands ECHO ON and ECHO OFF enable or prevent batch file commands from appearing on or *echoing to* the screen as your .BAT file is run. If you begin with an at sign (@), the ECHO OFF command will not even show up itself (@ECHO OFF). The main purpose of this command is to hide the seams and stitchery, while reducing the confusion of a new user by concealing the commands that are being executed beneath his very nose.

ECHO can also be used to display instructions or any other text for the user of your .BAT program to read. Simply include lines like, "ECHO This is some text, fella!" in your file at the appropriate points. If you want to insert a blank line in a series of text lines, enter echo . (the period is required) in your file. ANSI escape codes may also be used in the text you "ECHO" (provided the ANSI.SYS driver has been loaded via CONFIG .SYS) to really dress up your text (colors, brightness, blinking, reverse video, etc.).

The ECHO command works fine for concealing or revealing lines of text in your batch file. But if you want to conceal responses presented by DOS commands and other programs, you must use a different technique. Again, this is pure cosmetics designed to make a batch file operate as professionally as possible.

Actually, there are at least two techniques in the "art of not being seen." You could include the line CTTY NUL to start the concealment, insert your commands, and then use the line CTTY CON to bring things back to normal. The CTTY NUL command has the effect of more or less disconnecting your console (keyboard and screen) from normal DOS output and sending it to NUL, one of DOS's "standard output devices." The CTTY CON command reestablishes the connection.

Alternatively, you could redirect a command's output to the NUL device using the greater-than symbol. Thus if you did not want to see *1 file copied* or a similar response on your screen, you might use a command like this: COPY MYFILE.EXT D:\HOLD >NUL. (This command also works from the command line.)

ERRORLEVEL

The ERRORLEVEL is a result code number produced by some DOS commands and some third-party programs. The code lets your batch program know how a program turned out and take appropriate action. DOS can accept 0 through 255, for a total of 256 possible errorlevel codes. The IF ERRORLEVEL statement will be seen as "true" if the code generated is *equal to or greater than* the one specified. Thus, a line in your program reading IF ERRORLEVEL 5 GOTO :END will send the program to the label :END if the result code generated by the target program is 5, 6, or anything else between 5 and 255.

FOR. . .IN. . .DO

The basic use of the FOR command is discussed in Section 2-3, though it really comes into its own in batch files. Just remember that the idea is to get DOS to execute a command more than once, or to get it to execute the same command on a group or set of files.

The batch file format of the command is FOR %%*A* IN (*SET*) DO *COMMAND*, where *A* can be any character except the digits 0 through 9. *SET* can be just about anything—a series of file specifications (*.TXT *.BAK), a series of commands (COPY, DEL), a series of batch file variables (%1 %2 %3), or something else. The SET may be one or several items, but if several are used, they must be separated by a space or by a comma. Finally, *COMMAND* can be any DOS command in all its glory.

The FOR command is so powerful, and it can be used in so many clever ways, that it is worthy of an entire chapter—in a book about batch programming. Since this is not such a book, we will have to leave it here. But we cannot resist noting that although DOS does not allow FOR commands to be nested, you can fool DOS with a command like this:

```
for %%x in (%1) do command /c for %%y in (type pause) do %%y %%x
```

The trick is that the first FOR command runs a second copy of the command interpreter (COMMAND.COM) and *it* executes the second FOR command.

GOTO

The GOTO command sends DOS to a specified location in the program. Locations are specified by labels in the form *:LABEL-1*. The GOTO command is *always* followed by a label name (GOTO *:LABEL-1*). Probably the main thing to know here relates to the labels you choose. DOS does not read anything past the eighth letter of a label. So, as far as DOS is concerned, the lines GOTO BIGLABEL1 and GOTO BIGLABEL2 are identical. DOS simply goes to the first occurrence it finds of BIGLABEL and ignores the *1* and the *2*.

IF/IF NOT

The IF command lets your batch file test for conditions and take action based on what it finds. The command can test for three things. It can tell if one string of characters is exactly equal to another, whether a certain file exists, and whether a so-called ERRORLEVEL (exit code) number equals the number you have specified.

To perform the first test of whether one string of characters exactly equals another, you must use the *double* equals symbol (==). Thus, if your batch file is called TEST, and the user was supposed to enter test all, you would probably include the following four lines:

```
if %1!==! goto :warning
if %1==all goto :move
if %1==ALL goto :move
if %1==All goto :move
```

The first line here is designed to guard against the possibility that the user will not enter anything after *TEST*. Whatever is entered after *TEST* would be assigned to the DOS variable %1, so if there is nothing to assign, the statement in the first line would become !==! and the program would go to the label :WARNING. The remaining three lines are designed to provide for a user entering ALL in lowercase, uppercase, or mixed case.

You can ask DOS to check to see whether a particular file exists in a given location with the IF EXIST command. But you can combine this with a second command telling DOS what to do IF NOT EXIST, like this:

```
if exist c:\ed\good.txt goto :label-1
if not exist c:\ed\good.txt goto :label-2
```

Finally, there are tests for ERRORLEVEL numbers. The way through this problem is to think of ERRORLEVELs as *result codes*. One code may indicate success, while the other may indicate a poor result. Either way, you can test for the ERRORLEVEL produced by a command and have your batch file take action accordingly. You will want to see your DOS manual for the exact ERRORLEVEL numbers produced by commands, but the general batch file format is:

```
if errorlevel n command
if not errorlevel n command
```

The *n* in each of the above lines must be supplied by you, based on the ERRORLEVEL code numbers you are interested in. The *command* must also be supplied by you. It can be a GOTO followed by a label name, or CALL followed by a secondary batch file name, or ECHO followed by some text, or some regular DOS command like CD \LOTUS or DIR, or it could be some third-party utility. Whatever it is, the COMMAND is executed only if the IF condition is evaluated as "true."

PAUSE

This command stops a batch file and generates a prompt to *Press any key to continue*. This gives you a chance to repeat or continue a batch file, or gracefully exit by keying in Ctrl+C or Ctrl+Break. It is often used after a short instruction file has been TYPEd to the screen or after important information has been ECHOed to the screen.

It is nice to know, however, that you can effectively change the text that the command displays. You can work this magic by putting a line like `ECHO Jim, please press your X key now` immediately before the PAUSE command. Then make your PAUSE command read PAUSE > NUL to redirect its prompt output to DOS's NUL device.

REM

The REM or (REMark) command has two main uses in batch files. Its primary purpose is to let you add remarks and comments to a batch file. Whenever DOS sees a REM command, it ignores the line to the right of it.

Most good batch programmers take advantage of this fact to include the program's name, possibly a date, and any notes regarding the purpose or command syntax for actually running the program. This information is usually placed at the beginning of the file.

Similarly, it is always a good idea to take the time to include REM statements within a complex batch file to remind yourself of what is going on at a particular point or why the next active command was written the way it was. Even when you are writing .BAT files solely for your own use, it can be important to "comment" your files in this way, since it makes it much easier to edit or change a file six months from now, when you cannot remember exactly why you did something a particular way.

The REM command can also be used to temporarily deactivate a command line. This can be important in AUTOEXEC.BAT, when you want to boot up without loading a particular TSR. But it can also be very helpful in debugging a batch file since it lets you zero in on troublesome lines of code or commands.

You may also use a colon (:) instead of the characters "REM." Just make sure you follow the colon with a space and then your comment. If you don't, DOS thinks the colon signals a label name in the batch file. As you probably know, if you place the command ECHO OFF or @ECHO OFF before a REM command, the "REM" and its text are not be displayed on the screen as the file runs.

As you probably did not know, you can use the REM command to create a 0-byte file. If you were to key in rem > nada.txt at the command line, for example, the file NADA would be created and it could contain 0 bytes. The same syntax works within a batch file. The file itself is irrelevant. The benefit of this use of the REM command is apparent only when combined with an IF statement.

You can thus use a batch file to say, "If such and such is true, then create a file called TRUE.TXT" and use the command REM >TRUE.TXT to do it. Later on in the program, you can say, "If the file TRUE.TXT exists, then go do this; but if it does not exist, go do that." In a moment, I'll show you how to use this technique to control how often your AUTOEXEC .BAT (or any other .BAT) file does something each time it is run.

%0—%9 (Replaceable Parameters)

Believe it or not, DOS batch file replaceable parameters are easy to understand. The key thing you need to know is that DOS parses the command one enters to run a batch file and assigns each discrete character string to one of ten variables. These variables are designated %0 through %9. (Don't let the percent signs throw you—in this context, they are merely symbols, not percent signs.)

Thus if you run the batch file CLEAN.BAT by entering a command like `clean *.txt *.bak`, DOS automatically makes the following assignments: %0=clean.bat, %1=*.txt, and %2=*.bak. Should any of the replaceable parameters %0, %1, or %2 appear in the batch file itself—in lines like DEL %1 or COPY %2 D:\SAVE—DOS would act on them as if the assignments or substitutions were actually included in the file. DOS would thus see DEL %1 as DEL *.TXT and COPY %2 as COPY *.BAK. Note that, as discussed later, the SHIFT command can effectively increase the number of available variable slots.

%ENVIRONMENT-VARIABLE%

Variables can be put onto the DOS environment scratchpad with the SET command. Applications programs often use environmental variables to tell them where to store temporary files or how to behave in general. DOS uses the environmental variable PATH to tell it where to look for executable programs. You, too, can make use of environmental variables via batch files.

All you have to do is frame the name of the environmental variable with percentage signs like this: %PATH%. Now, PATH happens to be one of DOS's fixed environmental variable names. But nothing's to stop you or your batch files from creating environmental variables of your own choosing. Simply include the desired SET command in your batch file. Then you can use the value of the variable you have defined in your batch program.

Here's a quick example. Suppose that you are debugging a batch file and thus need to be able to turn ECHO ON and OFF. You want it off so you can make sure that all of your programming handiwork has been concealed; but you want it on to track what is happening to cause the program to malfunction. Ordinarily, you might bring the file into your word processor or text editor each time you wanted to change the status of ECHO.

But here's a better way. Simply include the line ECHO %X% in place of ECHO ON or ECHO OFF. Then, when you want to toggle ECHO on, enter the command `set x=on` at the DOS command line and run your batch program. To toggle ECHO off, enter `set x=off` at the command line. This is much easier than opening the file with your word processor each time you want to change your ECHO command. When the file is running perfectly, however, use your word processor to replace ECHO %X% with @ECHO OFF.

SHIFT

The SHIFT command lets you increase the number of replaceable parameters (variables) DOS can use in your batch files. Since the first parameter (%0) is always the name of the batch file itself, the actual number of usable variables is effectively nine. That's still a lot, but DOS lets you use even more with the SHIFT command. Imagine, for example, that you have entered a batch command followed by twelve replaceable parameter values.

You may have a total of 127 characters, including spaces, plus Enter, for a total of 128 characters on a command line. When you reach 78 characters on the line beginning with the DOS prompt, the text wraps around and appears on the next line down. DOS doesn't care—it's not a command until you hit Enter. For simplicity's sake, assume the command line reads TEST followed by the numbers 1.TXT through 12.TXT, each separated by a space.

The first time DOS looks at this line, it assigns TEST to %0, 1.TXT to %1, 2.TXT to %2, and so on. But it runs out of possibilities after 9.TXT has been assigned to %9. However, while it is not able to assign 10.TXT, 11.TXT, and 12.TXT to a replaceable parameter at this point, DOS remembers them.

Let's assume that your batch file runs some command against %1. Say, it is DEL %1. When DOS reads that line, it makes the substitution and executes the command DEL 1.TXT. If the next command in the file were SHIFT, the phrase "TEST" would drop off the list and 1.TXT would be assigned to the variable %0. Everything else would shift to the left as well, like marbles in Chinese Checkers. After the SHIFT command, 2.TXT would be assigned to %1, 3.TXT would be assigned to %2, and so on. In short, the SHIFT command lets your batch file process a variable, get rid of it, and shift everything else to a lower variable number.

Solving "Case" Problems

As is true with many programming languages, DOS's batch language pays attention to the case of the letters a user enters. You may not be aware of it, for example, but an uppercase *Y* is symbolized by a completely different ASCII code number than a lowercase *y*. A careful programmer thinks of this and makes provision for the program to accept either *Y* or *y* from the user.

Since a batch file that is limited to only the tools DOS provides is not interactive, you might think that you do not have to worry about the case of user input. Most of the time, in a simple batch file that does not accept replaceable parameters (variables), you don't.

But imagine that you have a batch file called GO.BAT that is designed to be used in the form GO LOTUS, GO WP, or GO COMM. Depending on the variable you specify, GO.BAT will take you to a program's directory and load the designated program. Even if you were the only one who was going to use GO.BAT, you would want to make provision for someone entering "LOTUS," "lotus," and "Lotus," for example. The following three lines are the traditional way of doing just that:

```
if %1 == LOTUS goto run_lotus
if %1 == lotus goto run_lotus
if %1 == Lotus goto run_lotus
```

You would have to include a similar set of lines for each possible variable (WP, wp, Wp, COMM, comm, Comm, etc.). And even then, the program would not be proof against typographical errors like "GO loTus."

The answer to this problem can be found in the DOS environment. Environmental variables can be used in batch files, as you know, and they are not case-sensitive. As long as the user gets the letters right, DOS does not care. Thus, the solution to the case problem is to include the line SET %1=ZZ *before* any lines evaluating %1.

I've used *ZZ*, but you can call your environmental variable anything you like. When the user keys in go lotus, %1 is equal to *lotus*, but thanks to your SET command, the environmental variable *ZZ* is equal to *lotus*, *LOTUS*, *Lotus*, or any other variation of case. Here are the core lines used to implement this trick. Notice that the last line clears the variable by setting %1 equal to nothing.

```
set %1=ZZ
if %ZZ%! == ! goto error_message
if %ZZ% == lotus goto run_lotus
   .
   .
   .
set %1=
```

Getting a Batch File to Count

DOS does not offer any built-in function for controlling how many times something is done or for testing whether some command or process has been executed. As noted earlier, however, you can often get around this limitation by using the REM command to create a 0-byte file with a particular name. If the file is created only after a certain thing has happened, your program can test to see if that thing has happened by testing for the existence of a file by that particular name.

The same technique can be used to get a batch file to count. Suppose, for example, you wanted your batch file to execute some command only every third time you ran the file. Here is the basic logic you would use:

```
@ECHO OFF
IF NOT EXIST TEST? GOTO NOPE
IF EXIST TEST1 GOTO ONE
IF EXIST TEST2 GOTO TWO
IF EXIST TEST3 GOTO THREE
GOTO ERROR
:NOPE
REM > TEST2
GOTO END
:ONE
REN TEST1 TEST2
GOTO END
:TWO
REN TEST2 TEST3
GOTO END
:THREE
REN TEST3 TEST1
ECHO This is the third time you have run this file.
GOTO END
:ERROR
ECHO Another "TEST" file exists;
ECHO Please delete it and try again.
GOTO END
:END
```

If you call this batch file TEMP.BAT, and key in temp at the command line, nothing appears on the screen the first two times. But you see the message the third time you run it. The cycle then starts over again.

SECTION

2-5

CRUCIAL TOOLS FOR
BATCH FILES

Although DOS doesn't appear to offer you all that much to work with when preparing batch files, as we have seen, clever use of the tools DOS *does* provide can make batch files do some remarkable things. Nevertheless, there comes a time when it is simply foolish to allow yourself to be limited by DOS alone.

Many programmers have come to the same conclusion, and as a result, hundreds of different .COM and .EXE programs have been created to supplement DOS's batch file offerings. The nice thing is that these tools are typically in the public domain, and you can obtain them for little more than the cost of a floppy disk, with no obligation to register the programs you like. They are also very easy to use. Best of all, doing so can make you look like a programming genius.

In this section we will look at some of the best little tools you may want to consider adding to your collection. Then we will offer a brief profile of the Extended Batch Language (EBL) package. All of these programs are available through Glossbrenner's Choice. But, really, with the exception of EBL, the specific program rarely matters. What matters is the *function*. There are, for example, many programs to turn a user's NumLock key on or off. There are lots of programs that can endow your batch files with the ability to ask a user to enter Yes or No. And so on.

The key thing to bear in mind is this: If there is a function you need to make your batch file do what you want it to do, chances are that any number of programmers have felt the same way and created a tool to provide it. The best way to look for such tools is via an online system like Compu-Serve or GEnie or a good bulletin board. User group and mail-order share-ware catalogues tend to lump all such little programs onto a disk called "Utilities," without taking the time to cite and explain each one. But on-line systems treat each program individually, making it easier to locate.

Batch File Utility Toolbox

Two functions most users need when preparing batch files are the ability to accept input from the user and to branch the program on the basis of that input, and the ability to feed keystrokes to a program the batch file is de-signed to run. A program called ASK.COM addresses the first require-ment, and FAKEY.EXE handles the other.

We will profile them briefly here. Then we will look at REBEEP, TUNE, WAIT, and WAITUNTL, each of which makes it easy to add pi-zazz and power to your batch files. Finally, we will introduce you to BAT2-EXEC.COM, a program by Doug Bolling that compiles your batch files into a .COM file for much faster execution.

ASK

This little program is used in the format ASK [*PROMPT LINE*], where you supply the prompt line text. For example, you might include the line "ASK Do you want to run Word Perfect now? (Y/N)" in your batch file.

If the user enters either a *Y* or a *y*, the ERRORLEVEL is set to 0. If the user enters *N* or *n*, the ERRORLEVEL is set to 1. (Any other answer causes the ASK prompt to appear again.) This allows you to test for the ERROR-LEVEL (result code) and have your program take action accordingly with lines like:

```
if errorlevel 0 goto run_wp.
if errorlevel 1 goto end
```

FAKEY

FAKEY lets you prepare a batch file containing the keystrokes a program requires to accomplish your goal. The "fake" in the name comes from the fact that you are, in effect, faking out or fooling the target program into thinking that the input it is receiving is coming from the keyboard instead of the FAKEY file.

This is usually better than redirecting required keystrokes to a program from a special file, as discussed earlier in this part of the book. For one thing, the redirection technique does not work with all programs. For another, with FAKEY you place all the necessary keystrokes in your batch file. There is no need for an additional file of recorded keystrokes.

FAKEY was written by System Enhancement Associates (SEA), the same people who invented .ARC files. A similar program called KEY-FAKE (produced by *PC Magazine*) also exists, but I like FAKEY better because it allows you to build in the delays that some programs require when they are booting up.

The way to use FAKEY is to think in terms of loading the keyboard with the keystrokes a program will need, before you call the program. You can load the keyboard buffer with any series of keystrokes you would enter yourself, including Esc and control codes.

WAIT and WAITUNTL

These are two very convenient programs. The command WAIT *n* will cause the system to pause *n* seconds before continuing. The command WAITUNTL *hh:mm:ss* will cause the system to wait until the specified time (hours, minutes, and seconds) before continuing.

Before using WAITUNTL, make sure that your system clock is properly set to the correct time. (Use the DOS TIME command.) Also, if you plan to put the system into suspended animation for any length of time, you might want to have your screen blank to preserve its phosphor. FANSI Console, discussed in Part 3, includes this ability. But there are many little screen-blanking utility programs designed to do this as well.

REBEEP and TUNE

Written by Mark Kelinsky with modifications by Ken Goosens, REBEEP displays the phrase *Press any key to continue. . .* while sounding an insistent two-tone beep. It is absolutely guaranteed to get a user's attention.

Many "beep" programs simply beep once and stop. That's fine for many applications. But not when immediate attention is required and you happen to be on the other side of the office. That's why I like to use REBEEP in the batch file I use to format floppy disks. It makes it very clear when one pass is done and the machine needs fresh blanks.

TUNE is one of my favorite ways to tone up a batch file. Programmed by Jeff Garbers, author of the original Crosstalk communications program, TUNE plays one of five tunes. It is activated by a line like TUNE *N.X*, where *N* is a number from 1 to 5 specifying the tune, and *X* is a number from 1 to 9 designating the speed at which the tune should be played.

Tunes 1 through 3 are phrases from the theme song for *Close Encounters of the Third Kind*. Tune 4 is the opening phrase of the famous funeral march. Tune 5 consists of the opening bars of a light melody I cannot identify. (I have my disk-formatting batch file play the funeral march when it encounters a bad disk.)

BAT2EXEC

This program, by *PC Magazine* contributing editor Douglas Boling, will compile your batch files into .COM files for added speed. When DOS runs a batch file, it loads the entire thing into memory and then starts at the top, reading and acting upon each line in turn. In order to act on a command, DOS must first read it and then "interpret" it by converting it into the machine language instructions the CPU requires. All of this takes time.

BAT2EXEC reduces the delays by making the conversion into machine language once and recording the result as a .COM program file. As with all compiled programs (BASIC, C, Pascal, etc.), once the process has been completed, you can't change the resulting file. The only way to make changes is to edit the "source code" (your original batch file) and recompile by running BAT2EXEC again.

To use BAT2EXEC, enter `bat2exec file.bat` where *file.bat* is the name of your batch file. The program creates a file called *FILE*.COM, using the same name as your batch file. If BAT2EXEC can't understand a line in the batch file, it prints an error message indicating the line in the file where it encountered the error.

Of course, you don't want to compile all of your batch files. BAT2EXEC should not be used on AUTOEXEC.BAT, for example, since it must remain a genuine batch file with exactly that name in order for COMMAND.COM to find it. Similarly, batch files that run TSRs should not be compiled, since the memory occupied by such a compiled file will be allocated to the TSR instead of being released once your compiled batch file finishes.

Real Power with EBL

If you plan to do much serious batch file programming, limiting yourself to DOS's offerings is like trying to play basketball with one hand voluntarily strapped behind your back. With skill, imagination, and agility, you can do some clever things. But frankly, why bother? Get yourself a real programming tool, like Frank Canova's Extended Batch Language (EBL). Learn to use it. Then, take no prisoners!

EBL is a complete programming language that lets you program in DOS the way you might in BASIC. If you are a user of VM/370, you will find EBL similar to that language's EXEC2. We can only begin to summarize EBL's features here, but you should know that in addition to all DOS commands, batch and otherwise, you have available over 45 *other* commands and functions. For example, consider EBL's IF command. The format is IF WORD1 CONDITION1 WORD2 CONDITION2 COMMAND.

Each word can be a fixed string of letters, or a variable, or a combination of both. And the conditions can be:

<   less than

>   greater than

<>   not equal to

=   equal to (not case-sensitive)

==   exactly equal to (case-sensitive)

Thus, if you are using EBL, all of the following IF statements compare correctly and execute their corresponding TYPE command. The first two statements initialize variables used in the IF commands:

```
%1 = ABC
%2 =
IF ABC = %1 TYPE The variable contains ABC.
IF %1 = abc TYPE This also matches.
IF 0 <> 00 TYPE These are different lengths.
IF 0 < 00 TYPE 0 has a smaller length.
IF 456 > 123 TYPE Numerically, 456 is bigger.
IF 456 < %1 TYPE ASCII value of 456 is smaller.
IF AABCD = A%1D TYPE Token substitutions are made.
IF %2 <> %1 TYPE Variables are different lengths.
IF .%2 = . TYPE This matches if var is empty.
IF BOX = BOX IF DOG <> CAT TYPE Did multi-if compare.
IF 1 + 2 = 3 TYPE Arithmetic results match.
```

EBL's functions are organized into four categories: console, string handling, system, and EBL control. (Please remember that these are just the functions. We have not included EBL commands like INKEY or BEGSTACK to load the keyboard stack.) Space does not permit a complete explanation, but if you've done any programming at all, many of the functions will reveal their meaning by their names. Please see Figure 2-5-1 for a complete list.

Figure 2-5-1 A Summary of EBL Functions

EBL Console Functions

CHARIN( )
COLOR(Names)
CURSOR.ROW( )
CURSOR.COL( )
EDIT(Field Color)
FIELD(Field Number[,Field Color])
KEY(Name)
KEYPRESSED( )
PLAY(Notes)
SELECT(Field Color[,Bar Color [,Arrow]])
WINDOW(X1, Y1, X2, Y2 [,Kind])

EBL String Functions

CENTER(String, I [, Pad])
COPIES(String, N)
DELWORD(String, N [,Length])
FIND(Sentence, Phrase)
LEFT(String, I [, Pad])
LENGTH(String)
LOWER(String)
REVERSE(String)
RIGHT(String, I [,Pad])
SPACE(String, N [, Pad])
STRIP(String [, Type [, Char]])
SUBWORD(String, N [, Length])
UPPER(String)
VERIFY(String, Reference)
WORD(String, N)
WORDS(String)   *(continued)*

(Figure 2-5-1 continued)

EBL System Functions

    CHDIR(Directory)
    DATE([Type])
    DIR(File [,Type [,Attribute]])
    EXIST(File)
    GETDIR()
    INT86(Intr, Regs)
    MKDIR(Directory)
    PEEK(Locn)
    POKE(Locn, Value)
    REBOOT
    RMDIR(Directory)
    SEEK(R/W, Posn)
    TIME([Type])

EBL/Control Functions

    NOT(Expression)
    TRACE(Type)
    VERSION()
    WHATFUNC()

Peeks, Pokes, Floating Point, and More

Extended Batch Language is simply terrific. The PLAY function, for example, plays a list of notes (up to 50 notes and rests can be played in the background) identical to those available in BASIC. The SELECT function lets the user move the cursor to select one item from a list of several. A moving bar indicates which item can be selected. The WINDOW function draws a rectangular area, in color, on the display. The INT86 function lets you execute an 8086 interrupt from your EBL batch file.

There are peeks and pokes, math functions, floating point functions, and the keyboard stack, which lets you load the keystrokes that programs will need onto a stack before they run. There is also a support bulletin board service for registered users, allowing you to contact EBL's author directly for help with your questions and problems.

Extended Batch Language is available as shareware. (The entire package, in compressed form, fits on a single 5.25-inch disk.) The registration fee is $82 and includes a bound, professionally-printed manual and all shipping and handling costs, plus a password to the BAT-BBS support bulletin board. The shareware version contains a demonstration program that would be impressive under any circumstances. But when you consider that it is all being done with EBL batch files, it is simply mind-boggling.

With EBL, you can create complete applications or menu systems or just about anything else you want—either for yourself or those you support—by "programming in DOS." The latest version of EBL is fully compatible with DOS 5 and DOS 6, but it can also be used with OS/2 in real mode, and with environments like PC Network, Windows, DESQview, and 4DOS.

PART III

TURBOCHARGED DOS

What You Will Learn

You can think of unadorned DOS, including the Ten Essential DOS Commands, as your computer survival kit. They are equivalent to the knife, compass, and box of matches given to troops in basic training—just before being left in the North Carolina swamps and told to survive on their own for three days. It's not always pleasant, but with the proper training, it can be done.

Personally, I think computing should be as pleasant as possible. The basic skills will serve you well. Indeed, you *have* to have them. But there is no reason to spend the rest of your computing life subsisting on snakes, crawdads, and the tubers you've clawed out of the ground. That's why, if given a choice between memorizing some complicated DOS command or using a simple PD or shareware utility, I'll always take the easy way out.

DOS is adequate, but it is certainly not inspired. To put it another way, if a giant bureaucracy were to create an operating system, it would create a set of tools just like DOS. The product would get the job done, but it would be as bland as cold porridge and about as intuitive as a tax form.

Life doesn't have to be this way. When you're using someone else's computer, you've got to be able to fend for yourself. You've got to know the basic DOS commands and be able to survive without your favorite utilities—unless you had the foresight to bring them with you.

But your own system is your castle. Your nest. You can customize and personalize it any way you want. After all, despite the trend toward replacing the mainframes of old with gaggles of linked-up, networked machines, your system is still a *personal* computer. So make the most of it!

Each of us is different, and I wouldn't dream of saying this is the way it has *got* to be. There are many ways to accomplish the same thing on a DOS machine. If you have found an approach or a technique you like, by all means, stick with it. However, in my opinion, computer books and magazines take diversity too far. Most publications say, in effect, "Well, you could do it this way. . . or that way. . . or some other way!"

No one is willing to stick his or her neck out and say, "Look, folks, this is how it should be done." Yet that is precisely the kind of guidance many users need. And that's what you'll find in this part of *Power DOS!*

The hobbyists—those who spend all their free time playing with computers—may disagree. But those of us with lives to live and businesses to run are inclined to say, "Don't bring me an interminable list of options. I'm too busy for that. You're the expert. Bring me the best. Tell me what I should do. That's what I'm paying you for, after all."

It is in that spirit that the following advice is offered. The information represents more than a decade of working with personal computers, augmented by a deep familiarity with public domain and shareware software and the unique powers it provides.

I certainly wouldn't insist that you incorporate every aspect of the following approach into your own way of doing things. But I guarantee that if you do, you will find that your DOS-based machine is easier to use, day in and day out, than any system running Windows or OS/2. You will be able to operate much faster. And without the resource demands (hard drive space, DRAM, and super-fast CPU) required for running Windows or OS/2 on a regular basis, your equipment will cost you far less as well.

Three Components for Turbocharged DOS

The turbocharged DOS approach involves three main components: system setup, command line tools, and file management. It requires a relatively small number of very good utility programs, most of which can be found as shareware or in the public domain. One or two commercial utility packages, like The Norton Utilities and PrintCache from LaserTools Corporation, are also helpful.

However, while the names of the specific programs cited here are important if you plan to duplicate or customize this particular setup, they are really part of a larger point. That point is to make you aware that commercial, shareware, and PD utilities and other tools of the sort discussed here exist, and if you take advantage of them, you will find that your computer is much easier—even fun—to use.

This part of the book concludes with a section devoted to an extraordinary program called QuikMenu. QuikMenu is available as both shareware and as shrink-wrapped, commercial software. In either case, its unique selling proposition is that it produces a snazzy, graphical interface that will make you think you are running Microsoft Windows 3.1. Unlike Windows, however, QuikMenu is always fast and responsive and does not require tons of extra memory and hard disk space. QuikMenu must be seen to be believed, and to make this as easy as possible, we've arranged to make it available for a mere $2. (See Part 9 for ordering details.)

SECTION
3-1

SETUP FOR CONVENIENCE

In this section, we'll look at two main topics: the directories you should create on your hard drive and the key lines you should include in CONFIG.SYS and AUTOEXEC.BAT.

Hard Drive Partitions

In years past, it was necessary to partition a hard disk into volumes (Drive C, Drive D, etc.) no larger than 32 megabytes each. DOS 4.x broke that barrier, and DOS 5 extended things even further, so that you can now have a Drive C as large as 4 gigabytes (4 *billion* bytes).

That's a nice capability. But, sad to say, it leads many users astray. It may seem logical to make your entire 200MB drive Drive C, but doing so robs you of the first tier of DOS's built-in filing system. It is much better, on a personal system at least, to divide that 200MB up into Drive C and Drive D, possibly allocating 100MB to each. That way, Drive C can hold the programs you use most often and Drive D can be used for storage.

If you have a 100MB drive, you might assign 80MB to Drive C and 20MB to Drive D, or you might divvy things up 50/50. The actual division is up to you, though you might start by totaling the number of bytes occupied by your main programs and then doubling the figure to come up with a rough estimate of the best size for Drive C.

Benefits of Multiple Partitions

There are at least two outstanding benefits to telling DOS's FDISK program to partition your hard disk into two different drives. First, by keeping less frequently used programs and files on Drive D, you simplify and shorten the output of the DIR command. That way, when you use DIR on Drive C, only directories containing the programs you frequently use are displayed.

Second, and at least as important, you simplify the subdirectory structure. That often means that you can get by with one less level of subdirectories and still keep things organized. For example, imagine that you want to store a set of old spreadsheets and a set of old text files.

If you had only Drive C to work with, you might create a directory called OLDSTUFF, and then create subdirectories branching off it called OLDLOTUS and OLDTXT. To keep your files organized, you might then add subdirectories branching off of OLDLOTUS for each of the last several years (89WKS, 90WKS, 91WKS, etc.). This is a great organizational structure. But it is cumbersome, as you will find out the first time you have to use a long CD command like this: CD\OLDSTUFF\OLDLOTUS\89WKS.

Now, rewind the tape and play it again on the assumption that you have both Drive C and Drive D. You've decided that you're going to use Drive D to store all your old files. You won't need a directory called OLDSTUFF, since you already know that everything on Drive D is old. (You could even use the LABEL command to give Drive D the label OLD STUFF.)

Therefore, you can create OLDLOTUS and OLDTXT branching off the root directory of Drive D. You could then use a command like CD\OLDLOTUS\89WKS instead of the longer command shown above. Drive D lets you eliminate an entire level of subdirectories while preserving your organizational structure.

Recommended Directories

If you currently have only Drive C, don't worry. You may find that your present setup is quite workable and prefer to keep things as they are. However, the next time you do a complete hard disk backup (see Part 5 of this book), you may want to consider repartitioning your disk into two or even three different drive volumes.

Now let's look at the directories you should create on Drive C and the files they should contain. I have a friend who keeps absolutely everything in Drive C, with nary a subdirectory in sight. It's a complete mess. But I wouldn't dream of advising her to change it. Oma, as I'm privileged to call her, is 87, and she gets along quite nicely writing letters and running the daylights out of a genealogy program she's using to prepare her family's history.

In my opinion, however, it is best to store as few files in your root directory as possible. With very few exceptions, the only files that absolutely must be there are CONFIG.SYS and AUTOEXEC.BAT. As we saw in Part 1, you can keep COMMAND.COM in a subdirectory and direct DOS to it via the SHELL command in CONFIG.SYS.

Let's assume that this is how you would like to arrange things. CONFIG.SYS must be your real CONFIG.SYS file. But there is an important trick to know regarding AUTOEXEC.BAT. The trick is to create a subdirectory called something like "STARTUP" branching off the root. Copy all of the programs you want to have loaded automatically on bootup into C:\STARTUP. Then create a batch file in that directory called AUTO .BAT (or some similar name) and make *it* do what you want an AUTO-EXEC.BAT file to do.

Finally, return to the root of Drive C and create a file called AUTO-EXEC.BAT that contains only two lines:

```
cd\startup
auto
```

This approach has at least two advantages. First, it lets you collect all of the little utilities and other programs you want to have loaded or run on bootup into a single directory (C:\STARTUP). That eliminates clutter in your root directory and it means you do not have to worry about specifying elaborate paths when activating a program in AUTO.BAT. Since the target program is right there in the STARTUP directory, there's no need to tell AUTO.BAT where to find it. (If you use AUTO.BAT to load a lot of programs, it can be convenient to put their associated documentation files in STARTUP, as well, for easy reference.)

Second, a very bare AUTOEXEC.BAT file of the sort I've recommended acts as a defense against programs that like to fiddle with the file. A well-mannered software installation program always asks for permission before adding anything to CONFIG.SYS or AUTOEXEC.BAT. But not all such programs are so polite. With a bare AUTOEXEC.BAT, however, it is easy to see what they have done.

You will need other subdirectories as well. Here is a summary of the directories you should create branching off the root directory of Drive C:

C:\BATS Put all of the batch files you use into this directory.

C:\DEV Store all your device drivers (files ending in .SYS, .DEV, etc.) and TSRs here. Some users prefer to call this directory "BIN" for "binary," but that's too bytehead for my tastes.

C:\DOS This is the place to store all of the files that were copied to your disk when you installed DOS. The Random House/Glossbrenner books on DOS will tell you which files you can safely delete to save disk space.

C:\SAVEROOT Use this directory to save copies of CONFIG.SYS and any other files you may have in your root directory, plus the complete contents of C:\STARTUP. This is just a precaution, of course. But on more than one occasion, when I've screwed up my CONFIG.SYS or AUTO-EXEC.BAT files, I have found it convenient to have extra copies tucked away in C:\SAVEROOT.

C:\STARTUP As discussed, this is the place to put all of the programs you want to have loaded in when you boot up, along with a file called AUTO.BAT that serves as your real AUTOEXEC.BAT file.

C:\UTILS This is the place for all of your utility programs and their accompanying documentation files.

In addition to these essential directories, you will want to create a directory for each of the major applications programs you use (C:\WP, C:\EXCEL, C:\DBASE, etc.), plus each of the major utilities discussed later, including their documentation and support files:

C:\CACHE for PrintCache from LaserTools Corp.

C:\FANSI for the complete FANSI-Console package

C:\LIST for Vernon Buerg's LIST package

C:\NORTON for Symantec's Norton Utilities

C:\QFILER for Kenn Flee's file manager

C:\NEWKEY for FAB Software's keyboard macroing program

C:\PKZIP for PKWARE's compression package

C:\LHA for the LHA/LHARC compression package

C:\ARC for the PKARC or ARCE compression packages

Figure 3-1-1 A Sample Drive C Arrangement

Here is an idealized summary of what you might see when using the DIR command on Drive C. Note that COMMAND.COM can be located in the C:\DOS directory if you use the SHELL= command in your CONFIG.SYS file. Certainly you will also have directories for application programs, possibly Windows, and several other things.

There may also be additional files in your root directory. But there should not be very many. Keep your root as free of files as possible. If you don't know where to put something, make a directory called C:\MISC and keep hard-to-classify files there.

```
Volume in drive C is DISK C
Volume Serial Number is 0000-0000
Directory of C:\
ARC             <DIR>        12-13-89    11:33p
BATS            <DIR>        06-16-93     7:38p
CACHE           <DIR>        03-21-92    11:49p
DEV             <DIR>        12-13-92    11:33p
DOS             <DIR>        03-21-91    11:49p
FANSI           <DIR>        12-13-91    11:33p
LHA             <DIR>        12-13-91    11:33p
LIST            <DIR>        12-13-91    11:33p
NEWKEY          <DIR>        12-13-91    11:33p
NORTON          <DIR>        03-22-93     2:06p
PKZIP           <DIR>        05-27-88    12:03a
QFILER          <DIR>        02-20-92     1:24a
SAVEROOT        <DIR>        03-01-92     8:00p
STARTUP         <DIR>        12-13-91    11:33p
UTILS           <DIR>        03-13-92     3:47p
AUTOEXEC BAT           76    04-16-92     6:53p
CONFIG   SYS          483    06-17-93     4:22p
     nn file(s)      nnnnnn   bytes
                   55906304   bytes           free
```

Installing FANSI-Console in CONFIG.SYS

Both CONFIG.SYS and AUTOEXEC.BAT are discussed at length in Part 1 of this book. We'll look at them again in Part 4 when we delve into maximizing memory usage, since these two files are the main tools at your disposal. Here, I'd like to focus on one particular line I recommend you use in CONFIG.SYS. Then we will look at several lines used to load important utility programs via AUTOEXEC.BAT. All of the lines discussed, and the programs they activate, are crucial to setting up your system for maximum convenience.

The key line in the CONFIG.SYS file is this:

```
devicehigh=c:\dev\fcon301k.dev /s=10000 /g=400 /r=250
```

This line loads Hersey Micro Consulting's FANSI—Fast ANSI or "fancy"—console driver into high memory. The driver is called FCON 301K.DEV, and it is located in C:\DEV with all the other device drivers. The meat of the matter is the collection of switch settings. The /S=10000 setting tells FANSI to blank the screen after about 10 minutes of no keyboard activity. That's not as much fun as flying toasters, but it is just as effective at preventing a single image being burned into your screen.

The /G=400 setting controls the duration of the computer's beep tone. By default, most PC beep tones last about a second. This setting reduces the beep (or "bell") to about a tenth of a second. If you wanted to eliminate the beep altogether, you could use a setting of /G=0.

The final switch is the most important of all. By using /R=250, you tell FANSI to set aside enough memory (expanded, extended, or conventional, depending on what you have) to recall 250 previously displayed lines. This pertains to FANSI's famous scroll-recall feature.

Once you have specified some value for the /R switch, you can hit your Pause key at any time, in any program, and put everything on "hold." You can then use your arrow and paging keys to scroll back through previously displayed screens. When you are finished, press Pause again (or hit Esc) to return to what you are doing. Or, if you see something you want to save, you can use other keys to mark off sections of the scroll-recall buffer, clip them out, and write them to a file.

I like to load FANSI as soon as possible—immediately after the commands that prepare and activate extended or expanded memory. That way, I can load FANSI into high memory but still be able to use the scroll recall feature to look at any messages that may have been generated by the rest of the lines in CONFIG.SYS. These lines typically disappear quickly as CONFIG.SYS completes and AUTOEXEC.BAT begins. Just remember, from the moment FANSI loads in with a line like the one shown above, it begins saving in its screen buffer the information that appears on the screen.

FANSI Will Change Your Life

It is simply impossible to overstate the impact that FANSI-Console and this simple CONFIG.SYS line will have on the way you use your personal computer. Never again will you be frustrated by a file directory that zips up the screen faster than a speeding bullet. Never again will you have to horse around with the DIR command's /P (for pause) switch or with passing it's output through the MORE filter. With FANSI loaded, you simply enter `dir` and let the command execute, then hit your Pause key, and scroll back through the file listing at leisure.

If you use bulletin boards or commercial online systems like Compu-Serve or GEnie, you can tell the online system to display your mail, its instructions, file directories, and other information that would normally race up the screen and off into the ether. But FANSI makes it easy to bring the text back for reading at a human pace. The same thing applies when you enter `type filename.ext` to look at a file on the screen, though you will find that LIST.COM offers an even better solution.

FANSI supports all of the features and control codes of DOS's ANSI .SYS driver, and much more besides. However, rather than risk confusing you by listing all of FANSI's features, I will simply say that the program gives you complete control over every aspect of your keyboard and screen, from key reassignment, repeat rate, and cursor speed to the number of rows and columns the screen displays and the fonts it uses.

There is simply nothing else like FANSI-Console. Yet it is available as shareware for $10. (The package is so packed with features and, at 250 pages, the on-disk manual is so extensive, that two 5.25-inch disks are needed to hold everything, even in compressed form.) If you decide to register, the cost is $75. Registration brings with it the commercial version of the product and a professionally printed, bound, and indexed manual.

The first version of FANSI appeared in 1984. But since Hersey Micro Consulting does little, if any, advertising for FANSI, magazine reviews are few and far between. No one knows about it. When FANSI is reviewed, however, the comments are uniformly positive. Writing in *Computer Shopper* (March, 1992), *New York Times* computer columnist Peter Lewis said of version 4.0, "Buy it!"

Feathering Your Nest with AUTOEXEC.BAT

The second tool for getting your system set up exactly the way you want it is AUTOEXEC.BAT. CONFIG.SYS lays the foundation; AUTOEXEC .BAT builds the structure. Here is the AUTOEXEC.BAT file that I use. It is a good model for following up on the work done by CONFIG.SYS and by the directory structure you have created. The lines are numbered for easy reference here, but, of course, they cannot be numbered in the file itself:

```
1.  echo on
2.  prompt $e[40;32m$n$g
3.  path c:\ed;c:\qfiler;c:\list;c:\dos;c:\norton;
       d:\utils;c:\bats;
4.  lh dpath30.com /p
5.  set temp=c:\
6.  set tmp=c:\
7.  lh mouse
8.  lh graphics laserjetii
9.  lh prtsc-lj
10. lh ced.com
11. nloff
12. send $e[$g39h ${Set FANSI-SHIFTLOCK$}
13. send $e[$g46h ${Set FANSI-Typewrite$}
14. send $e[$g6;50z ${Change FANSI-KEYRATE$}
15. send $e[$g0;62;46p
16. rem  The above command assigns . to > key.
17. send $e[$g0;125;62p
18. rem  The above command assigns > to } key.
19. rem  Toggle reassignments on and off with
       Alt-Ctrl-CapsLock.
20. pcache
21. cd\
```

Line by Line

Let's look at each line in this file in turn. The first line is really not needed, since DOS's default is to echo all .BAT lines to the screen unless you specifically tell it not to. I have included it to emphasize the fact that you want to see what's going on when AUTOEXEC.BAT loads. It is fine to use @ECHO OFF when preparing files for other users, but you definitely want to be able to see what's going on when your own AUTOEXEC.BAT loads in. If something seems amiss—or if something has gone wrong with your system—it can be very helpful to hit your Pause key and scroll back, courtesy of FANSI, through the screen text produced by AUTOEXEC .BAT.

The second line simply uses the PROMPT command to set the screen colors to green text on a black background. Either ANSI.SYS or FANSI-Console will respond to the commands you see here. If you prefer a different color combination or a more elaborate prompt, see your DOS manual, Part 2 of this book, or the Random House/Glossbrenner DOS books.

The PATH Command, Yet Again

Line 3 seems simple enough. And it is. But, as I have emphasized repeatedly throughout this book, the PATH command is truly the key to ease of use. The PATH command gives you "any-time access" to all of your most important programs, regardless of their location on your system. That way, you can preserve the organizational structure of keeping programs and their related files apart, but use them as if they were always located in your current directory.

With the PATH statement shown in Line 3, I can key in `ed filename.ext` to run my word processor against FILENAME.EXT, regardless of where I am. If FILENAME.EXT exists at my present location, PC-Write, my word processor, brings it to the screen. If not, I am given the option of creating such a file in the current directory.

I can key in `qfiler` at any time, and have that incredible file management program appear, focused on my currently logged location. I can key in `list filename.ext` at any time, and Vern Buerg's LIST program (located in C:\LIST) displays the target file on the screen.

I can use any DOS command, or any command in my C:\NORTON directory that contains all of the Norton Utilities. I keep all of my small utility programs in D:\UTILS, but all of them are available at any time, thanks to the PATH command. The same applies to my batch files, located in C:\BATS.

Line 4 lets me do the same thing with *data* files, which is why the program activated by Line 4 is called DPATH30. This is version 3.0 of the DPATH utility that does for data files what PATH does for program files. The /P switch in Line 4 tells DPATH30 to use the currently specified PATH, but there is an option to tell it to search through a different collection of directories instead.

With DPATH loaded, I can key in, say, `list appnotes.txt` and have the file displayed—even though APPNOTES.TXT is located in C:\DOS and I am currently located somewhere on Drive D. DPATH, in short, makes text and data files as accessible as PATH makes program files.

Lines 5 and 6 merely define (set) two variables for the environment. Some programs look for the TEMP or TMP variable to specify the location they should use when creating the temporary files they need to operate. I've used the root directory (C:\) as my specification, but you can use anything you like.

PowerPoint

Eliminating TEMP File Buildup

If you'd like to see the TEMP variable in action, key in `set temp=a:\` and put a blank disk in Drive A. Then log onto your hard drive and find a large text file. Key in `type filename.ext | more` and watch the drive light in Drive A come on. If the light does not come on, the text file probably isn't large enough. Display a few screens, but do not go to the end of the file.

Now open Drive A and reboot the system. When you're up and running again, put the floppy back in Drive A and do a DIR. You will see files with names like APAICHABH, APAICABM, and so on. These are the temporary files DOS created when you piped the text file through the MORE filter. Since you rebooted before the process was completed, DOS did not have a chance to erase them.

If you do not set the TEMP (and TMP) environmental variable, DOS and other programs create their temporary files in your currently logged directory. Since all of us are guilty of shutting off the machine or rebooting without properly exiting a program, temporary files can build up over time, robbing you of disk space.

It thus makes good sense to define TEMP and TMP as some specific location. You can then check that location periodically and clean out the garbage. I specify my root directory on Drive C because I view it every day. But you might create a directory called C:\JUNK and use it as your definition of TEMP and TMP.

Line 7 loads the Microsoft mouse driver program into high memory with the LH (LOADHIGH) command. Line 8 does the same with the DOS GRAPHICS command. Notice that GRAPHICS is followed by the name of the printer definition I want it to use (LASERJETII—for an HP LaserJet II printer). See your DOS manual for details if you are using a different make and model of printer.

Line 9 loads a little PD utility program called PRTSCR-LJ. This program overcomes the fact that when you hit your PrintScreen key (or Shift+PrintScreen), the printer does not automatically eject the page. This is true, regardless of the printer you are using. Fortunately, there is almost certainly a comparable page eject utility program for your printer. Contact your printer's manufacturer, or use the techniques presented in Part 9 of this book to find a PD or shareware version.

Line 10 loads Chris Dunford's CED into high memory. CED ("said") is the command line editor that almost certainly inspired Microsoft to create DOSKEY. One of the most aggravating error messages one can receive is *Bad command or filename.* DOS produces this message whenever you type a command incorrectly or tell it to do something with a file that it cannot find (usually because you made a mistake typing its name). Without CED or DOSKEY loaded, you have little choice but to retype everything from scratch. (DOS does assign editing commands to the function keys, but they are next to worthless.)

With CED or DOSKEY loaded, however, you can recall a command and edit it as you would a line of text in a word processor. You can make full use of the Ins and Del keys to insert and delete letters and words. And you can recall and then reissue a command you entered five (or more) commands back.

The average user will probably find DOSKEY perfectly serviceable, if a bit clunky. CED, in contrast, is fleet-footed and inspired. For example, with CED, there is no need to learn confusing special symbols like "$G" or "$B" to symbolize the greater-than sign or the pipe symbols. CED accepts the real symbols (>, |, >>, etc.). CED also accepts the standard DOS symbols for variables (%1, %2, etc.).

CED is simply a much better program. And since it matches every DOSKEY feature, I use CED. Mr. Dunford issued a new version of CED shortly after DOSKEY was introduced. He has placed the program in the public domain.

Using CED

In addition to setting up a circular command buffer that you can use to recall previously issued commands (just hit your up or down arrow keys), CED also lets you define command synonyms. (The DOSKEY term for this is "macros.")

For example, if you want the system to give you a directory every time you key in d (instead of DIR), you can load CED and key in `ced syn d dir`. From then on, each time you hit an upper- or lowercase d followed by Enter, your computer will act as if you had keyed in `dir`.

This only touches on CED's power. The program has lots of other features. But you should know that as good as CED is, the commercial version, PCED (Professional CED) is even better. Among other things, it offers an online help command, the ability to automatically log to a file every DOS command issued in a session, a "learn" mode that lets you save to a file the synonyms you have defined during a session for reloading later, and much else besides. The documentation for the public domain version is on disk. PCED customers receive a typeset manual. In both cases, the doc is well-written and complete.

Customizing the Keyboard to Your Liking

It's the little things that drive you crazy when using a computer. Why doesn't the PrintScreen key automatically send a form feed when it's done, instead of forcing you to manually eject the page by fiddling with the printer's front panel buttons? Why must the cursor move so slowly when you want to zip across the screen? And so on.

The answer, of course, is that some setting or design must be the default. That's true with any appliance. Makers of VCRs, microwave ovens, and similar equipment decide how the thing should work, and that's that. Users have no choice in the matter.

But computers are different. Not only are you much more intimately involved with your computer than, say, with your digital clock radio, you also have the power to change just about any default setting you do not like. The mistake so many people make is to view their PCs like their VCRs and adapt *themselves* to the hardware, instead of the other way around.

Lines 11 through 19 are designed to do just that. Line 11 runs a tiny PD program that turns off the NumLock key. On the original PC keyboard, this was essential because the Home, End, and other cursor control keys shared space with the numerical keypad. The "101 keyboard" that has become standard equipment for desktop systems today includes a set of dedicated cursor control keys, as well as those on the keypad. So toggling off the NumLock key may not be important to you. But I find it more convenient to use the keypad for cursor control, so I toggle the key off.

Lines 12 through 15 and Line 17 use the SEND.EXE program that comes with FANSI-Console to send control sequences to the FANSI driver. Unlike the PROMPT command, which transmits its escape sequences to the driver every time you hit Enter at the command line, SEND does its job just once. Using SEND also eliminates the need for separate files of control sequences to be "TYPEd" to the screen.

All of the control sequences shown in these lines are unique to FANSI. FANSI supports all the standard ANSI.SYS sequences, but it uses its own sequences for its many additional features. The nice thing is that you do not need to know anything about this FANSI "metalanguage."

The package comes with a program called FANSISET.EXE that lets you choose the features you want to activate or deactivate from a menu. FANSISET then outputs the proper control codes to a file, which you can incorporate into your batch files. It even labels each line for you ("Set FANSI-SHIFTLOCK," etc.). Here are the functions activated by lines 12, 13, and 14:

- Set FANSI-SHIFTLOCK   Forces the system to display the shifted character for *all* keys when CapsLock is on. Normally, for example, engaging the CapsLock does not affect the number keys across the top of the keyboard. With your CapsLock on, if you press the 2 key, you get a 2. Thanks to FANSI-SHIFTLOCK, however, when you press that key you get its shifted character, the "at" sign (@).

- Set FANSI-Typewrite   On a typewriter, pressing either Shift key will automatically disengage the shift lock. That's not the case on a computer, where the Shift keys have no effect on the status of the CapsLock. This FANSI setting corrects that situation. When FANSI-Typewrite is set, pressing either Shift key will disengage the CapsLock.

- Change FANSI-KEYRATE   This features sets the number of times per second a key will repeat when you hold it down. The setting applies to all keys, but it is often thought of as controlling the cursor speed. On many systems, you can control this function via your system's CMOS setup, but your choice of settings may be limited to Normal and Fast. FANSI-KEYRATE, in contrast, lets you select any number of times per second you want your keys to repeat. The default on most computers is 10. Here, I've cranked that up to 50.

Reassigning Keys

These are just a few of the dozens of options FANSI offers for completely customizing your keyboard. The program automatically increases the system's type-ahead buffer to 255 characters, compared to the default of 15. If you are a good typist and know your applications programs and DOS well, typing ahead can save time. There's a special FANSI-HANDICAP mode that enables "one-finger typing" by converting the Alt, Ctrl, and Shift keys to toggles.

And, of course, there is key reassignment. As lines 15 through 18 indicate, I have used FANSI to move the greater-than symbol to a different key

(}) and replaced it with a period. I do this because of a habit I developed years ago when writing books on a typewriter. On a typewriter, the period key produces a period whether shifted or unshifted. Consequently, when I'm typing something like P.O. Box, I keep the Shift key held down until reaching the *ox*. That works on a typewriter, but not on a PC, where the result is *P>O> Box*.

Moving the greater-than symbol to the position occupied by the right curly brace solves the problem. But what if you one day find that you need the } symbol? As line 19 reminds me, keyboard reassignment macros can be toggled on and off with the Alt+Ctrl+CapsLock combination. If you find this combination does not work in your program, you can easily use FAN-SISET to create two little batch files (MACRO-ON.BAT and MACRO-OFF.BAT) that will send the control codes needed to toggle the feature on and off. Shell out of the program, run the batch file, and then return.

PCACHE and Back to the Root

The last two lines of this AUTOEXEC.BAT file load PrintCache from LaserTools Corporation and then log onto the root directory of Drive C. We'll look at printer performance enhancers in Part 8 of this book. But I should say right now that if you routinely print anything more than a page or two, you *need* a print spooler program like PrintCache. The shareware equivalent, DMP, is very, very good. But PrintCache is faster and more feature-rich.

With PrintCache or a similar program loaded, you never need to wait on your printer again. I've set PrintCache to use a megabyte of extended memory as its buffer because this is the optimal size for desktop publishing. You can get by with a lot less. But whatever value you choose, you will find that you can tell your word processor to print 100 pages or more and be back at work on Page 101 in twelve seconds, instead of having to wait twelve minutes or more for the print job to be finished. The word processor passes the text to be printed to PrintCache, thinking it is the printer, and PrintCache spools it out to the actual printer.

The physical production of pages takes place in the "background" as PrintCache utilizes available CPU time. A pop-up window offers a thermometer graph of how much remains to be printed at any given moment, plus controls that let me suspend printing, clear the buffer, or send a form feed to the printer to eject a page. The program lists for $149 and is available from most mail-order software firms and computer dealers. The PC Zone, for example, offers it for $98. Call (800) 258-8088, 24 hours a day. LaserTools Corporation is located in Emeryville, California and can be reached at (800) 767-8004.

SECTION
3-2

TOOLS NEAR AT HAND

You must trust me on this. You can operate a personal computer comfortably and completely with just the Ten Essential DOS commands and four utility programs—Mark Hersey's FANSI-Console, Chris Dunford's CED, Vernon Buerg's LIST, and Kenn Flee's QFILER. In fact, as we will see in the next section, QFILER eliminates the need for most DOS commands, essential or otherwise.

Key Utility Programs

But, while QFILER is fast, for quick commands you are often better off using DOS and a few utilities. For example, the public domain utility RENDIR makes it easy to rename a directory. QFILER can do this as well, but if that is all you want to do, why wait even a few seconds for it to load? Other simple tools I personally use all the time include:

- COPYIT.EXE   Lets you copy an unlimited number of files to floppy disks, prompting you to insert a new disk as each disk in the drive fills up. You can copy on the basis of date or size, and you can tell the program to optimize floppy disk space by copying files in the most efficient order.

- DISKID.EXE   Used to change the serial number DOS places on a disk when formatting it.

- **MV.EXE**   One of dozens of available move utilities. Use it like the COPY command: MV FILENAME.EXT D:\DIRECTORY. Saves you the bother of copying a file and then deleting it from its source location.

- **NO.COM**   Written by Charles Petzold of *PC Magazine*, this program excludes the files you specify from a particular action. Thus keying in the command `no *.txt *.bat mv *.* d:\temp` would move every file in the logged directory to D:\TEMP, *except* files ending in .TXT or .BAT. The program works its magic by changing the attributes of the specified files to "hidden," executing the command, and then changing the attributes back again.

- **QDR.COM**   This program, Quick Disk Reformat, is another gem from Vernon Buerg. The program operates the same way as the DOS command FORMAT /U /Q, but it is much faster and does not prompt you for a volume label.

- **RENDIR.COM**   What a time-saver this program is. When you key in `rendir`, it prompts you for the name of the target directory and then for the new name you would like to use. The DOS alternative is to create a directory with the new name, copy all of the files in the old directory into it, delete the files from the old directory, and then use the RD command to remove it.

- **WHEREIS.COM**   I probably use this program more frequently than any of the others. There are lots of WHEREIS-type programs for locating files, and all work in the same way. You can specify either an exact filename or use wildcards (WHEREIS *.BAT, WHEREIS JAN*.*, etc.). The program will search every directory of your disk and tell you which files in which directories meet your specifications. If you have no joy on Drive C, key in `d:` to log onto Drive D, and hit your up arrow key to bring your WHEREIS command back to the command line, courtesy of CED or DOSKEY.

Other Utilities

There are other utilities I use less often. CHOP31, for example, lets you cut a text file into as many pieces as you want. CLEANUP searches your disk for the little 1- and 2-byte files that are the detritus of operating some programs. (At your option, CLEANUP deletes them, saving you anywhere from 2K to 4K of disk space per file, depending on the minimum allocation unit for your disk.)

The program DPROTECT prevents any program from writing to a specified drive, and thus offers nearly unbeatable protection against virus infections when running software of uncertain origin. (MS-DOS 6 includes two DOS programs, MSAV and VSAFE, to scan for, remove, and continuously protect against viruses. Windows versions are also included in the DOS 6 package. See Part 8 of this book for more information.)

FREE instantly reports currently available disk and memory space. LOOKFOR can search every file on a disk for the text you specify. It even lets you conduct a "proximity search" by specifying several words and the number of characters that may separate them. I use LOOKFOR or The Norton Utilities TextSearch program when WHEREIS fails. Finally, on those few occasions when I need to sort the contents of a file, I use Vernon Buerg's SORTF230 (Sort File, version 2.3). The DOS SORT filter pales by comparison.

Vernon Buerg's Famous LIST Program

Of course there are other utilities. Hundreds of them, in fact. You can't spend much time reviewing PD and shareware software without amassing quite a collection, almost inadvertently. You see something that works well and you think, "Hmm, that's pretty neat. I might want to use that some day," and the program ends up in your D:\UTILS directory. The problem is that when that someday arrives, you will spend more time locating the utility and figuring out how to use it than you will applying a program you know well to accomplish the same task.

For example, there is a utility that removes the leading white space from every line in a text file. It is helpful when you're dealing with a file in which every line starts at, say column 10, and you want to left-justify it.

The program does an excellent job, but I don't use it any more. I have found that I can do the same thing with my word processor by telling it to record and then repeat a series of keystrokes. The word processor is a bit slower in performing this task. But since I know the program so well, there is no "overhead" (searching for the utility, reviewing the instructions, and running the program)—so the total time involved is much less.

I bring this up because it illustrates a point I have made repeatedly about becoming a power user: Learn a few good programs and learn them well. There will always be some other program or some other way to do things. But while others are struggling to locate the perfect program for the job and figuring out how to use it, you will have accomplished the task and be on your way to other things.

Without question, one of those few good programs you should learn is Vernon Buerg's LIST. Make no mistake—software, all software, is a work of art. And as with movies, books, and music, the more talented the artist, the more striking the artwork. Vernon Buerg, a modest, unassuming man who for years didn't even request a registration fee or contribution for his programs, is a software artist par excellence. He has produced many wonderful utilities, but LIST is his masterpiece.

Using LIST

With a buildup like that, the program had better be able to polish your shoes, do the dishes, and TurtleWax the car. Well, it won't exactly do all that. But here I'll highlight a few of the things it *can* do for you, focusing on just those features that I personally find most useful.

First and foremost, LIST displays text files on your screen. If you put the program in C:\LIST and add that directory to your path, you will be able to look at any file at any time by simply keying in `list filename .ext`. You will use it to look at text files, batch files, and even .COM and .EXE files. And why would one want to view machine language .COM and .EXE files? To look for the exact phrasing of error messages, copyright dates, program-generated instructions, and possibly even the author of the program.

With a file on your LIST screen, you can zip to the bottom or back to the top with your Home and End keys. LIST does not care how large the file is—it spools to and from disk—so you can view a file that is 500K, 1MB or larger, if you like. Better still, you can use LIST to *search* that file for a particular word or phrase or other character string. All you need to do is press your F key and key in the text you want LIST to find. The first occurrence appears on the screen. You can then hit your A key to conduct the search "again" from your current location in the file.

When you have found what you want, you can position it on the screen, mark the top and bottom of the text you want to "clip out," and dump it to a file. This feature is very helpful in the normal course of things, but it is invaluable when you are presented with a file containing strange characters. LIST includes a "junk" filter that can be toggled on and off. Toggle it on to get a "clean" file, then mark the top and bottom of the file and dump the whole thing to disk under a different name. The new file will be cleansed of junk characters.

Other features include the ability to set a "bookmark" to which you can instantly return while viewing a file. You can also shell to DOS, change the display from 25 lines to 43 lines, expand tab characters, display a ruler line, and display two files at once in different windows.

LIST also accepts wildcards, so you can key in a command like `list *.txt` to look at every .TXT file in a directory. The key sequence

Ctrl+PageUp takes you to the next file, while Ctrl+PageDown takes you back to the previous file. Whatever string you have specified for your FIND text remains in force as you switch among files, making it easy to search several files.

Other file-viewing programs are available, both commercially and through shareware channels, but I can't imagine using a computer on a regular basis without Mr. Buerg's LIST program. LIST is widely available online and in shareware collections, so you can see what all the shouting's about for a mere $5. If you like what you see, Mr. Buerg requests a registration fee of $20.

NewKey, Briefly

Before leaving the subject of close-at-hand tools, I should say just a word about Frank A. Bell's shareware program, NewKey. This is a keyboard macroing program like ProKey that lets you define any key or any series of keypresses as anything you like. If you frequently perform repetitive, multi-keystroke tasks, NewKey can save you a lot of time. For example, suppose you wanted to be able to automatically format a 5.25-inch 360K disk and specify a standard volume label by pressing Shift+F1.

All you need to do is key in `newkey` to load the program. Then press Alt and your plus key (+) to pop up the program. Enter the key combination you want to define (Shift and F1 for our example), and NewKey goes into "learn" mode. Enter the commands needed to accomplish the task, and toggle NewKey's learn mode off with Alt and the minus (-) key.

That's it. The next time you enter Shift+F1, all the keystrokes you just entered will be repeated. Of course you can save your macro definition to disk. And, of course, you can arrange to have NewKey load it automatically each time you boot up. You can even use NewKey to edit the series of keystrokes you have defined as if you were working with a word processor. NewKey, in short, adds sophisticated keyboard macroing features to DOS and any other program. And that can save you tons of time in the course of a year, not to mention wear and tear on your typing fingers.

SECTION
3-3

FILE MANAGEMENT

On a day-to-day basis, most of your time is spent running applications software (word processors, spreadsheets, database programs, communications software, and the like) and doing *file management*. Power users are always moving from directory to directory, looking at and editing files, copying them, deleting them, renaming them, or moving them to a new location.

It really isn't stretching things too far to suggest that your hard disk is like your home and thus constantly in need of maintenance. To tell you the truth, most of the time I don't even think of my hard disk as a disk at all. To me, it *is* my system.

If a program leaves some temporary files behind, I remove them, just as I would remove a branch that fell on my roof. And, just as most of us think of our houses or apartments as an entirety we call home—instead of as a series of freestanding rooms—I view my disk as an integrated whole. At any given moment I could not necessarily tell you what each directory contains, any more than I could list every item in my living room. But I know it's there, and I have a pretty good general idea of what it contains.

As you know, I believe in keeping directory trees as shallow as possible, preferably no more than one and occasionally two directories deep. That makes it easy to move from one directory to another—from one "room" to another—with the CD command. But when I want to do some serious file management, I use QFILER.

Use a File Manager!

There are many, many file management programs, both commercial and shareware. Many people use the commercial program XTREE, for example, and Athena Software's Disc Director has quite a following. My purpose here is not to suggest that QFILER or any other program is necessarily better than another. The key point is that file managers *are* available, and it is foolish not to take advantage of them.

Since QFILER is the one that I personally prefer, I'll use it as an example of the power this category of software can place at your disposal. (With a registration fee of just $20, QFILER may also be the one to give you the most bang for your buck.) Like much of the very best shareware, QFILER was written by a professional programmer. Kenn Flee and his firm, Jamestown Software, produce custom applications for other firms to sell. If you have ever received a laser-printed name badge at a trade show or used a voice-mail system at a leading firm, the chances are you've already encountered Mr. Flee's work.

QFILER Basics

QFILER offers an easy, intuitive way to accomplish just about any file management chore you can think of. Indeed, with QFILER on your disk, you can pretty much forget about DOS. And you can almost forget about your keyboard, since the program lets you do just about everything with your mouse, if you so choose.

As an example, consider the screen shot in Figure 3-3-1. We are assuming that you have loaded the program into C:\QFILER; that you also have a copy of Vernon Buerg's LIST program in C:\LIST; and that these directories, as well as C:\DOS, are part of your PATH statement. If you want to use QFILER as a menu-driven front-end for compression programs like LHA, PKZIP, and ARC, those programs must be accessible via your path as well. (You may want to simply put the compression software in C:\UTILS.)

Figure 3-3-1 QFILER and the Directory Tree

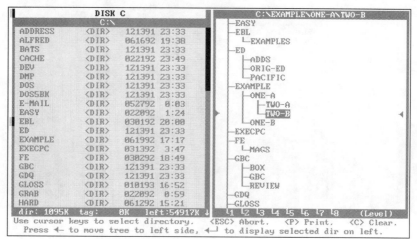

The screen shown in Figure 3-3-1 was presented after I logged onto the root directory of Drive C and keyed in `qfiler`. I then hit a single key to get the program to display the directory tree of Drive C in the right window. Notice that the path C:\EXAMPLE\ONE-A\TWO-B is highlighted in the middle of the right screen. That's where I moved the cursor.

When I hit Enter, the contents of that directory were immediately presented in the left window. My goal was to copy those three files to D:\ARCHIVE. So, as you can see in Figure 3-3-2, I used the mouse to bring up QFILER's drop-down help menus. I wanted to display a new directory in the right window. With a click of the mouse and a response to the program's prompt for the name of the new directory, the screen shown in Figure 3-3-3 appeared.

Notice in Figure 3-3-3 that QFILER displays two directories at once. You can cause the program to focus on and apply commands to one or the other by simply moving the highlight bar left or right with your arrow keys. Here, I've used the mouse to tag two files in the left window and clicked on *<C>opy* (not shown on this screen). QFILER asks whether I want to copy the tagged files or just the file currently under the highlight bar.

Figure 3-3-2 QFILER's Drop-Down Menus

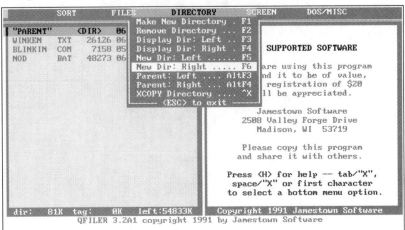

Figure 3-3-3 Two Directories at Once

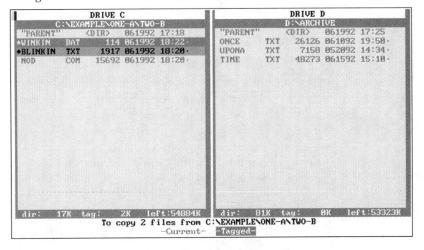

Using QFILER

That's all you have to know to use QFILER effectively. But let me tell you
when it really comes into its own. I rarely use QFILER to move around my
disk, but then navigating is easy for me because I refuse to create multilevel
directories. Most of the time all I need to enter is a command in the format
CD*DIRNAME* to get where I want to go.

But QFILER is an absolute godsend when you are cleaning out old files and doing other file management chores. Using the program is like being in a World War II-era headquarters with its huge, elevated map and people pushing wooden ships or tanks here and there with pool cues. QFILER lets you look down on the whole theater of operations and manipulate your files just as easily.

For example, imagine you have a directory filled with files of every kind —.COM, .EXE, .BAT, .TXT, and many with strange file extensions. Log onto the directory and key in qfiler. The file directory will be displayed in the left window, sorted, unsorted, or sorted in reverse alphabetical order, at your option. You can also tell the program to display just the *.TXT files or use some other expression to change the "mask."

You scroll or mouse through the directory until you come to a file that puzzles you. It's a .TXT file, and you'd like to look at it. With two keystrokes, QFILER will have it on the screen, displayed by Vernon Buerg's LIST program. (QFILER is designed to look for LIST in your path.) You can use all of LIST's features, and when you are finished, hit your Esc key to be returned to QFILER.

Now that you know what's in the file, you can copy, delete, rename, or move it. If you have told QFILER where to find your word processor or text editor, you can make changes in the file. (If you are using DOS 5 or DOS 6 and have not specified an editor, QFILER automatically loads the DOS EDIT program.)

You can also hide or un-hide it, make it read-only, or otherwise change its attributes. You can change its time and date stamps. Or you can tag it for some future operation, like a mass deletion of tagged files.

Should the next file you stop at be a program file, you can do all of these things, but you can also tell QFILER to run the program. QFILER prompts you for any parameters you may want to pass to the program before it runs.

You can change disk volume labels and rename subdirectories. You can create subdirectories. Or completely remove them and everything branching off them without first deleting all of their files. (QFILER issues suitable warnings when you are pruning your directory tree this way.)

Of course, you can shell to DOS. You can also tell the program to print a file or to print a directory listing. You can tell QFILER to *search* for files like a WHEREIS program. And you can call the UNDELETE program in DOS 5, DOS 6, or PC-Tools to recover erased files. With two directories displayed, QFILER will even automatically search for duplicates, tagging either all duplicates or only those that are newer.

In a similar vein, QFILER has a backup function that lets it compare, say, a directory on your hard drive with one on your floppy disk. The files you have tagged on the hard drive are compared to what's on the floppy and copied to it if they are newer, or if no floppy copy currently exists.

Making Compression Easy

Finally, QFILER makes dealing with compressed files a snap. To save floppy disk space, many programs today are distributed as a series of compressed files. Similarly, online users tend to prefer compressed files because they can often be downloaded in half the time. We'll look at compression options in more detail in Part 9 of this book. Right now what you need to know is that there are several techniques in wide use, so you must be prepared to deal with all of them.

Each technique requires a separate program, and each program has its own set of commands. QFILER cuts through the confusion by automatically recognizing the file extensions used by the leading compression programs and issuing the commands needed to deal with such files. (The compression programs must be on your disk and in your path.)

Thus, you can select, say, a file ending in .ARC and tell QFILER to "zoom" in on its contents. A list of the files contained in the archive will be displayed in the right window. You may then select the files you wish to extract or view on the screen. Similarly, you may tag the files you want to place in an archive and tell QFILER to do it for you.

Turbocharged Forever!

Today, DOS reigns supreme. Solid figures are hard to come by, but there are some 100 million DOS users. At this writing, in contrast, Microsoft has reportedly shipped about 20 million copies of Windows 3.1 and IBM has shipped even fewer copies of OS/2 2.0. (And, don't forget, just because people have received copies of Windows 3.1 or OS/2 does not necessarily mean that they are using the software, as *PC Week* columnist William Zachmann has repeatedly pointed out.)

Still, while stranger things have undoubtedly happened, it is all but inconceivable that Windows will fail as a product and disappear from the scene. Windows benefits everyone in the industry: hardware manufacturers, software houses, magazine advertising sales departments, and any other entity with a computer-something to sell. Even magazine columnists benefit. Having squeezed every tip, trick, and twist out of DOS, they now have a vast new and complicated topic to talk about.

Just ask yourself: Is there anyone who *doesn't* benefit from the Windows bandwagon or the OS/2 parade? The only person I can think of is the typical computer user. To put it plainly and simply, most computer users do not *need* Windows, OS/2, or any other Graphical User Interface (GUI).

Indeed, those products just add to the complexity of using your system. After all, if Windows is truly so easy to use, why is there such a market for Windows add-ons like the Norton Desktop for Windows, or Xerox's Rooms for Windows? Why does nearly every computer magazine now have a column devoted to telling readers how to configure Windows, how to overcome incompatibilities, and how to deal with a myriad of Windows-related problems?

There is no question that the world needs an operating system capable of accessing the power of today's 32-bit CPUs, and applications software to match. That product may be OS/2, or it may be Windows NT, or it may be something else. There is no question that most PC users will eventually install a copy of such an operating system, if only to be able to take advantage of the fact that all the best software will be developed for it.

But it is simply impossible to believe that 100 million people, most of whom use only a fraction of the power placed at their fingertips by their machines and their applications programs, will drop everything and migrate to Windows, OS/2, or some other operating system software. Even if you give the stuff away, people will not necessarily use it.

What seems likely is that DOS will be around and actively used by millions of people for many years to come. And most of those people don't even have what you now have—a specific procedure for turbocharging DOS!

SECTION
3-4

QUIKMENU: WINDOWLESS WINDOWS!

QuikMenu from OSCS Software Development is simply dazzling. It looks and acts like Microsoft Windows but is much faster and more responsive, while making far fewer demands on your system. It is exactly the kind of program to give to your non-power user friends who need an easy and enjoyable way to run their systems. It is the perfect tool to use when setting up a system for people who are essentially non-computer users. And it is so much fun that you may even find yourself using it on a regular basis. Who says real power users don't use menus!

Loading QuikMenu

When you load QuikMenu for the first time, the program searches your hard disk and automatically sets up sculpted 3-D menu buttons for the programs it recognizes. You can then add your own additional menu buttons, submenus, and program groupings. You have complete control over colors, whether menus "explode" or simply appear, and whether or not sound effects are used. You can even opt for different *fonts* in your menu button text.

QuikMenu is compatible with any DOS-based network (It even includes a network electronic mail feature!), and it is filled with clever utilities. These include a calculator, calendar (with an auto-reminder feature), phone book and dialer, and time log. You can even use .PCX graphics files as background "wallpaper," as shown in Figure 3-4-1. In fact, the commercial version of the program, QuikMenu III, includes over 150 ready-to-use icons and an icon editor that lets you create your own Windows-like icons from scratch or use any .PCX graphics file.

Most important of all, adding menu selections could not be easier. You will have to type in the name you wish to use for a menu button, but everything else can be done point-and-shoot fashion with your mouse.

Space won't permit a complete rundown of all QuikMenu features. But for an idea of what you can expect, see the QuikMenu approach to file management shown in Figure 3-4-2. With the QuikMenu File Manager, you can copy, move, rename, and delete files and directories. You can view and print text files or search for files using the Find option.

QuikMenu also offers a number of utility functions, including a nifty digital calculator and a phone book and phone dialer (modem required, of course). There is also a time log feature to make it easy for consultants and others to keep track of their billable time. There is a send/receive electronic mail feature for DOS-based network users. (When someone sends you a message, you will see a little envelope symbol in the upper left corner of the QuikMenu screen.)

But the utility many will find most useful is the QuikMenu Calendar. As you can see from Figure 3-4-3, you can instantly view past, present, and future years, and you can also attach memos and reminders to future dates. When you click on a date, the built-in QuikMenu text editor pops up to let you create your message or reminder. Once created, a little memo-page icon appears in the date's box on the calendar. If you opt to activate the auto-remind feature, QuikMenu will automatically display the day's reminders when you first power up your machine for that day.

As noted, when you first install QuikMenu, the program searches your hard disk for the executable files it recognizes and automatically sets up menu buttons for the programs it finds. You are then free to set up your own additional menu buttons. You can also create layers of submenus, making it easy to group a series of programs together, rather like the "desktop" approach used by some Windows utilities.

QuikMenu is not only pretty and fast and filled with thoughtful features, it is also fun to use. In many ways, it offers all of the gain of Windows with none of the pain. But you don't have to take my word for it. You can try QuikMenu for yourself for a cost of $2 for a 5.25-inch disk or $3 for 3.5-inch format. Please see Part 9 of this book for ordering details.

Figure 3-4-1 QuikMenu with .PCX "Wallpaper"

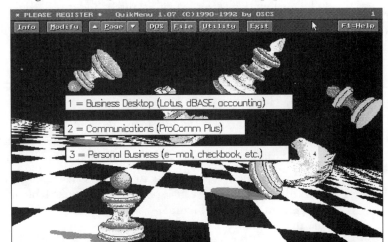

Figure 3-4-2 The QuikMenu File Manager

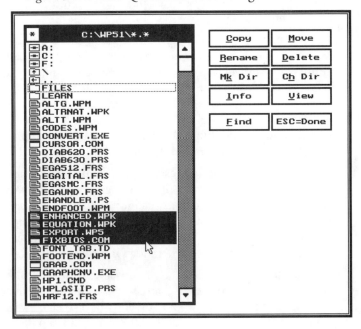

Figure 3-4-3 QuikMenu's Nifty Calendar Function

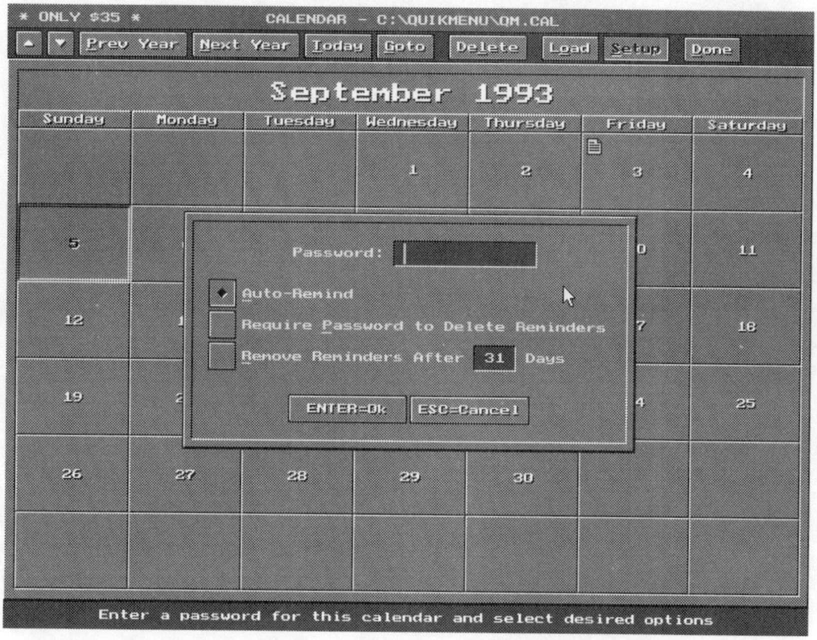

PART IV

MAXIMIZING MEMORY

What You Will Learn

Computer memory is both cheap and precious. At $30 to $40 a megabyte, it doesn't cost much to install. But once installed, it becomes incredibly valuable because, no matter how much memory you put into your system, you never have enough. Memory is always a scarce resource. And it has become even scarcer since the Fat Boys—Windows and OS/2—waddled into town. Today's operating systems and environments, and the programs they run, gobble up RAM the way Congress consumes tax dollars. The demand is insatiable and unending.

That's why, whether you've got 4, 16, or even 32 megabytes of RAM in your system, every megabyte counts. This part of the book will help. We're going to assume that you have at least 4 megabytes of RAM and that you are using at least a 386SX CPU, since most systems sold today have those characteristics.

We'll start with a brief explanation of key terms and concepts, some familiar and some new. Then we'll look at the memory management tools provided by DOS and available as third-party packages. We will conclude with two super tricks for getting the most out of the RAM you put into your machine.

BASICS: MEMORY, MEGABYTES, AND MORE

If it weren't for DOS, there would be no need to worry about getting the most out of your memory. That sounds like a strange statement, but it is largely true. Memory is a hardware component, so it is naturally the province of the operating system. But operating system software has not kept up with CPU hardware.

DOS was written to work with the Intel 8088, a chip introduced in 1979. The 8088 can address 1MB of memory. The 286 came along in 1982, with the ability to address 16MB of memory. The 386 appeared in 1985 with the capacity to address 4GB (gigabytes) of memory. But not until the introduction of DOS 5 in early 1991 did DOS offer any tools to let users take advantage of more than the original 1MB of memory space. DOS 6 continued the trend with the introduction of the MemMaker utility discussed later.

To this day, DOS and the programs that run under its control are wedded to that original 1MB, only 640K of which can be used for applications programs. DOS and most programs can make use of memory beyond the 1MB mark, but they can't *run* in that memory.

To do that, you must load in on top of DOS an environment like Windows, or replace DOS altogether with something like OS/2 or Windows NT. Of course, the programs you use must be written to run this way. Otherwise, you're pretty much back to DOS with the possible addition of Windows task-swapping (cooperative multitasking).

The question we need to address, then, is *DOS* memory management, and that requires a basic understanding of the DOS memory layout. You will find a complete explanation in the Random House/Glossbrenner books on DOS 5 and DOS 6. Here we will simply present a short refresher course. Then we'll look at memory hardware.

The Memory Layout

The key to understanding PC memory is *addresses*. A single cell of memory can store eight bits (one byte) of information, and every cell has a specific address. Memory cells are numbered sequentially, and as far as the CPU is concerned, one memory cell is the same as another, except for the byte of information it contains when the CPU comes calling. It follows, then, that a CPU could work with an infinite amount of memory. What limits a CPU is the largest address number it can specify. If it can't specify the address, it can't use the memory.

To specify an address, the CPU must send signals on the pins that connect it to the motherboard and to the outside world. The more address pins it has, the bigger the binary number the CPU can write, and the more memory cells it can address. The CPU in your computer thus sets the upper limit on how much memory can be used. Your budget sets the limit on how much memory is physically present to be used. But DOS sets the limit on how much your programs can use to run.

That limit is 640K. This is because of DOS's historical ties to the 8088 chip and its 1MB (1,024K) limit. The designers of DOS left 384K of CPU addresses for the ROM BIOS and hardware add-ons, like video and communications cards. (Remember, everything has to have an address, or the CPU can't see it.) It seemed like a good idea at the time, a time when 64K, one tenth of 640K, was considered an enormous amount of RAM.

Expanded, Extended, and UMBs

In very short order, however, software outgrew the 640K limit. Users demanded more power, more features, more pop-up help, more everything. All of which led to programs that required more than 640K of *conventional memory*.

The most successful solution was *expanded* memory. The idea was to add a lot of memory to the system on a separate board and to make that memory accessible through a "window" in the 640K of memory addresses DOS could use. A controller chip on the board would take care of swapping or "paging" chunks of this extra RAM in and out of the window. The extra hardware fooled DOS into actually using anywhere from one to 32 megabytes of memory to run programs. The programs, of course, had to be designed to use expanded memory, typically as defined by the Lotus-Intel-Microsoft (LIM) standard. The term you will hear most often is *LIM EMS 4.0.* This stands for the LIM Expanded Memory Specification, version 4.0.

The expanded memory technique can be used on any CPU from the 8086/8088 onward. With the introduction of 286-based machines like the IBM/AT, the CPU itself could be used to address memory beyond the 1MB mark. This memory continues the address column so that it "extends" beyond 1MB. Even though this is a more natural arrangement than paging memory in and out of a window in the address column, *extended memory* was virtually useless for years. About all one could use it for was as a place to put a RAM drive.

Everything changed with the introduction of the 386. This CPU, the first to be specifically designed for the personal computer market, incorporates memory management on the chip itself. This gives it the ability to remap physical memory to different address locations and to use what is actually extended memory to emulate expanded memory.

A 386 or better chip can also remap extended memory into any unoccupied addresses set aside for hardware add-ons in the top 384K of the first megabyte. This creates Upper Memory Blocks, or UMBs. The number and size of the UMBs available on your system will depend on the add-on boards you use and how many of your upper memory addresses are unoccupied. But almost every system has some free addresses up there, and they make the ideal place for little programs, utilities, and device drivers. That's why DOS 5 and DOS 6 provide the DEVICEHIGH and LOADHIGH commands for your CONFIG.SYS and AUTOEXEC.BAT files, respectively.

XMS: The Extended Memory Specification

In July 1988, the same companies (Lotus, Intel, and Microsoft) that had established the expanded memory standard joined with AST and other vendors to agree on a standard for extended memory access. The current version of the standard is called the Extended Memory Specification, version 3.0, customarily abbreviated as XMS. The HIMEM.SYS file supplied with DOS and Windows is the system's XMS driver. You must load this (or a third-party equivalent) via CONFIG.SYS to make DOS aware of your extended memory.

Figure 4-1-1 PC Memory Map

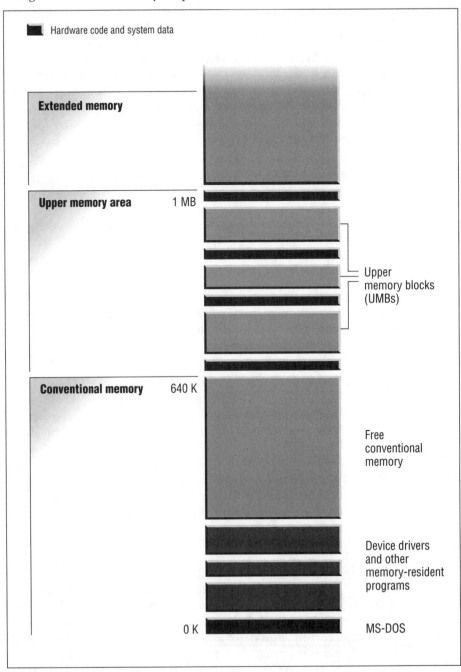

The XMS standard defines the functions DOS programs can use to access extended memory. It tells them how to reserve memory for themselves, how to transfer any amount of data from conventional 640K memory into extended memory and back, how to release extended memory when they're finished with it, and much more.

PowerPoint

Shadow RAM Explained

There's another neat memory remapping trick you should know about. Available on some 286 machines and many 386 systems, it's called *SHADOW RAM*. The goal is to speed up the system's access to various ROM BIOS chips, including the DOS ROM BIOS. Most add-on cards have a ROM BIOS of some sort that plugs into the memory column above 640K. For reasons of cost and marketing, many of these cards are designed to support the lowest common denominator: an 8-bit data path. That way they can be used in most machines in the PC family.

But 286 and 386SX machines have a 16-bit data path, and 386DX machines have a path that's 32 bits wide. The RAM in these systems matches their respective data paths. If the programming in an 8-bit ROM BIOS could be copied into 16-bit or 32-bit memory, the system could access it as much as four times faster. A speed difference like that is particularly significant in the case of the ROM BIOS on the video card.

The shadow RAM technique automatically copies the code in your system's ROM BIOS chips into extended memory. It then fixes up the addresses so that when the CPU accesses what it thinks is, say, the video ROM, it actually goes to the copy of that ROM in the faster extended memory. The RAM set aside for holding copies of the various BIOSes is called shadow RAM.

The technique can work quite well. But unfortunately, there are no standards. Some systems are designed to automatically appropriate as much as 384K of extended memory for use as shadow RAM. Other systems let you turn off this feature, when necessary, to allow applications programs to have access to that memory. *(continued)*

(Shadow RAM Explained continued)

The shadow RAM issue is particularly important to a DOS 5 or DOS 6 user, since the portion of extended memory that is often appropriated is the same portion into which one loads most of the operating system. As you will see in a moment, this is the HMA (High Memory Area), the first 64K of memory extending beyond the 1MB mark. If the shadow RAM in your system uses the HMA and cannot be disabled, then you cannot move most of DOS out of conventional memory.

Note that if the DOS MEM command seems to indicate that you have less memory than you know you have, shadow RAM may be the culprit. Remember, the extended memory that is used in this way is *replacing* eight-bit ROM memory. Therefore, MEM will report the memory occupied by these ROM locations, but it will deduct an equivalent amount from your extended memory. Indeed, since some other software is responsible for ROM shadowing, MEM may not be aware that the XMS memory being used for this purpose even exists in your system.

The High Memory Area (HMA)

You know about conventional, expanded, and extended memory. Now there is one more term to learn: the high memory area or HMA. The HMA is actually the first 64K chunk of extended memory. It owes its existence as a separately named entity to a fluke.

As we all know, DOS can address only one megabyte of memory, but 286, 386, and better chips can write address numbers much larger than that, thanks to a greater number of address pins than the original 8088 upon which DOS is based. Well, some years ago, someone figured out that, while you couldn't *start* a program outside the 1MB mark, you could *run* it there under DOS.

For historical reasons having to do with CP/M, DOS's distant ancestor, DOS divides the megabyte of memory it has to work with into 64K segments. The HMA trick starts a segment just inside the 1MB mark. 16 bytes inside, to be precise. The segment continues in linear fashion straight into the first 64K of extended memory.

By definition, the addresses in the HMA are greater than 1MB. So how does the processor manage to write those addresses without switching into non-DOS "protected mode"? The answer is the second part of the discovery. Thanks to the magic of the binary numbering system, to write one megabyte's worth of memory addresses the processor must use twenty address pins or lines. However, because of the way addresses are handled internally by the CPU, it was discovered that by selectively enabling and disabling the processor's twenty-first address line, one could address and gain access to that first 64K of extended memory in real or DOS mode. (This was actually a bug in the 286 design, but it is one bug that really did turn out to be a feature.)

In typical computer fashion, the first address pin of a chip is numbered A0. So the twenty-first address pin is numbered A20. It is the A20 address line that gets toggled on and off. And why would it ever be off? To keep the processor in "real," 8086/8088, 1MB DOS mode.

The hows and whys really aren't important, however. The fact is that the trick works and results in an additional 64K of space above the 1MB mark into which you can load certain programs, thus freeing as much as 64K of conventional 640K memory for other uses. Third-party memory managers like QEMM and 386Max have been using this trick for years. Microsoft has used it with Windows. (Indeed, the file WINA20.386 installed by Windows is a driver to let Windows and DOS share the A20 line. As long as Windows can find that file, it can run in enhanced mode.) But, with the introduction of DOS 5, loading most of DOS into the HMA became part of the standard PC configuration.

PowerPoint

Segment and Offset

In your journeys through PC memoryland, particularly when using DOS's MEM command or some third-party memory manager, you will inevitably encounter the terms *segment* and *offset*. You may or may not have to actually deal with these terms, but you should know what they mean. Here's a concise explanation.

Every memory cell has an address, and the content of each cell is limited to 8 bits (one byte). This means that each memory cell can contain a value ranging from 0 to 255. In the binary numbering system used by computers, 0 is eight zeros in a row (00000000) and 255 is eight ones in a row (11111111). That's a lot of writing. So for greater convenience, binary numbers are often represented using base-16 or hexadecimal notation. In hex notation, digits run from 0 through 9, plus the letters A through F, for a total of 16 digits. The last digit, F, stands for 15 in decimal notation. *(continued)*

(Segment and Offset continued)

Each place to the left in hex is some multiple of sixteen times the digit. We won't go into the hexadecimal numbering system here, except to say that zero is 00 and 255 is FF. (FF is sixteen fifteens, plus one fifteen, for a total of 255, decimal.)

Hex notation saves space. But whether you use hexadecimal or binary notation, one heck of a lot of bits and bytes are required to write just the 1 million addresses the 8086/8088 is capable of using, not to mention the gigabytes 386 and better chips can address. That's why hex notation is used to specify memory addresses.

The *way* it is used relates to the memory addressing scheme used by the 8086/8088 processor. Addresses within the first megabyte of RAM have two parts, each of which consists of a 2-byte hex value. Since the processor divides the 1MB of memory up into sixteen *segments*, the first part of the address specifies the segment number.

Each segment contains 64K (actually 65,536) unique addresses. (If you multiply 64 by sixteen, you will find that the product is 1,024.) The second 2-byte hex value specifies the actual cell address within the segment. The second value says, in effect, start at this specific segment number and count into the next 64K by a certain amount. That's why the second value is called the *offset* or the relative address.

Think of it this way: The segments are the chapter numbers of a book; the offsets are the page numbers within each chapter. We've all seen books and manuals where the pages are numbered 2-23, 5-64, 10-3, and so on, instead of being numbered continuously. Yet each individual page is uniquely identifiable in the index or table of contents. We turn first to the chapter and then to the page. PCs turn first to the segment and then to the offset. (It's actually a bit more complicated than that for the PC, but the concept is the same.)

Adding More Memory

Now let's take just a moment to consider memory hardware and the procedure to follow to boost the amount of memory in your system. Forget the technobabble you see in articles and books. Adding memory is a simple three-step process:

1. Turn your computer off, remove its cover, and look for a large group of identical chips or chips on mini-circuit boards plugged into your motherboard. Copy down the number stenciled on the backs of these memory chips.

2. Pick up the phone and call one of the mail-order memory merchants that advertises in a leading computer magazine. (A starter list of companies is provided later in this text.) Tell them how much memory you want to add and the identification number on the chips currently in your system. Then ask them for a price.

3. After your order arrives, repeat Step 1, only this time, consult the manual or booklet that came with your machine as to where the memory you have ordered should go.

Memory in More Detail

This oversimplifies things just a bit, but it drives home the central point about memory upgrades: The chips you add must be compatible with your system, and the compatibility information you need is stenciled on each chip. It will be a number like HM50256P-15 or UPD42100L-12 or something similar. It is the memory merchant's job to worry about what those code numbers mean and to make sure the chips you buy are compatible.

The reason I suggest turning off the computer and looking around inside is that it is the only foolproof way to tell what you've got and what you need. This information should be in the manual that came with your system. But if you have bought a low-priced clone, you may not have such a manual. And if you do, you may find that it appears to have been translated from the Chinese by someone who learned English by watching American cartoons on television.

Needless to say, one should not have a high degree of confidence that such booklets are conscientiously updated should the company's engineers make a design change. Someone once said, "Trust, but verify." I say, "Trust only what you see with your own eyes." Turn the system off and pull the cover.

SIMMs and Other Technologies

Memory chips are distinguished by three main characteristics. The first and most obvious characteristic is their physical form or "packaging." The original PC memory chips were DIPs, short for Dual In-line Package. These are the rectangular black chips with metal pins on either side. They look like Cubist caterpillars. They are supplied in a static-resistant plastic tube and must be inserted very carefully to avoid bending a pin. A notch on the top of the package guides you in the proper orientation.

DIP chip memory has pretty much faded from the scene. And a good thing, too, since it is a royal pain to install. If you happen to have an older machine that requires DIP memory, for heaven's sake go down to your local Radio Shack and get a chip-pulling tool. It will cost you less than $10 and will make inserting and removing chips much easier, to say nothing of helping you straighten the inevitable bent pin.

Single In-line Package memory or SIP chips came next. These are usually supplied as several chips on a small circuit board that is designed to be plugged into the motherboard by inserting a single line of pins.

The current technology, and the one that is undoubtedly used in your system if you bought your computer in the last two or three years, is represented by the SIMM or Single In-line Memory Module. This is a mini-circuit board measuring just a few inches long. It contains all of the chips in the module and plugs into the motherboard with a gold-fingered card edge, just like the boards you insert into your system's expansion slots.

Memory Speed

All memory chips are rated to operate at a certain speed, measured in nanoseconds (billionths of a second; abbreviated "ns"). Typical speeds are 60, 70, 80, 100, 120, 150, and 200ns. The lower the number, the faster the chip. And, of course, the faster the chip, the higher the price.

The key points to remember about chip speed are these: The speed of the memory you add is determined by your system design; faster chips work in place of slower chips, but slower chips do not work in place of faster chips. Faster chips do not, however, make your computer run faster than its rated speed, a characteristic that is determined by the system's internal clock, not by the speed rating on its RAM.

If you're not sure of the chip speed you require, look at the chips installed in your PC. Both chips and memory modules are marked with a speed rating as the last digit of the identifying number on top. For response times of 100ns or slower, the last zero usually is not printed, so a chip with a speed rating ending with "12" is rated at 120ns, while one ending with "80" is rated at 80ns. Again, you can usually trust the memory merchant to correctly interpret the information you provide.

SIMM Size

The one memory characteristic which you can choose concerns the capacity of the chips you install. Most motherboards today, for example, are designed to accept SIMM modules of either 256K or 1MB or a combination of the two. Thus, depending on the SIMM capacity you choose, you can fully populate your motherboard and end up with 8MB of RAM, or fully populate it with "higher calorie" SIMMs and end up with 16MB of RAM.

By mixing and matching SIMM modules of different capacities, you can increase your system's memory in 1MB increments from zero through 16MB. All on the same motherboard. Most motherboards today top out at 16MB, due to the limitations of the ISA expansion bus. But you may be able to add even more memory, if you can afford it, via a memory card in your system's 32-bit expansion slot.

The key consideration in almost every case is the manner in which your SIMMs must be arranged. Sometimes, especially if you are mixing different sizes of SIMMs in the same system, you need to put specific SIMMs in certain specific sockets or banks for the computer to recognize them all. You should find specific instructions in your motherboard documentation pamphlet. If not, call the company that sold you the machine for more information.

Note that a SIMM module usually has a number on its little circuit board. As you are looking at your system, take the time to copy down this number as well as the numbers stenciled on the chips themselves, since that information may be helpful in matching the SIMM module you need.

Finishing Up

Static electricity is the enemy of all ICs (Integrated Circuits), including memory chips. Fortunately, chips today are designed to be much more resistant to being zapped by static electricity. You don't have to wrap one end of a piece of wire around your ankle and attach the other end to a radiator or other "ground" these days. But it doesn't hurt to be cautious. If a spark leaps from your finger to the system unit as you are removing the cover, for example, it is not a good sign.

If static electricity is a concern, you can often solve the problem by leaving the machine plugged in to a grounded electrical receptacle and touching the power supply housing the moment you remove the cover. That should dissipate any potential static electric spark.

After you get your memory installed, be sure to check your work. Take the time to verify that the modules are installed in the correct positions, according to your manual, and that they are firmly seated. Check the manual to see if there are any jumpers you must change to make the new memory available to the system. (There probably won't be, but it doesn't hurt to read the manual's memory section thoroughly.)

Then, before you screw the cover back on, boot up. (Don't touch anything inside once the power is on.) Your next job is almost certainly resetting the CMOS to tell it about your newly installed memory. Again, check your manual for specific details. If all the memory appears to be there after you reset the CMOS and reboot, you can turn the system off and close it up. If the POST memory test stops short of what you think you should have, turn the system off and review the installation again to make sure the proper SIMMs are in the proper slots.

Merchants of Memory

I can't recommend any specific mail-order memory merchant because I've never had occasion to buy memory through the mail. But I can give you the numbers of some of the companies that advertise in *PC Magazine* and similar publications. Give them a call and ask for their most recent catalogue. Better yet, copy down the chip and SIMM numbers of the equipment currently installed in your system and contact the manufacturer for a quote on boosting your memory.

Make sure the company is prepared to refund your money if the chips don't work out. And don't hesitate to accept their advice on acceptable substitutes. A manufacturer may have been using only Toshiba chips at the time it designed and tested your system, even though NEC and NMB parts are completely compatible. As specialists, chip vendors are likely to have comprehensive information. Again, without endorsement, here are some of the companies you may want to call. TENEX is in Indiana, and Sigma Data is in New Hampshire. All the rest are in California:

First Source International: (800) 535-5892; (714) 588-9866

JDR Microdevices: (800) 538-5000; (408) 559-1200

L.A. Trade: (800) 433-3726; (310) 782-2880

Performance Memory Products: (800) 255-8607; (619) 931-7824

Sigma Data: (800) 446-4525; (603) 526-6909

TENEX Computer Express: (800) 776-6781; (219) 259-7051

SECTION

4-2

MEMORY MANAGEMENT
TOOLS

The fundamental goal in making the most of your memory is to free up as much 640K conventional memory as possible. This gives your DOS applications programs more elbow room and often results in increased performance. The reason is easy to understand, once you are aware of the techniques software developers have devised to cope with the constrictions of the 640K limit.

First, it is important to remember that just because DOS can give programs a maximum of 640K does not mean that programs will actually have that amount of memory to work with. A software developer must assume that DOS itself will occupy some of that 640K, not to mention a variety of TSRs, DOS housekeeping notepads, and various and sundry other items. Therefore, the guts of most DOS programs are designed to occupy considerably less than 640K. Say, 512K or less.

But what if the features of a program require more memory? What if the program is designed to have extensive online help, available at the touch of a hotkey, but the help information and the program itself cannot both fit into 512K of RAM? The solution many programmers use is to separate help files and other nonessential information or features from the main body of the program and bring them in on an as-needed basis as *overlays*.

179

Suppose you are running your word processor and you hit F1 for help. The program pauses, goes out to disk, and brings in the help feature. In doing so, the program lets the help feature overwrite or overlay part of the program or data that is already in memory. When you are finished using the help feature, the program brings in a copy of whatever it was the help feature overwrote, and you continue creating your document.

Overlays and similar techniques are clever solutions to the DOS memory limitation. But, no matter how fast your hard disk, a noticeable amount of time is consumed by bringing in overlays. Now here's the key point: If you can free up more conventional memory, your programs may be able to load in all of their overlays and keep them there, instead of having to bring them in from disk each time.

Similarly, with more conventional memory to work with, your word processor, spreadsheet, or database program may be able to deal with larger documents, worksheets, or a larger number of records at one time. That means you may not have to cut very large documents into separate, smaller pieces. And it means that you will not have to wait for disk access as you scroll through a spreadsheet or page back and forth through database records.

Available Options

At this point we know that the goal of memory optimization is to load as many things as we can into some location other than DOS's 640K of conventional memory. We know the available locations: upper memory blocks (UMBs) located above the 640K mark but below the 1MB mark, the HMA located just above the 1MB mark, and extended or expanded (windowed or paged) memory.

We also know what might be loaded into these locations. The items include the device drivers and TSRs we load via CONFIG.SYS and AUTO-EXEC.BAT, plus a number of things that come with DOS, including much of DOS itself.

The question now is, "How do we get the items in Column A into the locations in Column B and thus free up more conventional memory and save the world for democracy?" You have three choices. The first is to use the facilities DOS 5 and DOS 6 provide. The second is to use a third-party memory management package. And the third is to do nothing at all.

In this section of the book we're going to go into more detail about these options and show you some specific power user techniques for getting the most out of your memory. But let me start with a comment on that last "do nothing" option. I don't agree with it. In my opinion, the tools Microsoft provides, starting with DOS 5, are so easy to use that you should take advantage of them just on general principle. But the possibility of doing nothing does raise an important point. Namely, that the game may not always be worth the candle.

Optimizing your computer's memory usage is like working a jigsaw puzzle. There are certain basic things you can do, like loading DOS into the HMA. But fine-tuning your system—determining which TSRs should be loaded in which order to squeeze out the last kilobyte of conventional memory—can literally take hours. This is true regardless of the tools you use.

You might think that the answer lies with a third-party memory management package like QEMM or 386Max. And you may be right. Many third-party programs use tricks that are not available with DOS, and most of them make a valiant attempt to optimize your memory usage *automatically*. They attempt to calculate the best load order for your TSRs and alter your CONFIG.SYS and AUTOEXEC.BAT to make it so. (DOS 6's Mem-Maker utility uses the same approach to try to decide where everything you want to load should go.) And, since the main focus of these packages is memory management, their manuals typically contain much more information on the subject than the DOS manual.

But no memory management program can *automatically* produce the best, most efficient configuration for everyone. There are simply too many varieties of device drivers, TSRs, and hardware out there for things to be as simple as that. You will find, as I did with DOS 6's MemMaker, that the memory management program may attempt to load programs into upper memory that cannot function from that location. Yet the memory program has no way of knowing this. All it knows is that Device Driver A or TSR B will fit into an available upper memory block, so that's where the program puts it. In almost every case, whether you use Microsoft's MemMaker or a third-party utility, some fine-tuning by hand is likely to be necessary.

Third-party packages have other disadvantages. They involve an additional expense, and they add yet another layer of complexity, presenting you with yet another program to master. Their sophisticated tricks can cause problems when running some programs. And, as noted, while their automatic mode gives you a good starting point, you will almost certainly have to complete the optimization by hand.

That's why, before we delve into the depths of memory optimization, I want to say that you don't *have* to squeeze out every last kilobyte. There is no question that it can be worthwhile—and even enjoyable—to do so. But be aware that, after you have harvested the low-hanging fruit, you can spend a lot of money and a huge amount of time pursuing the last full measure of your memory—and that last little bit may not make one iota of difference in the way your programs run or the way your system performs.

So go for the easy stuff first, using the tools DOS provides. Then, if you still get *Out of Memory* or similar errors when you use your machine the way you want to use it, escalate the problem by getting a third-party package and/or really bearing down and testing different load orders for your device drivers and TSRs.

Managing Memory with DOS 5 and DOS 6

DOS gives you all the tools you need to free up an astonishing amount of conventional memory. You must have at least a 386-based system with at least 1MB of memory (640K conventional and 384K of extended). But if you do, two simple lines in your CONFIG.SYS file can immediately save you as much as 48K of conventional memory. DOS also gives you the MEM command so you can see what's loaded where.

Let's quickly review the tools. Some of them are files supplied with your DOS package; some of them are command lines you will want to include in CONFIG.SYS or AUTOEXEC.BAT:

HIMEM.SYS   This file is your XMS (Extended Memory Specification) driver. It is what makes extended memory available to your system. Remember, DOS processes the lines in CONFIG.SYS sequentially. Therefore, you must place the line loading this driver before any lines that use extended memory.

DOS=   This command line is used in your CONFIG.SYS file (DOS= HIGH) to tell the system to load most of DOS into the HMA. As we will see in a moment, the command DOS=UMB is needed if you want to use the Upper Memory Blocks created by EMM386.EXE or other UMB-providing software. The two settings can be combined as a single line reading DOS=HIGH,UMB.

DEVICEHIGH=   Used in CONFIG.SYS, this command line loads device drivers into any available Upper Memory Blocks (UMBs). To make it work, you must load software that provides UMBs. The UMB provider supplied with DOS is EMM386.EXE.

EMM386.EXE   Supplied with DOS, this file is both a program and a device driver. As a device driver, it is used with the DEVICE= command to emulate expanded memory (using what is actually extended memory), and to provide UMBs. As a program, it is used to get information on EMS usage and, if no EMS or UMBs are being used, to toggle its functions on and off.

LOADHIGH   This is a command for your AUTOEXEC.BAT file. It is used to load TSRs into UMBs. As with DEVICEHIGH=, you must first install a UMB provider and include DOS=UMB in your CONFIG.SYS file.

LOADFIX.EXE   This is a program supplied with DOS that is used to cure the *Packed file corrupt* message you may get when trying to run some older programs under DOS 5 or DOS 6. Programs that generate this message expect the lowest 64K of conventional memory to be occupied when they load in. Since DOS has traditionally resided in that location, this has not been a problem in the past. However, if you have loaded DOS into the HMA instead, DOS obviously will no longer live in the first 64K. LOADFIX fools the offending programs into thinking that the first 64K of memory is occupied.

MEM.EXE   The MEM command is DOS's memory allocation reporting tool. The command MEM /C, for example, will show you what's loaded where, how much space each item is taking up, and how much of each sort of memory is free.

MEMMAKER.EXE   Introduced with DOS 6, this is Microsoft's effort at a QEMM/386Max-style memory optimization utility. Two options are available—"express" and "custom." In either case, MemMaker attempts to arrive at the configuration that makes the most efficient use of the upper memory area (640K to 1MB) by trying thousands—even tens of thousands—of alternatives. In my experience, the CONFIG.SYS and AUTOEXEC .BAT files produced by MemMaker give you a good starting point. But you will still have to fine-tune these files by hand.

MSD.EXE   This is the Microsoft Diagnostics program, also included with DOS 6. Figure 4-2-1 displays the program's opening screen. Though it has many other uses, one of the pieces of information MSD provides is a report on the utilization of your system's upper memory area. MSD uses character graphics to display some of the information that the MEM command displays as a numerical table. Please see Figure 4-2-2.

Figure 4-2-1 DOS 6's Microsoft Diagnostics Opening Screen

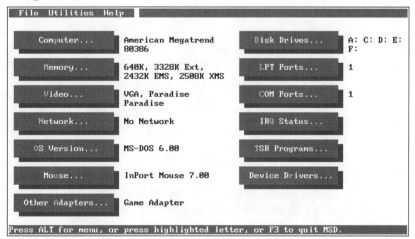

Figure 4-2-2 Microsoft Diagnostics and Memory Management

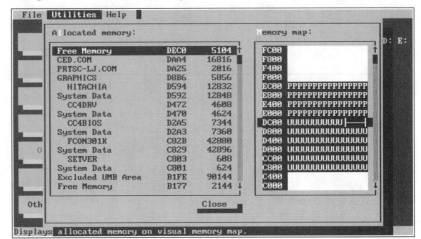

Using the Tools

The DOS manual does not make it immediately obvious how to begin using UMBs and the HMA. So if you want to get started quickly, here's what to do. Put the following lines in the following order into your CONFIG.SYS, using whatever paths are appropriate for your setup:

```
device=c:\dos\himem.sys /machine:1
dos=high,umb
device=c:\dos\emm386.exe i=e000-efff noems
```

Reboot your system. Then use the DOS MEM.EXE utility by keying in mem /c ¦ more. (Or, if FANSI-Console is loaded, enter the command mem /c and press your Pause key to put the system on hold while you scroll back through the display.) The MEM command will give you a report of your memory allocation: conventional, upper memory, EMS, and memory total. At the end of the report, you should see *MS-DOS resident in High Memory Area*. You should also see that you have a lot more conventional memory than you're used to.

HIMEM.SYS and the Machine

The three CONFIG.SYS lines shown above are all you need to load most of DOS into the High Memory Area (and thus save about 48K of conventional memory) and to remap what is physically present as extended memory into any empty address locations in the 640K to 1MB area. The next step is to fill those locations with device drivers and TSRs to free up even more conventional memory.

Before moving on to that step, however, let's take just a moment to discuss what these three key lines do and why they work. It is going to sound complicated, and I'm sorry to say, it is. But take heart. There are really only a few things you need to know.

Indeed, the only alterations you may need to make to these lines are in your /MACHINE: switch (in case a setting of 1 does not work on your system), and in telling the EMM386 driver to give you EMS memory and how much. Both EMM386 items are quite easy. To request EMS (expanded) memory, you simply specify RAM in Line 3 in place of NOEMS. That will give you 256K of EMS automatically. If you want more for your programs that use expanded memory, you may a enter the number of kilobytes you want. As long as you've got enough remappable extended memory in your system, you will have no problem. (For an exhaustive treatment of the all the settings and switches you can use with these and other DOS memory-related commands, see the Random House/Glossbrenner books on DOS.)

All right. Let's start with the first line. This tells the system to load DOS's extended memory driver, HIMEM.SYS. That makes memory above the 1MB mark available to DOS and implements the procedures for using it, as defined by the XMS standard. The /MACHINE:1 switch relates to the way your particular computer handles the toggling of the CPU's A20 address line. As you will remember, this is the address line that makes the first 64K (less 16 bytes) of memory lying above the 1MB mark available to DOS as the High Memory Area (HMA).

You may or may not need to use this switch to make the HMA available on your system. If DOS has been loaded into the HMA, a message to that effect will flash on your screen at bootup. You can also use the MEM /C command to verify that DOS is loaded into the High Memory Area. The bootup message looks like this:

```
HIMEM: DOS XMS Driver, Version 3.09—07/24/92
XMS Specification Version 3.0
Copyright 1988-1992 Microsoft Corp.

Installed A20 handler number 1,3.

64K High Memory Area is available.
```

If it is clear that the HMA is *not* available, then you have to either include the /MACHINE:*n* switch or change the number you have specified as your "machine." The README.TXT file that comes with your DOS package lists all of the available machine numbers and the computer brands to which they apply. (See Figure 4-2-3 for a complete list.) If you are in doubt, and if you have the time, you can simply start with /MACHINE:1 and continue through /MACHINE:16, rebooting and using the MEM /C command each time to see if DOS is loaded into the HMA.

Figure 4-2-3 /MACHINE: Switch Settings for HIMEM.SYS

Listed below are leading computer brands and the recommended number to use with them when using the /MACHINE: switch in the CONFIG.SYS line DEVICE=C:\DOS\HIMEM.SYS /MACHINE :*n*. If your computer is not listed, check the README.TXT file supplied with your DOS package, as it may include updated information.

The default value for /MACHINE: is 1 (IBM PC/AT), so you would not think that you have to specify it if that is the system you are using. Unfortunately, however, this is a murky area, so you may find that you do indeed have to specify the default value. If you like, you may specify a code instead of a number.

Make and Model	*Number*	*Code*
(A20 handler)		
Abacus 386	1	at
Chaplet		
Everex AT Plus 1800		
Everex Notebook ELX		
IBM PC/AT		
JDR 386/33		
OPT 386-25 motherboard		
Pak 386SX		
IBM PS/2	2	ps2
Datamedia 386/486		
UNISYS PowerPort		
PC380/33C		
PC350/33C		
PC 300/33C BIOS v. 1.14		
Phoenix Cascade BIOS	3	pt1cascade
HP Vectra (A and A+)	4	hpvectra
PC Limited	4	
AT&T 6300 Plus	5	att6300plus
Acer 1100	6	acer1100
Toshiba 1600 and 1200XE	7	toshiba
Toshiba 5100		*(continued)*

(Figure 4-2-3 continued)

Make and Model	Number	Code
Wyse 12.5 MHz 286	8	wyse
COMPUADD 386 systems		
Hitachi HL500C		
Intel 301z or 302		
Tulip SX	9	tulip
Zenith ZBIOS	10	zenith
IBM PC/AT (alternative delay)	11	at1
IBM PC/AT (alternative delay)	12	at2
CSS Labs	12	css
IBM PC/AT (alternative delay)	13	at3
Excel Computer Systems	13	
Philips	13	philips
HP Vectra	14	fasthp
IBM 7552 Industrial	15	ibm7552
Bull Micral 60	16	bullmicral
Del XBIOS	17	dell

Get an Extra 64K of Memory!

The second line in my recommended CONFIG.SYS file, DOS=HIGH, UMB, does two things. It tells the system to load most of DOS high into the HMA, and it establishes a connection between DOS and Upper Memory Blocks. You could accomplish the same thing with two lines: DOS= HIGH and DOS=UMB.

The third line, DEVICE=C:\DOS\EMM386.EXE I=E000-EFFF NOEMS, accomplishes three tasks. First, it loads DOS's UMB provider, EMM386.EXE. This software causes the CPU to remap extended memory into unused (and thus available) "reserved" memory addresses lying between 640K and the 1MB mark.

Second, with the I=E000-EFFF parameter, the line tells the EMM386 to include a 64K chunk of upper memory addresses that is normally reserved for onboard option ROMs. This is a real power user trick that most people do not know about. EMM386 will not normally use these addresses because IBM PS/2 computers use them for special BIOS extensions. But since this area is actually rarely used on non-PS/2 machines, it is almost always available.

You will see this more clearly when you consult the memory map provided later in this section. But all you really need to know is that telling the driver to use these addresses increases the number of available UMBs by 64K. The location specified by the hex range E000-EFFF is located 64K down from the end of the first megabyte of memory, just below the segment used by the system's ROM BIOS.

Third, the NOEMS parameter tells EMM386.EXE to provide UMBs but *not* expanded memory (EMS). If you want expanded memory as well as UMBs, replace NOEMS with RAM, or make the entire line read DEVICE =EMM386.EXE M9 RAM. The M9 parameter tells the driver to use the same 64K chunk of addresses specified by E000-EFFF as its page frame (or EMS window). You *must* specify M9, not the hex range, for this purpose. And either RAM or NOEMS *must* be included if you want UMBs.

EMM386 defaults to supplying 256K of EMS memory when you use the RAM parameter, but you can change that. All you need to do is include a number ranging from 16 through 32,768 on the line that loads EMM386 .EXE. The number specifies the kilobytes of EMS memory you want the driver to allocate, rounded down to the nearest multiple of sixteen. Thus, if you have 4MB of memory (extended memory) in your system, and you want EMM386 to use 2MB of it to emulate expanded memory, you use a command like DEVICE=C:\DOS\EMM386.EXE M9 RAM 2048.

You can check this with the MEM command or by keying in emm386 at the command line. EMM386.EXE will report that 1,984K of EMS memory is available. Add that to the 64K it has "used" by mapping it to the EMS page frame, and you have your 2,048K.

Get Yet Another 32K of Upper Memory!

The additional 64K of upper memory discussed above is available on most non-PS/2 systems. Since this is exactly the number of kilobytes needed for the EMS page frame, it simply makes good sense to use it for that purpose by including the M9 parameter in your command line.

There is another trick you may be able to use that will yield yet another 32K of upper memory that would not ordinarily be available. And that is to specify I=B000-B7FF. (Do not use this trick if you run Windows 3.0, since that version of Windows may corrupt any data stored in this region.) The first two lines in your CONFIG.SYS file would then look something like this:

```
DEVICE=C:\DOS\HIMEM.SYS /MACHINE:1
DEVICE=C:\DOS\EMM386.EXE i=b000-b7ff M9 RAM 2048
```

As explained earlier, you may have to use a different number for your "machine." The EMM386.EXE line tells the driver to use the 32K location specified by B000-B7FFF for UMBs, to use the location M9 for its EMS page frame, and to give you 2MB (2,048 bytes) of EMS memory (RAM). Notice the two "by request" ranges shown in the map of the Upper Memory Area below:

```
        Memory Ranges
        in Hex Format

640K    A000 - AFFF—VGA Graphics (64K)
704K    B000 - B7FF—available (32K) by request
        B800 - BFFF—VGA Text (32K)
768K    C000 - C7FF—Video ROM (32K)
        C800 - DFFF—available (96K)
896K    E000 - EFFF—available (64K) by request
960K    F000 - FFFF—System ROM (64K)
```

The map begins where conventional memory ends, at 640K. The first chunk of memory above 640K is set aside for VGA graphics. Then there is the 32K "by request" block, followed by more memory for VGA video. Because this 32K range is nominally set aside for use by video adapters, EMM386.EXE does not normally use it as a UMB. But it turns out that the original "set asides" in the PC's design were excessively generous. On many systems you can tell EMM386.EXE to use this address range and gain an *additional* 32K of UMB space.

Your system's video equipment may be different, and this 32K chunk may not be available. But it is certainly worth a try. Do a mem /c >prn first to record your base point. Then add I=B000-B7FF to your EMM386 .EXE line in CONFIG.SYS and reboot. Next, check your available memory again with the MEM command. MEM should report about 32K more of free upper memory than before. As a final test, load your favorite graphics program (not Windows). If that program works, there's a good chance you can use this range of addresses on your system.

The second available chunk of memory starts at C800 (the 768K mark). In this example, a total of 96K is available. This is the memory EMM386 .EXE will use for UMBs automatically. The amount available depends on the various add-on cards and other devices you use. On your system, you may have more or you may have less memory available in this area.

Finally, there is the second "by request" block. This is the block that EMM386.EXE does not normally use because PS/2 machines appropriate it for onboard option ROMs. But as discussed, you can tell the driver to use it either for UMBs with the I=E000-EFFF command, or for the EMS page frame by specifying M9 RAM.

Load 'Em Up!

The CONFIG.SYS lines discussed above really will do the trick for the vast majority of users. As noted, the only modifications you may have to make concern the /MACHINE:*n* setting and the settings determining whether or not you want expanded memory. It is important to emphasize, however, that there are all kinds of other switches and settings you can use with HIMEM.SYS and EMM386. Should you find that the above three lines do not work for you, it may be necessary to delve into the DOS manual or seek expert assistance.

We are going to assume here, however, that the lines suggested here do indeed work as advertised on your machine, and that you are now ready to start moving things out of conventional memory and into UMBs. It is at this point that the DEVICEHIGH=, LOADHIGH, and MEM commands really come into their own. For these are the three tools you will use to pack things into the Upper Memory Area.

From here on in, the process is largely a matter of trial and error. You set the system to load something high; then you reboot; then you use the MEM /C command to see if the item was indeed loaded high and to check on how much additional high memory is available. Next, you load an additional item or two high and repeat the process. (Don't forget, you may use the command mem /c >prn to direct output to the printer, or use a similar command to append output to a file.)

Fortunately, there are a number of general principles that can guide you along the way. First and foremost, it is important to realize that the Upper Memory Area is not one smooth, continuous block of empty memory. Instead, it consists of nooks and crannies and blocks of various sizes. The challenge is to fit your device drivers and TSRs into those fragmented spaces as efficiently as possible. (That's what DOS 6's MemMaker and third-party memory management packages try to do by automatically trying thousands of combinations.)

Second, because of this, it is generally best to arrange your load order by size. Start with the biggest device driver or TSR, and work down from there. This rule is complicated by two factors. First, some drivers and TSRs insist on being loaded before others or they refuse to work. Second, some TSRs need to have more space available when they load than they end up occupying. The Logitech mouse driver, for example, occupies only about 13K when loaded into upper memory. But to get it to load there, you must have at least 29K of free upper memory space available at the time. Unfortunately, there is really no way to tell beforehand whether or not a given driver or TSR will behave this way.

A third general principle is that there is usually no way to tell whether a given program can run from the Upper Memory Area until you test it. All of the TSRs supplied with DOS, including DOSKEY and FASTOPEN, may be loaded high. (The shareware programs CED and FANSI-Console may also be loaded high.) The same goes for all DOS drivers, except HI-MEM.SYS and EMM386.EXE. As for third-party programs, it's any-body's guess. The only way to tell is to test.

Remember, just because you can get a program loaded high, as reported by the MEM command, does not mean the program will actually work from that location. So before you build an elegantly structured memory allocation edifice, make sure that a program not only fits into upper memory but also operates from there.

Fourth, as suggested in Part 1 of this book, always make sure you have an "escape hatch" in the form of a bootable floppy disk. Anytime you start fiddling around with your CONFIG.SYS and AUTOEXEC.BAT files, there is a chance that something you have tried will lock up the system. That's why it is also a good idea to make backup copies of your currently working CONFIG.SYS and AUTOEXEC.BAT files. At worst, should things get hopelessly muddled, you can always get back to where you are right now.

Finally, take the time to produce printouts and make notes. If you charge into this project they way you and I and everyone else attack a new piece of software—head down and hell for leather—you are guaranteed to end up on the rocks. Memory optimization is a meticulous, painstaking process that demands to be performed in a methodical manner. So load your printer with paper, set aside a couple of hours, and have at it! Just re-member that no prizes are given for squeezing out every last byte or kilo-byte. There is so much low-hanging fruit that there's no need to strain yourself reaching for the upper branches.

Additional Memory-Saving Tricks

Speaking of low-hanging fruit, there are at least five additional lines you can use in your CONFIG.SYS file to free several hundred to several thou-sand bytes of conventional memory:

1. Do *not* use the SETVER.EXE command. When you install DOS, the program automatically inserts in your CONFIG.SYS file a line like DEVICE=C:\DOS\SETVER.EXE. SETVER.EXE is designed to fool some programs into thinking that they are running under a different version of DOS. This is a very thoughtful gesture on Microsoft's part, for nothing is more aggravating than to run a pro-gram and get an *Incorrect DOS version* error message.

However, unless you're getting error messages of that sort when SETVER.EXE is not loaded, you don't need it. If you do need it, be sure to load it high with DEVICEHIGH=. The program occupies about 400 bytes of upper memory.

2. Include the command STACKS=0,0 in CONFIG.SYS. A "stack" is an area of memory set aside as a storage area for a DOS interrupt handler. The storage area lets the interrupt handler restore the system to the state it was in before the interrupt was issued. Most systems do not need to set aside space in this manner, but if you do not include STACKS=0,0, DOS automatically allocates more than 1K of memory for this purpose.

3. The same reasoning makes it a good idea to include the line FCBS=1 in CONFIG.SYS. FCBS stands for File Control BlockS and refers to an outdated method of opening files. The DOS default is FCBS=4, at a cost of about 240 bytes of memory. By using the line FCBS=1, you countermand the default and save about 180 bytes. Obviously, if some program refuses to run because it cannot open a file, you will have to remove this line and let the DOS default come into effect. But FCBS=1 is certainly worth a try.

4. Use BUFFERS=32. Once DOS has been loaded into the HMA, that 64K segment of memory cannot be used by any other program. However, since DOS occupies only about 48K of that space, there is about 16K of additional room. Fortunately, DOS is designed to utilize that space by allocating it to whatever disk buffers you have specified. Since each buffer costs you about 500 bytes, you can specify about 32 buffers, and it won't cost you any conventional memory at all.

There is no single "correct" buffers setting. Everything depends on how you use your computer, so you may wish to experiment. It may be that BUFFERS=32 is fine on your system. Which is great, since those 32 buffers cost you nothing in conventional memory. Microsoft has some recommendations, however.

If your hard disk is larger than 80MB but smaller than 120MB, a buffers setting of 40 is about right. For disks larger than 120MB, a setting of 50 is recommended. After a setting of 50, according to Microsoft, diminishing returns begin to set in. If you decide to use DOS's SMARTDrive hard disk cache, you may want to reduce your buffers setting to about 10 for optimum performance.

5. Don't set LASTDRIVE= any higher than necessary. DOS allocates 88 bytes for every logical drive defined in your system. Thus, if you set LASTDRIVE= any higher than the actual number of drives you

plan to use, you will waste memory. For example, if you assume two floppy drives (A and B) and two hard disk volumes (C and D), plus one RAM drive (E), and one CD-ROM drive (F), your CONFIG .SYS file should contain the line LASTDRIVE=F.

6. Tell DOS to draw the memory it allocates for file handles (FILES=) from upper memory blocks. Each file handle you specify costs you 59 bytes of conventional memory. Now, thanks to UMBFILES.COM, you can tell DOS to take this memory from any available UMBs. Written by *PC Magazine*'s Jeff Prosise, this program was one of the first utilities to appear that was specifically designed to take advantage of the memory management abilities Microsoft introduced with DOS 5. It's a real beauty.

UMBFILES is the perfect way to make use of those little 2K upper memory blocks that are too small for anything else. Simply include the line FILES=8 in CONFIG.SYS. Then include in your AUTO EXEC.BAT a line like C:\UTILS\UMBFILES=32. A companion program, NUMFILES.COM, reports the number of file handles that have been allocated at any given time.

These two programs are available from Glossbrenner's Choice and via PC MagNet. See the November 26, 1991, issue of *PC Magazine* for a complete technical explanation of how they work. Also, do not forget to make a line using UMBFILES a permanent part of your AUTOEXEC.BAT file. Otherwise you may find some programs locking up for no apparent reason—until you realize that you have cut the file handles back to 8 with FILES=8 in CONFIG.SYS and neglected to use UMBFILES.

PowerPoint

Loading the Mouse into the HMA

If you have reduced the number of buffers to the minimum (BUF-FERS=3) because you are using a disk cache, you may be able to use the extra space in the HMA for your Microsoft Mouse driver. You will need Version 8.1 or above of the driver, and you will need to use the undocumented /U switch. Use a command in your CONFIG .SYS like DEVICEHIGH=C:\DEV\MOUSE.SYS /U. For AUTO-EXEC.BAT, use LOADHIGH MOUSE.COM /U. This will load all but 4K of the driver into the HMA space left by DOS and load the rest into a regular UMB.

QEMM, 386Max, NetRoom, and Others

DOS 5 and 6 do an excellent job of quickly and easily freeing up large chunks of conventional memory. They also gives you a large array of switches you can use to include this or exclude that range of memory addresses. But the switches are highly technical and require a good familiarity with hex addresses and DOS's memory layout. Nor is DOS capable of some of the tricks employed by some third-party memory managers.

All three of the top-rated memory managers—386Max, QEMM-386, and NetRoom—can squeeze more conventional memory out of most systems than can DOS. All three list for $99.95, with a street price of about $57. Each also offers a higher degree of automation, as they automatically calculate the best, most memory-efficient load order of TSRs and drivers.

Memory managers typically require several passes to optimize your system. You start with everything loaded as usual—all your device drivers and TSRs. Then you run the program, and it takes a look around. It will then place its own drivers in your CONFIG.SYS file and reboot your system. During the second pass, the program tries out the changes it has made, attempting to load device drivers and TSRs into UMBs. Then it reboots to make sure that they do indeed work from their new location. Finally, the programs rebuild your CONFIG.SYS and AUTOEXEC.BAT files and then reboot again.

Third-Party Tricks

These programs use some very interesting techniques. In the first place, third-party memory managers tend to take up less room than HIMEM .SYS and EMM386.EXE. Those two DOS programs occupy about 8K, for example, while most memory manager drivers occupy about 2K. Most also give you the option of reclaiming memory addresses set aside to support video graphics.

If you have an EGA/VGA system, you may be able to increase program-usable conventional memory to a maximum of 736K, provided you are willing to give up EGA/VGA graphics and pretend you have a CGA system. You can do this because DOS computers are designed to set aside 128K of Upper Memory Area addresses as video RAM (where the video card stores its screens).

But not all video cards and modes need all of that memory. Monochrome systems in 80-column mode use only 4K of that space, for example. CGA systems use 32K. But both EGA and VGA systems use 96K of RAM, starting immediately after the 640K mark. (See the previously discussed memory map, Figure 4-1-1, to get a better idea of this location.)

The crucial point is that since this chunk of memory is located directly above the 640K limit, it can be *added* to conventional memory. And that is what third-party memory managers do, at your option. Often you can toggle this feature on and off from the command line, so you can enable graphics capabilities (and reduce conventional memory to 640K again) when you need them.

The packages also have the ability to get DOS to draw from the Upper Memory Area (UMA) the space it sets aside for FILES= and LAST DRIVE=. QEMM-386 also includes an option it calls Stealth that creates a buffer in extended memory and a page frame-like window in Upper Memory. It then compresses the system ROM BIOS into the buffer and pages sections in and out of the UMA as needed. NetRoom has the ability to group related drivers and load them high as a set.

Here are the addresses of the companies that produce what are generally considered to be the three top PC memory management software products. I've played with all three programs, and each is quite good. You may wish to contact the companies for more information about their specific products:

NetRoom
Helix Software Co.
47-09 30th St.
Long Island City, NY 11101
800-451-0551; 718-392-3100

386Max
Qualitas, Inc.
7101 Wisconsin Ave., Ste. 1386
Bethesda, MD 20814
800-733-1377; 301-907-6700
FAX: 301-907-0905

QEMM-386
Quarterdeck Office Systems
150 Pico Blvd.
Santa Monica, CA 90405
310-392-9851
FAX: 310-399-3802

Is It Worth It?

Third-party memory management packages may be just what you need. I've worked with lots of them, and their automatic "optimize" modes, in particular, are quite impressive. A number of caveats apply, however. First, the nifty tricks such packages use to squeeze out the last kilobyte of conventional memory can result in incompatibilities and problems. If a program has decided to shrink the space occupied by the system BIOS and does so by removing the code needed to access your floppy disk drives, you could face a problem.

In addition, in an era characterized by greater and greater use of graphics, not many of us would want to disable EGA/VGA graphics memory, even if it meant an additional 96K of conventional memory. Besides, programmers who know they're going to need more than DOS's 640K are not going to assume that you have 736K of conventional memory in your system. They're going to include code to let their programs use EMS or XMS memory instead.

Finally, as when buying any major piece of software, I strongly urge you to read the reviews in leading magazines. Interestingly, if you look at the reviews of memory management software, you will find that in nearly every case the reviewer had to make several calls to the software companies' technical support numbers to produce an optimal configuration.

If a computer expert hired by *InfoWorld, PC Magazine,* or some other publication needs that kind of help in optimizing a typical hardware and software configuration, how much more help are you and I going to need? That's why I'm inclined to feel that if I had an extra $57 or so, I'd spend it on an extra megabyte of RAM instead of on memory management software. In most situations, the tools provided with DOS 5 and DOS 6 will serve you well until DOS is replaced by OS/2, Windows NT, "Windows NT Lite," or something else and the 640K limit disappears into the mists of microworld history.

SECTION
4-3

MAKING THE MOST OF
YOUR MEMORY

At this point, we're going to assume that you've either used the tools DOS provides or used some third-party package to free up as much conventional 640K memory as possible. The DOS kernel and DOS's disk buffers have been loaded into the HMA, and most of your TSRs and device drivers have found comfortable homes in UMBs. You have achieved your goal. You now have almost 600K of free conventional memory, and you deserve to give yourself a pat on the back.

But is that all there is? Well, yes, and no. If you regularly run programs that are able to take advantage of XMS or EMS memory, you may find yourself adjusting and otherwise fine-tuning the EMM386.EXE line in CONFIG.SYS as you allocate more or less EMS memory. You may also find yourself procrastinating, er, "tweaking your system," as you try yet another TSR load order to squeeze out another handful of free bytes.

But, by and large, you can rest on your laurels, content in the knowledge that many of your DOS programs will run better and possibly a bit faster now that you've given them more conventional memory to work with. That may very well be enough in your particular case.

But you should know that software exists to give you even more control. How would you like to be able to load, unload, activate, and deactivate your TSRs at will, without rebooting the system or worrying about which one happened to be loaded first? How would you like to be able to instantly jump from one program to another and back again in a nearly infinite shell game? It's enough to make anyone think twice about converting to Windows.

These are the two memory-related options we will focus on in this section. They amount to complete control over your TSRs and complete control over your applications programs (or apps, in computer-speak.) Only two programs are needed to provide this measure of control—Kim Kokkonen's TSR Utilities (also known as Mark/Release) and Shane and Sandi Stump's Back & Forth task swapper.

TSR Control

TSRs—Terminate and Stay-Resident programs—are a wonderful invention. The ability to pop up a utility program at the press of a hotkey combination, while you are in the midst of some other app, can be indispensable. I don't know whether Borland International invented the technique, but certainly that company's SideKick both established and popularized the concept. Why shouldn't you be able to pop up, say, a notepad, to jot down some idea while you are in the midst of a spreadsheet?

If the only alternative was to exit the spreadsheet and run your word processor or text editor to take a note, you either wouldn't bother, or you would force yourself to jot something down on a pad of paper. That's not bad, but it certainly is not using the technology. It makes much more sense to load a program like SideKick—which offers a notepad, a calendar, an ASCII table, and several other features—all on a pop-up basis.

The problem is that to this day there is no universally accepted standard for managing TSRs. Some still insist on being the first loaded. And, while some TSR packages include utilities designed to remove them from memory, those utilities may not work if the target TSR is not the last one loaded. In general, once you have loaded most TSRs, you're stuck, at least until you reboot with a different AUTOEXEC.BAT file.

That's why Kim Kokkonen's Mark/Release package is so convenient. Though copyrighted, it is not shareware. Mr. Kokkonen asks for no registration fee or contribution. Available from Glossbrenner's Choice and many other sources, Mark/Release at last gives users control over their TSRs. The concept is simple. When you load your TSRs, all you have to do is run the MARK program before each one. Thus, if you wanted to load

SideKick and the NewKey keyboard macroing program, you would put the following lines in your AUTOEXEC.BAT:

```
mark sidekick
loadhigh sk
mark newkey
loadhigh newkey
```

The MARK program places in RAM memory markers associated with the words SIDEKICK and NEWKEY. The two TSR programs are then loaded or loaded high after their markers. The markers serve as a reference point. Thus, when you want to remove NewKey, all you have to do is use the RELEASE program by keying in release newkey. All TSRs loaded after the *newkey* mark will be released from memory.

To look at the current status of your TSRs and memory marks at any time, use the supplied MAPMEM program. It shows you a table containing, among other things, the name of each TSR mark, the number of bytes it occupies, and the DOS interrupt vectors it uses. In this way you can easily see which program(s) will be removed from memory when you release a particular mark and the number of bytes that will be freed.

Once you have released a TSR, you can use the space it occupied for a different TSR. If you use MARK before loading that program, you can later RELEASE it and either reload the former TSR or load something else.

The latest version of Mr. Kokkonen's TSR Utilities fully supports use of the Upper Memory Area under Microsoft DOS, Digital Research, and most third-party memory managers. It also includes MARKNET and RELNET, a version of the Mark/Release pair specifically designed for those who want to release the Novell NetWare shell. There is also a program to disable a specific TSR but leave it in memory. Disabled TSRs can be activated again using the same program. A program called RAMFREE shows you how much memory is available, while one called DEVICE tells you what device drivers are loaded.

The point is control—control over your memory and control over your TSRs. There are commercial equivalents, but none does a better job than the TSR Utilities.

Task-Swapping, Big Time

Task-swapping is nearly as useful as multitasking. If you've ever shelled out of a program to run something else and then returned with the EXIT command, you already have a pretty good idea of what's involved. The two main differences between multitasking and task-swapping relate to the continuation of a process versus putting it on hold, and to the amount of hardware and software required.

Windows and OS/2 enthusiasts are fond of saying that their software lets you start a long database sort or spreadsheet recalculation and then load your word processor to start preparing a letter. Thanks to multitasking, while you are preparing your letter, the database or spreadsheet continues its work in the background. Or they may suggest that you can start a spell checker in your word processor and load your database to check a few records.

A task swapper, in contrast, lets you freeze any program right where it is and switch to another program by pressing a hotkey. Your spreadsheet, database, or word processor will not continue to operate in the background. But it will be exactly as you left it when you opt to return by pressing another hotkey.

At the risk of being labeled a reactionary, I have always felt that multitasking is a solution in search of a problem. The only time I personally ever feel a need for this capability is when I'm doing a long download from a remote system. It would be nice to be able to go on to other things, while the download takes place in the background.

But, wouldn't you know it, communications is the one thing that multitasking environments like Windows 3.1 have trouble with. That may change when Windows NT appears. But right now, the one multitasking capability I would like to have is not reliably provided by Windows. Yet, for acceptable performance, Windows requires a considerable investment in memory, hard disk, and video hardware, not to mention processor power and speed. OS/2 requires an even larger commitment.

I'm sorry, but I don't need to spend hundreds of extra dollars in hardware and software at this point for the ability to run my programs by clicking on cute little icons or conducting a database sort in the background. Truth to be told, I love to sort a large database because it gives me an excuse to get up from the computer and do something else while the machine is grinding away.

Should Windows NT prove to be a killer, I will willingly change my ways. But until (and if) that happens, I would rather stick with a program like Back & Forth Professional (B&F) from Progressive Solutions, Inc. This program is from the same husband-and-wife programming team that was responsible for such commercial successes as Take Charge! and Disk Commando. Small wonder that *PC Magazine* gave an early version of B&F top rating [*PC Magazine*, Oct. 30, 1990, p. 175].

This is a task swapper, par excellence. The shareware version will only use a little more than one meg of memory for storage and swapping. So that puts a de facto limit on the number of tasks you can load. The registered user version can take advantage of all the XMS and EMS memory you have. You will need a 512K system with at least one of the following: EMS memory, XMS memory, a RAM disk, or a hard disk. A mouse, modem, and color monitor are optional. If you want to load B&F into the Upper Memory Area, you will need DOS's EMM386, or some other UMB provider.

The features offered by Back & Forth Professional are far too numerous to mention. So let me just hit the highlights. The most outstanding feature is the sheer speed with which you can switch among tasks if you have EMS or XMS memory for the program to use. Applications programs pop up at the touch of a hotkey as if they were TSRs.

Assignable Hotkeys and Macros

You can assign each task its own hotkey combination and jump around your active task list as you please. You don't have to return to the main screen. Nor do you have to cycle through the list. If you are in your database program, for example, going directly to your word processor can be as easy as keying in Ctrl+W (or whatever hotkey combination you have assigned to the word processing program). To go back to your database, you might enter Ctrl+D from your word processor, and it instantly appears.

Via Back & Forth Professional, you can also define a series of macros to be used with each program you run. Thus, if your database program does not include a macro or programmable key function to make it easy to issue a frequently used series of commands, B&F can supply that capability.

In all, a total of 50 separate programs can be included on the program list, and you can run any twenty of them as active tasks at the same time. You can tell B&F to *automatically* load in your chosen selection of active tasks when it runs. That way, you can switch among tasks from the start, without the bother of first having to load each one by hand.

B&F includes a powerful print formatter and buffer that not only let you spool data to memory but also let you control how the text is formatted. You can also opt to have print output directed to disk. You can use B&F to clip text out of one program and paste it into another or save it to disk. It's not quite like the Dynamic Data Exchange (DDE) of Windows and OS/2, but it's probably more useful at this point.

You can use B&F to capture graphics screens. The screen images are saved as disk files, and they can be converted to PC Paintbrush (.PCX) format quickly and easily by B&F, should you want to use them with a desktop publishing program or graphics editor.

Back & Forth Professional/Test Drive is available as a three-disk set from Glossbrenner's Choice and many other disk vendors. You can also find a copy in the Zenith forum on CompuServe. Progressive Solutions, Inc., uses the Zenith forum to provide online support to users. A voice phone support number and support bulletin board are also available.

PART V

OPTIMIZING YOUR HARD DISK

What You Will Learn

Next to the CPU, your hard disk is probably the most important component in your system. It is, after all, the place where you keep your tools and
the place where you keep your "work product." Since using software tools
to create work product is what personal computing is all about, the hard
disk clearly plays a crucial role.

In this part of the book we will briefly review the fundamentals of how
a hard drive operates and how data is stored on its surfaces by DOS. Then
we'll charge into the changing landscape of hard disk interfaces to discuss
at length topics like ST-506, ESDI, SCSI, and, most particularly, IDE.
You will emerge from this section with a much better understanding of
what your drive is doing and how you can help it do even better.

Next we will look at the major options available to help you boost the
effective speed of your hard drive. We will show you how to tune up a drive
with a file defragmenter, and how to boost its responsiveness with a disk
cache. Then we will present a program for quickly and easily freeing up
space on even the most overstuffed drive, including the use of a program
that can cut the size of your .COM and .EXE files in half, with no decrease
in performance.

After that, we'll look at the best way to back up a hard drive: what it
costs, what to expect, how to implement a backup program, and so forth.
And we'll finish off with tips about using floppy drives that can save you
time, heartache, and money.

SECTION
5-1

HARD DISK BASICS

Most computer equipment seems to get more complicated to understand and use as time goes on. But just the opposite has happened with today's hard disk drives. The technology is more advanced than ever—drives are significantly smaller, faster, more reliable, and more capacious than even a few years ago. But far less effort is required on the part of the user to obtain peak performance from the equipment.

Indeed, with today's IDE drives, there is nothing you *can* do but plug them in, add the drive specs to your CMOS, partition them with DOS's FDISK, and run DOS's FORMAT program. You can forget about low-level formatting, bad track lists, sector interleave, terminating resistors, special twists in the data cable, and most of the other topics hard disk users have traditionally had to contend with. Today, all of those things are taken care of at the factory.

We'll have much more to say about IDE drives later. Right now, it's important to make sure that everyone has a basic idea of how hard disk drives work. (For more detailed information, see Glossbrenner's *File & Disk Management: From Chaos to Control* from Osborne/McGraw-Hill.)

Platters and Spindles

Hard disk drives consist of a stack of metal-covered platters stuck on a spindle. The spindle turns the platters at 3,600 revolutions per minute (or faster, in some equipment). That's the same as 60 revolutions per second or one revolution every 16.67 milliseconds.

Data is recorded and retrieved by read-write heads that literally fly over the surface of the platters on a cushion of air. These units are analogous to the record and play heads in a tape deck. The tiny spots of polarization created by a read/write head when recording data are called magnetic domains. The process of reading a disk is just the opposite of writing. As it flies over the disk surface, the head senses the magnetic flux changes recorded there, interpreting them as ON and OFF bits. In either case, whether reading or writing, it is crucial that the head be very close to the medium.

You don't have to be an engineering genius to figure out why this must be. Magnetic fields, unlike laser beams, cannot be focused with great precision. If the read/write head were, say, an inch from the disk, the only way to affect the medium would be to boost the strength of the magnetic field, increasing its *coercivity*. And that, of course, would inevitably magnetize a large swath of the disk.

So read/write heads must be small, and their fields must be relatively weak. That means they must operate very close to the disk surface. Just how close might surprise you: A human hair would seem like a log compared to the distance that separates a read/write head from the disk surface. That's why all hard disks are placed in sealed compartments equipped with sophisticated air filters. A single grain of pollen or particle of cigarette smoke would appear to a read/write head as a boulder in the road. The result would almost certainly be a head crash.

Tracks and Sectors

Disks are formatted to have tracks and sectors. Tracks are concentric circles ranging out from the center hole to the platter rim. Sectors are portions of tracks (arcs). Every track and sector has a number, and each of the read/write heads has a number. So, if you know the head, the track, and the sector number, you can locate any piece of data on the disk.

If you imagine a stack of four platters, you can assume that there is a read/write head for each side of each platter. The heads are attached to a comb-like arrangement that intersects the platter stack. As the "comb" moves in and out of the stack, all of the heads attached to it move as well. Read/write heads, in other words, do not move individually.

The mechanism used to move the head assembly in today's drives is a *servo-voice-coil actuator.* Imagine a stick lying on a table. One end is attached to a spring that is secured to the table. The other end is covered with a metal cap.

Now imagine an electromagnet placed an inch or two away from the metal cap. If you apply a small amount of electricity to the magnet, it will pull the metal-capped stick a short distance across the table against the resistance of the spring. If you apply a lot of current, the stick will be pulled a greater distance. If you cut the power completely, the spring will pull the stick back to its starting position.

That's basically what happens when your hard disk drive wants to move its read/write heads from one location to another. A voice-coil magnet of the sort used in audio speakers is used to pull against a spring to get the head assembly to the correct location.

For technical reasons, this approach usually requires that one side of one of the hard disk platters be devoted to servo data. Either that, or *servo* data must be permanently recorded on each side, between the real data tracks. The servo tracks act as magnetic bumpers to tell the heads where they are. The system uses this information to fine-tune the power applied to the voice-coil magnet to move the head assembly with great precision.

Servo-voice-coil technology results in faster access times and greater drive capacities. It also makes most drives "self-parking." When you power down the system, the voice-coil magnet goes dead, and the spring automatically pulls the head assembly to its at-rest, "parked" position over a spot on the disk that is never used to record data.

A Word About Interleave

In the past, perhaps the single most important step one could take to boost a hard drive's performance was to adjust its *sector interleave.* Since all IDE drives are set at the factory for a 1:1 interleave, this is no longer an issue. It is important to understand, nonetheless.

Imagine a circle divided into seventeen equal sectors. Each sector has an assigned number from 0 through 16. But the numbers are not necessarily sequential. Instead of 0, 1, 2, 3, and so on, the numbers may actually run 0, 6, 12, 1, and so forth. Sequentially numbered sectors, in other words, may be interleaved. The reason this technique was used in the past has to do with the slowness of the drive controller card and the computer itself. Older equipment cannot digest one sector of data right after another. Interleaving sectors introduces a small delay between the time the system reads Sector 1 and the time it must be ready to read Sector 2. IBM/XT-class machines typically have disks with a 1:6 interleave. AT-class machines might have a default interleave of 1:3.

The computers most of us use today do not suffer from these limitations. That's why your hard drive is almost certainly set to a 1:1 interleave, where sequentially numbered sectors are physically contiguous (0, 1, 2, 3, etc.).

Controllers and MFM and RLL Encoding

You should now have a broad, conceptual understanding of what's going on inside your hard disk drive unit. We really don't need to get much more technical than this. But we do need to discuss the rest of the hard drive system, for the spindle with its platters is only part of the story. There must be a mechanism to control the drive, to send its heads darting hither and yon to pick up or lay down the data you are dealing with.

All hard disk drives have a controller card of some sort. When you want to retrieve a file, DOS talks to the card, telling it which disk sectors it wants, and the card issues the necessary commands to the actuator to move the heads to the correct location. The controller card is intimately involved with the drive itself. It knows all kinds of things about the drive that DOS does not know and has no need to know.

DOS assumes, for example, that each track contains seventeen sectors. But the controller card may know that the bigger tracks, the ones farther away from the center spindle, actually contain 26, 28, 34, or some other number of sectors. Those tracks have the room, after all, and as long as the controller card is capable of fooling DOS into thinking it is dealing with seventeen-sector tracks through a process called "sector translating," all is well.

The disk controller is also responsible for the data encoding technique used by the drive. Older controller cards use a technique called Modified Frequency Modulation or MFM. Somewhat more recent cards use a technique called Run-Length Limited or RLL. The advantage of RLL encoding is that it allows a platter of a given size to hold 50 to 100 percent more data than would be the case with MFM encoding. That translates to faster access time, since more data is passing beneath the heads with each spin of the disk.

There are different techniques of RLL encoding. The key point is that if you use an RLL controller, you must get a drive that is rated for the more stringent tolerances RLL encoding requires. It is true that you can prepare and use an MFM-rated drive with an RLL controller, and things will seem to go well at the start. But over time, you may find that errors begin to creep into your data as the drive is pushed beyond its rated limits.

Happily, thanks to the overwhelming market presence of IDE equipment, none of this need concern most users today. As we will see, with an IDE drive, it is irrelevant whether the manufacturer has used 1,3 RLL; 2,7 RLL; 3,9 RLL; or some proprietary encoding technique.

IDE, SCSI, ESDI, AND ST-506

We know about the hard disk itself, and we know about the need for a controller card of some sort. Next we must spend just a moment on the topic of interfaces. A hard drive's interface is not really the connection between the controller card and the computer, though of course that connection must be defined. A hard drive's interface is the connection between the controller card and the drive itself.

As far as the computer and DOS are concerned, the device that plugs into the system at location X is a hard drive storage device. Requests for data are sent to location X, as is data to be stored. Neither DOS nor the CPU care about how the data gets to and from location X via the hard drive and its controller.

A hard disk interface specification thus defines the signals that pass between the controller and the hard disk, and which physical lines will be used for what purpose. The interface design is directly responsible for the speed with which data is transferred to and from location X in the computer.

Outmoded Interfaces: ST-506 and ESDI

The hard disk interface specification that was most popular in years past is known as ST-506. It was named after the 5-megabyte Seagate Technologies drive that first employed it, model ST-506. The original ST-506 drive was soon replaced by the ST-412, a unit that could store 10MB. So you may see the interface referred to as ST-506/412. This interface allows for a data transfer rate between drive and controller of 5 megabits per second. Note that that's mega*bits*. Because a bit can be thought of as a clock cycle, and megahertz refers to millions of cycles per second, you may also see data transfer rates expressed as megahertz. Thus 5Mb/s (5 megabits per second) is the same as a data transfer rate of 5MHz.

In more comprehensible terms, this amounts to about 625K per second with an MFM-encoded drive. If you eliminate the data concerned with sector addressing, error correction, and other overhead, the actual throughput of usable "real" data is about 522K per second. When RLL encoding is used, the actual "real" data throughput is about 798K per second. This was fine for old, slow, PC-, XT-, and AT-class machines. It is not acceptable for the machines we use today.

An attempt at improving on the ST-506 interface was made by the Maxtor Corporation and some 40 other disk manufacturers. This interface is called the Enhanced Small Device Interface or ESDI ("esdee"). The ESDI specification extended its reach into not only the speed of data transfer but also the means of data encoding on the drive. ESDI drives, in general, can store twice as much data in a given space, with a data transfer rate ("real" data) of 1MB per second or more. That's pretty good, and these two characteristics (large capacity and fast data transfer) have made ESDI drives popular as network file servers.

However, computer technology has leaped ahead. As a result, ST-506 is all but dead, except for replacement drives. And ESDI is considered moribund at best. According to *PC Magazine* (March, 1992), for example, industry leader Seagate Technologies does not plan to introduce any more ESDI drives. Like most other hard drive manufacturers, Seagate is looking ahead to the SCSI and IDE interfaces. We will too, starting with the Small Computer Systems Interface (SCSI, "scuzzy") and then moving on to IDE.

The SCSI Interface

The SCSI interface first came to the personal computer world's attention when Apple equipped each Macintosh with a "scuzzy" port. Indeed, many still mistakenly believe that SCSI is a proprietary Apple Computer interface. It isn't.

Officially known as ANSI standard X3.131-1986, SCSI grew out of the Shugart Associates Systems Interface (SASI, "sassy") developed in 1979 to connect 8-inch hard drives to some of the early personal computers and dedicated word processors. SASI went further than this, however. It was conceived as nothing less than a universal mass storage gateway. The idea was to eliminate the costly task of designing new controller cards each time a new drive came to market.

As SCSI evolved, the specification was enhanced to support tape drives, printers, coprocessors, optical disks, LAN connections, scanners, and other devices. In reality, SCSI is a complete *bus specification*. That means that it offers the equivalent of an extension to your computer's motherboard. Under SCSI, devices are daisy-chained together by plugging one into another.

That sounds great in theory. Unfortunately, at this writing, the reality is something else again. The trouble is that the interchangeability of equipment, which from its beginning has been at the heart of the SCSI concept, is still more promise than reality, at least in the DOS world. And this is where the danger lies.

SCSI is a fully-documented ANSI standard, but the standard is very flexible. So flexible and undefined, in fact, that three devices can be manufactured to the SCSI standard, and none of them will be completely compatible with the others. To add fuel to the fire, there is now SCSI-II (officially, ANSI standard X3T9.2/86-109). Characterized by the description "fast and wide," SCSI-II features a 16- or 32-bit data path (versus the 8-bit path of SCSI-I), a command queuing feature to let a controller accept new commands while in the midst of executing former commands, and a maximum device-to-device transfer speed of 40MB per second (versus the 4MB per second possible under SCSI-I).

Data transfer rates like that are enticing, to say the least. As is the simplicity of being able to plug one device into another's SCSI port and thus extend the system bus. But right now, it is a mistake to hope to be able to effortlessly connect a SCSI hard disk, CD-ROM, scanner, and tape drive to a single host adapter. It's possible, but trying to get multiple SCSI devices from different manufacturers to work together is asking for a major headache.

IDE: Today's Standard

Some time around August, 1990, the long-reigning standard that consisted of the ST-506 interface and MFM or RLL encoding began to crumble. The agent of change was the new IDE approach. The speed with which it took over was amazing, even to those in the industry. As one hard drive maker told me, "IDE just came out of nowhere!"

It didn't, of course. IDE, like any number of other interfaces you've never heard of, had been in the pipeline for years, but no one paid it much attention. (The first IDE drive appeared early in 1986 in a Compaq portable.) After all, we already had the SCSI interface with its electronics integrated onto the drive or the device, and the resulting performance was excellent.

It seems probable, however, that SCSI was seen as trying to do too much, too soon. At least in the IBM-compatible DOS world. SCSI not only improved performance by tightly integrating devices and their electronic controllers, it also attempted to implement an entire expansion bus.

SCSI may yet win out. In the meantime, IDE went to the heart of the market: improved performance and lower costs. That made it irresistible, particularly to the clone makers and mail-order firms, all of which compete on price in what is essentially a commodity market.

The Key to IDE's Success

Here's what you have to understand to appreciate IDE's success. In the past, hard drives and controller cards were purchased separately, whether by the user, the mail-order clone maker, the local computer dealer, or the brand-name manufacturer. The controller and the drive had to be compatible, and the controller had to apply a low-level format to the drive it was going to work with. This is a lengthy process, requiring fifteen to twenty minutes or more per drive.

Bad tracks had to be noted and mapped, and a computer printout had to be generated and taped to the drive. Then the disk had to be partitioned into Drives C and D, or whatever. And each partition had to be given a high-level format with DOS's FORMAT command. If software was to be bundled with the system, the programs had to be copied onto the drive.

These steps are very time-consuming and labor-intensive. But they were necessary if the company wanted to deliver a turn-key system to its customers. There is also the matter of the cost of a separate controller card. The margins are so thin on computers that even a 35-cent connector can be a major issue in system design. A dollar here, a few pennies there, and pretty soon costs are such that you can't sell the machine at a profit.

IDE (Integrated Drive Electronics) equipment changed all that. The drive and its controller were mated into a single package by the manufacturer and sold as a single unit. As you would expect, controller and drive are designed to work together to deliver the optimal performance. And the drives are delivered with their low-level formats already in place. That cut labor costs.

What's more, IDE drives typically connect to the motherboard via a simple pin header or socket. That further reduced the component cost of the computer. Better performance and lower costs made the choice of IDE drives a "no brainer" for most clone makers.

Why Drive Makers Love IDE

Drive manufacturers were equally enthusiastic. It is true that with IDE equipment, the drive makers supply both the drive and the controller, so they have to charge the OEMs (Original Equipment Manufacturers) a bit more. But the extra savings far outweigh the extra cost to an OEM. For their part, the manufacturers like the freedom the IDE approach offers them. Since they are in control of the complete package, they can do all kinds of things to optimize the unit.

They are free to use any encoding scheme they please to pack as much data as possible on a given disk surface. They can even alter the rotation rate of the platters when recording data on different parts of the disk. When a disk stack is spinning at a constant rate, data cannot be stored as densely on the larger, outer tracks as it can be on the inner tracks. That's because on the outer tracks more disk "real estate" is passing under the heads in a given amount of time than passes beneath them on the shorter, inner tracks.

The solution is a technique called *zone-bit recording* that involves writing to different zones of the disk at different rotational speeds. The result is a nearly uniform data density across the disk. Or, to put it another way, the outer, larger tracks can hold more sectors of data than the inner tracks, thus boosting the drive's capacity. The integrated drive electronics conceal this fact from DOS, which expects each track to have seventeen sectors containing 512 bytes of data each. DOS can't deal with disks that might have seventeen sectors on one track, 23 on another, and 31 on some other.

At this writing, most companies are manufacturing IDE drives using hardware that is either identical to or based on the designs for the ST-506 and ESDI units they produced in the past. The firms are in the enviable position of being able to pack more data onto the same drives they've been making for years—but selling the units for more money.

PowerPoint

Fooling the CMOS

An IDE drive must have the ability to fool DOS into thinking it is an ordinary, conventional drive. But this ability has an added benefit. In many cases, it means that you can tell your CMOS just about anything you want about the drive's heads, cylinders, and sectors, instead of being forced to use an official "drive type." Drive parameters may no longer matter, in other words, thanks to the ability of many IDE drives to alter the way they appear to DOS.

You will want to check with your computer maker or drive supplier to be certain, but you may be able to merely pick a drive type with a capacity the same as your drive and tell the CMOS that this is what you have. Among other things, this can help you get around the 1,024-cylinder limit imposed by DOS and most computer BIOSes. (A cylinder is a stack of tracks. So if your disk has 1,024 tracks per side, you have 1,024 cylinders.)

Just don't forget which drive geometry (cylinders, heads, and sectors) you have specified. Once you have formatted a drive using a given cylinder and head emulation, its logical configuration is cast in concrete and cannot be changed without reformatting. If your CMOS memory should disappear, you will not be able to access the drive again until you re-enter your CMOS information, specifying the same geometry you started with.

Your Basic Black Box

Of course, the IDE phenomenon has fed upon itself. Less than two years after their introduction, IDE drives had taken over not only the OEM market but the replacement drive market as well.

At this writing, there is no apparent downside to the trend. Everyone—drive maker, OEM, and consumer—benefits. Thus, when my trusty Seagate ST-4096 (80MB, 28ms) died a while back, I replaced it with a Western Digital Piranha 4200 (212MB, 15ms). A $20 host adapter card connected it to my system, and I couldn't be more pleased. If you're an old hand, though, using an IDE drive requires a little mental adjustment.

From the user's standpoint, an IDE drive is the quintessential black box. You have no idea what's going on inside it. All you know is that this black box will hold a certain amount of data and deliver it to your computer at a certain specified speed. There is no tweaking or tuning to be done.

So you don't need to know what data-encoding scheme is used. (Most IDE drives use some form of RLL encoding.) Nor do you need to know how many sectors are actually recorded on each track, or whether there are any bad tracks. The IDE electronics present a "perfect" drive to DOS. You don't have to worry about sector interleave, either, since all IDE drives are interleaved at 1:1.

Low-level formats are out as well. Indeed, you can completely ruin an IDE drive if you attempt to give it a low-level format. (You will have to send it back to the factory for repair and reformatting.) As I say, IDE is bound to be a little disconcerting to anyone who is accustomed to hands-on, low-level control. But ultimately, it is liberating, since it frees you from a whole set of concerns.

IDE Performance Considerations

The proof is in the performance, so if you are considering adding an IDE drive to your system, read the current magazine reviews thoroughly. Then buy the biggest, fastest IDE drive you can afford.

Hard drives are typically described in terms of megabytes and milliseconds. We all know what megabytes are. The milliseconds quoted refer to a drive's average access time. That is, how long, on average, the drive takes to find a random byte of information stored on the disk. In the not-too-distant past, a speed of 28 milliseconds (28ms) was considered the standard. But computer CPU speeds and hard drive technology are rapidly pushing that standard down to 15ms. (Some drive makers also report track-to-track seek speeds, but you can pretty much ignore them since they have little relevance to everyday life.)

You can think of the average access time as the amount of time that elapses between the time you press Enter when issuing a command and the time the program or DOS reads the data from the drive. If you use your computer in a way that does not involve much disk access, you may not be bothered by the difference between 28 and 15 milliseconds. But if you use disk-intensive software like database programs, in which hundreds of records must be retrieved or sorted or processed, a 13 millisecond difference is noticeable indeed. The slower drive will cost you an average of thirteen seconds for each 1,000 records you access, or an extra minute for every 4,600 records, and so on.

A drive's average access time is determined by the mechanism of the drive itself. Faster drives have faster, more precise head actuators, so they cost more. In my opinion, in today's computing environment, a 28ms drive is unacceptable. An 18ms drive is marginally so, but you will be much happier with a drive offering a 15ms average access time or less. Hard drive speed *does* make a difference.

Of course, performance characteristics cited by hardware manufacturers should be taken with a grain of salt or two. What you may not be aware of is the wildcard that IDE drives add to the normal mix of manufacturers' hype and cooked test results. This is especially relevant to that other measure of hard drive performance—data transfer rate.

The key thing to remember is that each and every IDE drive is a unique black box product. In the past, one could compare the average access time of a shelf full of ST-506 drives and have some sense that the results were a valid ranking of the speed of each drive. But with a given IDE drive, you don't know what the product is doing to produce the results you are getting.

For example, the electronics on most IDE drives include memory chips that serve as either a RAM buffer or data cache. This effectively lowers access time and raises data transfer rates. The buffer on one drive may be 32K, while the buffer on another may be 64K, while on a third drive, it may be as large as 256K. What's more, the memory may be used as a simple read-ahead track buffer designed to read in an entire track, on the assumption that if DOS wants one sector on a track, it will soon want another. Or it may be a much more sophisticated cache, with the intelligence to anticipate the next track that will be requested and read it in ahead of time.

Ultimately, of course, it makes no difference to you or me how a given IDE drive manages to deliver the goods. The key thing to be aware of is that any time a buffer or a cache is involved, the performance statistics that are quoted may not actually appear in your system. In other words, the statistics are not measuring the raw performance of the drive, as used to be the case with ST-506 equipment. They are measuring the performance of the drive along with a buffer or a cache.

That's the wildcard. We can use caches as an example. A cache is designed to anticipate the data you will need next and to automatically go get that data and, in effect, queue it up in random access memory. If the cache guesses correctly, when DOS asks for that chunk of data, it is transferred to the system at the speed of light. But if the cache guesses incorrectly, not only does the drive have to go get the data you want, there is a slight delay while the cache first checks in RAM and discovers it does not have the data you need.

Caches of any sort can vary widely in their "intelligence" and sophistication. And the performance of even the best caches ultimately depends on how you happen to use your computer.

To reduce the confusion and re-establish a level playing field, assume that the cache or buffer does not exist. When comparing drives, zero in on the internal, disk-to-electronics transfer rate. This is the rate at which data comes off the drive. It is measured in megabits per second (Mb/s), and the higher the number the better. Some very fast IDE drives have rates as high as 24 Mb/s (or 24MHz). That's as fast as the fastest ESDI drive. But an internal transfer rate of 10 to 15 Mb/s is more common.

Ultimately, however, "Your results may vary." The safest bet is to study the reviews of hard drives and computer systems in reputable computer magazines and to buy brand-name equipment. In today's market, with its hypersensitivity to price, if one drive costs more than another of comparable capacity, you can assume there's a very good reason.

The ATA Specification

Finally, you should know about something called the "AT Attachment" standard or ATA. ATA is an ANSI standard that defines the way an IDE drive should connect to your computer's ISA expansion bus. Remember that "IDE" describes a technology, not a system interface. (Technically, SCSI drives with their onboard controller circuitry are IDE drives.)

The ATA standard includes a command language and the electrical interface for connecting an IDE drive to a PC with a 16-bit ISA expansion bus. This is a parallel connection that delivers 16 bits at a time. It is one of the reasons why IDE drives perform so much better than traditional drives. The ST-506 and ESDI interfaces are one-bit wide serial interfaces in which data is delivered one bit at a time.

The ATA standard assigns data and control signals to the 40 lines in an IDE data cable. That cable can be used to connect two drives directly to an IDE connector built into the motherboard or to a small IDE adapter called a *host adapter* or *paddle board*. Though compatible with the ST-506 interface, the ATA standard adds new signals and commands specific to IDE.

You should know that IDE/ATA drives use a master/slave protocol to handle two drives on the same cable. Whichever drive is jumpered to be the "master" does all the data translating for both drives. Since most IDE drives are shipped set to serve as the "master," if you are adding a drive to an existing IDE system, you will almost certainly have to change a jumper on the new drive's circuit board to designate it as the "slave." (You can also buy IDE drives for IBM PS/2 Micro Channel PCs, but you must be sure to specify your computer model to insure compatibility.)

SECTION
5-3

INCREASING SPEED
AND SPACE

Now let's talk about performance and disk optimization. To be frank, the most effective single step most users can take to improve hard drive performance is to replace their current drives with newer, larger, faster models. To be realistic, that's out of the question for most of us since it involves hundreds of dollars of expense. But it is important to make that point.

Your hard drive is always important, but if you use your system heavily every day, its performance is absolutely crucial. With the possible exception of your video hardware, the performance of your hard drive is the most vital element in your sense of how fast your system performs. So, as expensive as it may be, upgrading to a newer, faster drive should not be out of the question.

I'm going to assume, however, that, like me, your Scottish blood rebels at discarding a piece of equipment before you have wrung every last second of usefulness from it. I'm going to assume that, for the nonce, you plan to hold on to whatever hard drive you have.

If so, I've got some really good news for you. Regardless of the type of drive that is currently in your system, there are three major steps you can take to improve its performance and its capacity. They are: defragmenting your files on a regular basis, installing a really good disk cache, and using a file compression program to store important but seldom-used files.

Defragmenting the Disk

It is in the nature of things for files to become fragmented over time. And it's not too difficult to understand why. The technique DOS uses to store files on a hard disk is analogous to the pigeonhole desks used by postmasters a century ago. Think of the pigeonholes as disk sectors, each of which is of an identical size. Now assume that each pigeonhole/sector is numbered sequentially. Imagine that on Monday you create a report with your word processor and save it to disk.

DOS will chop that text file into pieces and store each piece in its own sector. The pieces will be 512 bytes long, so unless the number of bytes in the report just happens to be divisible by 512, the very last sector will almost certainly contain some wasted "slack" space. But don't worry about that right now. Note that for the sake of simplicity, we're using the term "sector" here. In reality, DOS uses groups of sectors called allocation units or clusters.

Tuesday rolls around, and you create a spreadsheet which you save to disk. DOS stores the spreadsheet in the same way—cutting it up into 512-byte sectors—and places it next to Monday's report. At this point, all of the disk sectors of the report file and all of the disk sectors of the spreadsheet file are contiguous.

Wednesday arrives, and you decide to expand the report by adding data and text. The file becomes longer. When you save it to disk, DOS uses as much of the space formerly occupied by the file as possible. But the longer version of the file won't fit. More pigeonhole/sectors are required. So DOS uses the sectors immediately after the spreadsheet file.

At this point, the report file has become fragmented. The sectors that hold it are no longer contiguous. So, on Thursday, when you load the report into your word processor for a final revision, DOS takes just a bit longer to do the job. The reason is not so much the larger number of sectors the report now occupies as it is the *location* of those sectors.

DOS and the hard disk drive cannot load the report with a single read operation. Instead they must read the first group of sectors and then seek the next group, which is located beyond the group of sectors occupied by

Tuesday's spreadsheet. The problem becomes even worse over time. When you copy your report file to floppy disk for archival storage, you naturally delete it from your hard disk. The sectors in the two chunks of space the file occupied are now available. They are added to DOS's inventory of free space, and DOS tries to tuck pieces of files into them whenever it can. The result is even more file fragmentation.

Easier Undeletes

File fragmentation affects not only disk speed but the ease with which you can recover files that you have deleted, especially if there has been some disk activity between the erasure and your recovery attempt.

As you know, DOS maintains a file directory listing all of the files stored on a disk or in a hard disk subdirectory. Though not shown by the DIR command, each entry in the file directory contains the number of the first sector used to store the file. DOS goes to that sector and pulls in the first chunk of a file.

DOS then goes to a location with the *same* number in a special file called the File Allocation Table or FAT. There it finds the number of the *next* sector associated with the file. The process continues as DOS follows the file allocation chain until it reaches a location in the FAT that contains an end-of-file marker.

When you delete a file, DOS simply flips a one-byte flag in the file's directory entry indicating that "this space is available." The data in the sectors is not wiped out. File recovery programs operate by ignoring that little flag and running down the file allocation chain to make sure all sectors are intact—which they will be if you run an undelete program immediately after you erase a file. If you record and delete *other* files in the meantime, however, there is a chance that the chain will be broken. File recovery programs must then try to guess where each of the remaining sectors is located.

The Delete Tracking option provided with DOS 6's UNDELETE command and with the DOS 5 MIRROR command preserves the address chain information for deleted files, thus making it easier for UNDELETE to restore a file when requested to do so. But Delete Tracking imposes costs in terms of disk space, memory, and a slight delay each time you erase a file. Personally, I'd rather not pay the freight. By regularly defragmenting my disk, I get faster access and better file recovery using UNDELETE. I do not use Delete Tracking.

As you may know, with DOS 6, Microsoft introduced yet another level of protection: Delete Sentry. As discussed in Part 2 of this book, the Delete

Sentry option sets up a hidden SENTRY directory into which your deleted files are moved as you delete them. This means that, until that hidden directory fills up and the program starts kicking out the oldest files, you have nearly a 100-percent guarantee of being able to recover any deleted file. This is the ultimate in delete protection, though Delete Sentry will consume up to seven percent of your hard disk space.

Two Ways to Defragment a Disk

There are two main ways to defragment a disk. One is to use a program designed for the purpose. The other is to use the COPY or XCOPY command. Personally, I think all PC users should have a dedicated disk defragmenting program and discipline themselves to use it regularly. If your disk is badly fragmented, as it very well may be if it has seen heavy use and never been defragmented, the first time you run such a program the process may take the better part of an hour to complete. After that, if you run the program every other day or so, you will probably find that "defragging" takes less than a minute.

The three leading commercial disk defragmenters are the Norton Utilities, the Mace Utilities, and PC Tools. Beginning with DOS 6, Microsoft includes a version of the Norton defragmenter (Speed Disk) as part of DOS. Microsoft calls the program DEFRAG. When you run DEFRAG, you will see a screen very similar to the Norton Speed Disk screen shown in Figure 5-3-1.

All of these programs give you a visual representation of the status of your disk, with blank spots signifying pockets of empty space. (See Figure 5-3-1.) As they work to make files contiguous, the blank spots wink out as they are filled, while new contiguous blank spots appear at the end of the disk space. Of course, all three packages provide many, many more features than disk defragmenting, including disk caches to speed up reads and writes. Here are the addresses to contact for more information:

Norton Utilities (V.6.01)
Symantec/Peter Norton Computing Group
2500 Broadway, Ste. 200
Santa Monica, CA 90404
(800) 441-7234; (310) 453-4600

Mace Utilities (V.1990.1)
Fifth Generation Systems, Inc.
10049 N. Reiger Rd.
Baton Rouge, LA 70809-4562
(800) 873-4384; (504) 291-7221

PC Tools (V.7.1)
Central Point Software, Inc.
15220 N.W. Greenbrier Pkwy., Ste. 200
Beaverton, OR 97006
(800) 445-4208; (503) 690-8090

Figure 5-3-1 The Norton Utilities Speed Disk Defragmenter

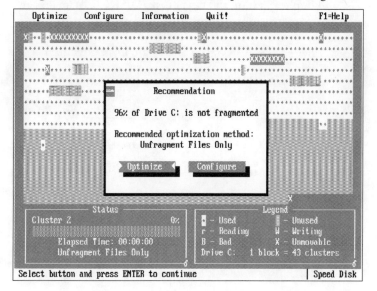

There's also a terrific shareware disk defragmenter and file sorter that deserves your attention, particularly if you do not have DOS 6 and find Norton, Mace, and PC Tools a bit pricey. Written by Michael Greve and David Rifkind, ORG quickly works its magic on virtually any drive (IDE, ST-506, SCSI) of any size. It automatically uses extended or expanded memory for its tables and buffers.

ORG also physically sorts your files in any order you please. You can even tell it to automatically delete .BAK files or files with some other user-specified extension to further clean up and optimize your disk space. The program does not run under Windows or DesqView, but it is compatible with QEMM, 386MAX, and other popular memory managers, including those provided by DOS. Online support is available via CompuServe. For a better idea of what ORG looks like, see Figure 5-3-2.

Whenever you copy a file from one location to another, DOS darts around the disk picking up the file's sectors and transferring the data they contain into memory. It then spits them out again, in contiguous order, as

it records them in the target location. If the target location does not have
enough free contiguous sectors, DOS has to fragment the file. But if the target location is empty, the file is stored in contiguous, non-fragmented form.

Only the COPY and XCOPY commands do this, since only they read
each file into memory before dumping it to a new location. The DISK-
COPY command, in contrast, reads each floppy disk *track* into memory
and duplicates it on the target disk. DISKCOPY makes an exact duplicate
of a floppy disk, fragmented files and all.

Figure 5-3-2 ORG, the Shareware Disk Organizer

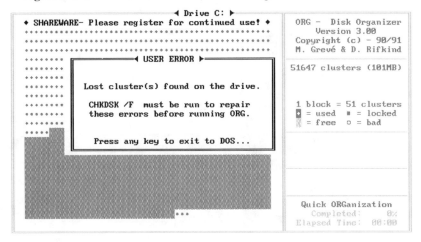

Thus, if you are going to make multiple copies of a floppy disk, make
your master with the COPY *.* command so all of the files will be contiguous. Then use DISKCOPY to make duplicates of the master. DISKCOPY
is faster than either COPY or XCOPY because it doesn't have to worry
about assembling each file. It just starts at the first track and reads in as
many tracks as your free conventional memory can hold.

If you don't have a commercial disk defragmenting utility, you can use
COPY or XCOPY to copy fragmented files to a new location. After you
have checked to make sure the copy operation was successful, return to the
source location and delete all the source files. Then simply reverse the process, by copying the files from the new location back to the now-empty old
location.

You will find that the shareware program QFILER can be a big help. It
has the ability to work with DOS's XCOPY command to copy entire
subdirectories, and it gives you the power to rename subdirectories. That
means that you can create a target location called C:\TEMP and then log

onto your WordPerfect directory (\WP). Key in `xcopy \wp \temp /s/ e`. This tells XCOPY to copy all the files in \WP to the directory \TEMP, including all subdirectories, whether they are empty or not.

Check your work, then use QFILER to delete the \WP subdirectory and to rename \TEMP to \WP. All of the files in \WP and its subdirectories will now be defragmented.

Install a Disk Cache

There are a number of techniques for implementing a disk cache, but they are all based on the fact that random access memory is much, much faster than the rotating memory of a hard drive. The idea is to get the information the CPU is going to need next off the disk and into RAM *before* the CPU or DOS calls for it. A good cache can boost the effective performance of your system by 50 to 300 percent, according to some estimates. A cache does, however, represent an additional layer of complexity.

There are two categories of caches and two general caching techniques. The categories are hardware-based and software-based caches. Prior to the advent of IDE disk drives, for example, a number of companies made circuit boards called "caching controllers." These cards were distinguished from ordinary ST-506 controllers by the large amount of memory they held and by the cache control programs burned into their ROMs. Most IDE drives, as previously discussed, have a cache of some sort built into their drive electronics. This helps boost the effective performance of their underlying drives.

Software caches are programs that load like device drivers or like TSRs. Most have the ability to use any type of memory as their cache (extended, expanded, or conventional). And most let you specify not only the kind of memory you want them to use, but also how large a cache you want them to create.

Most are also "write-through" caches. This means that, while they may store indefinitely in memory the information they've read in, when *you* want to record something on the disk, they pass it through immediately. The thought is that if they didn't, and there were a power failure or you had to reboot your system before they had actually recorded the data, that data would be lost.

Although you may be able to find an IDE host adapter with caching capabilities if you look very hard, today most people use software-based caches. These come in two basic flavors. The simplest is a track cacher, a program that automatically reads in an entire track whenever a sector on that track is requested. Thus, if a program wants sector 8 on a track, it will probably also want sectors 9 through 17.

DOS 5's SMARTDrive 3.13

Microsoft's DOS 5 includes SMARTDrive, Version 3.13. The cache is supplied as a device driver, SMARTDRV.SYS, that must be loaded via your CONFIG.SYS file. SMARTDrive 3.13 is a track cacher, and like all track cachers, it assumes that your files are not fragmented. If your files are badly fragmented and you use SMARTDrive or a similar program, you actually get hit with a double whammy. More time is required to assemble a file that has been fragmented into sectors scattered over four or five tracks, and more cache memory is required as a result.

Remember, SMARTDrive 3.13 and other track cachers automatically read in the entire track containing whatever sector they have been asked to find. So a fragmented file can cause SMARTDrive to give up four or five tracks worth of memory, when only one or two tracks might be required if the file were stored in contiguous sectors.

SMARTDrive 3.13 can indeed speed up your system. When I ran George Spafford's shareware program Cache Test, as discussed below, SMART-Drive improved disk performance by about eighteen percent, compared to the results with no cache loaded at all.

The *percentage* speed increase was the same whether I used a 25ms drive (Toshiba MK 134FA-1, RLL formatted to 65MB) or a 15ms drive (Western Digital 4200 Piranha, 212MB). The actual number of seconds required to complete the test was quite different between the two drives, of course, with the 25ms drive completing in 171 seconds and the 15ms drive completing in 127 seconds. So the slower your drive, the more aware you will be of any benefits SMARTDrive may contribute.

Unfortunately, SMARTDrive 3.13 is really not a very good program. Like many of the DOS and Windows utilities Microsoft produces in house, it is merely adequate and never inspired. There are many better solutions.

Undocumented Switches

If you decide to use SMARTDrive 3.13, however, you should be aware of two undocumented switches. These are the /P and the /B+ switches. Should you try to load SMARTDrive and receive an *Incompatible disk partition* error, try adding the /P switch to the end of the line loading SMART-Drive in your CONFIG.SYS, like this: DEVICEHIGH=C:\ DRV\ SMARTDRV.SYS 2048 512 /P. (The error can appear if your disk was partitioned with almost any other software but DOS's FDISK.COM.)

The other switch concerns *double buffering*. A program that is "well-behaved" goes through the operating system and the BIOS instead of accessing the hardware directly. SMARTDrive 3.13 is not well-behaved. It accesses the hard drive directly whenever it wants to read or write data. This can cause problems if you are using an older SCSI drive. If that is your situation, add the /B+ switch to your CONFIG.SYS line to force the cache to use DOS's normal disk buffers.

DOS 6's SMARTDrive 4.x

Microsoft received so much criticism for the inadequacies and incompatibilities of SMARTDrive 3.x that it really went to work and produced a much better (and substantially different) product—SMARTDrive 4.x. This caching software first appeared as part of the phenomenally successful Windows 3.1 package. And it is the version Microsoft includes with DOS 6.

The most obvious difference between version 4.x and previous versions is that 4.x is supplied as an .EXE file. This means it can be activated and deactivated from the command line or from a batch file. That's important because it is sometimes necessary to disable a caching program, as when you are about to defragment your hard disk.

Other improvements are more subtle. Version 4.x is still track-oriented. It still assumes that the data you or your program will need next is probably stored nearby the data you just asked for. But one can now specify the size (in kilobytes) of the tracks on your particular disk. SMARTDrive refers to this as its *elementsize*. (Multiply the number of sectors per disk track by 512 bytes per sector to determine the number of kilobytes per track.) You might specify this SMARTDrive option if you have two hard disks with different track sizes and you want to force SMARTDrive not to default to using the larger of the two.

You can also specify the size of the read-ahead buffer, adjusting its size to any multiple of *elementsize*. And you can explicitly specify the size of the cache you want SMARTDrive to use in DOS and in Windows with the *size* and *winsize* options. This lets you override the size settings that SMARTDrive uses when it starts up.

SMARTDrive 4.x also performs both read- and write-caching. The older version performed only read-caching. Basically, SMARTDrive 4.x will hold data in cache memory and not write it to disk until the cache either fills up or five seconds elapse. This fact represents a general change in thinking in the industry regarding caches with delayed disk writes. The current opinion is that the performance improvements made possible by delayed disk writes are well worth the minimal risk of losing unrecorded cache data to a power failure.

Delaying disk writes lets SMARTDrive 4.x improve performance, since it goes out to disk only during periods of inactivity, as when you are thinking or making notes or doing anything other than using the mouse or keyboard. The delay also gives SMARTDrive a chance to organize, sort, and consolidate planned disk operations in ways that minimize head movement and the number of rotations required to perform a disk write.

You will have to fine-tune SMARTDrive 4.x's settings to your system. (Use your DOS 6 manual and the copious online help DOS 6 provides on SMARTDrive.) But if you are using DOS 6 (or if you have Windows 3.1), you can get a taste of the software easily enough.

Simply log onto the directory containing SMARTDRV.EXE and key in smartdrv. This will load SMARTDrive in a mode to read- and write-cache your hard drive or drives. SMARTDrive implements only a read cache on floppy drives. The thought is that a floppy write cache is dangerous because a user can remove a floppy disk before a write has been properly executed.

DOS 6 Point

Is Double-Buffering Needed?

Notice that when you key in smartdrv a screen like the following appears:

```
Microsoft SMARTDrive Disk Cache version 4.0
Copyright 1991,1992 Microsoft Corp.

Cache size: 1,048,576 bytes
Cache size while running Windows: 524,288 bytes

              Disk Caching Status
drive   read cache   write cache   buffering
  A:        yes          no           no
  B:        yes          no           no
  C:        yes          yes          no
  D:        yes          yes          no
  E:        yes          no           no

For help, type "Smartdrv /?".

The memory-resident portion of SMARTDrive is loaded.
```

(continued)

(Is Double-Buffering Needed? continued)

You may find that your Windows setup program has automatically enabled SMARTDrive 4.x's double-buffering feature by inserting a line into your CONFIG.SYS file. If you do not see a *yes* in the column labeled *buffering*, however, you can safely remove the line. It reads:

```
device=c:\dos\smartdrv.exe /double_buffer
```

This line does not load SMARTDrive, only its double-buffering cache. Eliminating it will save you about 2.5K of conventional memory. You must still run the SMARTDRV.EXE program to load and activate the cache.

Better Solutions

SMARTDrive 4.x stacks up very well in cache comparison tests. Needless to say, it does a much better job than its predecessor. In fact, SMARTDrive 4.x is good enough to eliminate the need for a better cache, in some cases. Certainly you should try it and look elsewhere only if you become dissatisfied with your system's performance.

The point I want to make here is that there *are* other caching possibilities. Track cachers like SMARTDrive are fine, but better performance is usually delivered by caches with some "intelligence." Intelligent caches may do track-caching, but they also use a variety of algorithms and techniques to second-guess DOS and your applications programs.

For one thing, they monitor how the data their buffers contain is being used. They are perfectly capable of discarding information that has not been accessed by your program in a certain number of disk reads in favor of more sectors located nearer the information you are using at the moment.

Use SMARTDrive if necessary to make Windows run at an acceptable speed on your system. But look around for something better. You might start with HyperDisk, a shareware program from Roger Cross and Hyper-Ware. (See Part 9 of this book for ordering information.) HyperDisk can be disabled or enabled with a hotkey command, and you can add more memory to the cache from the command line at any time. HyperDisk also has some "intelligence" to bring to bear.

You might also consider the NCACHE program supplied with the Norton Utilities. When I tested it, it delivered a 44-percent improvement, compared to a non-cached system. I did not test the caches supplied with the Mace Utilities and PC Tools, but you should know that both packages include this kind of software.

PowerPoint

Cache Test

In a brilliant marketing move, Multisoft Corporation includes a benchmark program with its Super PC-Kwik package. The program automatically runs a battery of tests without the cache installed, and then does the same thing with Super PC-Kwik in place. The cache-based improvement can often be dramatic.

Unfortunately you cannot use Multisoft's benchmark program to test other caches. So I used a program prepared by an impartial third party. George Spafford's shareware program Cache Test really gives your drive a work-out. It creates a file containing, by default, 10,000 records of 32 bytes each. Then it performs seven tests, including a "butterfly read," a "crescendo read," and a random read/write test.

The total time required to complete all Cache Test tests is presented, and it is this figure that I have used to calculate the percentage speed improvements offered by the various caches discussed in the main text. It is as close as one can come to a level playing field, although, as always with caching software, your results will depend on how you actually use your computer. If you do a lot of database work, you may see a dramatic improvement from your cache. But if you spend most of your time creating text documents or spreadsheets, the speed increases will not be as obvious.

I next tested market leader Super PC-Kwik from Multisoft Corporation. When I limited the program to the same 2MB of extended memory used in the other tests, Super PC-Kwik produced a 42-percent improvement. But when I let it operate the way it wanted to, it blew everyone else off the board with a 60-percent improvement using a cache of over 3MB.

The way Super PC-Kwik wants to work is to take all of your extended memory. The neat thing is that you are safe in letting it do so, because the program loans that memory back to any program that requests it. Hyper-Disk, NCACHE, and the other commercial caches can be adjusted too, from the command line. But Super PC-Kwik dynamically changes its cache size based on conditions existing at the moment. It also has a very simple, "no-brainer" installation program that makes the process a snap.

The mail-order price for Super PC-Kwik is about $45 at this writing. (Super PC-Kwik is included in DR DOS 6 from Digital Research.) The mail-order price for the Norton Utilities is about $110. Competing programs are quite good. The Mace Utilities offer some tricks even Norton doesn't have, and people have written entire books on all the top-flight utilities PC Tools provides. I use them all. But if I had only $155 dollars to spend, I would get Norton and Super PC-Kwik. They are absolutely first rate and, in my opinion, absolutely essential to any power user. For more information on Super PC-Kwik, you can contact Multisoft at:

Multisoft Corporation
15100 SW Koll Parkway
Beaverton, OR 97066
(503) 644-5644; (800) 627-5945

PowerPoint

Make Sure VERIFY is Off

Whether you are using a caching program or not, it's a good idea to make sure that DOS's VERIFY setting is off. This setting determines whether DOS automatically checks to make sure that your files have been correctly written to disk. Since this is usually not necessary, the default setting is "off."

But it is always possible that some overly cautious third-party program has turned it on. That can put a tremendous drag on disk performance. Therefore, check the setting by keying in `verify`. If you get the message *VERIFY is off*, you're fine. If you are told that it is on, key in `verify off`. Then see if you can find the program that turned it on. Start by checking your AUTOEXEC.BAT file.

PowerPoint

Flash Memory

Hard disk caches will be a factor for many years to come. But in the future, we are sure to see greater use of *flash memory*. This is memory packaged on a 68-pin plug-in module about the size of a credit card and conforming to standards set by the PCMCIA (PC Memory Card International Association). It requires no battery backup and has an access time, at this writing, of 250 nanoseconds—far slower than the 80ns memory installed in most computers today but far faster than even the fastest hard disk.   *(continued)*

> *(Flash Memory continued)*
>
> Of course, if you assume a current cost of $40 per megabyte of memory, replacing a 100MB hard disk with flash memory would cost $4,000. That sounds absurd. On the other hand, more than a decade ago I paid over $2,000 for a 20MB hard disk "subsystem"—and felt I was getting a bargain.

Maximizing Disk Space

Earlier I mentioned that I was really rather happy when my 80MB Seagate 4096 drive died. It turns out that I may actually have been to blame. This particular drive is known to be quite rugged. But, like almost all hard drives, it is meant to be operated in a desktop machine that actually sits on a desktop. I may have signed its death warrant when I turned my desktop system unit on its side so that it stood vertically on the floor.

Gravity takes its toll as the weight of the platters pulls against the spindle, creating an uneven stress on the spindle bearings. The damage is slow but nearly inevitable. I have since switched to a real tower-style case, which allows my hard drive to be mounted horizontally. The case came with a robust power supply and twin fans and cost about $225. I simply pulled everything out of my desktop system and installed it in the new case.

Note that if you formatted the drive in the vertical position, you may have to reformat it when you change to a horizontal orientation. Back up your system before making any changes. Then, if you discover a large number of read errors when the drive has been reoriented, consider reformatting the unit and reloading your files.

As it happens, losing the drive probably turned out to be a good thing. I wasn't pleased about the hundreds of dollars it cost to replace it, but I would never have done so on my own. The fact is, though, that I had long been bumping up against the 80MB limit and had grown tired of hard disk triage. For more than a year I'd been pulling programs and files off the disk to make room for additional programs and files.

Of course, I could always restore those files when I needed them. But they were no longer quickly and readily available. It's rather like having a tiny room and a large attic. You're constantly having to shift things around in the attic to be able to bring down the stuff you need or want at a particular time. It can be done, but it is a nuisance.

Thus, it was a relief to have an excuse to buy a 212MB hard drive when the 80MB Seagate gave up the ghost. And my new drive is nearly twice as fast, to boot. We all pass through such transitional phases, and we all know that the only real solution is to eventually buy a bigger, faster hard drive. But, since prices keep coming down, it behooves every power user to wait until the last minute before upgrading. Here are some tips and tricks I've learned to prolong Replacement Day.

Use CHKDSK.COM to Recover Stolen Space

The DOS utility CHKDSK.COM is one of those programs you never *have* to run. It used to be the only DOS utility that would tell you how much memory you have free, a function now performed by the MEM command. But you should still run CHKDSK occasionally, because it can identify and correct problems you didn't even know you had with your hard disk.

The problems are actually twofold. One is the problem of lost allocation units or clusters, and the other is the problem of cross-linked files. Both can affect your disk's available capacity, and both should be corrected as soon as they are identified.

The command to enter is `chkdsk /f`. When CHKDSK encounters lost clusters, it will return them to your disk's root directory in the form FILE ####.CHK. Each file contains the equivalent of about 32 lines of text, though the files are not necessarily all text files.

Use Vern Buerg's LIST or your favorite editor to check the contents of the files. Delete any .CHK file that contains the funny characters of machine language. But proceed with caution if a .CHK file contains text. Don't delete such a file until you are sure it does not contain information missing from its parent file. If you have no idea of the name and location of the parent file, use a program like Norton's TextSearch or a public domain program like LOOKFOR to scan every file on your disk for the target text you specify.

Slack Space and Your Partition Size

The next thing to do in a space maximization program is to check your hard disk partition size. If you are not certain how much of your hard drive is devoted to Drive C, Drive D, and so on, run DOS's FDISK program and select the option that will *Display partition information.*

Partition size affects disk space because of the way DOS stores files. Previously we have spoken in terms of 512-byte sectors because this concept is easy to understand. In reality, DOS uses contiguous groups of sectors as its smallest allocation unit. (Prior to DOS 5, allocation units were called clusters.) The partition size determines how many sectors DOS uses as its allocation unit.

Thus, with a 1MB to 16MB partition, DOS uses eight sectors, accounting for 4K of space. On disks partitioned between 17MB and 128MB, DOS uses half that amount, or 2K of space for each allocation unit. Partitions between 128MB and 256MB use 4K allocation units; partitions between 256MB and 512MB use 8K allocation units; and partitions between 512MB and one gigabyte use 16K allocation units.

There are good reasons for this seemingly arbitrary scheme. The point is that, with allocation units of 2K, a disk partition of between 17MB and 128MB makes the most efficient use of available space. Why? Because the least amount of space a file may occupy is one allocation unit. Thus, on a 128MB partition, a file consisting of a single byte would occupy 2K of space. But on a partition of 512MB, that same file would occupy a full 16K of space.

The unused portion of an allocation unit is called slack space or disk slack. Because few files fit precisely into the number of bytes provided by allocation units, this is an unavoidable phenomenon. But there are two ways to minimize slack. First, you can get rid of unnecessary files, and second, you can combine several files into one large file.

As you know from Part 3, a little public domain program like CLEAN-UP can be used to run through your disk looking for those tiny 0-, 1-, and 2-byte files some programs leave behind. The program will give you the opportunity to delete each file or leave it, as you please. Gary Lieberman's shareware program CLEAN, in contrast, can be told to go after files based on their extension. You may specify any group of extensions you want, though .BAK, .$$$, and .TMP are good places to start. At your option, the program can either automatically delete matching files or prompt you for a yes or no in each case.

You might wonder how much space you can save this way. Obviously, it all depends on the programs you use and how actively you use your machine. Recently, however, I ran CLEAN and CLEANUP and recovered over 22K of disk space, formerly locked up in useless .BAK and 1- or 2-byte files. If you can afford the time, and if hard disk space is really tight, you might want to run programs like these via AUTOEXEC.BAT to clean the disk each time you boot up.

Preserving Space with File Compression

It goes without saying that all of us should spend some time each week cleaning out or otherwise dealing with the files that have accumulated on our disks. As you know from Part 3 of this book, QFILER is the program I like to use to do this. You can look at or execute any file from within the program and then delete it, copy it, move it, or compress it into an archive for compact storage.

Indeed, whenever I have the time, but at least once a month, I use QFILER to confront and deal with all of the files that have accumulated on my disk. Then I run a disk defragmenter to make all the remaining files contiguous. Finally I back up my disk to a streaming tape drive. It's just the thing to round out a workday. And when everything is shipshape and Bristol fashion, you have a wonderful feeling of satisfaction. Let the winds rage and blow. Let the cataracts and hurricanes spout. Your disk is defragmented and safely backed up.

As you are dealing with your files, however, it is important to be aware of your compression options. File compression techniques and algorithms predate the personal computer era. But the process really began to develop over ten years ago, at the beginning of the personal computer revolution. The driving force was the desire to reduce the amount of time required to transmit a program over the phone.

Why ship fresh orange juice north from Florida when you can turn it into concentrate and ask the consumer to add three cans of water when preparing a batch? Why pay to transport all of that water? Those of us who are so addicted to fresh-squeezed orange juice that we gladly pay to have the oranges themselves shipped in from the groves know the answer.

But that answer does not apply to the transport of files. In the computer world, there is absolutely no difference between a "reconstituted" compressed file and the original file. So why pay the freight to transmit, say, twice as many bits as necessary? It is much more efficient to transmit a compressed file and have end users "add water" by decompressing it and thus restoring it to its original state, once they are offline and not paying long distance or connect time charges.

What's more, with the compression techniques available today, it is possible to compress not one file but a large *group* of files into a single "archive." This has at least two benefits from the standpoint of a space-conscious hard disk user. First, it reduces the total amount of space actually occupied by each of the files in the archive.

Second, it greatly reduces the slack space on the disk because DOS is now storing only one file instead of half a dozen files or more. Let's assume that, on average, every individual file leaves half an allocation unit as unoccupied "slack." If your allocation units are 2K each, then six files probably occupy 1K more apiece than they should. That's a total of 6K. If you bundle those six files into a single large archive, the archive file may have 1K of slack, but you will have freed up as much as 5K of the slack space attributable to the individual files.

Plain File Compression and Storage

There are two ways to take advantage of file compression to preserve your hard disk space. Both are easy to apply, but one is much simpler than the other. We will look at the simpler technique first.

The quickest, simplest way to save disk space through file compression is to place into archives those programs and data files that you seldom use but still want to have readily available. Though compression ratios vary with the type of file and the compression technique, in general, you can look for compressed files to occupy 40 to 50 percent *less* space than in their uncompressed state. Compression is effective on nearly every kind of file, though text files usually show the most dramatic difference.

As for the program you use to effect the compression, in my opinion, there are only two choices. The first is Professor Haruyasu Yoshizaki's public-domain LHA or LHARC program. The second is Phil Katz's shareware PKZIP package. There are other compression alternatives, including ZOO, PAK, ARJ, and ARC. But LHA and PKZIP are more or less the de facto standards. And with good reason: both are very fast and both produce very tightly compressed files. As we will see later in this book, if you are an online communicator, you have to have access to a variety of compression programs. But when maximizing your hard disk space, you cannot go wrong settling on either LHA or PKZIP.

Now, I would be the first to admit that with their cryptic commands, compression programs tend to be among the most "bytehead" of programs. But most people do not need the multiple options that tend to complicate things. There are generally only four tasks you need to worry about with any compression program. You need to be able to put files into an archive and get them out again. And you need to be able to generate a list of the files contained in an archive and, possibly, to make an archive *self-extracting* so that it unfolds automatically when you key in the file's name.

We will present those four commands for LHA and PKZIP later in this book when we look at how a power user goes online. Right now, all you need to know is that with QFILER you can call up a directory of files, tag the ones you want to put into archive storage, and enter either Ctrl+L to use LHA or Ctrl+Z to use PKZIP. As long as the file compressing program you have selected is path-accessible, QFILER takes care of the rest. You can then delete the files you have tagged and put the newly created archive in a good place.

When you want to look inside an archive, use QFILER to bring the filename to the screen. Then use the key combination Ctrl+A for Archive utilities. QFILER automatically detects the kind of archive involved and gives you the option of adding files to it, extracting its contents, viewing a list of the files it contains, or zooming in to actually look at any text files that may be included.

Once you have created an archive, you may leave it on your disk and delete the files it contains. Or you may copy it to a floppy disk. It all depends on how often you think you will need to access the files in the archive.

Dynamic File Compression

The second way you can apply file compression technology is to use a program capable of compressing your files for disk storage but reconstituting them on the fly, as you need them. This way you get the best of both worlds: reduced storage requirements and nearly instant access to your files, as if they had never been compressed at all.

The faster your CPU and hard disk drive, the more pleased you will be with the dynamic file compression option. I've used it on my 386DX/25MHz system with its 15ms hard drive and have been amazed at the results. In most cases, it is impossible to tell that the files I'm reading or the programs I'm running have had to be decompressed between the time I issued a command and results appeared on the screen. Since compressing and decompressing files does require processor time, however, slight delays are sure to be noticeable on slow equipment.

The two best-known commercial products in this area are Stacker from Stac Electronics and SuperStor from Addstor. (SuperStor is included with Digital Research's DR DOS.) Both have list prices in the $145 range but sell through the mail for around $80. Here is where to get more information on both products:

Stac Electronics
5993 Avenida Encinas
Carlsbad, CA 92008
(800) 522-7822; (619) 431-7474

AddStor, Inc.
1040 Marsh Rd.
Menlo Park, CA 94025
(800) 732-3133; (415) 688-0470

DOS 6 Point

DOS 6's DoubleSpace Dynamic Compression

Beginning with DOS 6, Microsoft introduced its DoubleSpace disk compression utility that, the company says, can double or even triple your disk's storage capacity. DoubleSpace uses essentially the same techniques employed by Stacker and SpeedStor to create a "DoubleSpace" disk volume. (If you are already using a disk compression program, the DOS 6 manual shows you how to convert to DoubleSpace, should you want to do so.)

The utility consists of two main components. The program that you run to prepare and set up your DoubleSpace volume is DBLSPACE .EXE. The device driver that makes the DoubleSpace volume available to the system is DBLSPACE.SYS. When you key in `dblspace` at the command line, you will be given the choice of doing an express or a custom setup. The express option assumes you want to make Drive C your DoubleSpace volume; the custom setup gives you more control, allowing you to designate some other drive as your DoubleSpace volume.

The program will set to work compressing the target drive and adding the necessary lines to your CONFIG.SYS file. It will then reboot the system. When you next examine your DoubleSpace drive, you will find that it offers twice or even three times as much space as before.

DOS 6's DoubleSpace may not offer all the bells and whistles of other dynamic compression software, but it certainly does the job. The technology appears to be well proven and reliable, so you may want to use it on both your laptop as well as your main desktop system.

Nonetheless, you may want to wait until you really need DoubleSpace (or any other dynamic compression product). Regardless of how sound they may be, this kind of software adds yet another layer of complexity to your system. It is one more thing to go wrong; one more thing to cause some unforeseen incompatibility.

There is also the fact that the number of files stored on your disk tends to increase with the space available to store them. Which is another way of saying that most of us are lazy and tend to put off giving our disks a good cleaning until we actually start to run out of space. If you double your disk space now, it may be a year or more before you sit down and really go through things on a file-by-file basis.

(continued)

(DOS 6's DoubleSpace Dynamic Compression continued)

That's why I suggest that you not blindly install DoubleSpace as a matter of course. Put it off until you absolutely have to have the space it will provide. Think of it as a reserve tank of gas in your car to be used only when you really and truly need it.

The Matsumoto DIET

The shareware program I like for this application is Teddy Matsumoto's DIET. The program can be used as a standalone file compressor, but where it really shines is as a Stacker/SuperStor /DoubleSpace clone. But, unlike those disk volume-oriented programs, DIET is file-oriented. Which gives you a lot more control.

When DIET compresses a .COM or .EXE file, it stores the file under its original name. Though much smaller, the program file is equipped by DIET with a self-extracting header that begins to run the moment you key in the filename. This little bit of code automatically expands the program to its full size in memory. Thus, once it has processed .COM or .EXE files, DIET does not have to be in memory for you to use them as you normally would. (Symantec uses the same technique with its individual Norton Utilities programs.)

DIET can also compress data files and program overlays. However, if you want to look at those files or if you expect your programs to use them, then DIET must be loaded into memory as a TSR. DIET itself will then handle the compression and recompression of data files and overlays. If you have expanded memory (EMS) for DIET to use, the program will occupy only about 8K of conventional memory when loaded as a TSR.

I was prepared to be unimpressed, but DIET won me over immediately. Its commands are simple and its performance is outstanding, at least on a 33MHz machine with a 15ms hard drive. Mr. Matsumoto enlisted the advice of Professor Haruyasu Yoshizaki, creator of the LHA (LHARC) compression package, in completing his work. And, like "Yoshi," he asks for no registration fee or contribution, only that you use and enjoy the program. DIET thus offers the perfect way to see if a dynamic file compressor will work well on your system. The program is so good, it may very well be the only such software you need.

How to Use Dynamic File Compression

I should note here that for about $250 Stac Electronics sells an optional circuit board that is designed to take most of the compression/decompression burden from the CPU, but you will want to read the reviews carefully before investing. You may find that the board will not add noticeably to the benefits of using Stacker software by itself.

Indeed, with today's machines, speed should not be a problem. The principal downside to dynamic file compression is the additional layer of complexity it introduces. When this technique is in effect, it is no longer just you and DOS. It is you and DOS and some third-party program. That makes things complicated if something goes wrong.

What happens, for example, if a file becomes corrupted? If the file is a plain DOS text file, you stand a good chance of being able to recover some or most of it using a program like the sector editor, DiskEdit, in the Norton Utilities. With such a program, you can even search currently un-used sectors for text strings. (This often uncovers backup copies of files you may not have suspected existed.)

Most compression packages, whether dynamic or otherwise, include some sort of "fix-it" utility designed to restore a file to an uncompressable state so it can at least be read by the program. But if the utility fails, you're stuck. That's because all compressed files in their native state consist of the funny-looking characters of machine language. If the "garbage" the file contains cannot be uncompressed into readable text, you might as well throw it out.

I may be unduly cautious, but in my opinion, the best way to use a dy-namic compression program is to let it operate only on program files. Pro-gram files can always be restored from the floppy disks you used to load them in the first place. Data files—the report, the spreadsheet, the book chapter—that you create out of your own head can never be replaced. If something goes wrong, they must be recreated.

It is also important, as the documentation for most compression pro-grams points out, to proceed with caution when using disk defragmenters, caches, and some TSRs. Not that you should necessarily expect problems when you have a compression program loaded as a TSR, but it is suggested that you back up your disk just in case. That's one of the reasons I like DIET so much. You can run it against your .COM and .EXE files once, and then it's out of the picture. (A separate DIET command restores your program files to their former sizes.)

Though the total disk space savings will not be as great as Stacker, Super-Stor, or DIET can deliver when you load them into memory and give them complete charge of your disk, the complexity isn't nearly as great either. DIET, for example, can cut the space occupied by a .COM or .EXE file by 50 to 60 percent. In two minutes, I recovered nearly 400K by running DIET against the .COM and .EXE files in my \UTILS subdirectory alone. And there is no need to keep DIET in memory.

BACKUP TECHNIQUES

Your hard disk drive is probably the most important component in your entire system. After all, you may use your keyboard, view your screen, and print with your printer, but you *live* on your hard drive. Therefore, the admonition to regularly back up your hard drive is more than the gentle urging of a parent or school teacher who knows what's best for you. Though the warnings are repeated so often that we tend to ignore them, making backups is really important, serious stuff.

That's why, to my mind, there's really only one way to go: streaming tape drive. It's easy, automatic, and efficient—which means we are all much more likely to take the time to back up our drives. And, at prices as low as $250 for a tape unit, the technology is so affordable that you can't afford *not* to take advantage of it. Think of it this way: Given a choice of spending an entire work day trying to rebuild the data files on your disk or paying $250, which would you choose?

Most tape drives easily mount in an empty half-height drive bay, though freestanding units that can be cabled to an adapter card are also available. All you have to do is insert a tape cartridge, run the supplied tape backup program, and go home or out to lunch. When you come back, the onerous chore of backing up your hard drive has been done for you. Unfortunately, while the DOS and Windows backup programs supplied with DOS 6 will back up to floppy disks and to MS-DOS devices such as Bernoulli drives, the programs are not designed to back up to streaming tape drives.

DC2000 and DC6000 Tapes

As I said, figure on a cost of about $250 for the tape unit itself. To this, add about $20 to $40 per tape cartridge, depending on capacity. That's not too expensive as it is, but it is even less expensive than it seems, since you use the same tape cartridges over and over again.

All the leading tape backup systems are based on cartridges that use quarter-inch tape. The two main sizes of these quarter-inch cartridges are DC6000 and DC2000.

DC6000-style cartridges are about the size of a paperback book (about 6.4 by 4.3 inches). Cartridges of this size used to be called DC600, but have been renamed to achieve consistency with other cartridge styles. DC2000-style cartridges measure about 2.5 by 3.25 inches. A variety of factors determine how much data can be packed onto a single DC6000 or DC2000 cartridge. These factors include the number of feet of tape in the cartridge and the recording format (QIC-40 or QIC-80 or something else) used by the tape drive.

It is important to note, as well, that the software supplied with most cartridge systems has the ability to *compress* the data it stores. This can reduce the required tape capacity to about half of what would be required without using compression.

In most cases, you will find that a DC2000 system is the best choice for backing up a single-user PC. The cartridges can hold between 40MB and 640MB. But, to be safe, make sure you tell the vendor how large a drive you have, and ask about the capacity of the DC2000 cartridge using the tape unit he sells. Ask about the capacity of the tape when the data is not being compressed and the capacity when data compression has been invoked.

It may be that you can fit more data on your hard drive than can be stored on a single DC2000 tape. That isn't a huge problem, and it won't begin to affect you until your hard disk starts to get full. The key thing is to make sure that the tape drive software can split a backup over two or more cartridges. Most can, but you should definitely ask.

DC6000 cartridges are better for multiuser systems and PCs with larger hard drives. They can hold between 150MB and 1GB. The most important feature of DC6000 systems, however, is speed. These drives move information at rates nearly as fast as some hard drives. That means quicker backups and faster data restoration after disaster strikes.

DC6000 systems achieve this kind of performance by using a proprietary interface. That means you'll have to buy a special add-on card as part of the package. DC2000 systems, in contrast, typically plug into your hard drive/floppy drive controller card. (If you already have both an A and B drive, Y-coupling cables are available from the drive maker to let the cartridge system share the card with your installed drives.)

In general, newer DC2000 systems can transfer data at a rate of between 2.5MB and 12.75MB per minute, while a DC6000 system can operate at between 5MB and 30MB per minute. Personally, I don't think this is a severe disadvantage for DC2000 systems. Normally, you start your backup and go do something else for a half hour or more. Unless you're using your system every minute of the day, there is always the "downtime" you need to do a backup in the normal course of things.

QIC Standards

The DC standard determines the *physical size* of the tape cartridge. But there is another set of standards to look for. These are the standards promulgated by the Quarter-Inch Cartridge (QIC) committee, an organization made up of leading manufacturers. This standard refers to the *format* used to record the data. All of these standards are identified by the name "QIC," like QIC-100. If the tape drive follows one or more of the industry standards, you have a better chance that third-party software is available for the drive.

The two most popular QIC numbers you'll see are QIC-40 and QIC-80. Both apply to DC2000 tape systems, and both require the tape drive to work in essentially the same way (connected through your hard drive/floppy drive controller). QIC-80 represents a newer technology.

The number following the QIC designation indicates the nominal, non-compressed storage capacity of a cartridge. However, some cartridges are filled with more tape, so some extended-length QIC-40 cartridges may be able to store 120MB with data compression. The capacity of extended-length QIC-80 cartridges with data compression is about 250MB.

Other QIC size standards exist, but for single users, a tape system using DC2000-size cartridges and QIC-40 or QIC-80 tape formats is almost certainly the most cost-effective choice. Proprietary formats offer increased speed and tape capacity, but they tend to lock you in. QIC-format tapes, in contrast, can be read by any of the many hardware systems that support this format. They are also backward compatible, so you can trade up to a QIC-80 system one day and still be able to ready your QIC-40 tapes.

Tape Backup Software

Most tape drives come with the special software you need to activate the unit and set it to automatically back up your hard drive. However, it is wise to check when you order your tape drive to make sure the system includes its own backup program. If it does not, you'll have to factor in the cost of backup software.

Also, be sure to ask about the availability of adapter cables to let you install a tape unit and still have two floppy drives. Worst case, you can add an extra floppy drive controller. In short, ask your vendor how you can install an internal DC2000 system and still have the use of Drives A and B.

Also, make sure you know the proper software installation settings to integrate your new tape system with your computer. In general, even if a tape drive is attached to your floppy drive's "B" position, you should not tell your system about it when preparing your CMOS setup. Again, ask the vendor for specific instructions.

The software should be able to operate in unattended batch mode. It should also be able to perform an incremental backup, copying only those files that have not been previously backed up, based on the status of the archive bit. The ability to schedule a backup for a preset time may also be useful. And, of course, you should be able to restore as much as an entire disk or as little as a single file.

Finally, you should know that any magnetic medium, be it floppy drive or hard drive or magnetic tape, must be formatted before you can record data on it. Formatting a tape cartridge is easy but time-consuming. Therefore, you may want to consider paying a dollar or so more to get preformatted tapes when buying cartridges for your system. Just make sure that the formatted tapes you buy are indeed compatible with your particular tape unit.

Backup Procedures

I should also say just a word about the importance of establishing a *regular* backup procedure. The elaborate backup routines outlined in many magazine articles are largely a waste of time. There are really just a few simple points to keep in mind.

First, the most important items on your disk are those you have created. If some kind of glitch wipes out your hard disk copy of DOS or some other program, you can always restore it from your original floppies (or your backups of those floppies). But if a glitch hits the spreadsheet you were working on or your receivables database, and you don't have a backup, the data is either gone forever, or gone until you can painstakingly recreate it.

Second, you should always back up your most important files and put them in a safe place. I keep copies of all of my books on disks stored "off-site" in our barn. I keep another copy in a fireproof safe in the attic. And I keep a third copy on 3.5-inch disks near my computer in case I need to refer to them. This may sound a bit obsessive, but three copies is not at all a bad idea for archival storage.

I make a complete tape backup of my various hard drives about twice a month. Only one cartridge is required per drive, but three cartridges are associated with each of them. I simply erase and reuse the oldest cartridge each time. That seems to work well for me, but you may want to use five or seven cartridges, one for each day of the week. Everything depends on how much new information is added to your system each day or how extensively the currently recorded information changes. If you add large quantities of irreplaceable information every day, then you'd better make a backup every day.

I should make clear that I also make daily backups, but not of an entire disk. For example, I write a book chapter or an article using the hard disk. But before I power down for the night, I copy what I have written that day to a 3.5-inch floppy.

That's *my* system, and over the years I have found that it works quite well. Your situation may be different. The key thing is to develop the backup habit, whether to tape or to floppy, and to establish a regular procedure for backing up the entire system. Figure out how often you think your tape drive should be used, and just put "Back Up System" on your calendar at each appropriate date.

You really don't have to make a big deal out of backing up your hard disk. But you *do* have to do it.

THE BEST FLOPPY
DISK TIPS

Hard disks may be where we live, but floppy disks are still the currency of the realm. There is not a great deal that needs to be said on the topic. But there are a few tips and tricks that can make working with floppies easier. I'm going to assume that you know all about write-protect tabs and sliders, about not touching the exposed magnetic media with your fingers, and about the fact that spilled coffee, milk, dust, and temperature extremes do not sit well with magnetic media.

Format Disks a Box at a Time

Every computer user, and certainly every power user, should have a supply of blank, formatted floppies near at hand at all times. Personally, I use my 5.25-inch drive only to read other people's disks or to supply disks to those who do not have 3.5-inch drives. For data storage, I much prefer 3.5-inch disks with their protective hard plastic shell. You can drop them in a file folder, put the folder in a drawer, and not worry.

The one thing I don't want is to have to stop in the middle of a project to format a 720K disk. I want to be able to reach for a disk, slug it into the drive, record my files, and be on my way. That's why I periodically take the time to format ten or more disks in sequence. While the formatting is taking place, I can be cleaning up my office or doing some other low-impact chore that lets me cycle back to the machine to pop out a freshly-formatted disk and pop in the next one on the stack.

Since the DOS FORMAT program automatically asks if you want to format another disk, you really don't need any additional software. However, if time is of the essence, you may want to use a program like Sydex's shareware program FORMATQM. This "quick mass" disk formatter lets you use more than one drive at a time (both must be of the same capacity), does not ask for a volume label, and does not need confirmation before formatting the next disk. The moment it sees an unformatted disk in a drive, it goes to work.

PowerPoint

Feeding Commands to FORMAT.COM

You can speed up FORMAT's operation by recording your responses to its prompts in a file and feeding them to the program using a redirection symbol. Let's assume you've got two disk drives of identical capacity and you would like to format disks in both of them with a single command.

Key in `copy con:no.txt` at the DOS command line and hit Enter. Then hit Enter twice to record two carriage returns in the file. Hit your N key and follow by hitting Enter yet again. The file will contain four lines. You will have two apparently blank lines, an *N*, and the cursor will be on the fourth blank line. You *must* hit your Enter key as described to make sure that the invisible carriage return and line feed characters are in the file. Now hit F6 to close the file and write it to disk.

You can now run the FORMAT command automatically by keying in `format a: < no.txt`. That takes care of Drive A. Now create a batch file called TEST.BAT containing the following lines:

```
format a: < no.txt
format b: < no.txt
```

(continued)

(Feeding Commands to FORMAT.COM continued)

To format disks in Drives A and B, you need only key in test. No further input from you is required. For the sake of simplicity, I've used a stripped-down sequence here. Clearly, you can customize the FORMAT lines (FORMAT A: /U /Q) and the location of the file NO.TXT to suit your own system (< C:\BATS \NO.TXT).

If you have loaded DOSKEY or CED, once you key in test, you can repeat the formatting cycle and run TEST.BAT again by hitting your up arrow key once and then hitting Enter. Formatting disks doesn't get much easier than this.

Quick and Unconditional

When you no longer need the files on a disk, you can empty it by keying in del *.*, but this causes DOS to present you with an *Are you sure?* prompt that requires a response. You will find that it is much quicker to use Vern Buerg's QDR.COM (Quick Disk Reformat) or the command format a: /u /q. You might even want to record this DOS command in a batch file called Q.BAT. Make the single line read FORMAT %1: /U /Q. That way you can enter q a: to reformat Drive A or q b: to reformat Drive B. (For more information on this technique, consult your DOS manual regarding "replaceable parameters" in batch files.)

Note that this technique can only be used on disks that have previously received a regular, track-by-track DOS format. The quick switch (/Q) tells FORMAT.COM to merely wipe out the file directory, which can be done in a twinkling. The unconditional (/U) switch tells DOS not to save the information the UNFORMAT command needs to unformat a disk. That saves disk space and it saves time.

Double-Sided and High-Density

In the old days, there were only 5.25-inch floppy disks, and they came in two varieties: single- and double-sided. It didn't take long for computer users to catch on to the fact that there was no physical difference between them. Double-sided disks just happened to have been tested on both sides, while single-sided disks were tested on only one side. Since a single-sided test tended to turn up any serious media problems on both sides, and since single-sided disks were cheaper than double-sided, most power users bought single-sided media and formatted it double-sided.

That bit of background is important because a similar situation exists today. A 360K and a 1.2MB disk look the same. They are both 5.25-inch floppies with no distinguishing characteristics. Yet the high-density 1.2MB disks cost more. In the 3.5-inch arena, the disks do have distinguishing marks. A 720K disk has just a write-protect slider, while a 1.44MB disk has both that and a matching square hole on its opposite side. But, of course, the high-density disks sell for more.

Formatting a floppy disk to 1.2MB is easy, and some companies sell special tools designed to punch the necessary square hole in a 720K disk to make it appear to the drive as high-density media. Therefore, you might think that you can save some money by using less expensive double-density media as a high-density disk.

You might be able to get by in a pinch. But this is not a good long-term practice. The reason is that there is a very real physical difference between double-density and high-density media. The magnetic coating used for high-density disks is thicker and specifically designed to hold the "smaller bits" used in high-density recording.

You ignore this fact at your data's peril. If you want to save money on disks, buy them in bulk. Check the ads at the back of most computer magazines. You should be able to buy bulk disks in quantities as low as 25 and save a pretty penny in the process. Just make sure that the vendor offers a 100-percent lifetime guarantee of the disks' quality.

Post-it Tape to the Rescue

Finally, one of the best tips of all is to use 1-inch wide Post-it brand correction and cover-up tape from 3M for your floppy disk labels. The pressure-sensitive labels supplied with boxed disks are generally not removable at all. The "removable" labels sold by Avery/Dennison and other firms remain removable for about six months. After that, they tend to start bonding with the disk holder.

But Post-it tape both sticks forever and remains forever removable. And you can write on it with anything from a pencil to a felt-tipped pen. (If you use a pencil or a ballpoint, do your writing before you apply the tape to the disk. Otherwise you'll make a bad impression.) If you know you are going to keep a disk for a long time, you may want to type up a nice label. But you can't beat Post-it tape for short- to medium-term storage. It's also a great way to label your much-used video tapes, but that's another story.

PART VI

VIDEO AND KEYBOARD
CONSIDERATIONS

What You Will Learn

In computer parlance, the system's keyboard and screen are called the *console*. In all our concern over the power and speed of our processors, hard disks, and other equipment, it is easy to neglect this part of the system. Yet most of us spend most of our time working directly with the console. It is the primary means with which we interact with our machines.

Therefore, the console should be as comfortable and customized as you can possibly make it. None of us should have to put up with keyboard or screen behavior that is anything less than what we want. In this part of the book, we will show you exactly what to do to truly "have it your way."

First we'll lay a foundation for understanding. We will trace the path followed by a keystroke and show you how the action of your fingers at the keyboard ultimately results in a character being displayed on the screen. Then we'll zero in on the keyboard and show you how to inexpensively upgrade your equipment, should that be necessary, and how to redefine your keyboard layout to your liking. Finally, we will look at the options available for boosting video performance and include some pointed advice regarding the current turmoil in the video marketplace.

BASICS: FROM KEYPRESS TO DISPLAY

I've said it many times before, and I will say it yet again here: The most important computer-related skill one can develop is *touch-typing*. Mice, trackballs, and stylus "pens" are fine. But you will never enter data with a mouse or a trackball, and doing so with a stylus is a good way to develop writer's cramp. If you want to use a computer, you've got to be able to talk to the beast. And that means being able to type—comfortably, as naturally as you speak, without giving the process a second thought.

That said, there are a number of things you can do to power up your keyboard and make using it more convenient and enjoyable. Those techniques are discussed in Section 6-2. But to make them truly your own, it helps to have a basic understanding of how your keyboard works and how characters appear on the screen.

PowerPoint

Learning to Type

Typewriting is the universal computer language. The more fluent and facile you are, the more easily you will be able to use any computer and any computer program. So, to heck with hunt and peck.

Fortunately, computers are not only designed to accept typewritten input, they are also superbly suited to teaching typing skills. For a computer, presenting you with text to type and comparing the keys you hit to that text, timing the entire process, and calculating your accuracy and words per minute is child's play. This is undoubtedly one of the reasons why there are lots of typing instruction programs on the market.

I haven't looked at all of them, of course, but they would have to go a long way to beat the shareware program PC-FASTYPE by William J. Letendre. PC-FASTYPE's operating theater is a detailed color graphics picture of your keyboard that occupies about two thirds of the screen. The top third of the screen contains the characters or words you are supposed to type. (See screen shot below.)

A typing rhythm sound beeps in the background as the character you are to type next changes color and blinks on the keyboard. If you hit the wrong letter, an *X* briefly appears over the incorrect letter and a video game-like sound is issued. There are other details, depending on whether you select the beginner, intermediate, or advanced levels.

When the drill is over, hit any key to see your statistics and an analysis of your performance. The program can also be told to keep a log of your drills, making it easy to chart your progress.

The program includes lots of help screens and easy-to-use menus, and there is a well-written manual on the disk, including a tutorial about typing techniques in general. Registered users receive a professionally printed, bound manual.

Give it half an hour a day for two weeks or so, and you'll soon find that you're "in the groove." From then on, all of your PC operations will be easier, and you will become even more comfortable with your keyboard as time goes on.   *(continued)*

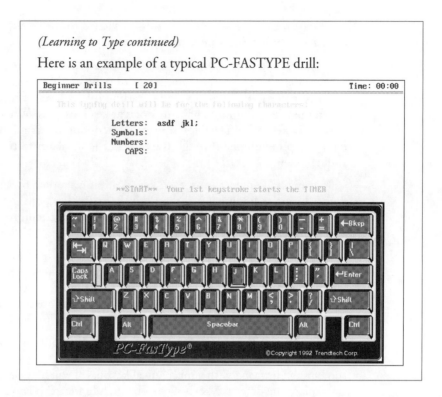

(Learning to Type continued)

Here is an example of a typical PC-FASTYPE drill:

Keyboard Technology

Of all a computer's components, the keyboard seems the most mundane and familiar. A Gibson Girl from the 1890s would not know what to make of a floppy disk. But she, and anyone else from that era, would instantly recognize a computer keyboard for what it is.

Yet there's a lot more to personal computer keyboards than most people suspect. Each of them, for example, is equipped with a microprocessor that is designed to scan every key position 60 times a second or faster. And I do mean *every* key position. Your left Shift and right Shift keys may be identical in function, but each has a unique "scan code."

The keyboard processor knows that a key has been pressed because pressing the key completes an electrical circuit. Each key is, in effect, an electrical switch that's on when pressed and off when released. The switch mechanism varies with the keyboard, but mechanical and membrane key switch technologies dominate the market.

A mechanical switch operates exactly as you would expect. The keytop is attached to a small plunger that is often tipped with gold. When you press the key, you move the plunger downward to complete a circuit by touching an electrical contact. A spring attached to the keytop pushes the key back up when pressure is removed.

Membrane keyboards, on the other hand, are designed around a single rubbery sheet that consists of two layers of polyester film, each with a silk-screened pattern of conductive silver carbon ink. A layer of insulation between the two membranes has tiny holes at key locations. When you push down on a key, a foam cushion squeezes the conductive membranes, pushing the top membrane through the hole in the insulator to make contact and complete a circuit.

In some implementations, each key location is marked by a little raised dome. Inside the dome is a carbon dot. Press the key, and the dome collapses, pushing down the carbon dot to complete the circuit between itself and the electrical contact below.

In general, keyboards that use mechanical switches tend to have a more tactile feel. There is a satisfying click when you press a key. Membrane keyboards can sound and feel mushy or rubbery. Indeed, to compensate for this, some computers equipped with such keyboards are designed to produce an audible click or beep via their speakers each time you hit a key.

Of course, with one-third fewer parts than their mechanical counterparts, membrane keyboards tend to be much less expensive. But, should something go wrong with a mechanical keyboard, you may be able to simply replace the defective key switch. If a membrane keyboard starts acting up, repair may be impractical, since all the switches exist on that single rubbery sheet.

On the other hand, it is important to point out that advances in recent years have made membrane keyboards much more reliable. Some even use mechanical spring actuators to provide a more solid feel. Honeywell, Key-Tronic, Tandy, IBM, and many other manufacturers now offer membrane-based keyboards.

Scan Codes

Keyboards are a matter of personal taste. The important thing is to be aware that you do not have to stick with the keyboard that happened to come with your machine, as we will see in Section 6-2. From the keyboard processor's standpoint, of course, it is irrelevant how you happen to complete the circuit for a given key. All it's interested in is determining the appropriate scan code and sending that code to the main system unit.

When you strike a key, the keyboard processor sends two signals to the keyboard port in the computer. One is a signal (Interrupt 9h) demanding attention from the CPU. This causes the CPU to run a keyboard servicing program found in the computer's ROM BIOS.

The other signal is the key's scan code. The scan code is an 8-bit value (one byte). But the keyboard's electronics rearrange it so it can travel to the computer in serial fashion (one bit at a time). That's why keyboard cables tend to be thin, compared to the wide *ribbon cables* used to connect parallel printers.

PowerPoint

Keyboard and Video Extension Cables

Only four wires are needed to connect most keyboards to the system unit. There's one for serial keyboard data, one to serve as a ground or "common," one for the keyboard clock signals that make sure your keyboard is in synch with the system unit, and one to provide electrical power. The extra pins you find on your round DIN or modular AMP keyboard connectors are not used.

Since the necessary connectors and shielded cable are available from Radio Shack and other electronics stores, you can make your own keyboard extension cable should you feel restricted by the cable that came with your system. But unless you're handy with a soldering iron, you'll probably be better off simply buying a cable designed for this purpose.

Global Computer Supplies, for example, sells an extension cable package that includes six-foot cables for power, monitor, and keyboard. The package for PC/XT/AT-style machines with VGA monitors costs $36, and the one for PS/2 equipment costs $40. For more information, call: (800) 845-6225. The company has locations in New York, California, Georgia, and Illinois.

Black Box Corporation offers even more flexibility. The company offers keyboard, video, and printer cables for nearly every kind of equipment. Standard lengths range from two feet to 100 feet, depending on the cable, and custom lengths are also available. A six-foot 5-pin DIN keyboard extension cable is $17.85, for example, but you can specify a custom length at a cost of $15.75 plus 35 cents a foot. Since longer cables yield weaker electrical signals, be sure to ask for technical advice before deciding on a cable longer than six to ten feet.

For more information, call the firm at (412) 746-5530. Black Box Corporation is located in Pittsburgh, PA.

The keyboard interrupt program causes the CPU to pick up the scan code byte at the keyboard port and take some further action. When you release a key, the keyboard processor chip sends another code to inform the computer of that fact. The complete scan code thus consists of a "make code" (sent when you press a key) and a "break code" (sent when you release it).

Make and Break

The use of make and break codes has a direct bearing on your ability to customize your keyboard. After all, there's no reason why the PC could not have been designed to generate a one-part, single-byte scan code for each key. But then there would be no way for the system to tell that you are still depressing a key, as you typically do when moving the cursor.

The make and break code arrangement solves the problem. The system is designed to automatically *repeat* a keystroke until it receives the break code indicating that you have released the key. The speed with which it does so is called the *typematic rate*. Now for the payoff: The typematic rate can be controlled by the user. If you want a faster, zippier keyboard response, you can reset the typematic rate with the DOS MODE command or you can use a third-party utility program.

As we will see in the next section, it's easy to dramatically increase your typematic rate. Once you have done so, returning to the default rate will seem like slogging through cold molasses.

Keyboard Macros

The reason you can alter your system's typematic rate is that the value your computer uses is determined by software. When your computer boots up, its ROM BIOS automatically places a certain value at a special location in memory. Then, when the system sees a make code that is not immediately followed by a break code, it consults that location to find out how frequently it should repeat the "made" key. The typematic rate can be changed by simply changing the value placed in that special location.

The *same* thing applies to the characters that are assigned to specific key codes. When the system receives a keyboard scan code, it consults a table stored in memory to tell it which character that code represents. But suppose you change the table? The computer is just a dumb machine. If you tell it, through software, that whenever it sees the scan code for a capital *A* it should display a lowercase *d*, it will do what you want without question.

With a little more software magic, you can not only swap letters around, you can assign complete commands or even a lengthy series of commands to a single keypress. Or you can simply assign a string of characters to a single key. You might, for example, assign the string "Every good boy deserves a favor" to your F1 key. Each time you pressed F1, the system would then display that phrase.

In computerese, this technique is called *macro expansion*. A single keystroke effectively expands to encompass multiple keystrokes. (From little acorns do mighty oaks grow.) As you are undoubtedly aware, the term everyone uses is *macros* or *keyboard macros*.

The main point is this: The PC's design makes it possible for you to have nearly complete control over your keyboard. Making alterations is easy. You can use DOS's ANSI.SYS driver or a third-party program. So there's no need to put up with a keyboard arrangement that does not satisfy you completely.

730 Unique Codes

Most keyboards supplied with computer systems today have 101 or 102 keys. Let's assume you've got twelve function keys, a separate numeric keypad, and a separate set of cursor control, Home, End, and related keys, for a total of 102. That's 102 different scan codes.

If you assume, as is indeed the case, that you can hold the Alt key down for nearly every one of these keys to produce a different scan code, that gives you 204 possible codes. If you continue the process by adding in the use of the Shift and Ctrl keys, you've got a couple hundred more possible codes. Now suppose you combine the Shift and the Alt and the Ctrl keys with various keys. How about Shift+Ctrl+F7? Or Shift+Ctrl+Alt+F12?

Your fingers may be pretzels by the time you enter keypress combinations like that, but you should know that these multikey combinations *also* generate unique codes. When you add up all the possibilities and remove the quirks and exceptions, a 101/102 enhanced keyboard can generate a total of about 730 unique codes.

We should note here that the reason so many codes are possible relates to what are called the status bytes. Located at the bottom of the PC's memory, these two bytes record the status of the following keys: Insert, Caps Lock, Num Lock, Scroll Lock, Alt, Control, Left Shift, and Right Shift.

Whenever you press any of these keys, the computer makes a note of the key's condition in the status bytes, even though nothing happens on your screen. Whenever you strike any key, the computer looks at its status bytes to see if any of these "shift" keys are engaged. When the keyboard-handling program picks up the scan code waiting for it at the keyboard port, it checks the status bytes and translates everything into a *2-byte* value.

Usually, the low-order byte (the rightmost eight bits) is the key's ASCII code value, while the high-order byte (the leftmost eight bits) is the keyboard scan code. The important point, though, is that with two bytes (16 bits), symbolizing a number as large as 730 is no problem. (If only one byte were used, the maximum number would be 256.)

Getting It On the Screen

At this point, we know that the effect of pressing a single key or a combination of keys is determined by what the system finds when it looks up the appropriate scan code in its keyboard table. Since that table exists in RAM, it can be altered, using the appropriate software. Therefore we can control the effect of any and all keystrokes by simply altering the table.

The same approach applies to the video portion of the process. You press a key, generating a scan code; the system picks up the scan code from the keyboard port and consults a table to determine the character this code represents. Now what? How does the character the system finds in its keyboard table end up on the screen? The answer lies in another table.

Most of us, if we thought about it for a moment, would realize that the information we see on our screens actually exists somewhere within the computer's memory. A display screen is thus nothing more than a window into a certain part of that memory.

The characters it shows us actually exist as on or off bits in the computer's RAM. When a bit is on, a corresponding part of the display screen lights up. When it is off, the corresponding part of the display is dark. By turning some bits on and some off in a part of memory that corresponds to a given region of the screen, characters can be formed. (A similar technique is used to produce characters on a dot-matrix printer.)

The special section of RAM that is reserved for storing the image that appears on the screen is called *video memory*. When in text mode, the typical screen is divided into a matrix 80 characters wide and 25 characters high, and a memory location is assigned to each character. One screen can thus contain a total of 2,000 characters ($80 \times 25 = 2,000$). Any of those characters can be changed at any time by simply changing its corresponding value in video memory.

Now, as we know, each character is made up of an array of dots. Different arrangements are used, depending on the monitor and the selected video mode, but this array is always called the "character box." It is measured by the number of dots that make up its width and its height. The dots are often called "pixels," short for "picture elements," and their physical size varies with the monitor. The smaller the dots your hardware can produce, the finer its maximum resolution.

PowerPoint

Dots and Pixels

Although the terms are often used interchangeably, "dots" and "pixels" do not always refer to the same thing. The inner surface of a monitor's screen is coated with multiple triads of red, green, and blue phosphor dots. These dots have no electrical connections. They are just tiny dabs of chemicals that have been placed very precisely on the glass screen. However, when they are struck by a beam of electrons, these chemicals glow in their respective colors.

The CRT's electron gun actually fires three beams, one for each color dot in a triad. The beams themselves are identical. What distinguishes them is that each is angled and aimed in such a way that it only strikes one color of dots. A piece of material called a *shadow mask* sits between the gun and the inner screen surface. The shadow mask contains a hole for each triad and is designed to insure that the dots in only one triad are affected by the beam at any given time.

A pixel, in contrast, is the smallest screen area whose color and brightness can be independently controlled. This varies with the video equipment and with the selected video mode. In some cases, a pixel may consist of several dots. In others, as when each dot is controlled by a single bit, a pixel may consist of a single dot or dot triad.

It is worth noting that one of the main features that distinguishes color monitors is *dot pitch*. Dot pitch is the vertical distance between two dots of the same color. The smaller the dots, the smaller the dot pitch, and the greater the maximum screen resolution. A dot pitch of 0.31 millimeters is the minimum acceptable standard today, but if you are buying a new monitor, hold out for a dot pitch of 0.28mm. Also, make sure that the vendor or manufacturer quotes the *vertical* dot pitch, not the horizontal dot pitch.

But what determines which specific pixels in a character box are turned on or off to create a given character? The answer lies in the ROM chips found on your video card. When the system receives a scan code from the keyboard and looks it up in its keyboard table, it sends the value it finds to the video card. The processor on the card looks up that value in its onboard

ROM. There it finds a pattern of on/off bits used to form the appropriate character. It then uses this pattern to create the character in video memory, and the results appear on your screen.

This is all very interesting, but what's the point? The point, once again, is the possibility of changing the tables. If you don't like the "font" your video card uses to represent characters on the screen, you can change it. All you have to do is load a *different* table of instructions on how to create characters, and tell the video card to use it in place of its own onboard ROM.

Always remember that what you see on the screen is a reflection of what exists in memory. If you change what's in video memory, you change what's displayed on the screen. This is true whether you are in character or text mode and dealing with character boxes, or in bitmapped graphics mode where every pixel on your screen can be turned on or off individually. (Windows, for example, is a totally bitmapped interface, making possible many different screen fonts.)

You should also know that in text mode, every character on the screen requires two bytes of memory. So, if one ASCII character requires one byte (which it does), and if a typical screen can hold 2,000 characters, then a total of 4,000 bytes (4K) is required per screen. With color video equipment, the extra byte for each character stores information about the foreground and background colors of the character box, and whether or not the character should blink.

Storing More Screens

From the beginning, PCs have been designed to store more than one screen or *video page* in memory. It has always been possible, for example, for programs to switch among several video pages by connecting a different portion of memory to the video hardware, redoing the display almost instantly in the process. But so far, neither DOS nor the PC itself has made it possible to recall information that has scrolled off the screen.

Yet, when you think about it, why shouldn't this be possible? If the screen exists in memory, why can't the data that piece of memory contains be copied to a different location and thus preserved? It can, of course. Indeed with a program like FANSI-Console, you can preserve and then scroll back through as many screens as your available EMS, XMS, or conventional memory accommodates. FANSI lets you specify a different set of screen fonts as well. And it also has a lot of power to offer regarding your keyboard, as we are about to see.

SECTION
6-2

KEYBOARD TIPS

Now let's zero in on the keyboard and on the power user techniques you can apply to make using it both easier and more enjoyable. Specifically, let's look at how and where to buy a replacement keyboard that's more to your liking, how to add zip to your cursor and all your other keys by resetting the typematic rate, and how to redefine keys and work with macros.

You will also want to see the discussion of Microsoft's DOSKEY and Cove Software's CED programs in Part 3 of this book. Both programs remember previously issued DOS commands and let you recall them to the screen for editing or to be reissued. Both also have a macroing facility, though CED's is much more intuitive and easier to use.

Sources of Replacement Keyboards

There's no point in pretending it's not so: The keyboards supplied with many computers today are little more than buff-colored, ergonomically shaped junk. To my knowledge, no one has ever bought a computer because it came with a particularly good keyboard. There is thus little incentive for a manufacturer to offer anything but the bare minimum, particularly since skimping on the keyboard can reduce the retail price of a system by $100 or more. Keyboards are like power cords. Every machine must come with one, but no one pays it any attention.

That's probably fine for most people. After all, if there were a huge public demand for superior keyboards, you can bet computer makers would start supplying them. If you spend a great deal of time at your computer, however, even if you aren't the world's fastest typist, the quality and design of your keyboard can make a huge difference.

Fortunately, power users *have* alternatives. For about $100, you can get a superior replacement keyboard from any of a number of companies, including firms like ALPS America, DataDesk International, Honeywell, Northgate, and Tandy. The keyboard you choose is largely a matter of personal taste. Some have a more tactile feel; some boast of their quietness. Compatibility is rarely a problem these days, and you will be amazed at how flexible and feature-filled a really good keyboard can be.

Northgate, for Example

My personal favorite is the Northgate OmniKey line. Models are available ranging in price from $89 to $129. Like most replacement keyboards, these generally conform to the layout of the Enhanced 101-Key Keyboard introduced by IBM when it upgraded the AT in 1987. But for me, there's a crucial difference or two.

The first is a large, IBM Selectric-style Enter key and the IBM-standard double-width Backspace key. Most important of all, Northgate makes a point of placing the twelve function keys down the left side where I like them, instead of across the top. Why anyone would want to reach up nearly to the keyboard's pencil tray to press a function key is beyond me. It's simply too much work.

With their metal base and ALPS click/tactile mechanical key switches, OmniKey models have a solid, satisfying feel. There is an option to change the locations of the Caps Lock, Alt, and Ctrl keys by pulling the key caps with a special tool (included) and flipping a DIP switch or two on the keyboard's underside. Two Dvorak layouts can be selected with those same DIP switches. (The company also sells keycap sets for Dvorak, Amiga, WordPerfect function keys, and foreign languages at about $15 a set.)

To minimize inadvertent screen prints, the PrintScreen key is designed to be pressed twice before a screen is sent to the printer. You can even change the rate at which a key repeats and the delay between the keypress and the beginning of the repeating key process.

All of the companies listed in Figure 6-2-1 make good equipment, and many may offer features of special importance to you. But, as *PC Magazine* [February 25, 1992] notes, "Northgate is the only company that thinks more carefully about keyboard design than IBM, and many users will find its various OmniKey models the only keyboards worth using." The magazine also pointed out that you can set these keyboards via DIP switches for compatibility with AT&T 6300 and Tandy 1000 models that won't work with some other replacement keyboards. In addition, all Northgate keyboards work at top speed with Novell networks.

Figure 6-2-1 Leading Suppliers of Replacement Keyboards

If you're serious about your computer keyboard, the companies listed below can help. Each of them makes one or more models of replacement keyboards for IBM-compatible equipment. Like the Northgate models discussed in the text, these units probably offer much more flexibility than the keyboard that came with your computer.

ALPS America
3553 N. First St.
San Jose, CA 95134
(408) 432-6000

Cherry Corp.
3600 Sunset Ave.
Waukegan, IL 60087
(708) 662-9200

Chicony America Inc.
3111 Miraloma Ave.
Anaheim, CA 92806
(714) 630-6662

DataDesk International
9330 Eton Ave.
Chatsworth, CA 91311
(800) 328-2337
(818) 998-4200

Honeywell Keyboard Division
4171 N. Mesa
El Paso, TX 79902
(800) 445-6939
(915) 544-5511

IBM/Lexmark
International Inc.
740 New Circle Rd. NW
Lexington, KY 40511
(800) 426-2468
(606) 232-6814

KeyTronic Corp.
P.O. Box 14687
Spokane, WA 99214
(800) 262-6006
(509) 927-5515

Maxi Switch Inc.
2901 E. Elvira Rd.
Tucson, AZ 85706
(800) 969-6294
(602) 294-5450

NMB Technologies Inc.
9730 Independence Ave.
Chatsworth, CA 91311
(818) 341-3355

Northgate Computer
Systems Inc.
7075 Flying Cloud Dr
Eden Prairie, MN 55344
(800) 548-1993
(612) 943-8181

Radio Shack/Tandy Corp.
1800 One Tandy Center
Fort Worth, TX 76102
(817) 390-3011

Doing It in DOS

DOS support for keyboard enhancement is thin at best. Yet since it's there, we have to deal with it, however briefly. As you will see, there are richer, more powerful, and more effective tools than DOS provides for taking control of the keyboard.

Using MODE to Set the Typematic Rate

Let's start with the technique for using DOS to boost the typematic rate. Two values are involved: The repeat rate and the amount of time the system delays after a key is pressed before it begins repeating it. You enter both values with the MODE command, like this: `mode con: rate=32 delay=1`.

The term "CON:" stands for the console (the keyboard in this case). The rate specification determines how fast a character is repeated. The default value, according to the DOS manual, is 20 for IBM/AT-compatible keyboards and 21 for IBM PS/2 machines. That's puzzling because the default typematic rate for the AT is 10 characters per second; 10.9 characters per second for the PS/2. The important thing, however, is that you may specify anything from 1 through 32 as your chosen value. The delay setting refers to how long the system should wait before it begins repeating a key. Valid settings are 1 (0.25 second), 2 (0.5 second), 3 (0.75 second), and 4 (1 second). The default value is 2, or half a second.

This is a very easy command to use. DOS must have access to DOS's MODE.COM utility, of course. The only caveat is that if you set the rate, you must also specify the delay, and if you specify a delay, you must also set a rate. It's an all-or-nothing proposition. It is also possible that changing the typematic rate may not be supported on your particular type of hardware. The only way to tell for sure is to try it.

Redefining Keys with ANSI.SYS

The ANSI.SYS driver supplied with DOS lets you accomplish four major things: set screen colors and attributes, set screen mode, redefine keys, and control the cursor's position from a batch program. Screen color control was discussed in Part 2 of this book, and the use of the ANSI driver in all its glory is fully described in the Random House/Glossbrenner DOS books.

Here we simply note that you can indeed use this DOS tool to reassign keys or to produce keyboard macros. A line like DEVICE=ANSI.SYS must be in your CONFIG.SYS file so the driver will be loaded when you boot up. And you may find it helpful to have a word processing program that can generate an escape code (ASCII 27) as a character that can be stored in a file, but you can also use the PROMPT command for that purpose.

The ANSI command used to set keyboard strings is: ESC[code;string; ...p. *Code* is one or more of the key codes listed at the back of your DOS manual or in the command reference sections of the Random House/ Glossbrenner DOS books. It is the code number of the key you want to redefine (plain, shifted, controlled or "alt-ed"). *String* is either the ASCII code for a single character, or a string of characters like DIR, enclosed in quotation marks ("DIR"). Following the string, you may wish to include one or more ASCII control codes, such as an ASCII 13, which adds a carriage return (Enter) to the string.

For example, the command ESC[4;"Dir C:";13p redefines the Ctrl+D sequence (key code number 4) as a macro that gives you a directory of Drive C. Note that an ASCII 13 at the end of the sequence adds a carriage return. If it were not there, the DIR command would not be activated, and you would have to press Enter by hand.

If your word processor produces a character for Escape, use it to prepare a file containing the single line shown above. Just remember to hold your Alt key down and tap in 27 on your numeric keypad to produce the ESC character. Save the file to disk, return to DOS, and use the TYPE command to send the file to the screen. You won't see anything, but when you enter a Ctrl+D, a disk directory appears.

If you don't have the necessary word processor, you may use the PROMPT command. The only thing you have to remember is to use "$e" to stand for the Escape character. At the DOS prompt, key in `prompt $e[4;"Dir C:";13p` and hit Enter. If your visual prompt disappears, key in prompt again to restore it. Now enter a Ctrl+D, and a disk directory will appear.

PowerPoint

Making Macros "Permanent"

Once you get the hang of it, redefining keys or loading macros into keys with ANSI.SYS isn't too difficult. After preparing a set you like, you can implement them each time you boot up using your AUTO-EXEC.BAT file. Prepare a text file containing the redefinitions/ macros you want to load and include a command in AUTOEXEC .BAT to TYPE that file to the screen. Or simply include a series of PROMPT commands in AUTOEXEC.BAT.

If you opt to use the PROMPT approach, make sure that your PROMPT lines appear *before* a command like ECHO OFF. If the ANSI driver is to see and act on the commands you have prepared, they must be echoed to the screen.

Doing It with FANSI-Console

As you know from Part 3 of this book, I feel that FANSI-Console from Hersey Micro Consulting, Inc., is essential to every user. It is certainly far more powerful than DOS. As it should be. After all, the program's various files and utilities occupy close to two megabytes. The on-disk manual occupies another 500K all by itself. And all of these files, utility programs, drivers, and documentation focus on one thing: the console.

There may be something FANSI cannot do to affect or otherwise customize your screen and keyboard, but I have yet to find it. Other utility programs or packages may offer a few FANSI-like features. The PC-Kwik Power Pack from Multisoft Corporation, for example, includes not only that firm's famous disk cache but screen and keyboard accelerator programs, as well as a scroll recall feature. But nothing else comes close to FANSI in power, features, and degree of control.

How FANSI Works

FANSI-Console has been under continuous development since 1983. The current shareware version is always the previous commercial version. It is never crippled in any way. The shareware version current at this writing is 3.01K. The present commercial version is 4.00I. You can get copies from most disk vendors, user groups, and online systems. Since it's such a large package, however, it is easy to be overwhelmed by all of your options. The following pointers will help.

Everything centers on the file FCONSOLE.DEV. This is the FANSI driver, and it must be loaded via your CONFIG.SYS file, as we saw in Part 3. FANSI completely replaces the screen- and keyboard-handling routines built into your system's ROM BIOS. It can be loaded into a UMB, and the program is smart enough to automatically select the best available type of memory (conventional, expanded, or extended) for its storage and work area. The amount of memory FANSI occupies can be reduced by telling it not to load the code needed for certain little-used features.

Again, as we saw in Part 3, you can specify the settings FANSI uses for certain features by including slash switches on the line that loads the driver. But you can also change and reset options from the DOS command line or via a batch file. The technique is nearly identical to the technique used to send color commands, key definitions, and macros to the standard ANSI .SYS driver.

Indeed, FANSI responds exactly like ANSI.SYS when presented with an ANSI.SYS command. Thus, if you wanted to, you could use the DOS PROMPT command to feed instructions to FANSI. There is a better way to do this, however. The FANSI package includes a program called SEND .EXE that is specifically designed to send commands to the driver once. PROMPT commands are sent every time the DOS prompt appears.

Fortunately, there is no need to sit down with a manual and figure out which codes to send to FANSI to make it do what you want. The package comes with a program called FANSISET.EXE that will prepare a file for you containing the necessary commands. Just enter a line like `fansiset codes.txt send`, and you are presented with a menu-driven screen that lets you opt to turn modes on or off, or specify values as appropriate. When you are finished, you can exit the program and use your word processor to incorporate the contents of CODES.TXT into your AUTOEXEC.BAT or other file. You may specify any filename you like instead of CODES.TXT.

Setting Key Rate and Key Delay

FANSI comes with a program called FASTKEYS.BAT that lets you quickly set your key repeat and delay rates. But you can also use FANSISET as discussed above. If you do, here are two of the lines you will find in CODES.TXT:

```
send $e[$g5;05z ${Change FANSI-KEYDELAY$}
send $e[$g6;45z ${Change FANSI-KEYRATE$}
```

Notice that FANSISET automatically "comments" the lines (the information in curly brackets) to remind you of what the codes after SEND are designed to do. The delay is measured in timer ticks. Since the timer operates at 18.2 ticks per second, and since the FANSI default delay is 9, the default delay is about half a second. That's the same as the default value for DOS and the MODE command; it's just measured a different way. Here, I've reduced the delay to 5 (;05z), or about 0.28 seconds. The repeat rate is measured in characters per second, and I've boosted it from the default of 10 to 45 (;45z).

The mechanics and actual values need not concern us. Use FASTKEYS .BAT in the form FASTKEYS *R D*, where *R* is the desired repeat rate and *D* is your chosen delay. Experiment until you find a setting that you like. Then either use FANSISET or edit FASTKEYS.BAT to record your values on disk so you can load them again at any time.

The point I want to make here is that DOS gives you only four possible delay settings and 32 possible rate settings. With FANSI, your available settings are effectively unlimited. If you stay with DOS, you will never be able to push your cursor around the screen any faster than 32 characters per second. With FANSI, you can crank the speed up as high as your hardware will go.

In addition, FANSI automatically implements *overshoot limiting*, a feature that immediately stops the parade of characters the moment you remove your finger from the key. That means that if you take your finger off the arrow key while it is in the middle of the line, you are far less likely to find your cursor at the end of the line.

Key Redefinition

When it comes to redefining keys with FANSI, you may use the PROMPT command exactly as you would with ANSI.SYS loaded. But you may also use FANSI's SEND command followed by an ANSI-like string. The reason I say "ANSI-like" is that FANSI offers commands in addition to the thirteen commands ($q, $t, $g, etc.) that ANSI.SYS supports. Nevertheless, there is still the nuisance of having to look up the scan codes for the keys you wish to redefine.

Fortunately, FANSI offers another alternative in the program FLAYOUT.EXE. When you run this program in the form `flayout test.lay`, you will be presented with a menu listing sixteen keyboard layouts ranging from *Enhanced 101-key Keyboard* to *Northgate OmniKey 102* to *Tandy 1000* to *Zenith Z200*. Make your selection, and a visual representation of your keyboard appears on the screen. Reassigning keys is as simple as moving one highlight box to the target key and the other to the key containing the value you wish to use.

When you exit, FLAYOUT records your settings in TEST.LAY. At your option, you can make your new settings effective immediately. That means that in the future, you can activate the assignments in TEST.LAY by entering `flayout test.lay` again and then exiting the program.

But FANSI offers an even more permanent alternative. To copy your new keyboard layout directly into the FANSI driver, you merely enter `flayout test.lay fconsole.dev`. The next time you boot the system and FANSI loads in, your new keyboard layout will be in effect. (I got tired of accidentally hitting the NumLock key, for example, so I used this technique to make it an End key.)

Should you need to use the original key definition, you can use a combination of your Control, Alt, and "Grave" keys—Ctrl+Alt+`. (The Grave is the French accent character that usually shares space with the tilde or "squiggle.") Then just strike the key in question, and its original character will appear.

PowerPoint

Feeding Keystrokes to Programs

One of the many powerful utilities that come with FANSI is KEYIN .EXE. KEYIN is designed to let you run programs from batch files by stuffing the keyboard buffer with the keystrokes the program will need. The technique is to enter KEYIN and then, on the same line, include the keystrokes you want to put into the buffer. On the next line, place the command needed to call the program.

You can use KEYIN to make the program you have called think you have pressed Enter, Esc, any function key, a space, or a string of characters. KEYIN will not work with programs that "flush" the type-ahead buffer when they load, so you will have to experiment. But when it can be used, it can be a great convenience.

The Best Way to Do Macros

FANSI-Console can be used to create keyboard macros in the same way that ANSI.SYS does. In both cases, it is a laborious process that is effectively limited to rather simple macro definitions. FANSI does offer the option of toggling your macro definitions off and on from the DOS command line, and it does increase the amount of memory available for storing macros. But the main advantage to both the FANSI and ANSI approaches is preservation of memory.

If you need true macroing power, it is a waste of time to fiddle around with FANSI or ANSI. You will be much better off loading a commercial program like ProKey or SmartKey, and better off still if you use Frank A. Bell's shareware program, NewKey.

Defining and editing macros with NewKey could not be simpler. Load the program via AUTOEXEC.BAT so it is always available during your session. Then, when you want to define a macro, use the Alt and Equals (Alt+=) key combination. A little window like the one shown in Figure 6-2-2 pops up. Press the key or key combination you wish to use as your target, and you are prompted to enter an optional descriptive phrase. Then enter the keystrokes you wish to record. Finish with the Alt and Minus (-) key combination to turn off NewKey's recording mode.

That's really all there is to it. No need to look up scan codes and no need to limit yourself to the simplicity imposed by the ANSI approach. Your macro will be in effect for the duration of your session, unless you opt to turn it off by popping up the NewKey control menu.

Of course, you can record your macro definitions to disk and load them in via NewKey at the start of the next session. You can even edit, merge, and elaborate on macros using NewKey's macro editor. It's as easy as using a word processor.

Figure 6-2-2 Popping Up NewKey

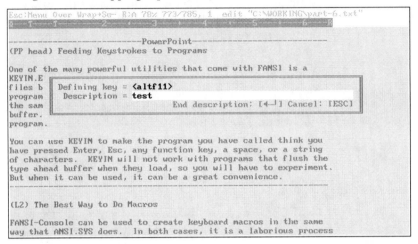

Among its many powerful features, NewKey lets you insert fixed-length pauses, nest macros and key translations, tell the program to wait while a floppy disk is being accessed, or tell it to beep (or not beep) at each keystroke entered during macro definition. There's even a cut-and-paste function that lets you cut screens out of one application and paste them into another. NewKey can also be toggled on or off, at your command.

The complete NewKey package, including an extensive on-disk manual, is available as shareware for about $5. If you like and use the program regularly, the registration cost is $43. Registration includes a commercial-quality, printed manual and support from the program author.

SECTION
6-3

UPGRADING
YOUR VIDEO

The performance of your video equipment can be *influenced* by software. By replacing your ROM BIOS software with a more skillfully programmed BIOS, FANSI-Console and other programs can increase the speed of screen display and scrolling. They can also give you control over your foreground, background, and screen border colors. In addition, there are many programs that can change your screen fonts and thus drastically alter the way text appears.

However, as powerful as the software approach is, video performance is ultimately a matter of hardware. That's why the single most important step you can take to bring your video setup into the realm of the power user is to replace your video adapter card. The cost, fortunately, can be as low as $100, but it can make a huge difference.

For example, in true component fashion, the systems I use have been expanded and modified over several years. If you were to pull a board from one of my machines and ask me where and when I bought it, I could not tell you immediately. I would have to first consult my files, where I keep the manual, any supplied software, and the receipt for each piece of equipment. (I'm not compulsive, but can see no point in not being organized.)

PowerPoint

Screen Fonts

I've experimented with programs that make all text appear as if it had
been carved by a medieval scribe or printed in a Moscow or Tel Aviv
newspaper. Screen fonts are fun but tend to be much more difficult
to read than your system's default font. The only font change I use is
one supplied with FANSI that replaces the slashed or dotted zero on
a system with a plain zero. Both the zero and the capital letter *O* are
designed to be distinct in this font.

In addition to being somewhat hard to read, screen fonts have no effect on your printer. So if you want your printouts to resemble what
you see on the screen, you will need to find a comparable cartridge
font or a soft font that you can download to your printer, and then
make that font the printer's default.

About a year ago, the video board on one of my machines began acting
up. It turned out that it was an old 8-bit card. I replaced it with a 16-bit
VGA/Super VGA card equipped with 512K of RAM. The total cost was
$106. The performance increase made possible by the wider data path and
extra memory was so dramatic, even in plain DOS applications, that I
threw out the perfectly good 8-bit card in my other system and replaced it
with a 16-bitter. When you're dealing with video equipment, software is
important, but hardware is paramount.

The Best Way to Upgrade

Use FANSI-Console and other programs for all they're worth. But if you
are still not satisfied with the speed of your video system's response, start
thinking about upgrading the hardware.

The first thing to check is your current video card. Does it plug into the
expansion bus with an 8-bit connector or a 16-bit connector? If it is an
older, 8-bit card, think strongly about upgrading to a 16-bit card. Few
upgrades offer a comparable bang for the buck. If you can afford it, try to
get a VGA/Super VGA card with at least 512K, and preferably a meg, of
memory. Inexpensive cards like mine top out at 512K. Others have more
capacity.

If you've already got a 16-bit VGA/Super VGA card, the next step is to
stop and think. If you spend most of your time either at the DOS command line or running DOS-based applications programs, the chances are

that you are perfectly happy with your screen performance in this mode. A 16-bit video adapter and FANSI or some other screen-accelerating software deliver all the responsiveness most people could want—in DOS and DOS applications.

In Windows or some other intensely graphic environment—like a desktop publishing program, a paint program, or a CAD program—your satisfaction level is likely to fall. Power users want to be able to zip around a screen with near-zero delay. Anything less makes us impatient.

If you find yourself becoming exasperated with the speed of graphics-intensive software, the next step is to consider installing a disk cache. You will be amazed, for example, at how much a cache like PC-Kwik can speed up the apparent responsiveness of Ventura Publisher or PC Paintbrush.

If you're still dissatisfied, I suggest you wait. Yes, wait. Or at least, consider waiting. Like everything else in the PC world right now, video standards and hardware are undergoing a major change. At this point, it is far from clear how it will all shake out.

As we're about to see, there are a number of hardware-related things you can do to dramatically increase video performance, particularly with graphics-based programs like Windows. But all of them are expensive, and at this point, none of them has become the next standard. If you can hold out for a year or two, a standard will certainly emerge. The technology will improve, and prices will fall. In short, unless a performance-enhancing upgrade is absolutely essential to your productivity and peace of mind, now's a good time to sit tight.

Hardware Upgrade Paths

Let's look at the options. Video adapter cards fall into one of three categories: frame buffer, accelerated, or coprocessed. Frame buffer cards are the least capable and least expensive. Unless you've already upgraded, you probably have a frame buffer card in your machine right now. Accelerated and coprocessed video adapters are significantly faster than frame buffer video adapters, and, of course, you pay for that capability.

One if the techniques video coprocessors and accelerators use to achieve higher speeds is to reduce the amount of data that needs to be transferred to the display system. But the main technique is to relieve the system's CPU of the job of generating screen images and moving data around in video memory. When you've got a microprocessor dedicated to the task of handling the screen, you can bet that your screen will scroll much more quickly. Indeed, since they are optimized for image generation, coprocessors and accelerators can often work faster than your main CPU.

The main difference between the coprocessor and accelerator approach is programmability. An accelerator is a fixed-function coprocessor that is usually designed to handle specific graphics chores related to particular programs and applications. The Windows accelerator boards you see advertised, for example, contain a chip programmed to handle Windows-related screen chores. Other boards are designed to work with AutoCAD.

A coprocessor board, in contrast, can be programmed to do anything. This versatility adds to the cost: Coprocessed boards start at about $750, while accelerator boards sell for around $200.

Probably the most important thing to remember when considering either an accelerator or a coprocessed video board is that each is unique. The standard frame buffer video cards most of us use, in contrast, tend to be commodities. Most VGA cards today come with special drivers to implement high-resolution displays with leading programs like Windows, Lotus, WordPerfect, AutoCAD, and others. That software may differ in quality and effectiveness among board makers, but the hardware is all pretty much the same.

This is not the case with accelerators and coprocessed equipment. Different video processing chips, support chips, and ROM-based programming make each card different. Some designs are simply better than others. Therefore, when you consider boards of this type, be sure to consult *PC Magazine*, *Computer Shopper*, and similar magazines for the latest reviews.

PowerPoint

Get the Latest Drivers

The software driver you use with your video card can have a major impact on performance. That's why it is crucial to get the latest and greatest version. (It is not uncommon for a newer version to produce a 50 percent performance increase, compared to the immediately previous version.)

Since it is not uncommon for hardware and software firms to produce updated drivers months after a product ships, the drivers packed with your program or with your video board may not be the latest available. Make a note of the driver's version number, file size, and date, and contact the supplier to see if a new version has come out. (You may be able to download the software from the vendor's bulletin board or via CompuServe.)   *(continued)*

(Get the Latest Drivers continued)

Also, if you have a choice of using one of the generic drivers that come with Windows or other programs and a driver created by your video board maker, go with the product-specific video board program. If your equipment supports both 16-color and 256-color configurations, try both types of drivers. You may find that the 256-color driver is faster, even though it's moving around twice as many bytes of information. The most logical explanation for this is that the board maker spent more time developing and fine-tuning that driver.

Unsettled Standards

Most systems sold today come with VGA video equipment since VGA is clearly the current standard. The next bump up is *Super VGA*, but there is no agreement on exactly what that term means. VGA resolution is 640 horizontal pixels by 480 vertical pixels. Super VGA is at least 800 by 600, but the term is also applied to a resolution of 1,024 by 768.

In addition, there is IBM's 8514/A standard (introduced in 1987) and its XGA standard (introduced in 1990). Both offer a resolution of 1,024 by 768, which is two and a half times as crisp as VGA. In the world of Sun, DEC, and IBM engineering work stations, resolutions of 1,280 by 1,024 are not uncommon. If you've got about $1,000, you can buy a board for your PC with capabilities like that.

Yet VGA is still the current standard. That means that, even if you have enough money to buy the most powerful video card made and a huge 20-inch flat-screen monitor, you can't count on benefiting from your investment with every program you run. It may be that a given program will only operate in VGA mode. Eventually, some incredibly high-resolution standard will replace VGA. But no one knows what it will be just yet, which is why I advise sitting on your wallet for a while.

Local Bus Wars

Finally, if the lack of certainty over video resolution and display mode standards were not enough, there is now a new hardware approach to consider. The approach is called the *local bus*, and it is easy enough to explain.

Nothing appears on your screen without the services of a microprocessor. In the vast majority of systems in use today, the microprocessor at the heart of the machine handles the screen. As we've just seen, however, one can reduce or eliminate that burden by installing an accelerator or a video coprocessor board. At this writing, adding a microprocessor in this way produces the highest video performance.

The local bus approach throws things back to the system's main CPU but with two critical differences. First, the CPUs that a local bus architecture has in mind are the top-of-the-line chips available today, and the even more powerful chips that will follow them. These chips have the necessary muscle. Second, the local bus approach envisions a road-widening project that would replace the sixteen-lane highway that now connects the CPU to the video with a 32-bit wide overpass.

In most systems today, the CPU communicates with your video card over a 16-bit wide expansion bus that operates at a clock speed of a mere 8 MHz. The local bus approach, in contrast, directly connects the video hardware with the system's CPU via a 32-bit circuit that operates at the speed of the CPU. On a 33MHz machine, the local bus approach can improve video performance 400 percent over a plain frame buffer card, just from the clock speed increase.

The problem is that, at this writing, at least three local bus standards are in the air. One is based on the OPTi chip set, another is being promoted by VESA (Video Electronics Standards Association), and the third is being pushed by Intel. The Intel standard is called PCI (Peripheral Component Interconnect). The OPTi approach essentially involves the simple installation of a direct 32-bit connection between video and CPU. The VESA and Intel approaches include bus mastering and other specifications that seem similar to full-blown expansion buses like EISA and IBM's Micro Channel. Indeed, the best way to think of the Intel and VESA standards is as extensions of the ISA and EISA architectures. For, as envisioned, they will not only accommodate video equipment but include slots for other peripherals requiring high rates of data transfer. Peripherals like hard disks and CD-ROM drives.

Clearly change is afoot. Something is going to happen. The data and video demands of today's software make it inevitable. But right now, no one—not even industry leaders—knows exactly what form that change will take or what standard will emerge. That's why it's a good idea to wait until the fog clears before making a major video upgrade investment.

PART VII

PRINTING

What You Will Learn

You can plot, plan, and compose all you want, but none of your creations will be "real" until you print them out. As computer users, we tend to focus most of our time and attention on the system itself. But that's like getting all wrapped up in the pen and disregarding the paper. For lots of computer applications, printing out the results of your labor is the final step. And the job is not complete until that step has been taken.

It is printing, then, that we will look at in this part of the book. We will start with a brief outline of the leading technologies for getting images on paper. Then we'll look at ways to boost printer performance, save money on printer necessities, and make any printer easier and more convenient to use.

Computer printing is such a vast and vibrant topic that you are all but certain to find something in the following pages that will save you time or money or both.

SECTION
7-1

PRINTER BASICS

There is no better demonstration of human ingenuity than the many ways people have devised to make it easier, faster, and cheaper to get images and symbols onto a piece of paper. In Thomas Jefferson's bedroom at Monticello you will find a device for duplicating pen strokes on a second sheet of paper as the original document is being created.

In the 1970s, I worked in a mainframe shop that used massive IBM printers to pump out everything from payroll checks to pink slips. Those machines printed using a rapidly rotating chain that held several copies of every letter of the alphabet. When operating under a full head of steam, the printers were quite noisy. But the noise could be put to good use. Not only could you feed in a stack of punch cards to print out large pictures of Snoopy or Santa Claus, you could get the printers to play "We Wish You a Merry Christmas" and "God Bless America."

The printers we use today are much quieter and much more powerful. In the PC world, most printing is done using one of three technologies: dot-matrix, inkjet, and laser. There are pen plotters, thermal wax printers, and numerous other approaches as well, but none of them is in the mainstream. In this section, we'll look briefly at the three major technologies. This will put you in a good position to take advantage of the performance-boosting and money-saving tips presented in succeeding sections.

Three Technologies: Dot-Matrix, Inkjet, and Laser

Dot-matrix printers or "impact" printers operate by literally hammering ink from a ribbon onto paper, just as typewriters have always done. The printhead is rectangular and consists of a single vertical column of tiny wires or pins. The pins can be pushed forward or withdrawn. When a pin is in its forward position and the printhead is hit with a tiny hammer, the pin is forced into the ribbon, creating a dot of ink on the paper.

Characters are created in stages: the printhead pushes forward the pins needed to create the first part of the character; the hammer strikes; the printhead moves to the right and pushes a different combination of pins forward; the hammer strikes again; and so on, until the complete character has been formed. The smaller the dots, and the more of them, the finer the resolution of the characters. Although it is still possible to buy a 9-pin dot-matrix printer, its output is really not acceptable for anything but first drafts and internal business use. Today, 24-pin dot-matrix printers are the standard, and their output is really quite good.

Inkjet printers take a similar dot-based approach. However, instead of a hammer, pin, and ribbon arrangement, they literally spray droplets of ink on the page through tiny nozzles that correspond to the pins of a dot-matrix printhead. There may be as many as 50 or 64 nozzles, each of them about half the diameter of a human hair. The ink is forced into a nozzle by a heated wire, which lies at the bottom of an ink reservoir and then expands when current is applied. When the wire gets hot, a bubble is formed, and as the bubble grows, it enters the nozzle lying directly above it. In some models, a piezo-crystal that expands when current is applied to it is used to force a droplet of ink through the nozzle. The process repeats an astounding 3,600 times a second for each nozzle. Because the ink droplet dots are so tiny—25 of them are needed to create the dot of a lowercase letter *i*—the output can be nearly as crisp as that of a laser printer.

For their part, laser printers use essentially the same technology found in photocopiers. A laser beam is focused on a rotating drum that is coated with an organic photoconductor. The photoconductor develops a charge of static electricity wherever it is struck by the laser. Particles of toner, which carry an opposite charge, are attracted to those locations on the drum.

When a piece of ordinary paper is passed over an arrangement of corona wires in the machine, it too, becomes charged. When this paper is pressed against the drum, the particles of toner are transferred. Heat is then applied to permanently fuse the toner to the paper. (That's why, if you ever get toner on your hands or clothes, you should be sure to wash with cold water, not hot.)

As with the other two technologies, characters are made from matrices of dots. (A resolution of 300 dots per inch or *dpi* is the current standard.) But a laser beam is not constrained by the physical size of a printhead. Therefore, laser printers can create a nearly infinite range of type sizes and designs. It all depends on how you program the laser. That programming is usually referred to as a *font*. All laser printers come with the programming for several fonts in one of their ROM chips. You can add more fonts by plugging in a cartridge containing more ROMs or by copying special *soft font* files from your computer into your printer.

Dot-Matrix Considerations

The main advantage of dot-matrix printers is that they are acceptably fast when producing plain text. And they are cheap—cheap to buy and cheap to operate. They offer the ideal way to pump out a rough draft of a long report, though the print production time will be slowed considerably if the report contains one or more graphic images. Dot-matrix printers can produce marginally acceptable graphic images, but they take forever to do so.

Since they produce their images by impact, dot-matrix printers can be used with multipart forms. Wide-carriage models can produce large spreadsheets and other wide documents without effort. Today's models even offer bypass slots to let you feed in a sheet of letterhead or an envelope, regardless of the continuous forms loaded into the printer's pin-and-sprocket mechanism. Most of today's models also include one to three built-in fonts. Some, like Epson's LQ570 and LQ1070, include scalable fonts as well.

The right printer, driven by the right software, can produce output that ranges from acceptable to quite good. But there is not much one can do about the noise of an impact printer, and, in general, the better the output, the more time is required to produce it.

Inkjet Considerations

The spray of an inkjet printer is all but noiseless. The paper-handling mechanism makes more noise than the printing itself. But what most vendors won't tell you is that most inkjet printers require specially treated paper or paper with a high clay content for best results. When sprayed onto ordinary paper, inkjet ink tends to be absorbed, causing the image to become fuzzy and washed out.

With treated paper or impermeable transparency acetate sheets, inkjet results can be superb indeed. Moreover, the size of the dots made by an inkjet spray is easier to control than the dots made by dot-matrix machines.

That means you can achieve higher resolutions. Due to differences in pin size and ribbon texture, you can't always assume that a dot-matrix printer will deliver the number of dots per inch its manufacturer promises. With treated paper or transparency "foils," however, most inkjet printers live up to their billing of producing 300 dpi, the same resolution delivered by most laser printers.

The reliability problems that plagued inkjet printers in the past have largely been overcome by better design. It used to be that if you left an ink-jet printer idle over the weekend, you could return Monday morning to find a clogged printhead. Today, if a printer is idle for a short time, the ink-jet head is "parked." The head is moved to the maintenance station of the printer, the ink that remains in the jets is pumped out, and maintenance fluid is pumped into the jets to prevent clogging.

Laser Considerations

When you add everything up, the main things that dot-matrix and inkjet printers offer is acceptable output and flexibility at a low cost. They are ideal for a home user who will be producing text-based output strictly for his or her own consumption. Indeed, as we will see later, if you've got the time, there are programs that can make even a lowly 9-pin dot-matrix printer produce elaborate fonts and 24-pin letter-quality output.

But I'm tempted to say that real computer users use laser printers. The power, the flexibility, the speed, the quietness, and even the price make the choice of a laser printer a "no-brainer" for anyone but the hobbyist, the dabbler, or the home user. At this writing, about $500 buys a feature-filled laser printer (like the Okidata 400 or the Panasonic KXP-4410) that puts real printing power at your fingertips.

Laser printers can't do multipart forms, of course. Instead, they can be used to produce filled in forms (blanks, lines, shaded areas, and all) with as many copies as you want. Most offer a bypass for printing envelopes, and with special software like GRAB Plus, this is a snap. As for labels, the answer is Avery/Dennison's program LabelPro and a supply of labels on single sheets. If large spreadsheets are a problem, as they may be since most laser printers use 8.5-by-11-inch paper, you simply tell the printer to print in *landscape* (sideways) mode using compressed type.

Interestingly, speed and resolution are not really distinguishing factors. A four-page-per-minute laser printer generates text at the same rate as a 320-cps dot-matrix printer. (This assumes that the page is completely filled with text, 4,800 characters in 60 rows of 80 columns). Lasers and inkjets now easily achieve 300-dpi resolution, and even inexpensive 24-pin matrix engines are able to produce output suitable for correspondence without hesitation or reservation—though laser and inkjet printers are better than dot-matrix at producing solid blacks.

At the high end, however, lasers really begin to pull away from rival technologies, particularly when it comes to speed. Most laser printers today easily produce four pages per minute. That's pretty much the baseline. From there, print rates climb rapidly to dozens of pages per minute.

Print speeds for complex pages are generally limited by the electronic speed of the printer's raster image processor (RIP). This is the chip that converts print commands to a raster (the electronic equivalent of the on-paper image in memory). RIP speeds are determined by the power of the microprocessor doing the work, the efficiency of the software driving the RIP, and the resolution of the output. Higher resolutions require more data and thus a longer processing time.

Faster laser printers use RISC (Reduced Instruction Set Computing) processors, such as the AMD 29000. These are often more powerful than the computer's main CPU. And, as with CPUs, the faster a given RIP chip operates (the higher the megahertz), the quicker it can compute and produce the instructions needed to drive the laser.

More Dots Per Inch

In the last few years, laser printer makers have begun to differentiate their products on output quality and resolution. As a result, there are now alternatives to the standard 300 dpi of resolution. For example, Hewlett-Packard's "resolution enhancement technology," introduced with its LaserJet III, makes ordinary 300-dpi resolution look sharper by varying dot size to reduce the jaggedness of diagonal edges.

Microtek's TrueLaser uses another approach—improving output quality by using true grayscale capabilities—to increase the apparent resolution of continuous-tone images. Instead of dithering—the use of a pattern of dots to simulate gray tones—gray scaling makes the smallest picture element dot-size rather than matrix-size. (Most dithering algorithms use a matrix of 4-by-4 or 6-by-6 dots as their pixel, reducing resolution to 75 or 50 dpi.) And then there's the Lexmark/IBM LaserPrinter 10, which can deliver a true 600-dpi resolution when suitably equipped. Yet even that is not the limit. LaserMaster offers custom RIPs that push ordinary lasers to resolutions as high as 1,200 dpi. (Typeset quality, by comparison, is around 2,500 dots per inch.)

PostScript and PCL

One cannot discuss laser printer technology without also discussing the two languages software packages use to talk to laser printers. These are PCL or Printer Control Language, developed by Hewlett-Packard for its LaserJet printers, and PostScript, the page description language developed by Adobe Systems.

PostScript is the more powerful of the two. Its many features make it most suitable for major-league desktop publishing applications, like generating professional-quality newsletters or preparing a mechanical for a brochure. Probably the most important of all PostScript features, however, is its use of *scalable fonts*.

With non-PostScript printers, if you want to use 14-point Times Roman for a subhead and 10-point Times Roman for your body text, a complete set of bitmapped characters for each of those two sizes must be given to the printer. The PostScript approach, in contrast, is to supply the printer with one set of generalized instructions for creating the Times Roman typeface. From this, the printer can create a Times Roman font of almost any size.

In addition, the PostScript approach is used across a wide range of equipment, making it possible for you to create a PostScript file on your PC and pass it to a print shop's typesetter. The same commands that operate a 300-dpi laser printer tell a high-resolution PostScript typesetting machine to create a page with 2,500-dpi resolution. That means you can create a document, preview it on your laser printer, and then give the file to a professional printer for typeset-quality output.

At this writing, there are two versions of PostScript—the original and PostScript 2, introduced in June, 1990. PostScript 2 adds more commands and standardized color functions. It also promises higher-speed printouts through improvements in file and memory handling.

In contrast to PostScript's multiplatform, multiresolution page description approach, HP's PCL is designed primarily to let PC software control an HP-compatible laser printer. The instructions it contains are preset for 300-dpi resolution on most printers. Since HP seems to expand and improve PCL with each major new model it produces, several versions exist. For example, the LaserJet III printers introduced in early 1990 use PCL 5. PCL 5 approaches PostScript in power by providing scalable fonts that can be mixed and rotated on the page. But at this writing, PCL 5 is so new and complex that few printer manufacturers besides HP use it.

The most widespread PCL version is PCL 4, popularized by the LaserJet II line. This version uses bitmapped fonts, so, as discussed a moment ago, you need a different font for each type size and for each typeface. That means either downloading soft font files to the printer or installing a cartridge containing a ROM with the fonts you need. (The original HP LaserJet used PCL 3, a version that can handle cartridge-based fonts but not downloaded soft fonts.)

Fortunately, if you have a PCL printer and you need to add PostScript capabilities, there are a number of options. We'll consider them in Section 2. Incidentally, the TrueType fonts included in Windows 3.1 are scalable and device-independent, like PostScript. Microsoft's TrueType FontPack adds an additional 44 scalable screen and printer fonts to those supplied with Windows. The company reportedly sells nearly as many units of the FontPack as it does of Windows itself.

Color Printing

I should also say a word or two about color printing. Traditionally, there have been two main ways to produce color printing from a PC. The easiest and least expensive is a special dot-matrix printer equipped with a multicolored ribbon. The most elaborate is a plotter equipped with a row of different colored pens that it can grab and use on command. In the past few years, inkjet printers have also been given color capabilities with multiple printheads and ink reservoirs.

A plotter is great at using color to highlight sub-assemblies in engineering plans and drawings. A dot-matrix printer does a fair, if laborious, job of producing color graphics. And inkjets do a decent job when printing on transparencies or treated paper. As always, the problem is a lack of crispness caused by the ink leaching into the page.

That's why high-end color printers use wax-based inks that are not absorbed by paper. Two technologies are currently in vogue: thermal transfer and solid-ink inkjets. The thermal transfer technique melts the wax-based ink from a page-wide ribbon called the transfer sheet. Solid-ink inkjets melt and then spray wax-based ink at paper. Once there, the wax quickly hardens, forcing the ink to stay put. Both technologies create 300-dpi images of excellent color saturation and uniformity. Most can print seven colors directly and thousands or millions more through dithering.

Color printing clearly has a place. But it isn't likely to really take off until someone invents a truly low-cost color photocopier. Few of us would want to face creating 50 copies of a report, the color pages of which had to be individually produced and tipped in by hand.

PowerPoint

Printer Term Primer

Every technology brings its own terminology. You may thus find the following brief definitions helpful when dealing with today's printing technology. The terms are not arranged alphabetically because some of the definitions build on those that preceded them.

Typeface   The specific design of a set of characters. Examples include Courier, Helvetica, Times Roman, Letter Gothic, and so on. Includes specifications for the degree of slant and thickness of line (stroke weight).

Type style   The degree of slant in a given typeface. Typically, upright (normal) or italic (slanted).

Font   A set of characters of a particular typeface, type style, stroke weight, and *size*. For example: 12-point Helvetica, 10-point Times Roman italic, 12-point Letter Gothic bold.

Portrait orientation   Printing in the normal way a letter-sized sheet is printed, with the 8.5-inch side considered the top of the page.

Landscape orientation   Sideways printing, in which the 11-inch side of a letter-sized sheet is considered the top.

Vector graphics   Graphic images that are stored on disk as a series of equations, one equation for each line. Squares and rectangles thus consist of four vectors. Circles and curves are stored by turning them into scores or hundreds of tiny straight lines. Vector graphic image files are relatively small, and, like PostScript fonts, they can be scaled up or down by using different variables in the vector equations.

Raster graphics   A raster is a pattern of scanning lines or rows of dots used to create an image on a TV or CRT. It is the dots, or dot-combinations (pixels), that are the key. In a raster graphic image file, every dot on the screen—even those used for the background—is, in effect, "described." Because most computer screens are raster displays (made up of dots), vector graphic images must be *rasterized* before they can be displayed. Paint programs, scanners, and most other visual input devices produce raster graphic images. Because they must contain so much information, raster graphic files tend to be rather large.   *(continued)*

(Printer Term Primer continued)

Halftone   The printed reproduction of a photograph or other illus-
tration. A snapshot or other actual photograph is like a painting. Colors or shade of gray blend and flow continuously as if they had been
applied with a brush. Printing such images could be a problem had
not someone invented *halftoning* in the 1850s. Halftoning atomizes
a photo into tiny dots. The process involves photographing the target
image through a fine-meshed screen.

The holes in the screen mesh are all the same size. Thus, the dots that
are produced on the negative are evenly spaced, measuring the same
distance from center to center. But the size of the dots varies with the
light and dark areas of the target photo. Areas that are all white in the
target show up as all-white dots. Indeed, depending on the fineness
of the screen, the "dots" in that part of the negative will not be distin-
guishable as dots. Since the human eye blends the dots together, the
printed results imitate the continuous tone original.

Dithering   This is the general process used by computer printers for
emulating halftone images. The key point is that the majority of
printers can produce dots of only one size. Thus, to emulate the vari-
able-sized dots of true halftoning, dithering uses what might be
called the "pixel approach" of grouping dots together in uniformly
sized areas called "spots."

By varying the number and location of black dots within each spot,
dithering can create the illusion of varying shades of gray on your
printer. Dithering can also be used to create a similar illusion on your
screen or color printer. By adjusting the number of white dots to red
dots in a spot, for example, dithering can produce shades ranging
from red to pink. Dithering algorithms in common use include
Bayer, Floyd-Steinberg, Burkes, and Stucki.

SECTION
7-2

PERFORMANCE
BOOSTERS

As with any piece of computer hardware, there are often a number of things you can do to tweak or otherwise improve the performance, ease of use, and output quality of your printer. We'll start with dot-matrix and inkjet equipment, then look at lasers, and conclude with a discussion of the various things you can do in DOS to improve printer performance.

Dot-Matrix, Fonts, and Letter Quality

According to industry reports, sales of 9-pin dot-matrix printers peaked in 1989 and have been either flat or declining ever since. It is clearly a dying category. Sales of 24-pin printers, on the other hand, have been fairly brisk, with unit shipments up nearly nine percent in 1991 and projected annual increases of between six and seven percent from that point on. For students, home users, and very small businesses, a 24-pin dot-matrix printer offers an admirable combination of speed, print quality, and price.

Still, if you have or can only afford a 9-pin machine, you will be pleased to know that there are a number of powerful options open to you, once you have the right software.

A program like Mark Harris's LQ (Letter Quality), for example, can make a 9-pin printer produce 24-pin output. Only eight pins are used when printing characters, so this program simply makes three passes when printing each line, shifting the paper ever so slightly each time. Printouts take three times as long, but the quality is exceptional. LQ includes 24 fonts (Gothic, Greek, Helvetica, Hollow, Script, etc.), plus a font-editing program to let you create your own fonts or special characters.

A program called ImagePrint takes things even further. Designed for use with either 9- or 24-pin printers, ImagePrint lets you print an IBM PC's extended character set in letter quality, including all standard text characters, mathematical symbols, national characters, and graphics characters. It provides all of the standard printer character attributes (10 or 12 cpi, bold, underline, italic, double width, and compressed), plus half-height characters for true superscript and subscript.

Fifteen standard text fonts are provided, including Cubic, Orator, OCR-A and OCR-B, outline, and block. And there are ten headline fonts ranging in size from 18 to 34 points (72 points equal one inch). There are also five ImagePrint print modes, including draft, low-quality three-pass, and high-quality six-pass for extra-dark printing. You can even preview your printout on the screen.

The third program you should know about is called OnSide. Like LQ and ImagePrint, OnSide is shareware. If your printer does not have the ability to print text sideways, then a program like OnSide can do it for you. It works its magic by converting any kind of text—whether it is a large spreadsheet or a plain report—into a bitmapped graphics image. As with LQ and ImagePrint, this takes a little time, but the results are usually worth the wait.

Inkjet Tips

Probably the most important tip regarding most inkjet printers is to *never* turn the printer off when it is in the middle of a print job. As noted earlier, many inkjet printers today have a self-cleaning procedure that goes into effect whenever the print head is idle for a short while. When the printer is turned off, it gives the printhead one last going over and then seals the nozzle area. Should you power down in the midst of a printing operation, the printhead may not be cleared of ink and sealed.

That can cause real problems the next time you turn the printer on and tell it to print. Should you find that a problem of this sort has occurred, however, consult your manual to see how to initiate the cleaning cycle. (It may be as simple as holding down the Shift key on the control panel and pressing the Cleaning key.) Repeat the cleaning cycle five or six times to clear any clogged nozzles.

If your printer does not have a clean or purge cycle, you might try removing the printhead and using a straightened paper clip to gently push on the ink bladder inside the cartridge. This forces some ink out onto the face of the printhead and, hopefully, clears the nozzles. If that doesn't work, use a Q-Tip dampened in alcohol to carefully clean the face of the printhead and the electrical contacts on the face. If you still have no luck, you will have to replace the printhead. Note that if your unit prints at 300 dpi, like the DeskJet 500, you should *not* touch the face of the printhead. The nozzles on a 300-dpi inkjet printer are quite small and quite fragile.

As discussed previously, inkjet printers produce the best quality output on transparencies or on paper with a high clay content. Standard office copier paper often qualifies, but text on cotton bond stationery often comes out fuzzy. The ink sticks to all the fibers it hits, and on bond paper the fibers aren't as flat as they are on photocopier paper.

Bond paper varies, so there's no guarantee, but one technique you might try for an important letter or document is rubbing the page lightly with a cotton cloth before printing. That loosens and removes stray fibers and, with luck, produces a much sharper printout.

Boosting Laser Printer Performance

Accelerator boards are available for those who need exceptionally fast graphics output from their laser printers. Such boards typically include a microprocessor like Intel's i960 RISC chip and as much as 2MB of extra printer memory. With list prices close to $1,000 (more than most people have paid for their entire printer), they are clearly a specialty item.

As an example, consider Output Technology Corporation's BetterYet IV, an emulation/accelerator package for Hewlett-Packard LaserJet II and III printers. BetterYet IV lists for $1,000 and offers four enhancements: PCL 5, PostScript, automatic switching between the two emulations for users operating in a LAN environment, and enhanced resolution of 600 by 300 dots per inch in both emulations. The company claims that the product speeds up throughput six to twenty times in both emulations.

BetterYet IV includes a board that plugs into the LaserJet's optional I/O port, plus a cartridge that fits into the machine's left font slot. This leaves the printer's right font slot open for existing or additional font cards. The BetterYet board includes 2MB of additional memory with SIMM sockets for up to 6MB more. The company does not sell SIMM modules, but they are easily obtainable from mail-order houses. You will need a total of 3MB on the BetterYet IV board for enhanced resolution under PostScript emulation. A call to the company confirmed that whatever other memory you have in your printer does not count toward this BetterYet total. For more information, contact Output Technology at (800) 468-8788.

Adding More Printer Memory

Probably the most popular enhancement for HP and compatible printers is adding more memory. If your printer came with half a megabyte (512K) of memory, adding an additional 1MB (for a total of 1.5MB) should be enough to print a full page of graphics. But there is really no point in stopping there. If you plan to add a PostScript capability, you will need a total of 2.5MB of printer memory. If you can afford to take your printer to 4.5MB, so much the better.

Two megs of memory, at this writing, will cost you between $140 and $245, depending on your printer model. (Printer memory is a bit more expensive than system memory because the kit includes a circuit board in addition to memory chips.) If your upgrade plans stop with adding more memory, you might request a quote from a company like Chips For Less, Inc., in Dallas, Texas, at (214) 416-0508. But you may want to wait until you have considered a PostScript upgrade as well.

PowerPoint

Why a Meg?

At a laser printer's highest resolution of 300 by 300 dots per inch, printing a single sheet requires 787,500 bytes of data. This assumes an active image area measuring 7 by 10 inches (half-inch margins top and bottom and three-quarter inch margins on the sides). And that 788K or so doesn't include memory for storing fonts and other system overhead. That's why you need at least one megabyte of printer memory to print full-page graphics.

Font Flexibility

More memory will improve your printer's performance, regardless of whether you use PCL or PostScript. This is especially the case if you use desktop publishing, paint programs, and other graphics-intensive applications. If you use your printer solely to produce text, the impact of more memory is far less noticeable. It's still important, though, as we will see later when we discuss print spoolers and print buffers.

If you even dabble in desktop publishing, adding PostScript capabilities to your HP or HP-compatible printer is very nearly essential. In our shop, for example, we use Ventura Publisher a great deal. It's a wonderful program, but it is infinitely easier to use when you are not limited to just a few sizes of a particular typeface.

That limit can be partially overcome by buying an add-on font cartridge containing a good selection of typefaces and fonts. But if what you really need for your document is a 6-point Times Roman and the smallest font in the cartridge is 10 points, you're out of luck.

More flexibility can be gained by purchasing downloadable soft fonts. But I've found there are at least three drawbacks to that approach. First is the extra expense. Font packages typically cost less than $100, but you often must buy several packages to get everything you need to prepare different kinds of documents.

Second is the tremendous amount of hard disk space downloadable fonts occupy. Though the industry seems to be moving to "fonts on the fly," most soft font packages today require you to create and store a file for each font you want. You can specify just about any point size you please for each typeface, but the program must perform a one-time creation process to prepare a file for that font. If you opt for a large number of typefaces and sizes, your computer may have to run all night to get the job done.

Finally, there is the additional time required to download the fonts to the printer before printing can begin. Ventura Publisher, for example, gives you a choice. You can either copy the fonts to the printer before you boot Ventura, or you can have the program itself do so each time you run it. Either way, there's an extra step and a delay.

With PostScript's scalable font approach, once you have selected the typeface in Ventura or some other program, you can specify almost any font size you want. The drawback here, though, is that since the fonts are made up on demand, PostScript printing can be very slow. That's why companies like Output Technologies offer accelerator/emulation boards capable of speeding up the process six to twenty times.

But at $1,000, packages like that are expensive. If you are willing to be patient with your printouts, you can add PostScript capabilities to your HP or compatible laser printer for as little as $300.

PowerPoint

Font Frenzy

The computer font industry has found renewed energy and is going great guns with new approaches and new products. The engine powering it all appears to be Microsoft's Windows 3.1 and the company's announced strategy to eventually bring everyone into the Windows camp. In a word, Windows has made it clear that fonts matter.

To font companies, this means that virtually every new PC user from now on will be introduced to fonts right from the start, since he or she will almost certainly find Windows pre-installed on the new machine. Longtime PC users are likely to be pulled into the Windows vortex as well, if only to be able to take advantage of the hottest new applications.

For the first time, the market for font-related products in the PC world will not be limited to desktop publishing experts and dabblers. Over the next few years, apparently, it will expand to include every PC user on the planet.

Personally, I'm not sure how many fonts I really *need* to prepare business letters, notes, magazine articles, and book manuscripts. They are certainly fun to play with, but one can't help wondering when the initial thrill of being your own compositor will wear off.

Companies like Adobe Systems and Bitstream Corporation will try to make sure that doesn't happen. Bitstream's MakeUp and FaceLift for Windows and Adobe's ATM (Adobe Type Manager) offer a tremendous amount of power and control over both screen and downloadable printer fonts. Adobe will even sell you a CD-ROM with all 1,500 fonts in the Adobe Type Library for $100. The catch is that only thirteen fonts are accessible right out of the box. To gain access to others, either on a package or individual font basis, you must contact Adobe to buy the necessary password. The product is called Type On Call.

Adobe has also announced plans to upgrade PostScript to include the ability to emulate Hewlett-Packard's PCL 5 printer control language. This will allow PostScript printers to print any PC or Macintosh document, regardless of whether it was designed for PostScript or PCL 5.   *(continued)*

> *(Font Frenzy continued)*
>
> In short, a great deal is going on in the font field, so you will want to proceed with caution. For more information, contact Bitstream at (800) 522-3668 or (617) 497-6222. Contact Adobe at (800) 833-6687 or (415) 961-4400.

How to Add PostScript

There are three main ways to add PostScript to a LaserJet or compatible printer. You can plug a cartridge into one of the printer's available front slots. You can use software that translates PostScript fonts into the LaserJet's native language, stores them on disk, and then copies them to the printer. Or you can throw your printer into overdrive by adding a special board to your computer and connecting it by cable to the printer's optional interface socket. The LaserJet Series II, IID, III, and IIID can use all three methods. The IIP, however, can't use the optional interface method. All three methods work with any application that has a PostScript software driver.

PostScript Cartridges

The simplest option is the plug-in cartridge. Turn the printer off; unplug all other cartridges; plug in the PostScript cartridge; and turn the printer on. Voilà! Instant PostScript printer.

The cost of the upgrade depends on your printer model and how much memory it currently contains. You may need to add between one and two megabytes of printer memory in the process. The cost also depends on whether you opt for Adobe PostScript or a clone. HP offers an Adobe-licensed cartridge for LaserJet models IIP, IID, III, or IIID at a list price of $695. If you have a Series II or compatible, consider the PostScript cartridge manufactured by Adobe itself. List price: $495.

Note that using a PostScript cartridge does not bar you from also using downloadable Adobe or PostScript-compatible soft fonts. For example, I use Pacific Data Products' PacificPage cartridge (street price: $300) on my LaserJet II. The cartridge includes the standard 35 PostScript fonts ranging from Swiss (Helvetica) to Century Schoolbook and Zapf Dingbats. But it also works with Adobe Type 1 soft fonts and with Bitstream's Fontware Typeface fonts. Indeed, all current PostScript cartridges, whether genuine Adobe PostScript or clones, can print Adobe's Type 1 soft fonts, although with differing levels of quality. For information on PacificPage, contact Pacific Data Products at (619) 552-0880.

For utilities that make using a PostScript printer easier, see the disk Printer 1, discussed in Part 9. Among other things, this disk contains utilities that let you copy a file directly to a PostScript printer from DOS or use your Print Screen key, two activities that are normally forbidden when you use a PostScript printer or put your printer into PostScript mode.

PowerPoint

PostScript and Other Screen Fonts

It's common sense, but it is worth repeating: Screen fonts and printer fonts are two different animals. For true WYSIWYG (What You See Is What You Get, pronounced "wissy-wig"), the screen and the printout should look pretty much the same, regardless of the fonts you have selected. But you need separate screen font files to make this possible. Otherwise an application like Ventura Publisher builds the screen from its own limited supply of fonts in an attempt to approximate your selection.

Fortunately, Pacific Data Products, Hewlett-Packard, and other cartridge font makers can usually supply you with the screen fonts you need. The cost is usually just enough to cover distribution expenses. Your cartridge vendor may even make the necessary screen fonts available to you online via a bulletin board or a system like CompuServe. In any case, before you buy a font cartridge of any sort, be sure to inquire about the availability of screen fonts so what you see really will be what you get when you print out your creation.

PostScript in Software

PostScript translation programs are available that convert instructions in PostScript files into PCL bit-image commands. The files are created and stored to disk. Then they are copied to your PCL printer. Their main advantage is that they turn any printer—even an old 9-pin dot-matrix machine—into a PostScript printer.

These programs are essentially PostScript language interpreters that run on your computer—using your main CPU—instead of in your laser printer. They thus shift the image-processing work from your printer to your PC. Most such programs are not licensed by Adobe Systems and are not true PostScript interpreters. Surprisingly, they not only work like PostScript but may generate pages faster. How much faster depends on the speed of your CPU. Generally, to match cartridge-based speeds, your CPU should be at least a 33MHz 386.

The leading PostScript software emulation programs include:

- UltraScript PC from QMS, (800) 631-2692. List price is $195 for the 25-font package; $445 for a version with 47 fonts.

- PreScript from Pan Overseas Computer, (201) 808-1900. List price is $195 with 28 fonts; $395 with 50 fonts.

- Freedom of Press from Custom Applications, (800) 873-4367. List price is $495 with 35 fonts.

- GoScript Select from LaserGo, (619) 450-4600. List price is $99 with thirteen fonts. GoScript Plus, with 35 fonts, lists for $299.

PostScript via Optional Interface

Minneapolis-based LaserMaster Technologies, Inc., is a longtime maker of high-performance laser printers (1,000 dpi!) and add-on boards. The company was one of the first to exploit the "slot for optional interface" (as the HP *User's Manual* puts it) found at the back of most LaserJet and compatible printers.

You will want to consult your own printer manual for the slot's specific location, but on my LaserJet II, it is at the back of the machine, right next to the serial interface port. The panel covering the slot is labeled "Optional I/O," and when it is removed, you can plug in a card that will connect your printer's laser engine directly to a special board in your PC. The Laser-Master package thus includes a board for your printer, a board for your PC, and cabling and software to tie everything together. The list price for the LaserMaster WinJet 300 package is $495, less than or equal to the list prices of most PostScript cartridges.

The main advantage of this approach is speed. If your printer is connected via a serial port, the top data transfer rate is 9,600 bits per second, so moving a 1MB bit image across that line takes about sixteen minutes. A parallel connection is about ten times faster, but moving a megabyte of data still takes nearly two minutes. A LaserMaster WinJet connection, however, is scores of times faster than a parallel port and hundreds of times faster than a serial connection. According to the company, it transfers up to 1.2MB per second.

LaserMaster calls this technology LPV, short for Line Printer Video. This is a reference to the fact that LPV is designed to drive a laser printer at the video data transfer rates. The company is seeking a patent on the LPV technology. The WinJet 300 package uses LPV technology and includes an enhanced version of Microsoft TrueImage, as well as PostScript language emulation. It is compatible with Hewlett-Packard Laserjet models II, IID, III, and IIID.

A product called WinJet 800 includes every thing WinJet 300 includes, plus 50 fonts, even faster printing, and the ability to turn your 300-dpi printer into an 800-dpi machine. LaserMaster's WinJet 800 lists for $795. (The company's WinJet 800 printer lists for $2,195.) Both WinJet 300 and WinJet 800 require at least a 386-based computer equipped with 8MB of memory and VGA video equipment. The company's thought is that users are better off adding more main system RAM than adding special printer memory, and that it is better to do your data processing with the main system CPU than with the printer's built-in microprocessor.

For more information, contact LaserMaster at (612) 944-9330.

PowerPoint

Paint It Black

The crispness and saturation of a graphic image printed on an HP or compatible laser is perfectly fine most of the time for most applications. But when you're ready to print your final version, possibly to paste into a mechanical or to use as a photocopying master, you will get better results if you refresh the toner development system first by printing four or five all-black pages.

Use your word processor to create an ASCII file called BLACK.TXT containing the lines of PCL code shown below. The "ESC" here stands for the actual escape character, an ASCII 27. It shows up on most screens as a little left-pointing arrow and can be generated by holding down your Alt key and entering 27 on your numeric keypad. All of the circles are zeros, not capital letter *O*s. And the case of the letter matters, so don't enter a capital *C* where you see a lowercase *c* below. The comments in the second column should not be entered. They are, for your information:

ESC &l0E	Sets top margin to 0.
ESC &l0L	Sets left margin to 0.
ESC *p0x0Y	Positions cursor at column 0, row 0.
ESC *c2400A	Horizontal rectangle size.
ESC *c3300B	Vertical rectangle size.
ESC *c0P	Fill rectangular area with solid fill.
ESC E	Reset printer.

When you have created the file, save it to disk and leave your word processor. Make sure your printer is in its native PCL mode (not PostScript). Then key in `copy black.txt prn`. If the file has been created correctly, you will get a solid black page with about one inch of white space at its top.

Enter the command again to print out a second black page and compare it with the first. The coverage should be even better. After four or five all-black pages, your system should be refreshed and ready to print that crucial graphic image.

SECTION

7-3

MONEY SAVERS

Years ago a colleague of mine in the corporate communications business created a film for Citibank, N.A., the nation's biggest bank, about the "office of the future." My friend did a great job. The production values were superb, and the film clearly said what the client wanted it to say. The only trouble is that, with more than a decade's hindsight, it is now clear that its projections of a paperless office were rather wide of the mark.

Today we go through more paper in our offices than ever. And each page we print not only consumes paper, it consumes ink and ribbons and laser toner as well. There are a number of ways to reduce these expenses, and that is what we will look at here.

For example, the quickest way for anyone to cut down on the amount of toner or ink used is to experiment with the darkness setting of the printer. Don't accept the default setting of your laser printer, for example. Go to your user manual and investigate how to reduce the setting below the factory default. Most laser printers have a darkness dial, accessible when you pop their tops to replace a cartridge. If you have a dot-matrix printer, you may be able to control how hard the hammer hits the printhead. Then experiment by printing the kind of material you normally print until you find the lightest acceptable setting.

As for paper, it is not easy to print on both sides of the Z-fold continuous forms used with dot-matrix printers, but nothing could be easier with a laser printer or an inkjet. When you print a test page with a desktop publishing package, save it. If you put these test pages in a neat pile near the printer, you can easily flip the pages over and load them into the paper cassette the next time you print a test page.

PowerPoint

Reset Instead of Form Feed

Here's a tip that can save you literally hundreds of pages of paper a year. Yet it is so simple, you'll wonder why you didn't think of it. (At least that's how I felt when it was first told to me.)

When you copy a file to the printer, the very last part of the file fails to print automatically because the number of lines remaining do not add up to a full page. The LaserJet's Form Feed light comes on, and you must take the printer offline and press that button to get the beast to disgorge the last bit of the printout. The Form Feed light comes on as well whenever you print the screen with your Print Screen or Shift+Print Screen keys. As we will see later, there's a simple free utility you can install to eliminate this problem when it is an inconvenience.

But sometimes, it's a mistake, as when you hit your Print Screen key by accident or otherwise send something to the printer you would just as soon went away. That's where the paper savings come in. If you do not want to spend a sheet of paper printing whatever is in the printer when the Form Feed light comes on, take the printer offline by pressing the Online button. Then simply press the Continue/Reset key until the word *Reset* appears in the LED window. The printer will come back online automatically, and whatever it was that was demanding a form feed will be flushed from the printer's memory.

PowerPoint

Scanners for Hire

Here's yet another way to save money on printer-related equipment: don't buy it. Specifically, if your desire for a top-quality, $1,500 flatbed scanner is strong but your wallet is weak, let someone else do your scanning for you. The inexpensive little hand-held scanners you see are fine for small jobs. But they are not up to the task of, say, scanning a design you want to use to desktop publish your own letterhead, business cards, forms, and so on. For serious work, you need serious equipment.

That's what scanner service bureaus provide. Typical charges are about $20 for a plain scan and $50 an hour for any touch-up work you may require. The result is a graphics file in whatever format you need for your word processing or desktop publishing program. Some firms will also create line art by hand for an extra fee.

Here are three companies you may want to contact to get a better idea of the services that are available:

AlphaGraphics (602) 293-9200

Genigraphics (315) 451-6600

Micrografx (214) 234-1769

Re-inking and Refilling

As a longtime business computer user, I can tell you that there is absolutely no need to replace your dot-matrix ribbon, your inkjet ink cartridge, or your laser's toner cartridge when printouts start to get faint. On occasion, time is of the essence, and we all must do whatever it takes to meet a FedEx deadline or complete a crucial project. But day in and day out, you can literally save hundreds of dollars by recycling your printer's ink-related supplies.

Re-inking Dot-Matrix Ribbons

In a pinch, you can rejuvenate the nylon ribbon on a dot-matrix printer by giving it a spritz of WD-40, the general-purpose lubricant you will find in any hardware store. This is certainly one of the oldest power user tips in computer history. I can tell you that it works, for I have done it numerous times. But it is messy, and the results are not instantaneous.

It is also not without a small element of risk, since to apply the WD-40, you must pry off the top of the ribbon cartridge. You will find that the inner mechanism is quite simple, but there is always the possibility that either the ribbon coils will spill all over the floor or that you will not be able to get the top back on without breaking something.

Spread a blanket of newspapers, and pop the top of the cartridge, being careful not to force anything. Use a full fan pattern when applying the WD-40, not the little red tube that fits into the sprayer. The main trick is to avoid applying too much lubricant. If you do, the WD-40 will pool in the cartridge and probably end up on your printout as a series of black splotches.

Reinstall the top of the cartridge and set it aside for a day or two to allow the capillary action of the nylon ribbon to absorb and distribute the WD-40. When you put the ribbon back into the printer, print a few test pages and examine their quality before deciding to trust the ribbon for real work.

Computer Friends Re-inker

A much better solution is to buy a ribbon re-inking machine of the sort sold by Computer Friends, Inc. The cost varies with the specific ribbon, but in general, you can expect to pay about $80. The ribbon snaps into place on a platform and the ribbon is threaded around the ink rollers. A small motor pulls the ribbon through the cartridge and around the rollers at a rate of one yard per minute.

List prices of computer ribbons vary widely, starting at around $3.25 and ranging upward to around $30 or more apiece. Thus, the payback period on a re-inker varies. The key point is that a nylon ribbon can be re-inked many, many times before the fabric itself begins to deteriorate. And the cost for each inking is usually about five to ten cents' worth of ink.

Based in Portland, Oregon, Computer Friends, Inc., can produce a re-inker for virtually any conceivable size or type of ribbon cartridge. The company also has professional and industrial models available, starting at $114. For more information, call (800) 547-3303 or (503) 626-2291.

PowerPoint

Default to Draft

One quick and easy way to prolong the life of your computer ribbon is to make sure that your machine is set by default to print in "draft mode." (See your printer manual for details.) Because draft mode puts fewer dots on the page, it uses less ink and takes less of a toll on your ribbon. You can always switch to letter-quality or near-letter-quality mode when necessary.

Refilling Inkjet Cartridges

Computer Friends and other firms let you work similar financial magic on inkjet printers. Black ink cartridges for the HP DeskJet, for example, list for about $10 each. But with the Computer Friends JetMaster cartridge recharging system, you can cut that cost to about $1.55 a refill.

The JetMaster ranges in price from $25 to $50, depending on your printer model and whether you want colors as well as plain black. It contains inks, a precisely graduated ink syringe dispenser, and an adapter to re-ink both black and three-color cartridges. The inks come in black, red, blue, orange, yellow, purple, brown, and green, in a variety of kits. Inks now available include waterproof and standard inks, both of which are guaranteed to meet or exceed original equipment manufacturer specifications. There is also a special bold black ink for really impressive printouts.

Recharging Laser Cartridges

The list price for an HP toner cartridge is an astounding $125 for LaserJet II models. I say "astounding" because the mail-order price is closer to $80. That's better, but it is still a lot of money. Fortunately, you can reduce that cost to about $40, and do the environment a good turn as well, by recharging spent cartridges.

This is not something you want to do yourself. But a growing number of companies can do it for you. (Please see Figure 7-2-1 for a list of possibilities.) Several years ago, you had to be careful to avoid companies using a "drill and fill" technique, in which a hole was drilled into the plastic cartridge and toner simply poured in. The plastic shavings from the drilling ended up inside the toner reservoir and eventually destroyed the drum.

In contrast, most companies today test the cartridge and then completely disassemble it, clean it, check the drum, and fill it with toner. Then they seal it in a light-proof bag, replace the felt on the fuser roller wand, pack everything up in the original box, and send it back to you. The best companies offer a 100 percent guarantee. Most will also either buy your spent HP cartridges for $5 to $7 outright or give you an equivalent credit.

Since many recharging companies put in lots of toner, you may find that your recharged cartridges last longer than the ones you buy at a store. Some firms offer extra-black toner for use when printing graphics. And colored toner (dark blue or brown), as well as magnetic ink toner for magnetic ink character recognition may also be available.

Of course, electromechanical equipment does eventually wear out. Depending on the model of printer you use, you may be able to recharge a cartridge anywhere from one to ten times before the photo-sensitive drum begins to show signs of wear. That's still a good deal, but there's an even better one available.

The best deal of all, in my opinion, is the Super Cartridge. This unit contains an extra-tough drum and is specifically designed to be recharged. The firm I've been using for the past few years, The Laser Group, Inc., sells the Super Cartridge for $70, charged and ready. When you return the cartridge for refilling, the cost is $35.

Best of all, the Super Cartridge carries a lifetime guarantee that includes coverage of any costs to repair your printer due to a Super Cartridge malfunction. By my rough calculations, I have already easily saved over $500 using the Super Cartridge, compared to the cost of buying a new cartridge each time, even at a mail-order discount. For more information, you can reach The Laser Group at (800) 527-3712.

Incidentally, using remanufactured toner cartridges will *not* void your printer's warranty. Both Hewlett-Packard and Canon, the company that makes most laser printer engines, have officially announced this fact. As a consumer, you cannot be forced to buy their cartridges. If anyone tells you anything different, contact your printer maker directly.

Recharging Tips

Whether you opt for the Super Cartridge or choose to recharge your spent HP cartridges, there are one or two things you should know. First, when your print quality begins to deteriorate, open the printer, remove the cartridge, and give it a firm shake in all four directions. This loosens up and redistributes the remaining toner and can result in the *Toner Low* message disappearing from the printer's LED screen for a while.

Second, *save* your fuser roller wands. The felt strip they hold will be replaced by the toner recharging company as part of the process. If you do not send back your dirty wand, you may be charged a dollar or so for a replacement.

Third, *save* all of your original cartridge packing materials, including the light-proof bag. You will need them to send the cartridge to the recharger when it is empty. It is very important not to leave a cartridge in direct light. Usually the drum is protected by a shutter on the cartridge. But you should know that even a few minutes of direct sunlight permanently damages any portion of the drum it hits. With regular room light, twelve hours of exposure is enough to do the job. That's why you should always store toner cartridges in the light-proof bag.

Figure 7-2-1 Laser Recharging Firms

Here's a geographically diverse list of many of the country's laser cartridge recharging firms. You may want to call several of them for price quotes and to inquire about any special products or services they may offer. All other things being equal, you might save a dollar or two on shipping costs by selecting the nearest firm.

Advantage Laser Products
2216 University Blvd.
Tuscaloosa, AL 35401
(800) 239-4027

American Expert Laser
606 Pinney Rd., Suite 201
Huntingdon Valley, PA 19006
(215) 947-8972

American Ribbon Co.
2890 Northwest 55th Ct.
Ft. Lauderdale, FL 33309
(800) 327-1013

BeeDee Enterprises
Hurricane Shores
Scottsville, KY 42164
(502) 622-4129

Black Lightning
RR1, Box 87, Depot Rd.
Hartland, VT 05048
(800) 252-2599

Chenesko Products
62 N. Coleman Rd.
Centereach, NY 11720
(800) 221-3516

CPR Recharge
902 Cutler Ct.
Waldorf, MD 20602
(301) 843-2800
(800) 794-1881 (Maryland only)
(800) 723-9253 (BBS)

(continued)

(Figure 7-2-1 continued)

Environmental Computer Supplies
1001 Louisiana Ave., Suite 407
Corpus Christi, TX 78404
(800) 521-3289

Heartland Laser
1716 Murray Hill
Manly, IA 50456
(515) 454-2576

The Laser Group
115 Crabtree Dr., Suite 100
Westmont, IL 60559
(800) 527-3712

LASERQuipt
7615 Washington Ave. S.
Edina, MN 55435
(800) 777-8444

Laser Research
8334-L Arrowridge Blvd.
Charlotte, NC 28273
(800) 462-7143

Laser's Edge
201 S. 23rd St.
Fairfield, IA 52556
(800) 635-8088

Omega Computer Services
4825 E. Indianapolis Ave.
Fresno, CA 93726
(800) 736-6342

Printworx
3322 S. Memorial Pkwy.
Huntsville, AL 35801
(800) 777-9679

Saving on Fonts

Whether you use an inkjet or a laser printer, you can usually save a bundle on fonts by buying your cartridges from a reliable third-party manufacturer. The Pacific Data Products 25-in-1 cartridge is a classic case in point. To get all the fonts provided by this product, you would have to buy at least 25 of the cartridges offered by Hewlett-Packard. Although they typically contain only four or five fonts each, HP cartridges are priced anywhere from $125 to $250 to $330 apiece. Even if you assumed an average cost of $100 per cartridge, you would have to pay $2,500 to get all the fonts contained in PDP's 25-in-1.

The 25-in-1 contains 172 fonts and twenty symbol sets in both portrait and landscape orientation. Point sizes range from 3.6 points to 18 points. Fixed and proportional spacing are supported, as are drawing tools. The inkjet (HP DeskJet 500) version of the product lists for $150 but is available at a street price of about $100. The laser printer version lists for $400 but is widely sold for about $270.

Pacific Data Products can be reached at (619) 552-0880 or on Compu-Serve in PC Vendor Forum D (GO PCVEND). The company has a particularly vigorous upgrade operation. When new versions of the products are introduced, current users can usually exchange their units for the newer version for as little as $75, depending on the product. If you are a current PDP customer interested in upgrading, you can call (619) 597-3450 for more information.

How to Get "Free" Fonts

I have to admit to being of two minds about fonts. On the one hand, when I'm preparing a document to be desktop published, I want to have every font in the world at my disposal. Otherwise my "creativity" may be cramped. On the other hand, I know that I don't actually use all that many fonts in the final document. (Some people go so crazy with fonts that their work ends up looking like a ransom note.) One can easily invest a great deal of money in cartridges and soft font packages, only to find that the money would have been better spent on something more useful.

One way to more or less have your cake and eat it too is to actively pursue shareware soft fonts. Anyone with a flair for design and a personal computer can create an outstanding typeface and make it available as shareware in one or more font sizes. Many men and women have done just that.

You will find their work in shareware collections and on online systems like CompuServe. And you will find that the field is both broad and deep. One of the best typeface/font collections available anywhere is Gary Elfring's 23-font collection. The man is a true artist.

The Elfring Shareware Font Collection

The Elfring shareware font collection includes Black Chancery, Broadway, Century Legal, Flourish, Helvetica (normal, bold, and italic), Script, Roman (normal, bold, and italic), a font of 18-point dingbats, and a font of commonly used symbols (arrows, check marks, pointing fingers, bullets, trademark and registered trademark symbols, etc.). Most fonts in the collection are 10 and 12 points.

The registration fee for the package is only $25, and it brings with it full telephone support. The package includes a soft font downloader (TSR Download) to get the font into your printer; a font information display program; a utility that examines soft fonts; printer drivers for Word-Perfect 5.1 and 5.0, MS Word 5.0 and 5.5, and MS Works; plus Windows, WordStar, PC-Write, Q&A, Ventura, and Pagemaker information. It also contains a tutorial that explains the basics of using soft fonts.

If you like what you see, you'll be interested to know that Elfring has nearly 50 other typefaces in font sizes ranging from 8 point through 30 points. Each font package is priced between $35 and $50, and there are versions for Hewlett-Packard inkjet printers as well as lasers. PostScript, PCL 5 scalable/Intellifont, and TrueType fonts are also available. (See Part 9 for information on obtaining these fonts, as well as a sampling of their appearance.)

Other Soft Font Utilities

The printer control and font loading program supplied with the Elfring package is excellent. But the shareware program Jet Pilot from Morton Utilities is equally remarkable. Jet Pilot can be installed as a pop-up TSR, or it can be run directly from the DOS command line. It gives you complete control of virtually every feature of your LaserJet or compatible printer. It can do everything from setting your top, bottom, left, and right margins, to rotating the printout by 0, 90, 180, or 270 degrees. Jet Pilot complements Elfring's TSR Download program because Jet Pilot deals with your printer's internal and cartridge fonts. TSR Download deals only with soft fonts. Between the two of them, you can do virtually anything you want with your laser printer, and you can do it *easily*.

Finally, you should also know about QFONT. Written by Kenn Flee, author of QFILER, this shareware program lets you design your own fonts or images, if you like. But you will probably use it most to *alter* existing soft fonts. Simply tell QFONT the name of the font file you want to start working on, and it brings up the letter *A* in its preview screen. The letter appears in the upper left corner as a reference and on the main screen for editing and manipulation.

With the letter on the screen, you can physically change each and every bit individually. Just click on it with your mouse. Or you can use the program's drawing tools to add lines, curves, ellipses, boxes, and other features. You can also cut and paste to create a unique design. But what you will find really exciting is the ability to change the *size* of the font.

QFONT can increase the size of a font up to a maximum of about 144 points (two inches). Horizontal and vertical dimensions can be changed independently, in case you want to create squashed or elongated characters. Similarly, you can cause the typeface to slant to the right or the left, and add shadowing or outlining. You can turn portrait fonts into landscape fonts. You can make the font bolder or lighter, or turn it into a reverse font (white characters on a black background).

When you select a change, the letter on the screen changes instantly to reflect it. That makes it easy to decide whether you like the effect or not. When you have made all the changes you want to make, you can tell the program to go through the font file and change all the rest of the characters, saving the font to a different filename on your disk. Then you can tell QFONT to download your new font to the printer and print a sample.

PowerPoint

PDP's FontBank Cartridge

As we have seen, Pacific Data Products (PDP) is a major player in the third-party font industry. One of the firm's most innovative products is likely to be of interest to anyone who uses soft fonts. The product is called the FontBank cartridge, and it is designed to combine the speed and convenience of cartridge-based fonts with the flexibility of soft fonts.

The FontBank contains flash ROM that is designed to be loaded with your favorite scalable and bitmapped soft fonts. At this writing there is a $299 version with 750K of flash ROM and a $399 version with 1.5MB of memory. The flash memory preserves the information you load into the cartridge without the need for electrical power. FontBank cartridges can be reprogrammed an infinite number of times.

To use FontBank with a program, you'll have to have a program-specific driver that supports the cartridge. PDP includes drivers for WordPerfect 5.1, Microsoft Word 5.0/5.5, and Windows 2.x/3.0 with the package. Additional drivers are sure to be available in the future.

SECTION

7-4

POWER PRINTING

As we all know by now, efficient, flexible printing is a matter of both hardware and software. Up to this point, we've spent most of our time looking at the hardware side of things. Now it's time to shift the focus and see what non-font-related printer software can do to increase speed and convenience. It's time to really turn on the power. We'll look first at print spoolers and then at those little utilities that can do so much to make printers easier to use.

First, Get PrintCache

The single most important piece of printer-related software you can install is a print buffer program. And not just any print buffer. The one to get is PrintCache from LaserTools of Emeryville, California. The program will simply blow you away.

The list price for PrintCache is $149, but the package is available from mail-order firms like PC Connection for $99. PC Connection has long been one of the very best mail-order firms in the business. You can place an order or ask for a catalogue by calling (800) 800-0004.

In computerese, PrintCache is a print spooler. Whenever you send something to the printer, either via DOS or Windows or from within a word processor, spreadsheet, or any other application, PrintCache intervenes. It accepts everything that the sending program dishes out and tucks it away in memory or on disk. When the last byte of data has been transmitted, PrintCache issues the signal the sending program expects to receive from the printer, indicating that the print job is done.

As soon as the applications program or DOS or Windows receives this signal, it is ready to go back to work. It has no way of knowing what actually happened to the data. All it knows is that the "printer" told it the job was done, and so the program—and you—are free to continue with other tasks. So, instead of waiting three minutes, you can be back at work in fifteen seconds. If you share a printer with several co-workers, the time required to print a job may be even longer. But with PrintCache, you can still be back at work in a few seconds. You can even exit the program and go on to something else. That's something many programs with built-in print spoolers do not permit.

As you go about those other tasks, PrintCache quietly begins spooling data to your printer. The program operates in the background, taking advantage of the tremendous amount of time the CPU remains idle. Like the interval between when you hit one key and then another when you are typing. I have not tried PrintCache on lesser machines, but on a 386SX/16 and a 386DX/20, the program's theft of clock cycles has no noticeable effect whatever.

PrintCache can use any kind of memory you happen to have—conventional, extended, or expanded. It can also use your hard disk as its temporary storage area, though you obtain the most impressive results if you opt for some form of memory. The program loads as a TSR, but you can choose whether to enable its pop-up menu or not. You can also specify the hotkey used to call the menu. The nice thing about the pop-up menu is that it lets you suspend printing if you like, and even flush the PrintCache buffer, deleting any data that remains to be printed. You can also use the menu to send to the printer a form feed telling it to eject a partial page.

PrintCache works with virtually any printer or plotter. It occupies as little as 6K of memory if you don't enable the pop-up menu; 16K if you do. It functions fine when loaded into an Upper Memory Block. And it really pushes the printer. When actually printing, PrintCache can complete the job 20 to 40 percent faster than Print Manager in Windows 3.1, for example. Small wonder that *PC Magazine* advises, "Replace the Windows Print Manager with PrintCache. . .the best print spooler on the market." For more information, contact LaserTools at (800) 767-8004.

DMP, the Shareware Spooler

If money's tight and you're willing to accept just a little less performance than that provided by PrintCache, try the shareware print spooler DMP from DMP Software. In my opinion, this is the best noncommercial print spooler available anywhere. Like PrintCache, DMP can use any type of memory or disk as its storage space. It's just not as fast as the commercial product, though it is much faster than printing without a spooler.

But DMP has one feature that PrintCache lacks: it can print a file to disk. Once the program is loaded, you can enter a command to redirect all output bound for the printer into a disk file. This is a great way to capture the text that appears on a program's screen. With DMP loaded and set, all you have to do is hit your Print Screen key and the screen will be printed to disk. You can then load the file into your word processor and clean it up by removing any ANSI codes or other non-text information. DMP has many other features besides. The key thing is that it works with *all* types of printers: lasers, inkjets, and dot-matrix.

PowerPoint

Don't Forget GRAPHICS.COM

The program GRAPHICS.COM and its companion file, GRAPHICS .PRO, which are supplied with DOS are designed to enable bitmapped graphics printing from DOS. When properly loaded, that means you can bring up a bitmapped graphic screen and make a copy of it by simply hitting your Print Screen key or Shift+Print Screen. If you try this without first loading GRAPHICS .COM, the your printed results are likely to resemble nothing so much as a pig's breakfast.

The format of the command is GRAPHICS *printer profile switches.* If you have an HP LaserJet II, for example, you might enter `graphics laserjetii` or `graphics c:\dos\graphics.pro\laserjet ii`. Consult your DOS manual or the Random House/Glossbrenner DOS books for details. The key thing is to tell GRAPHICS.COM not only the name of your printer but also the location of GRAPHICS.PRO if that file is not in the current directory.

You might also want to experiment with the /R switch. This tells GRAPHICS.COM to reverse the image so that it prints whatever is black on the screen as white on your paper. The default setting is black on white. But, depending on the kind of things you print with Print Screen, you may be able to save time and conserve toner or ink with the /R switch. Again, see your DOS manual for more detail.

Tiny Utilities

There are also a number of small, single-function utility programs that can make working with a printer a much more pleasant experience.

For example, one of the most aggravating things about using the Print Screen key is that you have to fiddle with the printer to get it to actually print. This is because the printer is normally set to think of a single page as 55 lines or so, and the Print Screen key has sent it only 25 lines. The printer, in short, is waiting for a full load before it hits the road.

If you have a LaserJet II, you can solve the problem with Steve Grant's little PRTSCR-LJ utility. It occupies just a little over 2K and can be loaded into a UMB. The program automatically issues a form feed signal to the printer after whatever is on the screen has been printed. It prints the entire screen, even if you are in 43- or 50-line text mode, and it treats video control characters as printable characters, not as printer control codes.

Sending a Form Feed

A similar form feed-related problem occurs whenever you copy a file to the printer from DOS, or whenever you redirect DOS output to the printer with the greater-than sign (>). The last few lines are always left in the printer. And you must manually take the printer offline, press the Form Feed button to make the machine print, and then put the printer back online again before you can continue.

There are a number of ways around this vexing little problem. You might, for example, use your word processor to create a little one-byte file called FF. The file would contain only a single ASCII 12 character (the form feed control character), entered by holding down your Alt key and tapping 12 on the numeric keypad. You could then issue a form feed with the following command: `copy ff prn`. You could even turn that line into a batch file called FF.BAT. That way, you could send a form feed by simply keying in `ff`.

Alternatively, you can send a form feed, or almost any other printer control character or sequence, directly from the command line. Key in `copy con: prn` and hit Enter. Then use your Alt key and numeric keypad to enter the desired printer control codes. Finish by hitting your F6 key to end the process. DOS will then send the codes you have specified directly to the printer.

The most elegant solution of all takes a little more work. But it is worth it. That solution is to create a tiny file called FF.COM. Once created, every time you key in `ff`, the program sends a form feed to the printer.

Here's what to do. Load DOS's DEBUG program. At the DEBUG dash prompt (-), begin keying in the lines shown below. When you key in rcx, DEBUG will respond with *CX 0000* and give you a colon prompt. Respond with 08 as shown, then w, then q. (Note that only zeros are used below, no capital *O*s.)

```
N FF.COM
E 0100 B4 05 B2 0C CD 21 CD 20
RCX
08
W
Q
```

You can also create a DEBUG script by typing these lines into an ASCII file called FF.SCR. Then issue the command debug < ff.scr. The results are the same in either case: a little eight-byte file called FF.COM.

Once this file has been created, make sure there is a copy in your DOS directory or in some other directory that is in your path. That way, you can key in ff to send a form feed to the printer regardless of your current location on the system.

Eliminate *No Printer* Delays

If you accidentally hit your Print Screen key when there is no printer attached or when the printer is not online, DOS tries repeatedly to establish a connection before finally giving up and giving you an error message. By default, DOS keeps things locked up as it tries twenty times, but you can reduce that number to one time with the 1TRY program we are about to create.

The lines below have been numbered for easy reference. To create the file 1TRY.COM, first create an ASCII text file called 1TRY.SCR containing the information in Lines 1 through 15. Then use the command debug < 1try.scr to create 1TRY.COM. Do not enter the line numbers in your file, and make sure that you leave a blank at line 10:

```
1. A 100
2. MOV AX,0040
3. PUSH AX
4. POP ES
5. MOV DI,0078
6. ES:
7. MOV BYTE PTR [DI],01
8. MOV AH,4C
```

```
 9. INT 21
10.
11. RCX
12. 10
13. N 1TRY.COM
14. W
15. Q
```

You can control the number of retries by changing the 01 at the end of Line 7 to a higher number. (Do not set it to 0, however, since this sends DOS into an endless loop.) You can also control the printer designation. The program assumes LPT1. To change this to a different printer, look at the end of Line 5. The 0078 shown here stands for LPT1; change it to 0079 for LPT2; to 007A for LPT3; or to 007B for LPT4.

Dealing with Envelopes

Today, with PCs everywhere, you'd think that the typewriter would be a thing of the past. But there are at least two tasks that are all but guaranteed to keep it alive. One is the need to fill out multipart forms, like Federal Express air bills. The other is the fact that generating addressed envelopes on a laser printer can be a royal pain in the keyboard.

All HP LaserJets are designed to accept envelopes. In fact, some are designed to accept special envelope cassettes. But unless you routinely send out a lot of mail, there is not much point in getting a special cassette. Most of us simply need to send out a few letters a day, and it is often more trouble than it's worth to try to address an envelope with a laser printer.

That's what makes Grab Plus, a shareware program from ZPAY Payroll Systems, so exciting. All you have to do is load Grab Plus into memory as a TSR and prepare your letter. When you are ready to generate an envelope for the letter, you press a hotkey combination and Grab Plus pops up onto your screen. You see two windows. One offers a quick summary of available commands. The other is a highlight box that you can move over the inside address in your letter.

Adjust the box with your function keys, hit another key to confirm your decision, and Grab Plus automatically sends the text in the highlight box to the printer. All you have to do is place an envelope in the manual feed slot and Grab Plus prints the address you have picked out, properly positioned in landscape mode, on the envelope. Depending on your preferences, Grab Plus automatically prints your return address in the upper left corner as well.

Doing Labels

There are at least three ways to produce pressure-sensitive labels. One is to buy a dedicated label-making machine and hook it up to one of your parallel ports. Another is to delve into your word processing or desktop publishing program and figure out how to print a label of a given size on your own. The best, most cost-effective solution, however, is usually to get a dedicated label-printing program.

Your choice depends on the amount of power and flexibility you need. But in my opinion, you can't go far wrong with LabelPro from Avery/Dennison. Versions are available for both laser and dot-matrix printers. Each has a list price of $99.95. (The street price is closer to $45.) And, of course, both versions are designed to print on Avery/Dennison label stock. Talk about giving away the razors to sell razor blades!

This might be a problem were it not for the fact that Avery/Dennison label products are widely available, even from stationery discount stores, and they come in many different sizes. The 3M company is big, but at this writing, Avery/Dennison owns the pressure-sensitive label market. Prior to their merger, Avery and Dennison dominated the market. As a single entity, they have a hammer lock.

Only the laser printer version of LabelPro can produce bar codes. But both dot-matrix and laser versions supply a large number of graphics files to dress up your labels. And both accept .PCX graphics files you create, and merge data from dBASE, WordPerfect, or the comma-delimited files produced by most database programs. That means that doing labels for mass mailings is not a problem.

Indeed, the only problem with this or any other label-printing program is the matter of label sheets. (The problem does not come up with pin-fed continuous form labels.) When you print on sheets of labels, you have a choice. Either you can print an entire sheet of labels or you can print one label. But if you print only one label and remove it from the sheet, you will not be able to reliably run the sheet through again. In other words, you can't use the sheet-fed approach to print only one or two labels. It's pretty much all or nothing.

In our shop, we cope with this in two ways. With friends, relatives, and close business associates, we use LabelPro to run off an entire sheet of identical address labels at one time. The sheet is then filed under the person's name, and we go to the file whenever we want to send him or her a letter.

When a single laser-printed label is required, we print it on a sheet of labels. Then we use the rest of the sheet as fodder for the typewriter. Not every piece of correspondence, after all, needs a laser-printed label.

I can't say enough for LabelPro. It's quick and easy to use. It lets us preview a label graphically on the screen. And the results are excellent. If your needs are more demanding, however, it can pay to check the leading computer magazines for other label-producing software. In the meantime, if you'd like more information on LabelPro, you can contact the company at (800) 462-8379 or (818) 915-3851.

The Mail Machine Alternative

LabelPro lets you preview label designs and incorporate .PCX image files. But it does not let you use your own fonts. Nor can you use a mouse. At least not in the versions current at this writing. If you'd like capabilities like these but do not want to pay commercial software prices, you may want to consider the shareware program Mail Machine (MM).

Among other things, Mail Machine can print envelopes and labels of any size acceptable by your LaserJet, up to 8.5 by 14 inches. Support for most standard size envelopes and labels is built into the program, plus support for most Avery forms. In addition, MM lets you print both addresses and return addresses on envelopes. (You don't have to do just labels.) As with LabelPro, the addresses can be entered manually, or they can be imported from a file created by a database or spreadsheet program.

Mail Machine supports six lines of address information on each label. Label addresses are optional and can be entered manually, or they can be retrieved from text files, the same as with envelopes. MM also gives you the option of automatically printing the U.S. Postal Service PostNet bar code in the correct position on your envelopes and labels. That can speed mail delivery because it allows your mail addresses to be scanned and read by machines similar to those now used at grocery store checkout counters.

In addition to printing addresses, you can also specify any number of original messages or comments. And the messages can be printed anywhere on the envelopes or labels, using any available fonts. For example, you might want to print messages like DO NOT BEND, NO COMMERCIAL VALUE, HAPPY HOLIDAYS, OPEN IMMEDIATELY, or HERE IS THE INFORMATION YOU REQUESTED.

Mail Machine lets you use any soft fonts, but it supports the fonts built into your printer and cartridge fonts as well. You can print envelopes and labels with any combination of available fonts. And, as with LabelPro, you can use PCL and PC Paintbrush graphics files to add logos and artwork to your labels.

Save Paper, Save a Tree

Anyone interested in saving both money and paper should know about STP—the "Save a Tree text Printer" program. STP can print eight normal pages on a single sheet of paper. It does this by using very tiny (though still legible) type, and by printing on both sides of the page.

During the first pass, the odd-numbered pages are printed, and the even-numbered pages are stored in memory. The program then prompts you to turn the pages over and put them back in the paper cassette. It then prints the even-numbered pages. As I said, the type is very small. But STP can be ideal for printing documentation, since you can take in eight pages at a glance and thus more easily locate the piece of information you seek.

Printer Sharing

Finally, I should say just a word or two about how to share a printer between two different systems. Our office revolves around two 386 computers and one HP LaserJet Series II printer. I work at one system while Emily, my wife and business partner, works at the other. Being reasonably intelligent people, we could see no point in buying a separate printer for each computer.

The answer, until recently, was a simple A/B switch. When the knob was turned one way my system would be connected to the printer. When it was turned the other way, Emily's system could print. Needless to say, it was a nuisance to have to check and possibly change the switch every time you wanted to print something.

That's why the Printswitch from Black Box Corporation was such a blessing. This is an intelligent switch that lets you connect one computer to two different printers, or two computers to the same printer. The Printswitch automatically connects whichever computer wants to print. If two computers want to print at the same time, it gives preference to the one that put in the request first. But as soon as the first job is finished, the second machine's output is accepted.

The cost is $140, or only slightly more than I paid for the mechanical A/B switch some years ago. In a two-computer, one-printer setup, the convenience of the Printswitch cannot be matched. If your needs are more elaborate, or if you are equipping a network, even more powerful printer switches are available from Black Box. For more information or to request a catalogue, call (412) 746-5565.

PART VIII

COMMUNICATING

What You Will Learn

It's not uncommon these days for computer retailers and mail-order houses
to automatically include a 2,400-bps modem as part of the system packages
they offer. Like mice, modems are used for promotional purposes ("Buy
this system and get a modem free!"), and as deal sweeteners ("If you'll buy
today, I'll throw in this modem absolutely free. Whadaya say?").

Modems, in short, have become a commodity. At least those of the 2,400
bits per second (bps) variety, and the same thing is happening to 9,600-bps
and 14.4-Kbps modems as well. That's all to the good, for a computer really
isn't complete without a modem. Indeed, I have long felt that, for most
people, online communications represents the highest and best use of a personal computer. As I have explained in numerous books over the years, no
other computer application can add so much to your personal and professional life.

Yet most modems today, even those belonging to card-carrying power
users, are gathering dust in closets or sitting in expansion slots, uncon-
nected to the telephone lines they were designed to tame. Part of the problem is that the modem, serial card, and communications program needed
to go online constitute a separate subsystem with its own terminology, settings, procedures, and requirements. This presents a rather steep learning
curve, and all for what?

Once you've climbed that curve, what can you expect to find on the
other side? Most people have no idea. And most of those who have gained
a glimmer from a magazine article or two don't find the offerings compelling. At least not compelling enough to subscribe to commercial systems
like CompuServe, GEnie, or Prodigy, or to ferret out free bulletin board
numbers, to say nothing of even taking time to connect their modems.

Of course, just as a newspaper account of a baseball or football game
cannot hope to convey a true sense of what it was like to be there, no magazine article can convey the true excitement of being online. The only way
to really know whether it's worth learning PC communications is to actually sample the online product. But you can't sample the product until you
learn how to communicate. It's a Catch-22 of classic proportions.

This is surely one of the reasons for the dismal growth record of online
systems over the last decade. Consider: There are today some 100 million
IBM-compatible computers in service, plus millions more Apple Macin-
toshes and other non-DOS machines. When equipped with a modem, every one of them has the ability to communicate. Yet, even by the most
generous of calculations, the total number of actual subscribers to online
systems barely tops two million. Add in a million or two more for good

measure, if you like. It won't make any difference. The number of online users is still but a tiny fraction of the total who are equipped to go online if they had any interest in doing so.

We're not about to solve this problem here. But this part of the book can certainly make it easier for you to sample communications, often for free, so you can judge for yourself whether you wish to delve any deeper. It will give you what you need to start using that modem or to buy a new one.

If you would like more detail, there are several Glossbrenner books that may be of interest. For a book-length treatment of all the possibilities the online world holds, see *The Complete Handbook of Personal Computer Communications, 3rd Edition.* For information on obtaining online information, see *How to Look It Up Online.* Both are published by St. Martin's Press. You may also find the tips and tricks stuffed into the *Master Guide to GEnie* [Osborne/McGraw-Hill] to be of value.

We will start with an explanation of the concepts you need to have to be comfortable with PC communications. Then we will look at the three commercial systems every PC user should consider. After that, we'll consider why you may want to think about replacing your serial communications card, and we'll explain many of the terms that make modem ads so confusing. We'll touch briefly on communications software as we look at file transfer protocols and downloading files. Then you'll see how easy it is to uncompress a ZIPped, ARC'd, or LHARC'd file, once you know the right commands. Finally, we will offer an introduction to free bulletin board systems, including tips on finding the best BBS numbers.

SECTION
8-1

COMM BASICS

Despite the apparent steepness of the learning curve, going online these days is much easier than in years past. Though there have been some major improvements in speed, the fundamental technology hasn't really changed all that much since the mid-1970s. People are also much more familiar with the hardware and the basic concept. I remember when *The New York Times* used to take pains to define the word *modem* when it appeared in a general interest story. No longer. Most computer users today know that a modem is a black box needed for connecting a PC to the telephone system. Even non-computer users have at least heard the term, thanks to the regular reports of electronic break-ins perpetrated by bright young criminals.

In short, the fact that computers can communicate over the telephone system has become common knowledge in the past few years. But even many longtime communicators have only a vague idea how the machines accomplish this feat. Let's see if we can shed some light on the process.

> *PowerPoint*
>
> ## Get ProComm!
>
> It goes without saying that, as with every other computer application, you need communications software to communicate. Communications programs are often called "comm programs" or "terminal programs" (because they fool a mainframe host system into thinking they are one of its own terminals).
>
> Comm programs tend to be overstuffed with features, and there are lots of choices in both the commercial and shareware realms. I've used many of them over the years, and, hands-down, the one I like best is ProComm from Datastorm Technologies, Inc. The package is a real shareware success story. Issued exclusively as shareware in the mid-1980s, ProComm became so popular that it went commercial several years ago. Today, according to industry analysts, ProComm holds between 50 and 70 percent of the data communications software market.
>
> ProComm versions 2.4.3 and ProComm Plus 1.0 are still available as shareware. They may very well serve all of your needs. The latest commercial version at this writing is ProComm Plus 2.x. In my opinion, some version of ProComm is the program to have. Good as its competitors may be, there simply isn't any point in fooling around with anything else. The company maintains a support forum on CompuServe (GO DATASTORM).

Going Online

Regardless of what you plan to do once you get there, regardless of the kind of system you plan to call, the fundamental goal of going online is always the same: You want to establish a connection that will transport the characters and commands you type at your keyboard to a distant computer—and transport that computer's responses back to your screen. A variety of systems and components are needed to achieve this goal.

The process can best be explained by following the bits of data used to symbolize a character as they travel from your keyboard, into the system unit, and out the back door to the modem. We usually think of binary digits as *1*s and *0*s, but physically, they consist of high- and low-voltage pulses.

As long as those pulses stay within the computer itself, everything is fine. Where you begin to run into difficulties is when you want to make the bits flow outside the system unit. They usually have enough energy to slide down the cable leading to the printer. But you cannot count on them to travel much farther than the eight feet recommended by most printer manufacturers. You might get away with a parallel printer cable of up to fifteen feet long, but if you go much beyond that point and fail to install a line driver or booster unit, you risk data corruption.

As for feeding those voltage pulses into the phone line, forget it. In the first place, everything inside the computer is set up for the bits to roll along in parallel formation. That takes eight wires at least. But most phone hookups have only two wires, and even special, high-quality leased lines have only four.

In the second place, things are pretty quiet inside the computer, electrically speaking. Each bit can be the electrical equivalent of a whisper and still be heard. In the big wide world of telecommunications, however, there is a lot of electronic noise and electrical resistance that would make your average computer bit inaudible.

Necessary Conversions

The solution is to perform a conversion. Two conversions, in fact. First, the natural parallel paths of computer bits must be changed from eight-all-at-once to one-at-a-time. You've got to convert from a parallel data format to a serial data format, in other words. Second, each bit has got to be changed into a more rugged form suitable for telephone transmission. Since phone systems were designed to handle sound, that's what the bits must be changed into.

There is a piece of equipment to handle each conversion. The first transformation is executed by a microchip called a UART (pronounced "you-art"). This stands for Universal Asynchronous Receiver-Transmitter. UARTs are the central element of your serial card or serial port. Most IBM-compatibles can accommodate up to four serial ports, named COM1 through COM4. IBM PS/2 and other MCA machines can handle up to eight.

It is the UART that is responsible for getting each eight-bit unit lined up, adding two bits of what for now we can think of as packing material, and sending the entire 10-bit package out the door. There is a difference among UART chips, as we will see later. But for the present, we'll assume they are all alike.

The second conversion, the one from electrical signals into sound, is performed by a modem. This term is a compression of the words *modulator/dem*odulator, and it refers to a device for changing outgoing computer voltage pulses into sound and incoming sound into voltage pulses.

You can think of these sounds as a high-pitched tone and a low-pitched tone, if you like, though in reality things are more complex. The details of the modulation techniques are not important, but it is helpful to know that modems deal in two sets of paired tones or frequencies. One pair of tones is for outgoing and one pair is for incoming information.

These two sets are referred to as the modem's "originate" and "answer" modes. For communications to take place, one modem must be set to originate and the other must be set to answer. Thus, regardless of who calls whom, if you want to establish a connection with a friend or colleague, one of you will have to be set to answer and the other to originate.

By convention, the system you call is referred to as the "host system" regardless of its size or function. It could actually be a computer identical to your own. In almost every case, if you are calling a remote host, your modem should be set to originate. Again by convention, the modems attached to any system designed to receive incoming calls will be set to answer. Either that, or their automatic answer feature will be enabled.

Cables and Plugs

Modems are usually connected to the computer by a cable that is plugged into the *RS-232 interface* on the card containing the UART. This is pronounced "R-S-two-thirty-two," and it stands for Recommended Standard number 232. Its official name used to be RS-232, revision C, a designation you will find on some communications products as RS-232-C. But that name was changed in 1987 to EIA-232D. No one seems to have noticed, since RS-232 is still the most frequently used designation.

The standard was developed by the Electronic Industries Association (EIA), the Bell System, and the computer and modem industries, and it is nearly universally endorsed. It specifies that an RS-232 interface must consist of 25 pins or sockets, and it describes how each pin must be wired, what signals it will carry, and so forth.

Most systems use a DB-25 connector. However, since the standard does not specify the type of connector, and since only nine pins are required for normal modem operations, you will see some nine-pin connections. The DB-9 connector is found mainly on IBM AT serial adapters and some laptops. Generically, these kinds of plugs are called *miniature D-shell connectors* because they look like an elongated *D*. In any case, it is through this portal that your system's bits come and go. A second cable leads from the modem to the telephone jack. Thus, the modem stands between the computer and the telephone system, modulating and demodulating sound and computer signals.

PowerPoint

Male and Female Considerations

The ports and connectors at the back of an IBM-compatible computer can often be confusing. Both the serial port and the parallel printer port may use DB-25 connectors. Similarly, DB-9 connectors are also used to hook up most monitors.

Here's how to tell the difference without taking the computer apart. The serial ports in most machines are male. They have either nine or 25 *pins*. The printer and video ports are always female and have nine or 25 *sockets*.

DOS 6's Interlink Program

Microsoft's DOS 6 includes two features specifically aimed at laptop users. The DOSX 6 POWER.EXE program conserves battery power on your laptop when applications and hardware devices are idle. If your machine conforms to the Advanced Power Management (APM) specification, POWER.EXE can save you up to 25 percent of the power that would normally be consumed. If yours is a non-APM machine, your power savings will be about five percent.

DOS 6 also includes a program called Interlink that represents Microsoft's attempt at creating a laptop-to-desktop file transfer program on the order of Fifth Generation's Brooklyn Bridge package or the Hot Wire package from Datastorm Technologies, Inc. Both of these third-party packages include the cables you will need. For more information contact Fifth Generation at (800) 873-4384 or Datastorm Technologies at (314) 474-8461.

DOS, of course, includes only the software. To use the program, you will need to buy a three-wire serial cable, a seven-wire *null modem* cable, or a bidirectional parallel cable. The Interlink lets you connect two computers through their serial (RS-232) or parallel ports. One computer then becomes the "server," while the other becomes the "client." The client machine has complete control of the server, including full access to its disk drives and the ability to run programs on the server machine.

In most cases, the server is the desktop machine and the client is the laptop. The idea is that you might use your laptop computer to gather data in the field and put it into your database program. Back at the office, with your desktop and laptop machines connected via Interlink, you would use your laptop machine to call up a database program on the desktop unit and merge in the data you've collected on your laptop computer.

Interlink is not a bad program, and, if you happen to have a spare cable lying around, you may wish to try it. It is worth noting, however, that software of this sort first appeared several years ago when most desktop systems lacked 3.5-inch floppy drives. Laptops, of course, are rarely equipped with anything else.

Today, when almost every computer of every sort is equipped with at least one high-density, 1.44-megabyte, 3.5-inch drive, you may find that it is easier to use floppies as your medium of data exchange instead of fiddling around with cables and the Interlink program. Though, an Interlink-style program could be a big help when you're loading up your laptop's hard disk or otherwise transferring large amounts of data.

PowerPoint

Null Modems and Terminal Programs

The reason you need a null modem cable to connect two RS-232 serial ports is that these ports expect to be talking to a modem. That means they expect to send data on a certain wire and to receive it on another. Thus, if you want two computer serial ports to communicate, you've got to fool each of them into thinking that they are actually talking to a modem. The null modem cable does this by reversing certain connections.

The relevant pins in a 25-pin connection are pins 2 and 3, pins 4 and 5, and pins 6, 8, and 20. If you are reasonably handy, you can create such a cable yourself. But, as with electrical extension cords, you will probably find that it is cheaper to buy a null modem cable than to buy the parts and assemble it yourself. Contact Black Box Corporation at (800) 552-6816 if your local computer store or Radio Shack doesn't have the cable you need. *(continued)*

(Null Modems and Terminal Programs continued)

Once you have a null modem cable, all you really need to transfer files is a communications program. Simply cable the two machines together and load your comm software on each one. Enter the command in each case that puts the software into *terminal mode,* and you will be able to upload and download files to and from either computer.

The serial ports on your two systems can almost certainly operate at a speed of 9,600 bits per second (bps), but more than likely, they can go at least as high as 19,200 bps (19.2 kilobits per second) and probably as high as 38,400 bps. You may want to experiment with even higher speeds. In any case, with no modem in the connection to limit you, you might as well operate at the highest possible speed both systems can support.

Public Data Networks and Packet Switching

It can be thrilling to imagine having the power to connect with any communicating computer in the world. But one phrase will bring you back to earth: long distance charges. Clearly, if one had to pay regular long distance rates for personal computer communications, the only systems most of us would call would be the bulletin board systems in our own neighborhoods.

Fortunately, although most systems can be reached by direct dial, there's usually no need to make your connection that way, thanks to the public data networks (PDNs). The PDNs use a technology called packet switching that is specifically designed to allow one computer to talk to another and to do so inexpensively. As long as both locations are within the continental United States, for example, the cost of using a PDN has historically been as low as $2 an hour during non-business, evening hours. That's about three cents a minute.

The two leading public data networks in the U.S. are Telenet, owned by U.S. Sprint Communications Corporation, which in turn is owned by GTE and United Telecommunications, Inc., and Tymnet. Tymnet was long owned by the McDonnell Douglas Corporation, but that firm sold the operation to British Telecom several years ago. Thus you will now see the term BT Tymnet. In Canada, the leading network is Datapac, owned and operated by Telecom Canada. Other companies, like CompuServe and General Electric, operate networks as well, but all work in essentially the same way.

You don't need to know a great deal about the PDNs, but it's important to have a broad familiarity with them. You will be using a PDN virtually every time you connect with a major commercial system—and you may be able to use one to reach distant bulletin board systems (BBSs) in some cities as well, thanks to Telenet's PC Pursuit program.

Data Packets and the Virtual Circuit

A packet-switching network consists of hundreds of computers and thousands of modems. The computers and modems are scattered all over the country and connected to each other by high-speed (up to 56,000 bits per second or 56 Kbps) data lines. Each location on the network is called a node, and if you live near a medium to large city, the chances are there is at least one node within your local calling area.

When you and your computer dial one of these local nodes, one of the modems at that location answers the phone and you immediately hear a high-pitched tone, often followed by a gravelly noise, through your modem's speaker. Your modem senses these sounds and establishes a connection with the node modem at your chosen speed. As soon as that happens, the noise stops. Next, you will probably see the word CONNECT on your screen. This comes from the modem to tell you that everything is ready for you to begin your session.

At that point you and your computer are in direct contact with the node computer, and after keying in some preliminary information, you are free to tell the network node which commercial system you wish to talk to. The node computer then patches you through to your target system, using the most efficient network route available at the time. In the target system's computer room—let's say it's Palo Alto, California where Knight-Ridder's DIALOG system is located—the phone rings and one of DIALOG's modems answers to complete the connection.

The word *efficient* is the key here, since the efficiencies made possible by packet-switching technology are one of the main reasons using a PDN is cheaper than placing a conventional long distance call. When you make a voice call, an actual physical circuit must be established between your phone and the person you are calling. This requires lots of switches and a lot of wires leading to a lot of different places. But the result is a circuit that's as real and complete as any you ever assembled in seventh grade science class. And of course the circuit must remain in existence for the duration of your call, tying up all of the physical resources involved in making the connection.

Computer-to-computer calls are different. Because they communicate digitally, their transmissions can easily be chopped up into discrete units or packets. Like the counterman at a hardware store pulling lengths of rope off a spool and cutting them to a uniform size, the node computer cuts your computer's data stream into uniformly sized packets of bits. It then stamps them with the address of your target system and a packet sequence number, and sends them on their way.

PDNs follow an international recommended standard called X.25 (pronounced "X dot twenty-five"). The standard specifies, for example, that a PDN packet always contains 128 bits. Padding characters are used to round out the packet when necessary to bring it up to that level. When a packet comes into the node computer from a remote system, the computer strips off any irrelevant bits, checks the packet's address, and channels it to the correct caller. This is why a network node computer is often referred to as a Packet Assembler/Disassembler or PAD.

A single PAD may have many incoming lines but only two or three high-speed lines connecting it to the network. However, since each packet is unique, the packets from several callers can be interleaved. What's more, they can be shot out into the network in different directions as the PAD strives for maximum efficiency in the face of ever-changing network load conditions and traffic patterns.

Other node computers at various locations in the network receive the packets, check their address, and relay them to another node or to the host system itself. Thanks to the address and sequence number, however, the packets are received by the correct host in the correct order, regardless of the route each packet took to reach its destination.

The result is what's called a virtual circuit. In most cases, when you use a packet-switching network, the connection between you and a host system appears to be identical to the connection that would exist were you to dial the remote system directly, even though an unbroken, continuous physical connection between the two never actually exists.

The ASCII Code Set

You can't spend much time in the personal computing field without running into the term *ASCII*. We've used it frequently throughout this book to signify a plain text file. That is the term's most common meaning. When you get into communications, however, you need to know a little bit more about ASCII than that.

The American Standard Code for Information Interchange or ASCII (pronounced "as-key") is the system that makes it possible for computers and computer equipment of all kinds to talk to each other. Other coding systems exist, but none is as universal as ASCII. (The ASCII code set is yet another achievement of ANSI, the American National Standards Institute.)

The code is simplicity itself. It functions by assigning a number to each lowercase letter of the alphabet, each uppercase letter, the numbers from 0 through 9, and most standard punctuation marks. There is also a code for a blank space, one for a carriage return, and one to cause the paper in a printer or the text on your screen to move up one line (line feed). There are several other codes as well that need not concern us here.

As you know, computers communicate in eight-bit units called bytes. Without getting into the binary numbering system at this point, take it on faith that it is possible to represent any decimal number from 0 through 255 using different combinations of eight 1s and 0s. Each byte, then, is a number. And since we know that each number represents a character in the ASCII code set, one byte equals one character.

Binary or Machine Language Files

Because the ASCII code is used to represent text, the term ASCII has become synonymous with "text." An ASCII file is a text file and contains nothing that cannot be displayed on the screen. ASCII files can be exchanged and viewed at will among all brands of computers.

Not so with *machine language* files. Machine language, too, is made up of eight-bit bytes, but any correspondence between those bytes and readable characters is purely coincidental. Machine language is the language of the CPU. You can display it on the screen, as when you TYPE a .COM or .EXE file, but the images you see are meaningless.

Of course, just to keep things interesting, there is a third type of file that mixes both ASCII text and machine language. Spreadsheets like those created by Lotus, Quattro, or Excel are good examples. So are the "native mode" document files created by many word processors. The machine language or binary codes found in these files are inserted for its own use by the program that created them.

For example, a word processing program might insert a binary code to symbolize a soft hyphen. Soft hyphens come and go as text is adjusted to fit between the margins. A hard hyphen, in contrast, is one you enter yourself, and the program does not remove it. Both look the same on the screen, so how can the program tell the difference? By tagging the soft hyphen with an invisible machine language code.

You don't see these codes when you are using the program, of course. But if you TYPE the file to the screen in DOS, they are visible. That's why it is crucial to create the files DOS reads, like CONFIG.SYS or AUTO-EXEC.BAT or any batch program, as pure ASCII text. It is also the reason why you must do the same thing when preparing a message you plan to transmit online. Always use your word processing program's ASCII text mode when creating a message you plan to send as text. If you fail to do this, your recipient may find your message unreadable.

That's just about all the basic technical background you need to be able to use your modem and your communications software with greater confidence. There are many other details, of course. But you will now have a much easier time figuring out how they all fit into the big picture.

SECTION

8-2

ONLINE POSSIBILITIES

Before moving on to matters of communications hardware, let's take just a moment to peer over the top of the learning curve. Once you get online, you will find that an entire electronic universe lies at your feet. Or at your fingertips. There are literally thousands of planets, moons, and suns to explore. As you begin your travels, however, you will find it helpful to keep one central concept in mind. Everything in the online world eventually falls into one of two categories: communications or information.

Communications and Information

Communications includes such things as electronic mail, online forums and Special Interest Group (SIG) message boards, fax and telex connections, computerized conferencing, and real-time CB-like "chat."

Information includes everything from the latest stock quotes and newswire stories to vast databases containing transcripts of television shows and world-wide radio broadcasts (translated into English). It includes instant access to tens of thousands of journals, newspapers, and magazines dating back ten to twenty years or more. Trademarks, patents, chemical formulas, conference reports, directories, government publications . . . the list goes on and on.

Indeed the list is so extensive that it is only a slight exaggeration to say that you can find out anything you want to know simply by sitting in front of your personal computer. And you can do it from virtually any location in the world, thanks to satellite uplinks, cellular modems, and all the other components of our worldwide communications system.

PowerPoint

Hire an Information Broker

Vast quantities of information are available, to be sure. But it's not cheap, and finding the answers to your questions requires a great deal of skill, knowledge, and experience. You *can* do it on your own, particularly if you concentrate on just one database or one online system.

But this is one field that often does take rocket scientists and brain surgeons. Or more to the point, it takes an artist. Online information retrieval is, and always will be, more art than science. Searching a major league database can also be quite expensive. Some patent databases, for example, charge as much as $5 a minute or more.

That's why, if you want to really take advantage of this incredible resource, you will hire a professional searcher. You'll pay much less and be much happier with the results than if you try to do it yourself. Though the term is a misnomer, the professional you should look for is called an *information broker*.

If you need to find someone local, start by checking with the librarians at your local libraries. The bigger the library, the better. If you have a choice, start with the reference librarian. Fortunately, thanks to computer communications, geography need not be a limiting factor in hiring a broker. You may thus want to order a copy of the *Burwell Directory of Information Brokers*. The cost is about $60. Contact Burwell Enterprises at (713) 537-9051.

Though aimed at people entering the profession, *The Information Broker's Handbook* by Sue Rugge and Alfred Glossbrenner [Windcrest/McGraw-Hill] contains a great deal of information that can guide you in locating, interviewing, and hiring an information broker. It also tells you what to look for and what to expect in the way of services and costs.

Recommended Systems

There are at least 500 separate online systems, and among them, they offer over 4,000 databases. But don't let the numbers intimidate you. As is so often the case, some version of the 80/20 rule applies. Most people spend most of their time using just a few systems.

As explained later, I strongly suggest that most brand-new online communicators get their feet wet using free bulletin board systems. BBSs can be a bit wild and woolly, but you can't go too far wrong if all you're spending is your time.

If you're ready to move beyond BBSs, or if you are simply feeling adventurous, there are three systems to start with. These are CompuServe, MCI Mail, and the Knowledge Index.

CompuServe

The CompuServe Information Service (CIS) is probably the oldest general interest online system. That's important, because over the years it has attained a critical mass. General Electric's GEnie, America Online, Delphi, and other smaller systems have a great deal to offer, often at lower prices. But *everyone* subscribes to H&R Block's CompuServe.

There are a number of reasons, starting with the fact that everyone is on the system. I know that sounds like circular logic, but the main reason many people all over the world subscribe to CompuServe is to be able to send messages to friends and business associates. The more people you can reach via CompuServe, the greater the incentive to subscribe. The greater the incentive, the more people subscribe. That's what I mean by "critical mass"—at some takeoff point, the reaction begins to feed on itself.

But it doesn't stop there. If "everyone" is on CompuServe, then that's the place that Ziff-Davis wants to be with its PC Magnet, a system that, among many other things, lets you download programs published in *PC Magazine.* It's also the place that, say, Hewlett-Packard, Microsoft, Lotus, and many other hardware and software makers want to be to offer online support to their customers. That makes the system even more desirable and leads to even more subscribers.

The Role of the SIGs

It is difficult to say just what it was that attracted a critical mass to CompuServe in the first place. But certainly the system's SIGs or "forums" were and are a major drawing card. An online SIG is like an electronic user group or club. It can be devoted to any topic. CIS has over 300 SIGS. Most of them are computer-related, but a hefty proportion are devoted to non-computer subjects like organic gardening, education, wine, coin collecting, political issues, and music.

Within each SIG, you can read and exchange messages with members on a wide range of topics. You can engage in real-time "chat," or attend a real-time presentation by some famous person or leading figure in your field. And you can upload (transmit) and download (receive) files from the SIG library. Since the message board and the library collection can be searched by specifying one or more keywords, it is fairly easy to find the information or files you want.

It is impossible to overstate the importance of online SIGs and the impact they have had on the online world. You can get news, weather, and sports information from your local newspaper. But the only way to get all the benefits offered by an electronic SIG is to go online.

When everything is said and done, SIGs really are the best thing online. SIGs alone are reason enough to climb the online learning curve. That's why all general interest online systems have SIGs of some sort.

Subscriptions and Costs

You can subscribe to CompuServe for $2 per month, plus connect time. Connect time is billed at $12.80 an hour for a 2,400-bps connection; $22.80 for 9,600 bps. Or you can opt for the Standard Pricing Plan, and pay $7.95 per month, plus applicable connect time. The key is that your $7.95 per month gives you unlimited access to a wide range of services, including news, weather, sports, two complete encyclopedias, *Consumer Reports*, stock quotes, American Airline's EAASY SABRE, the Electronic Mall, and electronic mail. As long as you stay within the basic services and don't send any more than about 60 messages a month, you never need pay CIS another dime.

An initial subscription costs $39.95. It includes your manual, a copy of CompuServe Information Manager (CIM) software, a credit that gives you your first month free ($7.95 value), plus a credit for $25 worth of connect time using features not covered by the Standard Pricing Plan.

If you happen to know a CompuServe subscriber, however, you can take advantage of the Member-Get-a-Member plan. Under the plan, you can get the subscription package for $25 instead of $39.95, and your friend receives a credit of $25 on his or her account. Just tell the salesperson your friend's number when you call to sign up. The numbers to dial are (800) 848-8199 or (614) 457-0802. Phones are manned until 10 PM Eastern time each day.

If you are a brand-new user, start with the Standard Pricing Plan. The flat fee will remove any pressure you might feel from the connect time clock ticking away, and you can cancel at any time. With your first month's subscription free and a $25 credit, you can really get to know the system. The most you can lose if you decide CompuServe is not for you is $39.95. However, if you find that you are spending $10 per month or more, change your account to the Executive Option.

This involves a commitment to spend $10 per month on the system, and your $7.95 counts toward that total. The Executive Option gives you access to special discounts and features. Even though you may never take advantage of the Executive Option, if you're spending $10 per month anyway, you might as well have those benefits.

For general information, you can call CompuServe at (800) 848-8990 or (614) 457-8650. You may also want to check recent computer books for coupons good for free CompuServe connect time, as well as the materials that came with your modem or communications software for other CompuServe subscription offers. Often these free offers include an account number, a temporary password, and a certain amount of free time. They can thus eliminate the need to buy the $39.95 startup kit. Once you are on the system, you can key in GO RATES at any time for free information.

The Four Best CompuServe Tips

Three of the best quick tips for using CompuServe are: key in GO IND to reach the system's index; "join" every SIG you enter; and key in GO IBMFF to access the File Finder feature for SIGs devoted to IBMs and compatible equipment. The fourth tip concerns using CIS's electronic mail feature.

When you reach the Index, open your capture buffer and opt to receive the entire system index. (Consult your comm program manual if you do not know how to open the capture buffer and record incoming information to a file.) When the complete index has been safely recorded, choose to search for topics of interest and specify the word "SIG" or "forum." This will give you an index of all SIGs currently on the system, plus the commands needed to reach them instantly.

The first time you enter a SIG, you are presented with welcoming information that explains what the SIG is all about. Eventually, you see a menu containing an item labeled *Join*. When you select this item, you are asked to key in your name, and within seconds you are a member of the SIG. There is no cost or obligation for joining a SIG, but you may not be able to download files from the SIG library until you do. So you have nothing to lose by joining.

There are lots of ways to locate files on CIS, but keying in GO IBMFF is the best technique when you are looking for computer-related information and public domain and shareware programs. This feature automatically searches the libraries of all of the many SIGs devoted to IBM-compatible topics. The feature is menu-driven and pretty easy to use.

But as is the case with any online system, it helps to have some idea of the terms the uploader probably used when tagging the file with "keywords." So, before you set off in search of a program or file, think for a moment. What term or terms would the person who uploaded the file you seek have used?

You want to be as specific as possible, but not so specific that your search does not pick up relevant files that do not carry those keywords. Yet, if the term you opt to key in is too general or used in many different ways in the industry, you could end up with a list of 500 or more files.

The only way to perfect your file-finding skills is to practice. Take your best shot. Then pay attention to the results. Refine your search approach and try again. But always bear in mind that the file you want may not exist on the system. In any case, you will find that the File Finder feature makes it easy to look for files and call up brief file descriptions.

When you see something that interests you, make a note of the SIG name, the SIG library number, and the name of the file. Then key in GO followed by the SIG name. Join the SIG if you are not already a member. Key in DL followed by the library number at the SIG prompt. When you are in the target library, key in DOW followed by the name of the file you want to download. The best protocol to choose is CompuServe Quick B or B+. The next best choice is CompuServe B. The third best choice is XMODEM. Check your comm program manual for details on the protocols you can use, but note that ProComm 2.4.3 supports both the CompuServe Quick B and B protocols. (If all this sounds confusing, read on. Downloading and protocols are covered below.)

Making the Most of Mail

The fourth tip concerns the best way to handle electronic mail. Regardless of the online system you use, there are two ways to deal with electronic messages. You can either read and respond to a message immediately. Or you can capture the message to disk, sign off, print it out, compose a reply, and sign on again to transmit your reply to your correspondent. Both approaches have their place. For routine correspondence, acknowledgments, and short notes, replying immediately is often the most time-efficient. (Just key in `reply` at the prompt that appears after the letter has been displayed.) For more lengthy, well-thought-out missives, however, it does not make good sense to wrestle with the crude line-oriented text editor most systems offer.

Instead, use your word processor to create an ASCII file containing your reply. Then sign on and transmit it to the other person's mailbox. Now, here's the tip. When you want to transmit a text file to CompuServe's mail system, do not opt to upload it. Instead, select the *Compose* option from the mail menu. The system will think that you want to enter text. The way to "enter" text, however, is to do an ASCII upload at this point, telling your comm software to transmit the text file you have just prepared.

As far as CompuServe is concerned, the transmission looks like a very fast typist is on the line. But the system doesn't care. When the transmission is finished, key in `/ex` to tell CIS you want to exit its editor. Then respond to the prompts for the recipient's ID and your chosen subject line. If you like, you can eliminate even this step by including that information as the first two lines of your prepared text file (TO:700123,456 and SUBJ: How's Trix?). You can even include */EX* at the far left of the last blank line of the file to send the letter immediately. Then you only have to respond to a quick confirmation prompt.

PowerPoint

Let TAPCIS Do It

CompuServe users have carried online automation to new heights. Over the years, programmers have taken advantage of the electronic medium to work as a group, hammering out the code for programs to keep your CompuServe bills as low as possible.

The most successful of these projects is TAPCIS. TAPCIS can be configured to automatically pick up your mail and then stop by your favorite forums to pick up any messages people may have left for you on the forum message board. It then signs off, giving you the opportunity to read and reply to your mail and messages. Then it initiates the second phase. It signs on and automatically distributes your replies to the proper places. TAPCIS can also be told to go get specified files in forum libraries or to upload files on a prepared list.

(continued)

(Let TAPCIS Do It continued)

The point of TAPCIS is to keep connect time charges to the absolute minimum, and it does a splendid job. It is so popular that Compu-Serve modeled its own CompuServe Information Manager (CIM) package on TAPCIS. There's an entire forum devoted to TAPCIS. Just key in `go tapcis` to get there. It's a great place to pick up the latest tricks and tips from enthusiastic users and from the support staff of this shareware program.

TAPCIS can also be used as a general communications program, though you will be much happier with ProComm. If you are a GEnie user, you should know that a program called Aladdin does for GEnie what TAPCIS does for CompuServe.

MCI Mail

Whether you're a businessperson, professional, or hobbyist, if you're going to be online, a CompuServe subscription is a sine qua non. But CIS is definitely not the last word in general interest online systems. GEnie has some remarkable offerings, and it charges only $5 a month for its basic services. You can request a free GEnie information packet by calling (800) 638-9636. America Online, Delphi, and many other systems, including Sears/IBM Prodigy, are also worth investigating.

You may want to explore each and every one of these other systems. But if you're in business, your next subscription after CompuServe should be to MCI Mail. MCI Mail is far from being the only dedicated electronic mail (e-mail) system, but it is far and away the best. That's why if you can't reach someone on CompuServe, there's a good chance that he or she is on MCI Mail.

MCI Mail offers you access to virtually any form of electronic message communication you could want. Plain e-mail is a given. As is the ability to send faxes anywhere in the world. With MCI Mail's Fax Dispatch feature, you can specify portrait or landscape mode for the entire message or for any page or pages within the message. Landscape mode lets you send spreadsheets containing up to 169 columns and up to 39 lines per page.

PowerPoint

X.400 Connections

MCI Mail has been one of the leaders in implementing the X.400 standard. This is the international standard for preparing and addressing e-mail messages. It makes it possible for letters prepared on one system to be sent to recipients on another system without human intervention. Thus, MCI Mail subscribers can communicate with subscribers to mail systems run by AT&T, Telenet, and CompuServe, among others.

Of course the connection operates in both directions, though often an additional fee is assessed for letters sent this way. CompuServe charges about fifteen cents to send a message to other CIS subscribers. Sending the same size message to an MCI Mail subscriber costs $1, an 85-cent difference.

Eventually, it is hoped, a sort of universal e-mail directory will be implemented. That would eliminate the need to subscribe to several different e-mail systems. All you would have to do would be to specify the recipient's name, and your system would figure out where to send your message. The X.500 standard has been created for precisely this purpose, but so far, no one has implemented it.

With MCI Mail, you can also send and receive telexes and TWX messages. (MCI owns Western Union International.) You can also use the system's EDI (Electronic Data Interchange) feature. (If you have to ask, you don't need to know.) Should you want to send a paper message, you can tell MCI Mail to print your letter at a location near your recipient and place the missive in the mail.

Or you can opt for overnight courier delivery. If you like, you can place your letterhead and signature on file with MCI Mail. You can then tell the system to print a letter using these graphic recreations of your letterhead and signature. (The same signature graphic can be used with fax messages, too.) Mass mailings, whether electronic, printed, or a mixture of both can be done very easily. Indeed, if you routinely send letters to the same group of people, you can place their names on a list and simply specify the list as your "address" the next time.

On July 1, 1992, MCI introduced 9,600-bps connections and binary file transfer features. Formerly the top speed was 2,400 bps, and the only way to do a file transfer was with Lotus's Lotus Express program. Those limitations no longer exist, and to the company's credit, the file transfer protocols the system supports are ZMODEM and Kermit. (Other protocols are scheduled to be included in the future.) ZMODEM is absolutely the best error-checking file transfer protocol available, as we will see shortly.

The cost of an MCI mail subscription is $35 a year. Access is through a toll-free 800 number, and there are no connect time charges. Instead, MCI Mail charges by the number of characters sent. It thus costs you nothing to read your mail. You are billed only for what you send. MCI Mail is truly a remarkable system. For more information call (800) 444-6245 or (202) 833-8484.

MCI Mail Tips

One quick tip for using MCI Mail is that when signing on, you can specify your user name and password on the same line as long as you separate them with double slashes. Thus, when prompted to *Please enter user name*, you can enter `jsmith//pword`, where *pword* is your password. If you simply enter `jsmith`, you are given a prompt requesting your password.

Signing on this way will save a little time. But the best tip one can offer for using MCI Mail is to take full advantage of the system's HELP command. Sign on and open your capture buffer. Then simply key in `help`. Additional command options will then appear. For a list of all help information available, for example, key in `help files`. The Help Index command is also very useful. For information on uploading and downloading, key in `help file transfer`. And so on.

You will also want to tap into MCI Mail's bulletin boards. These are not interactive, in that you cannot usually post messages of your own, but they often contain useful information. Start by keying in `view mci mail news`. You will see a numbered list of files placed on the system by the company. Enter the PRINT command, followed by a number or combination of numbers to view the files. Type `help` at the View prompt for a list of commands and what they do.

PowerPoint

The Internet and Cyberspace

Shortly after you enter the electronic universe, you are bound to encounter the term "The Internet" or just "Internet." The Internet is a worldwide collection of thousands of computer networks that are in constant communication with each other. Because it is subsidized by governments and universities, usage is either free or very inexpensive.

Users of any of the Internet networks can reach users on any of the other networks, either by the traditional "store-and-forward" process of electronic mail or in real time. It is also possible to search for and download files (lots and lots of files), bulletin board messages, "newsgroup" discussions, and many other things using the Internet, but doing so requires a deep familiarity with the system. (Internet has been called "the only functioning anarchy in the world.")

Consequently, the main value of the Internet for typical online users is as an electronic mail system. In recent years, CompuServe, MCI Mail, and many other commercial systems have established Internet connections, allowing their subscribers to correspond electronically with Internet users.

The Internet began with the Defense Department's Advanced Research Projects Agency's ARPANET. Started in 1969, this was the first system to use packet-switching technology to connect widely scattered systems, most of which were either on university campuses or at the offices of large defense contractors. Over the years, many other networks were connected to the system.

In 1983, ARPANET was split into two networks, MILNET for the military and ARPANET for the researchers. Together they formed the Internet. The military wanted a reliable network that wasn't constantly being changed. The researchers wanted the freedom to experiment with networking. Electronic gateways and bridges were installed to connect the two nets.

There are currently nearly 2,500 separate networks connected to the Internet, worldwide. Most are at government agencies and universities, and usually you have to be an employee of one of these bodies to get an account. It is the Internet that Robert T. Morris, Jr., a graduate student at Cornell, was convicted of bringing down on November 2, 1988, by injecting a "worm" into the system.   *(continued)*

(The Internet and Cyberspace continued)

In June, 1990, ARPANET itself was taken down, by design. Having served its purpose and having given birth not only to the Internet but to the modern computer telecommunications industry, it was switched off.

If you are really interested in tapping Internet resources, contact Ursula Finkemeyer, President, Bear Software at 70564,604 on CompuServe, or at ugf@bearsw.com on the Internet. The Internet mavens on CompuServe tend to hang out in the UNIXFORUM. See Section 12 of that forum's message board.

You may also be interested in the book *The Whole INTERNET User's Guide & Catalog* by Ed Krol, published by O'Reilly & Associates, Inc., 103 Morris Street, Suite A, Sebastopol, CA 95472. This 376-page book sells for $24.95 and is the most complete guide to the Internet system published to date.

For excellent and entertaining treatments of networks and what it's like to enter *cyberspace*, a term coined by William Gibson, read the following novels:

Shockwave Rider by John Brunner

True Names by Vernor Vinge

Neuromancer by William Gibson

Count Zero by William Gibson

The Knowledge Index

Most general interest online systems offer some form of information retrieval. But much of the time, the databases involved are not in the major leagues. That's fine. They answer the needs of many people. But if you want professional quality, industrial-strength information, you may have to go elsewhere.

If you happen to fall into that category, let me share what is undoubtedly one of the best kept secrets in the online world. It's a system called The Knowledge Index (KI), and it gives you off-hours access to a hundred or more of the databases found on its parent system, DIALOG. Better still, regardless of the database you access or the number of records you opt to view, you are charged a flat rate of $24 an hour.

There is a one-time subscription fee of $39.95. This brings you the KI Starter Kit. The package includes your documentation, a disk for practicing

KI searches, the quarterly KI newsletter, and two free hours of search time. That's a very good deal, since connect time is normally billed at $24 an hour, including telecommunications or packet-switching costs. And $24 an hour is in itself a good deal as online charges go in this area of the electronic universe. KI does not levy an annual subscription fee. All charges are billed to your chosen credit card.

KI is available each weekday between 6:00 P.M and 5:00 A.M., your local time, and all day during the weekend. You can use the system via menus or opt for the quicker command mode. And the databases you have access to are quite impressive. They include the full text of the *Harvard Business Review*, Books in Print, Standard & Poor's, Consumer Drug Information, Legal Resource Index, Canadian Business and Current Affairs, AIDSLINE, Facts on File, Who's Who, the King James Bible, Japan Technology, the Philosopher's Index, and MEDLINE (National Library of Medicine). All KI databases are identical to the databases available through DIALOG.

The Knowledge Index, in short, offers you inexpensive, non-prime time access to *real* full-bore databases. It is incredibly useful. But if you find that it does not suit your needs, the most you can lose is $39.95 and two hours of your time. To request information and a subscription packet, call (800) 334-2564 or (415) 858-3785. While you're at it, ask for an information packet on DIALOG. If you are a latent information junkie, the DIALOG catalogue will give you a high that will last for weeks.

PowerPoint

Other Options

The electronic universe is vast. But, as you might imagine, a number of firms have published directories of databases and online systems. One of the very best is the *Directory of Online Databases* from Gale Research. A semi-annual subscription is $199, but you may be able to find a copy in your local library's reference section.

This is the famous Cuadra Directory, formerly published by Cuadra/ Elsevier. It presents comprehensive, authoritative summaries of online databases to help you select the databases and online services that are best for you and your clients.

You can reach Gale Research, Inc., at (800) 877-4253 or (313) 961-2242. Gale Research specializes in directories of all kinds. Be sure to ask for the company's current catalogue.

SECTION
8-3

UART CONSIDERATIONS

Like everything else about computing, comm cards (serial cards) and modems used to be simple. Now comm cards can contain different UARTs, and modems have become self-contained computers with more programming commands than BASIC. And I said the technology hadn't changed. Well, it hasn't, really. What has happened is the onset of "featuritis," the same dread disease that afflicts our televisions, VCRs, and microwave ovens.

Competitive pressures have forced modem manufacturers to take full advantage of now-amortized development costs, greater chip integration, and economies of scale to offer modems of incredible power at incredibly low prices. The power/price ratio is all to the good. The problem is that when you just want to go online, all those features can get in the way. A similar phenomenon has occurred in communications software, with similar results.

The upside of all this is that today, no matter which modem you buy or which comm program you install, you can pretty much assume the product will have all the important features. The look and feel of the product and its capabilities at the margins of performance are still important factors. But you no longer need to worry about, say, whether a modem is Hayes compatible, or whether a communications program has a scripting capability for automating its operations.

UARTs and the NS16550AFN

Unfortunately, this "What, me worry?" approach does not yet apply to serial cards and their UARTs, or to the UARTs found on internal modem cards. In a nutshell, old-style UART chips cannot buffer data. New-style chips can, and that buffering ability can be crucial to high-speed communications, particularly if you want to run your comm program in the background while you go on to something else.

Two chips constitute what we can call old-style UARTs. Both are made by National Semiconductor. They are the 8250 and the 16450.

The 8250 is the eight-bit chip that was the centerpiece of the serial port in the original IBM/PC. The year was 1981. The PC ran at a blazing 4.77 MHz, and 300-baud communication was the norm. With the introduction of the higher speed AT in 1984, however, it was necessary to move to the faster, 16-bit 16450 UART. That chip has remained the serial card standard ever since. CPU speeds have risen dramatically, of course, but the speed of the expansion bus has remained fairly close to AT levels, so a faster UART has not been necessary.

The popularity of high-speed modems, however, and the increased use of multitasking pretty much spelled the end for the 16450. Imagine yourself as part of a bucket brigade. The person behind you hands you a bucket of water. You turn and pass it to the person in front. So far so good. You get another bucket, but now when you turn to hand it off, the person in front of you is busy talking to somebody else. He can't take the bucket from you just yet. Meantime, the person behind you is shoving yet another bucket your way.

So what do you do? What the 16450 does when it cannot get the attention of the CPU is to drop the character it is holding, thus freeing itself to accept another character from the modem. And what is it that has suddenly distracted the CPU? Well, it could be your word processing program or some other software you are multitasking under Windows, DesqView, or OS/2.

The solution is simple, when you think about it: Use a chip that is equipped with a buffer or holding tank. That way, when "buckets" are being pressed into its hands by the communications link, the chip can store its contents until it can get the CPU to come and take the data away. That chip is the National Semiconductor 16550AFN UART. The 16550A, as it is often called, sports a 16-byte onboard buffer. The buffer operates on the first-in-first-out principle. When properly programmed by your communications software, the chip has the ability to send and receive data all by itself for up to three milliseconds at 38.4 Kbps.

FIFO Enable/Disable

The communications program you use must be able to work with the 16550A's FIFO buffer if you want to be able to take advantage of this feature. ProComm Plus and Windows 3.1 are designed to work with the UART buffer enabled, if you have a FIFO chip. But Windows 3.0 does not, so the buffer must not be enabled. (You can improve the multitasking performance of Windows 3.1 by editing the 386Enh section of SYSTEM.INI to add the line *COMBoostTime=10*. That gives your comm program more time to handle UART interrupts.)

Programs that are not compatible with an enabled FIFO buffer make your machine appear to lock up. That's because some programs expect the UART to issue an interrupt (a signal to get the CPU's attention) before each character.

If the chip's FIFO buffer is enabled and filled, it sends one interrupt, expecting the comm program and CPU to come and get the entire 16 bytes. The comm program sees one interrupt and thus accepts one character. Then it waits for the next interrupt, unaware that there are fifteen characters ready to go. The UART, seeing that its buffer has not been emptied as expected, puts the comm line on hold and waits, creating the electronic equivalent of a Mexican standoff.

Fortunately, there are solutions in the form of little public domain utility programs. The two I like best are the COMFIX package from the Support Group and the UARTTOOLS package from Milliways! Software Systems. They are not the end of the world (or the universe), but they are clean, quick, and invaluable.

With the Support Group's UARTID, you can instantly find out what kind of chip serves as the UART for each of your COM ports. CHECK-IRQ will tell you what IRQ (Interrupt Request) number each port is using. BIOSFIX will make it possible to use COM3 and COM4 if they happen to be located at some strange address in your machine. The Milliways! package includes FIFON.COM to enable your UART's buffer; FIFOFF.COM to disable it; and FIFOSTAT.COM to determine whether the buffer is currently enabled or disabled.

If you have a very new PC or serial card, there is a good possibility that you don't have a single UART chip at all. Instead, your manufacturer may have used a single "super" chip. The VLSI (Very Large Scale Integration) Western Digital 16C552, for example, includes the equivalent of two 16550AFN UARTs, plus a parallel port, all in a single chip. If the UART ID or a similar program reports that you do not have a 16550A, the VLSI chip may be the reason.

Change Chips?

If you discover that you have an old-style UART, there's really not much point in upgrading unless you find that your current equipment is dropping characters. If you are having a problem, and if you suspect the UART, an upgrade may be in order. Though, naturally, you will want to make sure that your comm software supports UART FIFO buffering.

Check with the maker or vendor of your serial card for confirmation, but you will usually find that it is technically possible to upgrade to a 16550A from a 16450. If you're reasonably handy with a chip puller, and if your 16450 is socketed, not soldered, you can buy a 16550A for about $15. Contact Jameco in Belmont, California at (800) 831-4242, or JDR Microdevices in San Jose at (800) 538-5000.

If the chip is soldered in place, the only way to upgrade your current equipment to replace the board. If the UART is soldered into your motherboard, you might consider adding a new comm card and connecting your modem to that. There is no need to disable the motherboard-based port, but it might be helpful to set it to COM3 or COM4, if possible. That way you can set your new board to COM1 or COM2. You might consider a company like TSD Systems in Longwood, Florida, as a source for your new board. For information, call (407) 331-9130. Or you might want to peruse the pages of *Computer Shopper*.

PowerPoint

COM2 Advantage

The COM port you use can have an effect on throughput. By connecting your modem to COM2, for example, you can get slightly better performance. Tests have shown that at high speeds, with a clean, noise-free connection, COM2 connections are about seven-percent faster than COM1 connections.

The reason is that COM2 and COM4 use IRQ3, which has a higher priority and will therefore be handled faster than IRQ4 used by COM1 and COM3.

SECTION
8-4

SORTING OUT MODEM STANDARDS

In this section we'll look at the many standards that confront anyone buying a modem today. The main question you have to ask yourself about modems is simple. Do you want a top-quality, brand-name modem for about $50 or one for about $250? In my opinion, there's not much point in fooling around with anything in between.

A Simple Answer

Your $50 will bring you a 2,400-bps modem with all the features you need to tap into any online service or BBS. For $250 you can get a unit with a top actual speed of 14,400 bps (14.4 Kbps). But when the modem's built-in compression program is enabled, the effective throughput can be as high as 38,400 bits per second. Without special hardware, your PC's comm port cannot operate any faster than that. For about $25 more, you can get the same model in a version equipped to send and receive faxes.

Which one should you get? You can forget the interminable hemming and hawing you'll find in computer magazines. Believe it or not, the answer is quite simple. Either you want high-speed data communications or you don't. If you don't, buy the 2,400-bps unit. If you do, there's no point in fiddling around with anything less than a 14.4-Kbps unit with built-in data compression capabilities. A send/receive fax feature is purely optional. If you have at least two phone lines, though, you may be better off getting a separate fax board for about $100. That way both fax and modem can be used at the same time.

If you are new to data communications, you should know that all modems are downwardly compatible. A 2,400-bps modem can also operate at 1,200, 300, and even 120 bits per second. A 14.4-Kbps model can operate at 9,600, 4,800, 2,400, and so on. Thus, while you won't be able to operate at 14.4 Kbps with every system you call, you will be able to connect at that system's highest supported rate.

Internal or External?

The only other major consideration is whether to get an internal, card-mounted model or a freestanding external unit. With no case, LEDs, or external power connections, internal modems tend to be about $20 cheaper. They also occupy no space on your desk. If you opt for an internal modem, make sure it can be set as any comm port (COM1 through COM4). If the unit can only be COM1 or COM2, and those ports are already in use on your system, you will have to rejigger your hardware and software.

If you've got the desk space and the extra $20, I think you'll be happier with an external unit. You won't have to give up an expansion slot to another heat-producing card, and you will find that the LEDs on external units are invaluable in finding out what's going on. For example, once you've loaded your comm program, the SD (send data) light will flash each time you hit a key. If it doesn't flash, you know you have a loose connection or some other problem. There is also the fact that an external modem can be used with any make, model, or size of computer.

PowerPoint

The Modem to Buy

To summarize, you should get either a 2,400-bps modem or a 14.4-Kpbs modem with built-in error correction and data compression. The first kind of modem is easy to identify. For the second kind, look for a phrase like this: "14,400 V.32bis with V.42bis." A modem that offers V.42bis will also include V.42. If such a unit also supports MNP 5, so much the better.

If you opt for a model that includes the ability to talk to fax machines, make sure you get one that can both send and receive. Ideally, it should be able to perform both functions at a top speed of 9,600 bps, though to keep prices down, some companies make units that send at 9,600 bps but receive at 4,800 bps. Be sure to ask.

Modem Specifications

The terms and specifications that make modem ads so confusing—terms like V.22, V.32bis, V.42, and MNP—refer to the signaling and error-correcting techniques used by the various units. Modem terminology has never been easy to understand, but in the past few years it has become a complete mess.

Part of the problem is that one must now be concerned with much more than just the modem's top speed. Today, due in large measure to the incredible speeds modems achieve over ordinary phone lines, we must also be concerned with built-in error correction. And we must think about data compression, since that can boost the effective throughput by 400 percent.

The other part of the problem is that there are cryptic terms for each of these specifications, and they all sound the same. In the case of V.32 and V.32bis or V.42 and V.42bis, the terms really *are* the same, save for the French "bis," which translates roughly as "again" or "the same, but slightly different." That wouldn't be too bad if V.42bis referred to a speed twice that of V.42. But it doesn't. As we will see, V.42 is an error-correcting protocol and V.42bis is a data compression standard.

How We Got Here

The confusion is increased by the fact that even the standards that refer to speed actually cover more than just the modulation technique used to achieve a certain rate of communications. They also deal with how the connection is negotiated, what to do when the phone line suddenly becomes noisy, how to do it, and so on.

Even this state of affairs might be manageable. But it represents only half the story. Conflicting or multiple standards have always been part of the story. Years ago, thanks to the hegemony of AT&T, North Americans followed the Bell standard for 1,200-bps communications, while Europeans followed one hammered out by the International Telephone and Telegraph Consultative Committee. This is an arm of the United Nations, and it is known as the CCITT, an acronym of its French name. (This is pronounced by saying each letter: "see-see-eye-tee-tee.")

A court decision making it legal for customers to attach non-AT&T equipment to phone lines added to the momentum. With the break up of AT&T some years later, there was no longer a body with the power to both set and enforce standards. As the technology developed, increasing speeds first to 2,400 bps and then leaping ahead to 9,600 bps, companies began to develop their own, proprietary standards.

Communicating at 9,600 bps over ordinary, crackly phone lines is a tricky business. For to fit more bits into a second of time, each bit must be "smaller." The smaller the bit, the more easily it can be knocked for a loop by a little bit of line noise. That meant that sophisticated error-correction techniques were mandatory. There is always more than one way to do things, so companies like U.S. Robotics, Hayes, and Telebit developed different modulation and error-correcting approaches that became the basis of their proprietary standards.

The catch, of course, is that it takes two modems to communicate. So, for a while, if you wanted to be able to communicate at 9,600 bps, you had to decide on a modem maker and then buy at least two of his boxes. Often at a cost of $1,500 or more apiece. Many companies with significant communications needs found this worthwhile, however, because it let them eliminate expensive leased phone lines and save large sums on long distance connections due to the faster throughput.

In the meantime, Tymnet was working on its X.PC protocol and Microcom was developing a competing product called MNP (Microcom Networking Protocol). The central feature of both is error correction, though they include many other feature besides. Committees, particularly those focused on technical issues that concern a multimillion dollar market, are not quick to produce their results.

But over time, the CCITT issued its recommendations for international standards governing high-speed communications, error correction, and data compression. CCITT standards typically begin with either an *X* or a *V*, as in X.25 or X.400 (the standards for packet-switching hookups and electronic mail formats, respectively) or in V.32. They are pronounced like this: "x-dot-twenty-five," "vee-dot-thirty-two," and so on.

The Nub of the Problem

Now, here's the problem. The essence of computer communications is compatibility. Without nearly universal agreement on how things will be done, no communication can take place. So, in today's marketplace, modem makers have to make their products compatible with everything that went before. Like most computer equipment, modems tend to last a very long time. There are still hundreds of thousands, if not millions, of high-speed modems in service that support only older or proprietary protocols.

Of course, almost every modem in use today can communicate at 2,400 bps using either the AT&T Bell standard or the CCITT standard, and many can deal with both. But the point of buying a high-speed modem is high speed. The goal is to be able to communicate with any modem at the highest speed it can accommodate. That isn't always possible, but it is certainly one of the reasons why so many standards appear in modem ads today.

Fortunately, these things have a way of sorting themselves out. In the opinion of many, the current state of confusion cannot last, if only because customers tend not to buy when they are badly confused. High-speed data communications over ordinary telephone lines is a well-established reality. And the advent of inexpensive 14.4-Kbps modems with built-in error correction will send many of the old 9,600-bps models, with their proprietary protocols, into retirement.

A consensus is clearly forming around the V.32bis standard for speed, the V.42 standard for error correction, and the V.42bis standard for data compression. In my opinion, the market won't have it any other way. As for the future and the possibility that history will repeat itself, there are indications that modem communications have just about reached the limit of what is physically possible. (Of course, that's what they told us about 2,400-bps and then 9,600-bps communications.) More than likely, the next battles will be fought over a different technology, like fiberoptics and ISDN (Integrated Services Digital Network) implementations.

> *PowerPoint*
>
> ## V.FAST, the Ultimate Standard
>
> In the not-too-distant future, Study Group XVII of the CCITT is scheduled to release its recommendation for the next modem standard. Informally known as V.FAST, it is expected to provide for signaling of at least 19.2 Kbps, though 24 or even 28 kilobits per second is considered a possibility. With data compression, a rate of 28 Kbps would yield an effective throughput of 113,000 bits per second over regular phone lines.
>
> No one knows what the standard will be called officially. Noting, however, that it is close to the absolute maximum data rate that ordinary copper cable can support, some wags have dubbed it "V.LAST." It may well be that modems will have finally reached their limit.

Quick Reference

Since the millennium is sure to be slow in coming, you may find the following list of terms helpful in deciphering a modem ad. You may or may not decide to buy, but at least you'll know what they're talking about. The list is followed by brief explanations of key terms:

Bell 103	300-bps U.S. Standard
Bell 212A	1,200-bps U.S. Standard
V.21	300-bps standard used outside the U.S.
V.22	1,200-bps standard used outside the U.S.
V.22bis	2,400-bps CCITT Standard
V.32	9,600-bps CCITT Standard
V.32bis	14,400-bps CCITT Standard
HST	14,400-bps U.S. Robotics proprietary standard
V.FAST	19.2- to 28-Kbps CCITT Standard (expected in 1993)
V.42	CCITT error correction protocol
MNP 4	Public domain error correction protocol that is incorporated as a less powerful subset of V.42
V.42bis	CCITT data compression protocol
MNP 5	Microcom's data compression protocol

1,200- and 2,400-bps Standards

No one communicates at 300 bps these days, and very few operate at 1,200 bps. So the Bell 103, Bell 212A, V.21, and V.22 standards simply are not a factor. Modems made in the U.S. typically support the two Bell standards, but not the two CCITT standards.

AT&T had developed a standard for 2,400-bps communications as well, but the company was broken up just when 2,400-bps communications was gaining momentum. AT&T no longer had the clout to impose its standards, so modem manufacturers joined the rest of the world and endorsed the CCITT V.22bis standard. That made V.22bis the first true "world modem standard."

V.32 and V.32bis

The V.32 standard is designed for 9,600-bps communications. But it includes a protocol that allows the two modems to automatically "fall back" to 4,800 bps if the phone connection is too noisy. However, there is no provision to "spring forward" should the noise situation clear up.

Modems supporting the V.32bis standard can talk to V.32 modems at 9,600 bps or at 4,800 bps, if necessary. But one of the key elements of the V.32bis specification is the ability to not only fall back but to also spring forward. Two V.32bis modems begin their session by negotiating the data rate they will use based on current line conditions. They try for the highest speed connection possible, which is 14.4 Kbps under this protocol. But if the line is too noisy, they may establish communication at 12,000, 7,200, 9,600, or 4,800 bits per second.

The modems monitor the connection continuously. Should they sense that the noise situation has improved, they will "retrain" themselves and spring forward to a higher speed. Basically, V.32bis modems act as your agents to insure that your data is always being transferred at the highest speed the phone connection allows.

U.S. Robotics HST (High Speed Technology)

U.S. Robotics, one of this country's most respected modem makers, introduced the Courier HST in 1986. The original model operated at a top speed of 9,600 bps using the proprietary HST protocol. Other modem makers had their 9,600-bps protocols as well, but for one reason or another, U.S. Robotics emerged as the standard before V.32 became established. Several years later, the company boosted the speed of the Courier HST to 14.4 Kbps.

Perhaps bowing to the inevitable, the company now offers at least three models of Courier modems. One supports only HST. One supports only V.32bis. And one, the Courier Dual Standard, supports both HST and V.32bis. The proprietary 9,600-bps protocols developed by Telebit (PEP —Packetized Ensemble Protocol), Hayes (Hayes Express 96 V series), and CompuCom (CSP—CompuCom Speed Protocol) are simply not major players in today's market.

V.42 Error Correction

The CCITT V.42 standard is designed to increase the reliability of V.32 and V.32bis communications by adding error-correcting techniques. The standard is based on the Link Access Protocol M (LAPM). But, by way of an "annex" document, the standard also includes MNP 4 (see below) as an alternative, fall-back error protocol. It seems clear that the inclusion of both LAPM and MNP 4 is the result of a political decision worked out by the CCITT study group.

In any case, it means that V.42 modems can implement error correction with MNP 4 modems, even if the V.42 modems do not specifically support MNP 4 themselves. Naturally, the two do not use the more powerful V.42 error-correction protocol. During the opening negotiations at the start of the call, the modems figure out whether the V.42 protocol can be used between them or whether MNP 4 has to be used.

Microcom Networking Protocol (MNP)

The Microcom Networking Protocol is a complete hierarchy of standards. It starts with MNP Class 1, an error correction protocol that is no longer used by anybody, and runs all the way up to MNP 10, a protocol for coaxing the highest performance from poor connections, especially those found in cellular phone systems.

MNP 2, 3, and 4 deal with error control. The company has placed them in the public domain, so any modem maker or software producer is free to implement them. MNP 4 is probably the most important since it offers both error correction and some data compression.

MNP 5 offers industrial-strength data compression. It can cut the time required to transmit a file in half, effectively doubling data throughput. However, since you can easily compress files with programs like PKZIP or LHA, and since sending those files with MNP 5 enabled can actually slow transmission, it is hard to see what benefit it offers. In some cases, MNP 5 has been known to try to expand compressed files.

The remaining five classes of MNP need not concern us here.

V.42bis

Although you would think that V.42bis would be closely related to V.42, this is not the case. The V.42bis standard is a CCITT data compression protocol. The V.42bis protocol can quadruple effective data throughput. The connection may use a raw data speed of 14.4 Kbps or less, but, thanks to compression, much less data needs to be sent.

The modem on your end compresses the data as it comes out of your machine and sends it down the wire. The V.42bis modem on the other end accepts the data, decompresses it, and sends it to its computer.

Thus, the connection between the two modems may be 14.4 Kbps, but the connection between each computer and its modem is even faster. Theoretically, modems could send their computers data at a rate of 57.6 Kbps, but the maximum speed a standard comm port UART can handle is 38.4 Kbps. That's why you can expect that if you buy a V.32bis modem with V.42bis compression, the maximum effective throughput will be 38.4 Kbps. And that assumes squeaky-clean phone lines.

It is important to point out that V.42bis has nothing to do with MNP 5, the Microcom offering for data compression. Indeed, V.42bis is more efficient than either MNP 5 or MNP 7. And, unlike MNP 5, V.42bis performance does not suffer when you transmit files that have already been compressed. It simply passes them on through.

PowerPoint

Modem Tips

If you opt for a high-speed modem, take the time to thumb through the manual. Try to get some idea of what all the various commands and switch settings mean. Then, save yourself some time and trouble by calling the customer service number for the system you want to connect with. Tell them the kind of modem you have and the name of your communications software, and ask them how to set things up to access their service at top speed. Online services have a financial interest in getting you connected, so you may find them quite helpful.

If you have Call Waiting on your modem line, always be sure to disable it by "dialing" *70 or 1170 at the start of your session. Call Waiting will remain disabled for the duration of the call. See the front of your phone book under *Tone*Block* for more details, and consider getting a second phone line if you are a heavy modem user.

(continued)

(Modem Tips continued)

If you are a portable or laptop user, consider leaving your printer at home the next time you travel. If you need a printout, you can almost always send yourself a fax, care of the hotel's fax machine. If your modem does not include a fax capability, send the fax via MCI Mail, CompuServe, or some other online system.

If you want to be able to dial up your main computer from a distant location, see if your main system's comm program includes a "host" mode. A simple command, for example, puts ProComm into host mode. The first time you try this, be sure to test the arrangement by calling your desktop system from a nearby phone. Then post a sign on your machine warning of dire consequences should a well-meaning do-gooder turn it off while you are away.

PowerPoint

Using Cellular Phones

With the necessary connecting hardware, any modem can communicate over a cellular phone. However, the interruption of the signal caused when one cell hands off to another as you drive down the road will break the modem-to-modem connection unless both systems are using special protocols and software. Spectrum Cellular Corporation of Dallas, Texas, has been a leader in cellular modem communications, so you may want to call them at (800) 233-2119 or (214) 630-9825.

However, you may also want to wait until the market settles down. Two approaches to cellular packet switching exist, for example. They are Cellular Data, Inc.'s Cellular Plan 1, and an IBM-led consortium's CelluPlan II. There is no question that cellular data communications is going to be a huge market once the major issues have been settled. If at all possible, wait until the smoke clears before taking the plunge.

PROTOCOLS AND COMPRESSION

You will never be able to take full advantage of an online system until you know how to upload and download files. Electronic mail is wonderful, but the real riches lie in the files you can download from a distant system. For someone new to computer communications, this presents two challenges. First, you have to use a file transfer protocol to effect the download, and second, in order to use or read the file, you often have to uncompress it once you are offline. Fortunately, both techniques are easily mastered once you have the right software and know which commands to enter.

How Shall We Communicate?

I once had a French professor who had a genuine gift for languages. On the first and only day during the term that he spoke English to the class he told us of meeting an equally gifted friend in Cyprus. "Which language shall we speak?" was the first line of their conversation. We were all mightily impressed. (I think I lasted about two weeks before switching to Latin.)

In a way, computers are multilingual as well. But the "languages" are called protocols. A communications protocol is simply an agreement on how things will be done. The two most common protocols consist of the communications settings of 8/N/1 and 7/E/1. Translated, this means "eight data bits, no parity, and one stop bit" and "seven data bits, even parity, and one stop bit." Numerous other combinations of settings are possible, but these are the two that nearly every system offers.

X-ON/X-OFF Flow Control Protocol

When you move into the realm of data transfer, where one system transmits a quantity of bytes to another as a continuous stream, more advanced agreements are necessary. The simplest is the start/stop X-ON/X-OFF protocol. The *X* here stands for *transfer* as in *Xfer*.

This protocol gives both machines some measure of control over the data flow. If MCI Mail is transmitting to you all of your electronic mail messages, and your computer is having difficulty accepting and storing all the incoming data, your machine may send MCI an X-OFF signal. By agreement, when the MCI mainframe receives that signal, it suspends the transmission. When your machine is ready again, it sends an X-ON signal telling MCI Mail to resume.

These signals are really ASCII codes. An X-ON is an ASCII 17 or Control-Q. An X-OFF is an ASCII 19 or Control-S. (The ASCII code numbers from 1 through 26 are the control codes Control-A through Control-Z.) These bytes are recognized as control characters and are dropped from the data stream. The X-ON/X-OFF technique is usually referred to as *software flow control* because it is the communications software on either end that issues and responds to the signals.

Most online systems and BBSs support X-ON/X-OFF. However, this protocol is far less important now than it was in the days of teletypewriters and slow computers with slow disk drives. In fact, with today's super-intelligent high-speed modems, the X-ON/X-OFF protocol can cause serious problems.

That's because the modems themselves are now smart enough to monitor the contents of the data stream instead of simply passing it through to the computer. If an ASCII 17 or ASCII 19 happens to occur in a binary file that you want to transmit, your modem assumes it is a control code and drops it from the data stream. Therefore, you should probably make sure that software flow control is disabled in both your modem and in your communications program.

Scripts and Control

But wait a minute. What happens if you're blasting a long text file into MCI Mail at 9,600 bps and the MCI mainframe temporarily finds that it cannot accept your data that fast? If your software flow control is disabled, there is no way for the MCI computer to signal your system to suspend transmission. The result could be that most of your file gets lost, and you have to start again.

Two things ameliorate this situation. First, modem technology isn't the only technology to have advanced. Thus, the likelihood that this kind of situation will develop is relatively small. Second, most communications programs these days include dialing directories (menuized phone books) and a scripting capability.

A script is basically a batch file for communications software. With a script, you can automate virtually every aspect of an online session from dialing the proper phone number, responding correctly to prompts for your account number and password, and issuing commands to pick up your mail, download a file, or anything else. Since a script can also be used to automatically reset both your modem and your comm software, you can, in effect, use a different configuration of settings for each system you dial.

Thus, if you find that you need to have software flow control enabled when using MCI Mail, you can prepare a script to do it. Put *MCI Mail* in your dialing directory, and whenever you select that item, your script will automatically configure your modem and software accordingly.

Hardware Flow Control

There is another protocol we should touch on briefly: hardware flow control. In every online session, there are three connections. There's the connection between your computer and your modem; the phone line connection between your modem and the remote modem; and the connection between the remote modem and its computer. Hardware flow control concerns the first connection, the one between your computer and your modem.

Most modems, and all high-speed modems, have data buffers—little bits of memory into which they can place data to smooth out the flow. In addition, for maximum throughput, it is common to set things up so that the computer and the modem transmit data to each other faster than the speed being used on the phone link. For example, your computer may be sending data to the modem at a rate of 19.2 Kbps, while the modem is talking to the remote modem at 9,600 bps. Some kind of flow control between your computer and your modem is thus essential.

Software flow control is one option. Your high-speed modem can probably be set to respond to X-ON/X-OFF signals issued by your computer and vice versa. But, for the reasons explained above, this is rarely a good idea. That's why most modern comm programs and modems support hardware flow control.

The concept is simple. Among the nine wires in the RS-232 interface that are actually used to connect a modem and a computer are two that are designated Request to Send (RTS) and Clear to Send (CTS). The voltage on these wires can be either high or low. By toggling the voltage levels on these wires, the modem and the computer can tell each other to stop or to resume data transmission.

Remember, hardware flow control is strictly between your computer (the Data Terminal Equipment or DTE) and its modem (the Data Communications Equipment or DCE). It has nothing to do with the remote system. Hardware flow control is by far the better of the two options, but, of course, your communications software must support it for it to work.

PowerPoint

Capture Buffers

Often when you are online you want to preserve whatever is being displayed, whether it is a letter someone has sent you or a system announcement. Some people solve this problem by hitting their Print Screen key each time the remote system displays a screen of text, but that is absolutely the wrong way to go about it.

All comm programs today offer a *capture buffer* feature. Before you tell the remote system to display your mail, you enter a command to your comm software. The program prompts you for the name of the file you want to put the incoming data in. Then you tell the remote system to display your mail, and your software records it to disk. Then you close your capture buffer with a command to your comm program and sign off.

When you're offline, you can edit the file. Print it with your word processor. Copy it to the printer. Or upload it to someone else. If you have a fax modem, you can even send it to a fax machine. So, if you are a new user, be sure to check your comm program manual for instructions on how to capture incoming information to disk.

Error-Checking Protocols

Technically, any time you record incoming information on disk you are downloading, and any time you transmit information (as opposed to typing it) to a remote system you are uploading. However, usually these terms refer to a process that involves transferring a binary, machine language file under the control of an error-checking protocol like XMODEM.

In most cases, if a noisy phone line causes some characters to be garbled when you are capturing text information to disk, little harm is done. Most of the time you can easily figure out what the text says, even with some of the characters missing. However, even one garbled character in a binary file can render it useless. That's why some form of error control is essential.

We won't go into detail, but in general, an error control protocol chops a binary file up into packets of bytes. It then calculates a *checksum* on the basis of the binary digits in those bytes and sends both the packet and the checksum to the remote computer. The remote system opens the packet, performs the same calculation on its bits, and compares the checksum it gets with the one sent by the other computer. If the checksums match, the next packet is sent. If they don't, the remote system tells your system to send the same packet again.

Naturally, numerous systems have been devised for implementing this basic technique. And still other protocols have been created that treat the entire file as a packet and offer additional features besides.

Fortunately, it isn't necessary for most online users to know all of the details. Indeed, there are only a few basic things you need to know to become an ace downloader. First, most online systems and BBSs offer several different protocols. ("Which language shall we speak?") Whichever one you pick, your own comm software obviously must support it.

Second, ZMODEM is the best choice in almost any situation. Should you be in the midst of a ZMODEM download and suddenly get disconnected, you can sign back on, opt to download the file again, and ZMODEM will pick up right where it left off! You almost have to see it believe it, but I've seen it and it works.

Third, XMODEM is the lowest common denominator, the one supported by virtually every online system. But XMODEM is not very good at mainframe-to-PC connections. If you have a choice, select XMODEM 1K or XMODEM-CRC instead of plain XMODEM.

If you are talking to a mainframe (as opposed to a BBS), you are probably better off with Kermit, a protocol specifically designed for this kind of connection. If a proprietary protocol, like CompuServe's B and B+ (Quick B) is offered and your comm software supports it, select that, since it is likely to be optimized for that particular system.

Quick Handles on Protocols

Until you gain more experience online, all you really have to remember is to opt first for any proprietary protocol, second for ZMODEM, and third for XMODEM 1K. Failing that, plain XMODEM still does a very good, if not super-efficient, job. Still, the details are important, so here's a quick summary of the leading protocols used by online systems today.

XMODEM   Created by Ward Christensen for PC-to-PC communications in the early days. Sends data in 128-byte packets. Calculates a simple checksum. Not good with mainframes because mainframes don't always send continuously. If a mainframe does not respond to ten requests to continue, plain XMODEM will "time out," that is, quit. Relaxed XMODEM, designed by John Friel (author of the comm program Qmodem), is more tolerant of mainframe delays.

XMODEM-CRC   XMODEM with a more robust error-checking method called a CRC (Cyclical Redundancy Check). Error-free transmissions 99.9 percent of the time. Since most versions fall back to plain XMODEM if XMODEM-CRC is not supported on the remote system, you can select this on your computer and XMODEM on the remote when a CRC version is not offered. It's always possible that the system designers simply forgot to include "CRC" in their description.

XMODEM 1K   Designed by Chuck Forsberg, creator of YAM (Yet Another Modem program) communications software. The same as XMODEM-CRC, except that it uses 1K-packets (1,024 bytes) instead of 128-byte packets. Produces a faster throughput, provided the phone line connection is decent. On a noisy line, however, it can actually result in longer transmission times.

YMODEM BATCH   Chuck Forsberg's warm up for ZMODEM. Based on XMODEM 1K, YMODEM sends the filename ahead of the file data, allowing you to specify an entire list of files you would like to download. (The alternative is to enter a separate download command for each file you want.)

YMODEM G   A streaming protocol that sends the entire file before checking for errors. YMODEM G handles the nitty-gritty of getting the file off the disk and into the modem (or vice versa), and it supports batch transmissions. But it relies on your high- speed modem's built-in facilities (MNP 4, MNP 5, V.42bis, etc.) to take care of the error checking.

ZMODEM   Chuck Forsberg's masterpiece. Commissioned by Telenet and then placed in the public domain, ZMODEM is designed to be used on a wide variety of systems operating in a wide variety of environments (modems, timesharing systems, satellite relays, wide-area packet-switched networks, etc.). Lets you specify a large group of files for batch downloading.

Uses a 32-bit CRC for even greater accuracy than XMODEM-CRC's 16-bit algorithm. Sends data continuously until the receiver interrupts to request retransmission of garbled data. Varies the size of each packet to continuously adapt to the noise on the phone line.

Does not pad the last packet to bring it up to a requisite size, so the file recorded to disk is the same size as the file you asked to download. Can pick up where it left off if interrupted.

KERMIT   Named after Jim Hensen's famous frog. Developed at Columbia University under the direction of Frank da Cruz and released into the public domain. Specifically designed to smooth out the differences in incompatible systems, most notably between PCs and mainframes. A version called Super Kermit supports sliding windows that let your computer send packets continuously, instead of sending a packet and waiting for confirmation from the remote system before sending the next packet.

Super Kermit sends and listens for packet acknowledgments from the remote system at the same time. If there is a problem with a given packet, it is resent. The sequence of packets does not matter, since the protocol provides for assembling them in their proper order. The development of Super Kermit was funded by The Source, a now-defunct system that, sadly, was about ten years ahead of its time.

PowerPoint

Adding ZMODEM and CIS B/B+

Although ZMODEM and CompuServe's B protocols have been placed in the public domain, you may find that your communications software does not offer them. Not to worry. There's a very good chance that you can add these protocols to your current software using two shareware programs.

There are basically three ways to accomplish this. Your communications program may include the option of adding one or more external protocols. That is certainly the best approach. Failing that, you may be able to shell to DOS from within the program. If so, you can shell out and run an add-on protocol program at the appropriate time.

(continued)

(Adding ZMODEM and CIS B/B+ continued)

Finally, your comm program may include a feature to let you call your word processor to prepare electronic mail. If so, you may be able to substitute the name of an external protocol program for your word processor when configuring your comm software. That way, at the appropriate time, you can enter the command to call your word processor and actually activate an external protocol program.

If your comm program offers any of these three possibilities, there's a good chance that you can add support for ZMODEM and CIS B/B+ to your current setup, using the shareware programs DSZ from Chuck Forsberg and OZBEXT from Ozark Software.

Compression: ZIP, LHA, ARC

File compression, like binary file transfer protocols, is a complicated topic. However, since there is no need to be familiar with all the details, you will find that dealing with compressed files is much easier than you might imagine. Indeed, all you need is a small collection of programs and a few simple commands.

A file compression program does two very desirable things. First, it squeezes a file down to as little as half its original size. Sophisticated algorithms are used, but the concept is easy to understand. Consider the word *the*. In an uncompressed file, it occupies three characters or bytes. But it is a common word that occurs quite often in most text files. If a program could substitute a single character for *the*, the size of the file could be reduced considerably.

That's what happens when a file is compressed. When it is uncompressed, the single character is read and expanded into its original *the* form. When the technique is applied to the file as a whole, the file can be squeezed down to half the size of the original. That means that only half the time is required to upload or download the file. The size reduction that is possible varies with the file and with the compression program used, but the reductions are almost always substantial.

Second, and equally important from an online user's perspective, file compression software has the ability to store *many* files in a single compressed library or archive. This means that when you want an entire program package, with the program, the documentation, the configuration utilities, and so on, you do not have to download each file individually. You can download a single archive, sign off, and then extract the files the archive holds, restoring them to their original form.

File Extraction

That's really all most people need to know about how the overall process works. The key question is how to deal with a compressed file or archive once it has been downloaded from a remote system. All you need are the right programs and a few very simple commands.

As you might expect, a number of compression techniques are used. The most popular are LHARC (.LHA or.LZH files), PKZIP (.ZIP files), and ARC (.ARC files). Other techniques, like ZOO, PAK, and ARJ, are less common, but the same approach applies. That approach is to download the file and sign off the system. Then extract the files in the archive using the appropriate program. The file extension of the downloaded file will tell you the program to use.

The programs are LHA.EXE, PKUNZIP.EXE, and ARC.EXE or ARC-E.COM. Virtually any online system that offers compressed files also offers the utility programs you need to extract them. LHA or LHARC is in the public domain. The next two are shareware. ARC-E.COM is a public domain utility created by Vernon Buerg specifically to extract files from .ARC files. It is available separately, but it is also now included with the main ARC package.

My suggestion is to obtain these programs and place them in your UTILS directory or some other directory that is in your path. That way they are always at your disposal. Download the file or files you are interested in having. Create a directory called TEMP. Then apply the appropriate extraction command to the file and extract its contents into TEMP.

What confuses most people about using extraction programs is all the features they include. With the exception of ARC-E.COM, each is designed to not only *remove* files from archives but to *create* archives as well. Thus, there are commands for viewing a "verbose listing" of an archive's contents, extracting individual files, freshening files by replacing them with newer versions, and so on. None of these options need concern you if you are new to this game. All you want to do is to *extract* files. That makes it simple.

Assuming you have copies of all three main programs in a directory that is in your path, and assuming that you have created a new directory called C:\TEMP, here are the commands to enter. You don't actually have to specify the file extension, since the program searches for it automatically:

- LHA E *filename.ext* C:\TEMP
- PKUNZIP *filename.ext* C:\TEMP
- ARC E *filename.ext* C:\TEMP

Self-Extracting Archives

The file compression and archiving field is so well covered by public domain and shareware programs that there is virtually no room for a commercial equivalent. And even if a commercial equivalent did exist, its success would depend on how widely it was adopted. As it is, if you want to download programs, files, games, graphic images, and anything else from a BBS or commercial online utility, you've got to have the programs to extract .ZIP, .LHA, and .ARC files.

There is, however, a small exception—*self-extracting* archive files. All three major compression programs have the ability to create self-extracting archives. These are .EXE files that automatically extract when you key in the filename. As with all archives, the original remains unaffected by the process.

The nice thing about self-extracting archives is that the user does not need to have a separate program to perform the extraction. Thus, a shareware author can put a program up on a board or in a library and not worry about whether or not the downloaders own ARC, LHARC, or PKZIP. If you can type a filename, you can extract the program. And making an archive self-extracting adds only about 2K to the size of the file when it's done with LHARC.

Self-extracting files have not yet begun to dominate file libraries—probably because the necessary commands are buried so deeply in the program documentation. But here's a tip. If you have the LHARC package, create your archive with the command `lha a filename *.*`. Then enter the command `lha s /x1 filename` to make it self-extracting. When you are finished, you will have *FILENAME*.LZH and *FILENAME*.EXE on your disk.

PowerPoint

QFILER and Compression

The shareware program QFILER is known primarily as a file manager. However, it also has the ability to deal with compressed files. As long as the necessary file extraction program is in your path, you can move the QFILER highlight bar to a file and enter a Ctrl+A for *archive utilities*. The program automatically senses the correct utility based on the extension of the target file.   *(continued)*

(QFILER and Compression continued)

You can then opt to add files, extract files, view the filenames in the archive, test the archive, or zoom in and read one or more of the archived files. A number of programs have been created to serve as "front ends" for archiving utilities, but with QFILER you don't need them, and you don't need to learn yet another program.

SECTION
8-6

TAPPING INTO BBSs

Bulletin board systems comprise the most fascinating part of the electronic universe. Each is, in effect, a mini-online utility, in the tradition of CompuServe, GEnie, Delphi, and other commercial systems. Yet most are housed in a PC very much like your own. And, although some boards levy modest membership fees, most can be used free of any charge, save for whatever you must pay your long distance phone carrier to make the call.

The only difference between your PC and the one hosting the BBS is that the BBS system operator or sysop (pronounced "sis-op") happens to be running bulletin board software and has made an effort to make his or her board's phone number known.

By some counts, there are over 32,000 BBSs in North America, and thousands more overseas. No one knows for sure because there is no formal structure and because anyone with a computer and a modem can set up a board dedicated to any topic at any time. There are boards devoted to every major religion, hobby, brand of computer, sexual persuasion, political opinion—you name it. BBSs exemplify freedom of the press in the 1990s. There is no topic that cannot be discussed, no subject that is taboo. With the exception of using a board to publish credit card numbers, or to transmit bootleg copies of commercial software and other illegal information designed to defraud, almost anything goes.

Enjoying the Board

I realize that this makes bulletin boards sound quite racy and anarchistic. Without a doubt, some of them are all that and more. But the vast majority of BBSs are put up by generous people—after all, when you use a board, you are using someone else's PC—who thoroughly enjoy offering electronic hospitality. Sysops *want* you to call. They have prepared a place for you, and they want you to come and enjoy it.

And enjoy it you will. Some sysops make a special effort to be entertaining. That's why it is a good idea to make sure that you have a line like DEVICE=C:\DEV\FCONSOLE.DEV or DEVICE=C:\DEV\ANSI.SYS in your CONFIG.SYS file before you go online to "work the boards." With an ANSI driver loaded, you are able to partake of the incredible graphics you will find on some boards. Otherwise, you are stuck with plain text.

The ANSI graphics option offered by many boards can be a lot of fun, and I heartily urge you to sample the offerings. However, transmitting ANSI graphics control codes and data does require more time. So when you get down to business with a board that you want to access regularly, you will probably want to opt for text instead of graphics.

Getting Good BBS Numbers

Bulletin board systems offer an opportunity to enter the electronic universe at the lowest possible cost. Instead of paying connect time fees to a leading online supplier, you can dial a nearby number, sign on, and receive many of the benefits of a commercial online system.

The key is to find a list of "good" numbers, by which I mean numbers that are still connected to operational boards. The attrition rate among new sysops is high. Many novices publish their board numbers only to find that they really don't want to make the required commitment.

The ephemeral nature of bulletin boards is a fact of online life, however, and it simply means that you must pay particular attention to the freshness of the BBS phone lists you use. Because of this, books and magazines are not usually very good sources. The lead time between the submission of the last bit of copy and the publication date can be three months or more, and inevitably many of the numbers are out of service by the time the book or magazine hits the stands.

Use the Technology!

The best place to get good bulletin board numbers is from bulletin boards and online systems. The electronic medium is ideally suited to providing up-to-the-minute information, and a number of people have dedicated themselves to providing current, accurate, validated BBS numbers. The most famous list of BBS numbers is undoubtedly the Darwin Systems list, created by Dr. Peter Olympia. Dr. Olympia is a chemical physicist by training, but he is also one of the leading experts in the XBASE language and applications. (The XBASE language includes dBASE, Clipper, FoxPro, and other dialects.)

He created the Darwin Systems BBS list over eight years ago, and it has been updated twice a month ever since. The filename to look for is some variant of USBBS*nn*, where the double *n*s are replaced by numbers. The list is so well established that shareware authors have created programs to parse the list and convert it to a ProComm dialing directory.

That means that you never need to key in the actual phone numbers. You can try a board by simply picking a menu item off your ProComm phone book/dialing directory. You can even tag several interesting boards and tell ProComm to continuously dial the numbers in sequence until you get an answer.

Many boards carry the Darwin systems list. But you may also be able to find it on CompuServe. Key in `go ibmbbs` to get the IBM-compatible BBS SIG. Then key in `dl` to call up a list of available file libraries. One of them is dedicated to BBS lists. (At this writing, Data Library 7 is the one with the BBS listings.) Then search on the keyword *Darwin* to locate the name of the file you want to download.

If you would like a complete listing of the BBS lists in the library, open your comm program's capture buffer, and then key in `cat/des`. The screen contains information like the following:

```
[72470,250]
PCPBBS.EXE/Bin Bytes: 57780, Count: 2320, 27-Jan-92(26-Jul-92)

   Title    : pc pursuitable bbs list
   Keywords : BBS LIST PC PURSUIT ACCESS

   This self-extracting file contains a list of almost 3,000
   bbs's which are accessible via PC Pursuit. This file is
   updated weekly.

[70007,4634]
SUPRT3.ZIP/Bin Bytes    : 10807, Count: 236,    08-Jul-92

   Title    : Technical Support BBS List for July 92
   Keywords : SUPRT SUPPORT TECHNICAL TECH BBS LIST VENDOR
              VENDORS SOFTWARE HARDWARE
```

Technical Support BBS List for July 1992

Lists over 300 BBS's that are run by Hardware, Commercial
Software, and Shareware Vendors around the country. It lists
the BBS number, modem type if it is PC Pursuit-able, whether
any serial numbers are needed to access the BBS, and what
products the BBS supports.

It is a monthly publication from the Digicom BBS 812-479-1310

Upl/Auth: Gary Barr

[71565,1532]
MED492.ZIP/Bin   Bytes: 14095, Count: 70, 02-Apr-92(04-Apr-92)

    Title   : Latest Black Bag Medical BBS list - April 1, 1992
    Keywords : MEDICAL FIRE EMS RECOVERY SCIENCE ALCOHOL AIDS
    DISABILITY BBS LIST

    Latest Black Bag Medical BBS list current of 04/01/92. The
    list contains over 380 systems with interests in medicine,
    science, Fire/EMS psychology, recovery, AIDS, and Disabili-
    ties. ENUMERABLE interesting systems. All numbers have been
    verified within the last 14 days. Now in its sixth year of
    publication. Those prefering to download an ASCII version of
    this file can find it in MEDSIG within Library 2.

      UPL/AUT Edward DelGrosso M.D.
      Black Bag BBS (1:150/140)
      302-994-3772 NEW NUMBER !!!! 4 nodes
      CIS 71565,1532

[76326,3266]
VETLIN./AscBytes:624,   Count: 70, 02-Sep-91

    Title   : listing of vetlink BBSs
    Keywords : VET VETS VETERANS VETLINK

    A sysem of Vetlink BBS's run by Veterans for Vets. Alot of
    good info including VA information. Download the Namvet News
    which is published every month. If you're a former Vet, Active
    Duty, Nam, or whatever, you are welcome. Welcome to Non Vets
    also.

[70160,301]
ALL.EXE/BinBytes:16128, Count: 848, 27-Jan-91

    Title   : 50 Match Dating BBS Listings
    Keywords : MATCH DATING ADULT BBS MAIL CHAT UPLOAD DOWNLOAD

    50 BBS's that specialize in match dating and may offer adult
    sections...Information is by state, city, system name, sysop
    (if known), time of operation, features of system, baud rates,
    and time of operation... A legend key is provided.

[72331,2346]
DTPBBS.ZIP/Bin   Bytes: 12160, Count: 168,   04-Dec-90

```
Title    : A List of Desktop Publishing BBS.

Keywords : DESKTOP PUBLISHING DTP BBS CLIP ART CLIPART VENTURA
           PAGEMAKER
```

A list of BBS's with significant collections of clip art images, and/or significant conferences concerning desktop publishing topics. Current as of December 1990. Author: Frank Atlee. Source: Infinite Perspectives BBS. Uploader: John McAdams.

```
[76703,633]
SCOUTS.BBS/Asc    Bytes: 5142,   Count: 105,    02-Dec-90

Title    : Latest SCOUTS.BBS list of Scout oriented BBSes.

Keywords : BSA GSA GSUSA LOCAL BBS LISTING CAMPING HIKING
           NETWORKS RBBS
```

BSA & GSUSA BBS systems. SCOUTS.BBS listing. Listing all "known" BBS systems with Scout-oriented interest areas (messages, files, echos, etc). This listing is posted in the IBMBBS & OUTDOORS forums, and has been DLed more than 300 times since Jan 90. All additions are welcome. Contact Steve Souza (76703,633) for more info or to have your board included in this listing.

The original list contained scores of files. I've edited it here to save space while at the same time demonstrating the breadth and depth of subjects covered by the BBS field. Among the files not shown above are ones focusing on BBS numbers in specific areas of the country and of the world. Not only were there lists for Japan and for South American countries, there was a list for BBSs in the Commonwealth of Independent States (the old Soviet Union).

The *Computer Shopper* List

The best *printed* list of BBS numbers is the one found in any issue of the Ziff-Davis publication, *Computer Shopper*. This magazine is a bargain hunter's dream and nightmare. Published in tabloid size, each issue regularly runs to 800 pages or more. The editorial content is surprisingly good—if you can find it amidst all the ads. And the ads are worthwhile, too, though they will drive you crazy as you thumb back and forth looking for the best deal.

Nevertheless, for as long as I can remember, *Computer Shopper* has published an extensive, accurate list of BBS numbers in each issue. The reason the numbers are so reliable is that any sysop who wants to be listed must contact the list producer every two months indicating that his or her board is still online. If the sysop fails to do this, the board is dropped from the listing. Boards are listed by state and area code, and each listing includes a paragraph describing the BBS's special focus, if any. International boards are covered as well.

PowerPoint

Computer Shopper List — Electronic

Ziff-Davis is an incredible company. It has moved rapidly to take full advantage of the possibilities the electronic medium offers by creating ZiffNet, an online system that is accessible via CompuServe and that features much of the material developed for the company's many computer magazines. You can search for and download software, articles, and product reviews, all for a membership fee of $2.50 per month, plus connect time.

Among the articles offered are the *Computer Shopper* bulletin board lists. However, there's a trick to avoiding a full $2.50/month subscription. If all you want are articles from Ziff-Davis publications (*PC Magazine, PC Computing, PC Sources, PC Week, Computer Shopper*, and all the Macintosh-related magazines), you can get them on a pay-as-you-go basis. Just sign on to CompuServe and key in `go complib`.

This will take you to the Ziff-Davis Computer Library, the CompuServe version of a database long produced by Information Access Company (IAC), called Computers ASAP. The service is menu-driven, but it is an "added-value" service, which means there's a surcharge for using it. Bottom line: You can use the Computer Library to locate the most recent *Computer Shopper* list and do an ASCII capture to download it to your machine. Your cost will be about $3.50.

The list is organized by area code. But once the file is on your disk, you can use Vernon Buerg's LIST.COM program or your word processor to search for boards devoted to topics of interest. Add them to your comm program dialing directory and tell your software to keep dialing until it gets a *CONNECT*.

BBS Culture and Viruses

The sysop and bulletin board community represents a culture all its own. There are leading personalities, procedures, special slang, and traditions. There are even bulletin board networks, like FidoNet, with more than

13,000 *nodes*. FidoNet users routinely upload messages addressed to correspondents in distant states, but they upload them by calling their local FidoNet node, so no expense is involved.

In the wee small hours of the morning, during "mail time," all of the FidoNet nodes call each other and exchange messages. As a result, your correspondent can call his or her local node and receive your message without the need to make a long distance phone call. FidoNet even has international nodes. (The FIDO BBS program that makes all this possible was created by Tom Jennings and named after his dog. No kidding.)

There are boards devoted to virtually any topic you can imagine, including those that offer interactive games, dating services, even digitized photographs and artwork (some of them X-rated) that you can download and display on your screen with Graphic Workshop or some other program. There is a sense of propriety, however. Most serious sysops require users to send in a written request before they are granted access to the racier libraries.

Of course, some BBSs charge small membership fees. And then there is the virus problem. Though vastly overblown by the general interest media, most of whom are cyberphobic, viruses do exist and they can cause problems. The key to safe computing is to make sure you know where your software comes from. On GEnie, CompuServe, and most other commercial online services, there is little need to worry. Not that a virus couldn't slip through, but you at least have the assurance that every file is tested for viruses before being made available for downloading.

A good BBS sysop is equally conscientious. The key to it all is to impose a delay between the time a file is uploaded and when it is available for download. There are programs the sysop can run against a file to test it for all known viruses. And responsible sysops do just that before allowing you to download something that came from another caller. Sysops also check uploaded files to make sure they are not pirated versions of copyrighted, commercial software. And, of course, they look for stolen credit card numbers.

In some respects, the virus scares of recent years have had a beneficial effect. They have made everyone much more aware of the problem and caused most sysops to take steps to prevent it. Yet, despite your precautions, should you ever have any doubts about whether your system has been infected, the programs to get are John McAfee's SCAN and CLEAN. The first searches every nook and cranny and every file in your system for viruses. The second is designed to remove any nasties SCAN finds.

As you would expect, SCAN and CLEAN are updated continuously. To get the latest copy, check into the VIRUSFORUM on CompuServe (GO

VIRUSFORUM). McAfee Associates runs the forum, and you can always find the company's latest programs there. When you register the programs, you automatically receive updates as new viruses appear.

DOS 6 Point

DOS 6's Anti-Virus Utilities

Beginning with DOS 6, Microsoft started supplying anti-virus software with DOS. Both a Windows-compatible and a DOS version are included in the MS-DOS 6 package, and both were licensed from Central Point Software, Inc., creators of the best-selling PC Tools. The software has the ability to scan for and remove hundreds of viruses. It also has the ability to sit in memory and monitor your system for a virus intrusion.

The programs are impressive. But there is one niggling detail— updates. As the DOS 6 manual says, "New viruses are discovered regularly. You can update the virus detection capabilities of Microsoft Anti-Virus by obtaining the necessary files from Central Point Software. For more information, see the coupon at the back of this guide."

One of the nice things about the McAfee anti-virus package, in contrast, is that you can sign on to the McAfee BBS or the VIRUS FORUM on CompuServe and download updates as soon as they are released (usually once or twice a month).

Plugging In with *Boardwatch*

The only way to really plug into the bulletin board world is to regularly work the boards. But that's time consuming, even when you enjoy it. That's why you may want to consider Jack Rickard's *Boardwatch Magazine.* This is a professionally published, full-sized magazine that normally runs 60 to 70 pages. Each issue contains hardware and software tips, profiles of interesting boards, announcements of new electronic services, and an extensive, current list of board numbers. Plus Mr. Rickard's pungent opinions on anything that comes to hand.

I wouldn't recommend *Boardwatch* for a complete computer novice, but if you've had a little experience, you may find that it's just the ticket. You'll find it on many major newsstands. Subscriptions cost $36 a year (12 issues) or $3.95 per copy. Contact:

Mr. Jack Rickard
Boardwatch Magazine
5970 South Vivian Street
Littleton, CO 80127
(800) 933-6038 (subscription orders only)

Cutting Costs with PC Pursuit

CompuServe, GEnie, and many other online services over the years were created to boost off-peak usage of large data processing systems. During non-business hours, usage drops off precipitously on the systems created by CompuServe to handle the remote data processing needs of banks and other institutions, and on General Electric's world-girdling GEIS information and e-mail network. Or at least that used to be the case. Today, the CompuServe Information Service and the General Electric Network for Information Exchange return millions of "found" dollars to their parent companies each year.

U.S. Sprint's Telenet/Sprintnet unit has been successful doing exactly the same thing. When everyone goes home for the day, usage of the company's packet-switching network drops dramatically. So the firm found a way to make the network available to BBS users during off-hours.

The program is called PC Pursuit (PCP), and it lets BBS users dial a local Telenet node whenever they want to access a distant bulletin board. The network connects the local node with a node in a distant city. Then the node in that city dials the number of the board and connects it to you through the network. The procedure is: local call to local node, network connection to distant node, local call from distant node to target BBS. And the net result is no long-distance charges.

Membership in PCP involves a one-time fee of $30 and a monthly fee of $30. The monthly fee gives you 30 hours of free, non-prime-time usage. Family Memberships are $50 and give you 60 hours of non-prime-time usage. A program for handicapped users costs $30 a month and includes 90 hours of non-prime-time usage. If you go over your limit, connect time is billed at $3 an hour. If you opt to use the system during prime time, the cost is $10.50 an hour.

Non-prime-time, PC Pursuitable hours are 6 PM to 7 AM, your local time, Monday through Thursday; and 9 PM Friday until 7 AM Monday morning, so you get Friday night and the entire weekend. If you really get into BBS-ing, PC Pursuit can save you a lot of money.

For more information, connect with your local Telenet /Sprintnet node. If you are on at 2,400 bps and set for 7/E/1, key in @ ("at" sign) followed by your Enter key when you connect. If you are at 8/N/1, key in @D and hit your Enter key. When prompted for your terminal type, enter D1, the type for all PCs. The network prompt, an "at" sign (@), then appears.

Now all you have to do is key in `c pursuit`. That connects you with the PCP bulletin board. As you are told, use *Sprint Guest* as your user name and *outdial* as your password. You are then able to explore information files about PCP at no cost. If you like what you see, you may subscribe then and there. Or you may dial the following toll-free number to talk to someone about the program: (800) 736-1130. For round-the-clock voice access, dial (800) 877-5045. That's the technical support number, but the person who answers will be able to route your call as necessary.

Be a Good BBS Citizen

Finally, it is important to realize that a good bulletin board is a labor of love. Yes, it is someone's hobby. And yes, no one asked the person to put up a board. You are within your rights to do nothing but pillage a board's file collection and offer not a byte in return. But to do so is to spit on the spirit that animates the bulletin board community.

For more than anything else, BBS-ing is a cooperative enterprise. The sysop may provide the computer and the modem. But it is the callers—the *people*—who make the board. If everyone simply signed on and took everything they could, offering nothing in return, most boards would cease to exist.

Fortunately, the BBS spirit is quite strong. Most people are perceptive enough to realize that a given board is only what they make it. So they are generous with their time, uploading files they have found that others may be interested in, participating in conferences and message exchanges, and generally becoming part of the community.

Indeed, you will find that after you have sampled many, many boards when you are just starting out, you will settle into accessing three or four favorite boards on a regular basis. If you really get into it, one or more of those boards will become your "home," and other members of the community will always know that they can reach you there.

At that point, bulletin boarding becomes more than a leisure pursuit, it becomes a way of life. You may not want to get that deeply involved. But you're more than welcome to sample the online offerings and then make up your mind. Believe me, sysops all over the world are waiting for your call.

PART IX

THE POWER DOS TOOLKIT

What You Will Learn

Throughout *Power DOS!*, we've cited and discussed many shareware tools. This part of the book offers more detail, where necessary, and provides you with the information you need to obtain the software.

The programs are widely available from online systems, BBSs, and user groups. But as a convenience to readers, we have pulled together all the crucial packages and made them available as a ten-disk set. The set is called the Power DOS Toolkit (PDT), and it is available for $25. Non-PDT programs cited elsewhere in the book are also covered. You will find a quick-reference chart organized by program name at the end of Section 9-4. Section 9-5 contains the order form to use for the Power DOS Toolkit and other disks.

SECTION
9-1

REFLECTIONS ON POWER USERDOM

It's amazing what can be done with a piece of wood, a block of stone, a bolt of fabric, and thousands of other materials—if you have the right tools. Much the same could be said of the typical personal computer system. With the right software tools, a PC can perform miracles. Or at least appear to.

At the system level, we're not after anything quite so spectacular. What we want is a PC that is all but transparent—a system that responds so quickly and is so natural to use that it doesn't get in the way of whatever work we're trying to accomplish. After all, every bit of the time and energy we expend wrestling with the system, trying to bend it to our wishes, could be more profitably devoted to the real task at hand.

How many pieces would a cabinetmaker be able to produce if every time he picked up a chisel, a plane, or a saw he had to stop and think about how it should be adjusted and what hand motions were needed to apply it to the work? You can't ignore your tools, of course. You've got to keep the cutting edges sharp and the attachments well organized. But whether you're using a wood chisel or a PC, you shouldn't have to give the tool itself much thought. It should fit so comfortably that it becomes an extension of your hand or of your brain.

A *Real* Power User

As I said at the beginning of this book, that's what being a power user is all about. Some PC enthusiasts are so intense, they spout DOS commands, software switches, and hardware specifications the way sports fans spew out baseball statistics. They revel in the differences among different DOS versions and are thrilled at the prospect of spending hours squeezing out 1K more of conventional memory. To which one might respond, "Who cares? Get a life!" A *real* power user is interested in getting the job done—quickly, completely, and with as little effort as possible.

Achieving that goal requires a certain amount of knowledge. You've got to have the right information. But you also need the right tools. The previous parts of this book contain the "right information" about DOS, memory, hard disk drives, and many other topics. They also refer to numerous software tools.

Shareware Tools

Some of those tools are commercial programs like the Norton Utilities, PrintCache, PC-Kwik, and Avery LabelPro. But most are shareware or public domain software. It is these programs that are the focus of this part of the book. Here you will find more information on the programs cited, but not fully described, elsewhere.

As we will see, the programs can be obtained easily and inexpensively. When you decide to register the ones you particularly like, you will find that the requested fees are quite small, particularly when compared to the prices charged for commercial software. And with shareware, there is always the opportunity to develop a personal, professional relationship with the person who created the program.

When you purchase a commercial program, you're simply buying a product. When you register a shareware program, in contrast, you become a patron of the software arts. Sending a programmer the registration fee he requests because you have looked at, admired, and really appreciate his art is no different than buying an original painting or sending a check to Michelangelo because you really dug the paint job on the Sistine ceiling.

So I urge you to register. Even if the requested fee is a niggling $5 or $10. The money might buy the person a large pizza or a six-pack of beer. Small enough compensation for all the time the program will save you. But as most shareware authors will tell you, it's not really the money so much as the fact that someone out there liked the program enough to take the time to say so.

So many public domain and shareware programs are available, particularly utility and "power DOS" type programs, that most programmers have trouble just getting people to try their stuff, let alone getting them to register. There is also the fact that not all programmers are equally talented or equally committed to their work. As a result, there's a lot of mediocre software.

The kicker is that good, bad, incompetent, and superb creations are all presented on the same terms. When you search for programs on CompuServe or any other online system, for example, the list that appears gives every file equal billing. The only way to discover the gems is to download the lot, run each one, read the documentation, and, often, contact the programmer to get a sense of his or her professionalism.

Most users with lives to lead and jobs to do don't have time for this exhaustive vetting process. And many users have yet to develop the depth of experience needed to know what to look for. Besides, it doesn't make sense for each individual to re-invent the wheel.

That's why the Glossbrenner's Choice collection was created. Its goal is to offer users the kind of guidance they need to take full advantage of the riches of the shareware world. Glossbrenner's Choice (GBC) includes only the best programs in their class, each one personally tested and selected from hundreds of similar packages.

All of the programs in the collection are widely available. You'll find them in user group libraries and in mail-order catalogues. Or you can use the tips and techniques presented in Part 8 to locate and download them from bulletin boards or commercial online systems.

However, as a convenience to readers, the collection is also available on disk directly from GBC. The cost is $5 for 5.25-inch and $6 for 3.5-inch disks. Since it costs the same to mail out a disk that is half empty as it costs to mail one that is packed full, GBC disks are typically stuffed to the gills. It is important to leave some space to allow for new program versions, which are inevitably larger than their predecessors, but you would be amazed at how many bytes you can pack onto a disk using an archiver like LHARC. (All GBC disks use self-extracting archive files, so all you have to do is copy the *-Z.EXE file onto your hard disk and key in the filename.)

SECTION
9-2

THE TOOLKIT
PROGRAMS

It is impossible to overemphasize the importance of having the right tools. You have got to be able to scroll back through previously displayed screens or previously issued DOS commands. You have got to be able to instantly view and search through any file. A disk cache, a print spooler, a disk defragmenter, a keyboard macroing program, and a file manager are simply essential to anyone interested in high-performance, low-effort computing.

That's why it makes sense to offer all of these functions in a single ten-disk package. The package is called the Power DOS Toolkit (PDT), and the cost is $25 for 5.25-inch and $30 for 3.5-inch disks. These are the programs that, in my opinion, every power user should have. (Individual Toolkit disks are also available separately for $5 or $6, depending on disk size.) The PDT package includes the following GBC disks:

Disk Name	Disk Title
CORE 1	FANSI Program files, CED, and Vern Buerg's LIST
CORE 2	FANSI Documentation, PC-DeskTeam, and PC-Window
CORE 4	QFILER and Associates
CORE 5	Newkey
UTILS 1	Quick Shots Collection
UTILS 2	Larger Programs I
UTILS 8	Disk Maintenance Tools
UTILS 9	System Configuration Tools
UTILS 10	HyperDisk Disk Cache
PRINTER 1	Printer Utilities

CORE 1—FANSI, CED, and LIST

Mark Hersey's FANSI-Console, as you know from Parts 3 and 6, is the package that gives you complete control over your keyboard and screen. You can use it to quickly and easily redefine any key, expand the keyboard type-ahead buffer, and control the keyboard's delay and repeat rate to really add some pep to your cursor. The program automatically speeds up screen writing by between 1.4 and eight times. It includes a screen save feature that blanks the screen after the number of minutes you specify.

You can control many other keyboard and video settings as well, but the single most important FANSI feature is one-button scroll recall. With FANSI loaded (via CONFIG.SYS), you can instantly put everything on hold and use your arrow and paging keys to scroll back through previously displayed screens. If you like, you can mark off and clip out portions of those screens and write them to disk. Or you can run the included DEJAVU program to write the entire screen buffer to disk. (Then edit it with your word processor.)

ProComm, the communications software I use, includes a scroll recall feature. But I still use FANSI when I'm online, since even ProComm can't beat the simplicity of just hitting your Pause key to freeze everything and scroll back through electronic mail messages or lists of files in online libraries. The number of screens FANSI can save depends on the amount of memory you allocate for the purpose. FANSI automatically uses EMS, XMS, or conventional memory based on its own determinations, though you can tell it what kind of memory you want it to use if you like. (The disk includes a Glossbrenner quick-start instruction file.)

CED is the DOS command editor from Chris Dunford. The program was cited in Parts 1 and 3. Basically, it does everything DOS's DOSKEY program does, and it does it better. The first version of CED was introduced in 1985, and it was almost certainly the inspiration for DOSKEY. As a conversation with Mr. Dunford confirmed, the latest version of CED was updated to make sure that CED ("said") beats DOSKEY in every way.

I won't go into detail here, but both CED and DOSKEY let you recall and edit previously issued DOS commands. The crucial difference is that the Microsoft product requires you to learn and use symbols like GG or $B. CED, in contrast, accepts real DOS symbols (>>, ¦, etc.). CED also accepts variables in the same format DOS uses for batch files (%1 through %9). DOSKEY requires you to use dollar signs instead of percentage signs. There is also the fact that CED synonyms (DOSKEY's macros) can include other CED synonyms as part of their definitions.

Vernon Buerg's LIST program is cited in Parts 2, 3, and 5. Any number of file listers are available from Public Domain (PD) and shareware sources, but none tops LIST. It's fast. It's flexible. It's filled with features that you may use or disregard, at your discretion. I use it to search for information in files, to clip out sections of files and write them to disk, and to clean up files containing "garbage" characters. For example, by default, LIST filters out non-text characters in what it displays. If you know the file contains garbage characters, you can use LIST to create a clean copy. Simply bring up the file, mark the top with Alt+M, hit your End key to go to the bottom of the file, mark the bottom with Alt+B, and then enter Alt+D to dump the marked text to disk under a new filename.

To my mind, FANSI, CED, and LIST are the three most valuable programs any user, power or otherwise, can have.

CORE 2—FANSI Documentation, PC-DeskTeam, and PC-Window

You will find all of the FANSI program and support files on CORE 1. The documentation is so extensive, however, that it must be located on a separate disk, CORE 2. Also included are the SideKick clones, PC-DeskTeam and PC-Window. These are TSRs that offer a pop-up notepad, an ASCII table, a calendar, and an alarm that you can set to remind yourself of some task or engagement. The pop-up notepad is particularly useful since it lets you enter and record notes while you are in the midst of some other program.

CORE 4—QFILER and Associates

Kenn Flee's QFILER is cited in Parts 3, 5, and 8. The program gives you complete control over your hard disk and almost eliminates the need to learn DOS commands. QFILER is the program to use when you want to copy, move, or delete a group of different files. It automatically displays both the source and the target directories in windows on your screen, so you can see exactly what's going on.

You can also use the program to create, delete, or rename subdirectories (or move entire subdirectory branches); change file attributes, names, and dates; locate files with a WHEREIS function; or easily move around your directory tree. You can even execute programs from QFILER—just point and shoot.

QFILER is set up to automatically call QFLIST (supplied) or Vern Buerg's LIST (see CORE 1); DOS's UNDELETE; and all of the leading file compression programs. These are the Associates supplied on the disk, and they include what you need to deal with ARC, ARJ, LZH, PAK, and ZIP files. This means you can use QFILER to select and view files on the screen, recover erased files, and look inside and/or extract the contents from archived files. There is much more besides, including drop-down menus, quick commands, and mouse support.

CORE 5—Newkey

Newkey is a keyboard macroing program that is easily on a par with commercial products like ProKey and SmartKey. (It is covered in Parts 1, 3, and 6.) Newkey has a ton of features, but basically, you load the program by keying in newkey. Then, when you want to define a macro, use the Alt and Equals (=) key combination and a window pops up. Hit the key or key combination you want to define, and Newkey returns you to the DOS prompt or to your program. But Newkey is watching and recording your keystrokes. When you have finished, hit the Alt and Minus (-) key combination to turn off Newkey's recording mode.

That's all there is to it. Once you have defined a key or key combination, each time you enter it the keystrokes you have recorded are entered. The package includes a program for editing, merging, and storing the macros you have defined, so you can easily reload them at some future time. Newkey takes the nuisance out of repetitive computer chores.

UTILS 1—Quick Shots Collection

This disk contains dozens of small, single-purpose programs. There are over 100 files in all, far too many to describe individually. The eleven files on this disk discussed in earlier parts of the book are:

MV   Moves files from one location to another, eliminating the need to first copy a file to a new location and then delete it.

NO   Prevents DOS from acting on a particular file or group of files (NO.COM). For example, keying in `no save.txt del *.txt` causes DOS to delete all files ending in .TXT, except SAVE.TXT.

ONBOOT   Chris Dunford's program to let you arrange to have your AUTOEXEC.BAT file run different programs, depending on whether you are doing a warm reboot (with Ctrl+Alt+Del), a cold reboot (when you hit the reset button or first turn the machine on), or during the first boot of the day.

FREE   One of many programs to instantly tell you how much space is free on your disk.

QDR   Vernon Buerg's quick floppy disk reformatter.

REBEEP   For use in batch files. Displays *Press any key to continue. . .* while sounding an insistent beep. The beep does not stop until you press a key.

REBOOT   The little program we showed you how to create with DE-BUG in Part 1. Use it in a batch file to reboot your system.

RENDIR   Lets you rename hard disk directories from the DOS command line.

TUNE   Improves the tone of your batch files by playing one of five tune phrases at a specified speed. If you like, you can opt to play several phrases with a single TUNE command.

WAIT/WAITUNTL   For batch files. Lets you specify either the amount of time the program will wait until proceeding to the next step or when it should do so.

WHEREIS   A program to scan the entire disk for the file specifications you enter. Wildcards are supported, of course. There is no quicker way to locate a file, provided you have some idea of its name.

You will also find programs to change file attributes, calculate subtotals of the bytes in the files in each subdirectory (DISK.COM), or determine the totals for files ending in .WKS or .TXT or something else. (If you have DOS 5 or above, you can achieve the same thing by using the DIR command.) NODUPE.BAT deletes duplicate files between the source and target disks or subdirectories. PI-COMP offers a much better way to compare the contents of two disks than DOS's DISKCOMP command.

SIZE calculates the floppy disk storage requirements for a specified group of files, which is usually different than their byte total due to the target media's file allocation unit (cluster) size. FDATE lets you change the date of one or more files to anything you specify.

LOCATE searches through every file for the text you specify. The six-file Patriquin SUPER-Search package offers virtually every known method for finding a file or text. NL and CAPSLOCK turn NumLock and CapsLock on and off, and STATLINE tells you on the screen when NumLock, Caps-Lock, or Scroll Lock are on, in case you have an old-style keyboard with no lights. FAKEY, which I think is better than a competing program called KEYFAKE, lets you feed keystrokes to your programs. You can use FAKEY from the command line, but it really comes into its own in batch files.

UTILS 2 —Larger Programs I

This is a disk of larger utility programs. But, while their numbers may be fewer than UTILS 1, they are just as important. Perhaps most important of all is the Mark/Release package that gives you complete control over TSRs. As discussed in Parts 1 and 4, Mark/Release lets you remove TSR programs from memory without rebooting.

UTILS 8 —Disk Maintenance Tools

This disk contains CLEAN (not the McAfee virus-removing program) and CLEANUP, two programs designed to search through your disk for the tiny 1- and 2-byte files that programs often leave behind. (You may also specify files with whatever extension you want.) The programs then either automatically delete them or prompt you for permission in each case. The programs were cited in Parts 3 and 5. Remember, even a 1-byte file occupies one complete file allocation unit (cluster), and the smallest unit available is 2K, so eliminating junk files like these can free up a lot of disk space.

Also on the disk is DISKID (Part 3), a program to let you change the serial number DOS adds to a disk as part of the format process, and FORMATQM (Part 5), a mass floppy disk formatter.

Perhaps most important of all, this disk includes DIET and ORG, both of which were discussed in Part 5. If you have DOS 6, you may prefer to use the DEFRAG.EXE program that comes with your operating system software package since it is essentially the same as Peter Norton's Speed Disk. However, if you have DOS 5 or below, you will find that ORG offers an impressive alternative to Speed Disk or DEFRAG.

As you know, DOS 6 also includes a dynamic disk compression program called DoubleSpace. The program works quite well, but you are required to place at least one of your hard disk volumes completely in its control. If that makes you nervous or if you use DOS 5 or below, you will definitely want to try DIET on this disk. DIET lets you compress program files to save disk space and then run those programs from their archives. It can handle both program and data files, squeezing them down to about half their former size.

UTILS 9—System Configuration Tools

All of the programs on this disk are discussed in other parts of the book. AUTOCON lets you conveniently reboot under the control of the CONFIG.SYS and AUTOEXEC.BAT files you specify. (A similar facility is built into MS-DOS 6, but AUTOCON gives you much more flexibility.) BAT2EXEC compiles DOS batch files into machine language programs for faster execution. In addition, a compiled batch program cannot be altered by other users.

PopDOS, from the creator of Mark/Release, lets you add a "shell to DOS" feature to many programs that do not support it. Tom Walker's XPATH offers two crucial features. First, it lets you create a DOS path of any length you wish. Second, it lets you temporarily add disks and directories to your normal path.

This can be extremely helpful when you are testing a new program that you have stored in a new directory, and you want to be able to use that program from any location on the disk. Use XPATH to add that directory to your path; do your testing; then use XPATH to remove the directory from your path.

Also included is Jeff Prosise's UMBFILES, a program that lets you tell DOS to take the space it allocates for the FILES= statement from the upper memory area. A companion program, NUMFILES, will tell you at any moment how many FILES you have specified. (See Part 4.) Finally, this disk also contains the UART-related utilities discussed in Part 8. With the COMFIX and UARTTOOLS packages, you can find out whether any of your COM ports has the 16550A National Semiconductor UART, and what interrupt they are using. You can also toggle that chip's FIFO buffer off and on. (See Part 8 for details.)

UTILS 10—HyperDisk Disk Cache

UTILS 10 contains two programs: Cache Test and HyperDisk. The first gives you an accurate benchmark and performance report to use when comparing various disk caches, both among themselves and versus DOS. The second is a full-blown disk-caching program that many feel offers better performance than even Microsoft's SMARTDrive, Version 4.x.

According to *Computer Shopper* (July 1992), HyperDisk "may be one of the most valuable pieces of shareware that you can get because it speeds up everything you do. . . and it goes Microsoft one better because it's faster than SMARTDrive. Standard Computers is so taken with it that it ships HyperDisk with every one of their Windows workstations. Standard knows a good thing when it sees it, and so should you."

PRINTER 1—Printer Utilities

Finally, there are the crucial printer utilities. This disk contains the form feed program (FF.COM) and the 1TRY program discussed in Part 7. (The instructions in Part 7 show you how to create these programs on your own using DEBUG.) FF.COM sends a form feed character to the printer, forcing it to eject a page. Put it in a directory in your path, and you can send a form feed from any location on the system.

The program 1TRY.COM lets you limit to one the number of times DOS tries to print the screen after the Print Screen key is struck. (Normally, DOS tries twenty times, tying up your computer if no printer is attached or if your printer is offline.) This is especially useful for portable and laptop users.

Equally important, the disk contains the DMP print spooler. As discussed in Parts 3 and 7, this program increases the speed with which DOS returns control of your system to you after you have opted to print something. DMP also lets you redirect output bound for the printer to a disk file.

There is also PRTSCR-LJ, the TSR discussed in Part 3 that automatically sends a form feed to your laser printer each time you hit your Print Screen key. And there is a TSR called PrintBuddy that lets you configure your printer on the fly, even in the midst of running another program. There is a program that prints graph paper (to your size specs) on a laser printer, and one that automatically uses the ZIP codes specified in a text file to print the appropriate bar code on the page. And there is a collection of short utilities for those using Epson-compatible dot matrix printers.

Finally, there is a clutch of PostScript-related software, including programs to let you copy a file directly from DOS to a PostScript printer and to allow you to use your Print Screen key to send the screen to such a printer. There is a program to convert .GIF graphics files into PostScript format, one to test your printer's dpi resolution, and a TSR pop-up to let users of Pacific Page's PostScript cartridge switch from PostScript back to PCL, even in the midst of a program.

QuikMenu Special Offer

As you know from Part 3 of this book, QuikMenu from OSCS Software Development is not only dazzling—it offers what amounts to "Windowless Windows." That is, QuikMenu gives every computer user most of the benefits of Microsoft's Windows with none of the delays or the vast memory and hard disk space requirements. (You can even run Windows from QuikMenu, if you like.)

When you load QuikMenu for the first time, it automatically searches your hard disk for programs it recognizes and sets up sculpted 3-D menu buttons for those programs. You can then add your own additional menu buttons, submenus, and program groupings. QuikMenu gives you complete control over colors and sound effects and even lets you select different fonts (built in) in your menu button text.

QuikMenu is compatible with any DOS-based network and also includes a network electronic mail feature. Plus it is filled with clever utilities, including a calculator, calendar (with an auto-reminder feature), phone book and dialer, and time log. The QuikMenu file manager feature will simply blow you away (copy, rename, move, delete, view, etc., all with a simple mouse click). You can even use .PCX (PC Paintbrush) graphics files as background "wallpaper." This is a truly outstanding piece of software.

I am so impressed with QuikMenu that I've made special arrangements to offer it to readers of this book at a rock-bottom price. The cost is $2 for a 5.25-inch disk or $3 for 3.5-inch format. See the order form later in this part of the book for details.

SECTION
9-3

SPECIAL APPLICATIONS

The programs in the Power DOS Toolkit will serve you well. I have no doubt that they will completely fulfill most of your needs. However, there are other utilities and programs to consider, all of which are available from the usual shareware sources or from Glossbrenner's Choice.

The Core Collection

The Core Collection contains the system-related programs I feel are absolutely essential to any serious computer user. Four disks from the Core Collection are included in the Power DOS Toolkit. Other Core Collection disks of interest are profiled here.

CORE 8—Extended Batch Language (EBL-Plus)

EBL-Plus lets you program in DOS in ways you never dreamed possible. Colorful windows that use bounce bar selection, pop-ups, fill-in-the-blank fields, buttons, and action bars are easily created. Enhanced arithmetic, string, system, file I/O, and error recovery functions are built in. EBL-Plus has over 100 built-in commands and functions. (The program was cited in Part 2 of this book.)

EBL executes batch files up to five times faster than COMMAND .COM. But for even greater speed, Canova's Seaware Corporation offers a reasonably-priced EBL compiler to turn your files into .COM programs. Of course, EBL fully supports all of DOS's batch file commands and conventions, but if you're serious about batch files, why hobble yourself by using only DOS?

CORE 10, 11, 12—Back & Forth Professional (3 disks)

As discussed in Part 4 of this book, Back & Forth Professional (B&F) is the task-switching program that leaves the DOS 5 and DOS 6 Shell in its dust. With multitaskers like DESQview and Windows, programs can continue to run in the background, even when they are not on the screen. Task switchers, in contrast, rapidly swap programs in and out of memory at the touch of a key. Task switchers thus give you most of the benefits of true multitaskers, with much less complexity and with many fewer demands on your computer hardware.

B&F makes full use of EMS (expanded) or XMS (extended) memory, and assignable hotkeys let you instantly flick from one program to another, almost as easily as you change channels on a TV with your "clicker." You can put up to 50 program partitions on the B&F menu, twenty of which may be used simultaneously. This means that nearly every program can, in effect, be turned into a pop-up TSR. You will need at least 512K of conventional memory in your system, plus a hard disk. EMS and XMS memory will let B&F operate even faster.

PC Magazine [13 Oct. 1992] compared all the leading task switchers, including DESQview, Software Carousel, WordPerfect Office for DOS, and Back & Forth. It said, "if you don't need resizable windows or multitasking, your most powerful and most flexible choice is Back & Forth Professional. This cleanly designed package. . .lets you define up to 50 programs that you can run in separate DOS sessions. . .You may want to use Back & Forth even if you never run anything more than your word processor, because its macro feature can automatically expand abbreviations or correct misspellings as you type."

Utilities and System Tweakers

There are probably more utility programs in the shareware and public domain world than programs of any other type. That's a problem, because often a dozen or more programs have been created to deal with the same problem. The trick is to find the best of the lot. The Power DOS Toolkit contains five disks of utility programs, but there are two others that may be of interest, UTILS 5 (Larger Programs II) and UTILS 7 (Laptop Solutions).

UTILS 5—Larger Programs II

You can think of this disk as a companion to UTILS 2, for it's another collection of larger gem-quality utilities. XEQ lets you store .COM files inside a single file to save disk space. But it also lets you execute those programs without removing them from the file. You can use the command synonym feature of CED (available on CORE 1) to make XEQ even easier to use. ASK, a program discussed in Part 2, lets you solicit user response from your batch files.

SCRNCH also stores many programs in a single file, and unlike XEQ, SCRNCH compresses the files in the process. You can use SCRNCH and XEQ together for maximum space conservation and convenience.

CT is a "command trapper" program that records in a disk file all commands issued from your keyboard. This lets you keep track of the commands issued during one or more sessions with a machine. COPYIT is ideal for copying files from a hard disk subdirectory to a series of floppy disks. It not only fills each disk efficiently, it also prompts you to insert a new disk when the current one becomes full. (COPYIT was discussed in Parts 2 and 4.) PCOPY is a much more powerful version of DOS's COPY and XCOPY commands.

UTILS 7—Laptop Solutions (3.5-inch only)

What are the five biggest problems portable computer users face? You'd be better off asking a group of theologians about the nature of God. I accepted the challenge, however, from the editor of *Portable Computing*, and the response to the resulting article was overwhelming.

Here's the answer to the "That's all, folks," battery surprise with NiCAD, a program to track battery usage and warn you well before it's too late. There is also CLAP to "bulk up" the cursor so you can't miss it on your laptop screen. The LHARC compression package eliminates disk space woes by nearly doubling your hard and floppy disk capacity.

And, of course, there is FANSI-Console to give you complete control over not only your screen but your keyboard as well. FANSI also makes up for the lack of keys on a laptop by letting you assign ASCII codes to any keypress combination.

Printer Productivity

Since virtually every computer user owns or has access to a printer, and since printers can do so many wonderful things, it is quite understandable that there would be a large number of printer-related shareware programs. The Power DOS Toolkit contains PRINTER 1, a disk of essential utilities. But there are also programs for more elaborate or more specialized purposes.

GRAB 1 and 2—Grab Plus (2 Disks)

Printing envelopes on a laser printer can be a royal pain, to say the least. But a wonderful program called Grab Plus makes short work of them. Load Grab Plus into memory as a TSR and prepare your letter. When you're ready to do the envelope, press a hotkey combination and Grab Plus "grabs" the address from your letter and prints it on the envelope. It even prints your return address in the upper left corner if you wish.

Grab Plus is available on two disks, GRAB 1 (the main program disk) and GRAB 2 (optional add-on modules). The add-on modules consist of an address database program and a program designed to produce labels. The database can accept input from most database programs, or you can use data you enter yourself. The Laser Label program is designed to print labels on Avery/Dennison stock. It can take its data from the Grab database, utilize soft fonts, and produce postal bar codes. If you're in doubt, start with GRAB 1. You may find that it fills all of your needs.

LASER 1— Elfring Fonts, CHART, and KEYCHART

This disk contains one of the best typeface/font collections available anywhere—Gary Elfring's 23-font collection. The package is discussed in Part 7 of this book. Figure 9-3-1 contains the text fonts. Some, but not all, of the dingbats and special symbols are shown.

The Elfring package also includes a soft font downloader; a font information display program; a utility that examines soft fonts; printer drivers for WordPerfect, MS Word, and MS Works; plus Windows, WordStar, PC-Write, Q&A, Ventura, and Pagemaker information. It also contains a tutorial on the basics of using soft fonts.

You'll also find CHART and KEYCHART, two handy little programs that generate printouts showing you which keys to enter to produce specific "dingbat" images after you have activated the dingbat font. CHART presents its information as an ASCII table. KEYCHART uses a keyboard-like display.

Figure 9-3-1 Elfring Soft Fonts

Black Chan 12 & 14 point	ABCDEFGHIJKLMNOPQRSTUVWXYZ abcdefghijklmnopqrstuvwxyz 123456789!'$x&()?
Broadway 18 point	**ABCDEFGHIJKLMNOPQRSTUVWXYZ abcdefghijklmnopqrstuvwxyz 123456789!#$%&()?**
Century Legal 12 point	ABCDEFGHIJKLMNOPQRSTUVWXYZ abcdefghijklmnopqrstuvwxyz 123456789!#$%&()?
Flourish 12 point	ABCDEFGHIJKLMNOPQRSTUVWXYZ abcdefghijklmnopqrstuvwxyz 123456789!#$&()?
Helv 10 & 12 point	ABCDEFGHIJKLMNOPQRSTUVWXYZ abcdefghijklmnopqrstuvwxyz 123456789!#$%&()?
Helv Bold 10, 12, & 18 pt	ABCDEFGHIJKLMNOPQRSTUVWXYZ abcdefghijklmnopqrstuvwxyz 123456789!#$%&()?
Helv Italic 10 & 12 point	*ABCDEFGHIJKLMNOPQRSTUVWXYZ abcdefghijklmnopqrstuvwxyz 123456789!#$%&()?*
Script 12 point	ABCDEFGHIJKLMNOPQRSTUVWXYZ abcdefghijklmnopqrstuvwxyz 123456789!#$z&()?
Dingbats 18 point	©®®™™●●∙○○○■■▪□□□▶◀▲▼▶◀▼ £¢¥°†‡§¶→←↑↓⇒⇐⇑⇓☒☑⊘∭丫✔√✂✄ ❶❷❸❹❺❻❼❽❾❿②③④⑤⑦⑧
Roman 10 & 12 point	ABCDEFGHIJKLMNOPQRSTUVWXYZ abcdefghijklmnopqrstuvwxyz 123456789!#$%&()?
Roman Bold 10, 12 point & 18 pt	**ABCDEFGHIJKLMNOPQRSTUVWXYZ abcdefghijklmnopqrstuvwxyz 123456789!#$%&()?**
Roman Italic 10 & 12 point	*ABCDEFGHIJKLMNOPQRSTUVWXYZ abcdefghijklmnopqrstuvwxyz 123456789!#$%&()?*

LASER 2—TSR Download, Jet Pilot, and Font Selector

This disk contains Elfring's TSR Download, which lets you select and download soft fonts on the fly, then return to your application. It works with LaserJet, DeskJet, and compatible printers, and any soft font file. It can also compress font files and then decompress them as needed, saving disk space. And it can rotate or create landscape versions of your soft fonts from their portrait equivalents (important if you use a LaserJet Plus or LaserJet II).

Jet Pilot from Morton Utilities is an equally remarkable control program. It can be installed as a pop-up TSR or run directly from the DOS command line. Jet Pilot gives you complete control of virtually every feature of your LaserJet or compatible printer. It complements TSR Download because it deals with your printer's internal and cartridge fonts, while TSR Download deals with soft fonts.

The third package on LASER 2 is Quicksoft's Font Selector for PC-Write. If you use PC-Write, you'll find that this program makes it easy to prepare the printer definition files you need for creating special effects in your PC-Write documents.

LASER 3—QFONT, Fontloader, and STP

QFONT, a program from the creator of QFILER, allows you to design your own fonts or images. But you'll probably use it most often to alter existing soft fonts. You can use your mouse to physically change each and every bit individually, or use the program's drawing tools to add lines, curves, ellipses, boxes, and so on. You can also cut and paste to create a unique design.

But what you will find really exciting is the ability to change the size of the font, up to a maximum of about 144 points (2 inches). You can also create squashed or elongated characters, make the typeface slant right or left, add shadowing or outlining, turn portrait fonts into landscape fonts, and create lots of other special effects.

Fontloader does more than just download fonts. You can enter a single Fontloader command to download the target font and resize it to between 8 and 24 points. You can also rotate the font, turn it upside down, print as white on black, and do many other things. Fontloader provides a quick way to produce font effects while saving disk space. By altering a font on the fly as it is sent to the printer, it eliminates the need to store each version of the font as a separate file.

STP (Save a Tree Printer), discussed in Part 7, can print eight normal pages on a single sheet of paper. It does so by using very tiny, though legible, type—and by printing on both sides of the page. STP is ideal for documentation, since you can take in eight pages at a glance and thus more easily locate the piece of information you seek.

MAIL MACHINE

Mail Machine (MM) is similar to the commercial program Avery Label-Pro. It's designed to automate the production of labels for mass mailings or other purposes. You can even produce special effects or otherwise spiff up your labels, since Mail Machine can be made to use just about any soft font.

MM can print envelopes and labels of any size acceptable by your LaserJet or compatible printer, up to 8.5 by 14 inches. Support for most standard envelopes and labels is built into the program, plus support for most Avery forms. MM also gives you the option of automatically printing U.S. Postal Service bar codes on your envelopes and labels.

PRINTER 2—LQ and ImagePrint

The two print enhancement packages on this disk do some amazing things with a dot matrix printer. LQ (Letter Quality) by Mark Harris gives you at least twenty different fonts on an Epson, Imageprinter, IBM Proprinter, C. Itoh, Star, and many other brands of dot matrix printers. These include Courier, Roman, Sanserif, Palatino, and even real Greek. Harris had the inspiration that three passes with a 9-pin printer can produce the equivalent of one pass with an expensive 24-pin printer—it just takes longer.

ImagePrint is designed to produce up to six different fonts on almost any popularly used printer. The shareware version comes with one font (cubic). A registration fee of $20 brings you six fonts and telephone support.

PRINTER 4—On-Side (Sideways printing)

This is a shareware version of Funk Software's well-known Sideways printing program for dot-matrix printers. It comes from David Berdan and Bill Willis of Expressware. This is a super program that is a must for anyone who uses Lotus and similar electronic spreadsheet programs. It prints text files sideways as well.

Communications and Bulletin Boards

It is not uncommon for modems to be bundled with some kind of communications software, often drawn from the shareware world. So if you have a program that you like, by all means stick with it. But if you have yet to step into the electronic universe, I think you ought to start with ProComm. As discussed in Part 8, ProComm is far and away the market leader. With the shareware versions offered here, you can get to know the program at virtually no cost. Then, if you like what you see, you can purchase the commercial version and not have to master a lot of new commands.

COMM 1—ProComm 2.4.3

ProComm Version 2.4.3 is the latest shareware version of the product. It's fast, flexible, and a lot of fun to use. You will like the way the programmers have anticipated your needs and you will be thrilled by the responsiveness of the software.

This version supports a wide variety of transfer protocols (Kermit, several varieties of XMODEM, YMODEM, CompuServe B and B+, for example), not to mention a variety of mainframe terminal emulations. It does not offer built-in support for ZMODEM, but there is an easy way to add this feature (See COMM 2.)

COMM 2—ProComm 2.4.3 Utilities

The main ProComm 2.4.3 package comes with several utility programs. But users have written many ProComm utilities of their own. The best ones are on COMM 2, including PRCMDIR, a program that takes lists of bulletin board system numbers and automatically inserts them into the ProComm dialing directory. PRCMDIR can be "trained" to parse any list, as long as all the information about the board is on a single line.

This saves you the trouble of keying in a lot of numbers yourself. It means that you can import a list of numbers, tag the ones you want, and tell ProComm to start dialing. ProComm dials each number until it gets an answer. Once you disconnect, it picks up where it left off, removing the successful number from its queue. Also included is ZRUN.COM, a program that allows ProComm 2.4.3 to support the ZMODEM protocol.

COMM 3—The Communicator's Toolchest

This disk makes life online much easier. First, it gives you what you need to extract the files contained in the .ARC, .LZH, .ZIP, and .PAK archives that you download from online systems. (See Part 8 of this book.) Second, it includes the *complete* LHARC package, so you can not only extract but also create .LZH files and self-extracting .EXE archives on your own. (LHARC is the de facto compression standard.)

Third, it lets you add the ZMODEM protocol to nearly *any* communications program by using Chuck Forsberg's DSZ. Fourth, with OZBEXT it lets you add support for CompuServe's B+ (Quick B) protocol to virtually any comm program. It includes programs to view RLE and GIF graphics files (popularized by CompuServe) either offline or while you are downloading them.

There are also a number of helpful utilities like BOMBSQUAD and DPROTECT to help you avoid virus-infected programs. And there's COMSTA.COM, a program to tell you how much time is required to transmit a given file at a variety of baud rates. There are even programs you can use in batch files to cause your system to log on at a particular time of day and thus save on connect time and long-distance rates.

COMM 7—TAPCIS

TAPCIS ("tap-sis") is designed to make it easy for you to deal with electronic mail and make the most of CompuServe forums. As explained in Part 8, using TAPCIS is a three-step process. First you tell it to sign on, pick up your electronic mail, and check forums you have specified for messages addressed to you. After doing so, TAPCIS signs off and thus stops the connect time meter.

Second, review the information TAPCIS has gathered and draft replies using the built-in editor. The third and final step is turning TAPCIS loose to sign on again and automatically upload your e-mail and forum message replies. TAPCIS can do lots of other things as well. The whole idea is to make using CompuServe as easy and inexpensive as possible. (There is a TAPCIS support forum on CompuServe.)

COMM 10—Compression Programs: PKZIP, LHARC, and PAK

The benefits of compression or "archiving" programs are discussed in Parts 5 and 8 of this book. They can cut the time needed to transmit a program package nearly in half. And they can be a real boon if you are bumping up against the limit of your hard disk's capacity. They even make it easier to do hard disk backups, since the compressed file occupies less space on a floppy disk or tape and requires less time to copy.

This disk contains the *complete* PKZIP, LHARC, and PAK compression packages. These enable you to compress collections of files, make the resulting file self-extracting, and otherwise manipulate things. In my opinion, all archives should be compressed with LHA (LHARC), since it is the most efficient. And all should be made self-extracting .EXE files, so the user does not need to have a particular compression program on his or her disk.

Thus, what most people need can be found on COMM 3, The Communicator's Toolchest. That disk gives you the programs needed to extract files from all the leading archives, plus the complete LHA package to let you not only extract but also create archives. If these needs fit your profile, get COMM 3 instead of this disk. But if for some reason you need the complete compression packages, you will find them here on COMM 10.

MAXIHOST—BBS Package

If you merely need to gain access to your own system from a remote location, you can use ProComm's "host" mode. When this mode is activated, ProComm sits waiting for your modem to answer an incoming call. As the owner of the system, you can set things up so that you have complete access to the computer.

If you need a more powerful BBS function, or if you want to let others call your system, I recommend MAXIHOST. MAXIHOST was written by Don Mankin specifically for consultants, attorneys, small-business owners, and others who need remote access to their own systems. The program supports up to 500 users and lots of protocols. The one drawback is the need to prepare a text file of commands to set up the system. However, the program comes with such a file, which you can easily edit to customize to your needs.

WILDCAT—BBS Package (2 Disks)

If you decide to "go public" with your BBS, then WILDCAT is the program to consider. WILDCAT is a zippy, feature-filled bulletin board system designed for anyone who really wants to become a sysop. It has thousands of loyal users and supporters. I particularly like the sysop control panel that appears when you are running the program.

Graphics Tools

Computer graphics can be a real time sink, yet few applications are as satisfying. And when you combine a graphics paint or display program with online communications, you find that the collection of images you can download, clip, manipulate, and print is nearly endless. CompuServe has multiple graphics forums, for example, each one of which has multiple, classified libraries of images people have created or scanned into their systems.

Often, the images or image collections are specifically offered as clip art that you can clip out and insert into your own productions. Some are shareware, but many are in the public domain.

The best way to proceed, in my opinion, is to download the graphics files that sound interesting. Then run Steven Rimmer's Graphic Workshop to view them on the screen. The program supports all of the most popular graphics file formats and has the power to convert from one format to another.

When you find something you like, use Desktop Paint by the same author. This program converts everything to black and white, but it gives you much of the power found in commercial packages like PC Paintbrush. (In fact, it even *looks* like PC Paintbrush.) A mouse, though not required, is essential. Yet another program from Mr. Rimmer, DTP256, is designed for color images. It is not as powerful as the black and white version and does not include as many features, but the results are really incredible.

GRAPHICS 6—Graphic Workshop

Graphic Workshop (GWS) from Steven Rimmer's Alchemy Mindworks, is designed to help IBM-compatible users deal in nearly any kind of graphics file. To use the program, you'll need one of the following graphics cards or compatibles: CGA, Hercules, EGA, VGA, Paradise Plus, Dell Super VGA, ATI VGA Wonder, ATI VGA Edge, or Headland Video 7.

But that's about all you'll need. The program comes with drivers to support most impact and laser printers. And it detects and uses expanded memory if you have it. Like the commercial program, HiJaak, Graphic Workshop lets you convert files from all the leading graphics paint or word processing programs used on IBM, Macintosh, Amiga, or other systems (files ending in .MAC, .IMG, .PCX, .GIF, .TIF, .EPS, .WPG, .MSP, .CE, .LBM, and .IFF). But unlike HiJaak, GWS lets you view the images as well. In addition, it lets you rotate, flip, reverse, and control the dither of most images.

DTP—Desktop Paint

Desktop Paint (DTP) will simply blow you away. I'm not kidding. DTP is absolutely fantastic. Using a Microsoft-compatible mouse, you can load files in the MacPaint, GEM Ventura, PC Paintbrush (.PCX), .TIF, or Word Perfect Graphics (.WPG) formats and modify them to your heart's content.

Perhaps you want to add some text? You have three typefaces to work with (Swiss, Courier, and Dutch), in sizes ranging from 6 to 36 points. (Not all typefaces are available in all sizes.) You can clip out a section of an image and re-size it. Or you can load one of the supplied images in the DTP image Gallery.

The program offers all the following paint program features: cut, spray paint, text, paintbrush, roller, erase, line drawing (three widths), and editing or painting at the pixel level. You can also set gradient and fill patterns and bring up a grid.

DTP offers more than enough power for occasional image clipping, editing, and creating. It may very well be all you need. If not, it serves as an excellent introduction to those high-priced commercial paint programs.

DTP256—Desktop Paint for Super VGA

DTP256, also by Alchemy Mindworks, is the Super VGA version of Desktop Paint. It produces 256 colors and lets you control the red/green/blue balance of each one. Think what a great time you'll have working with 256-color images!

To run DTP256, you'll need a Super VGA card with at least 256K of memory, and preferably 512K or 1MB. The package comes with the necessary software drivers for cards compatible with Western Digital/Paradise Plus or Professional, ATI VGA Wonder, Tseng Labs 3000 series, Trident 8900 series, and Headland Video 7 and 1024i.

DOS and Computing Skills

DOS commands can be obscure, to say the least. Thus, even though you really only need about ten commands to run your computer, there may be times when you need to extend your DOS knowledge. Also, it wouldn't hurt to learn to type!

EDUCATION 4—The DOS Tutor

The DOS Tutor from Computer Knowledge can help you learn DOS completely. With colors, sound, optional quizzes, and conversationally written text, it takes you from bootup through batch files, covering along the way such topics as subdirectories, DOS variables, the BIOS, and the most crucial DOS commands. This is without a doubt the best DOS tutorial program going.

EDUCATION 5—DOS Practice and DOS Summary

DOS Practice from Skill Software is not so much a tutorial as one extensive, extremely clever game of Trivial Pursuit. Like that game, it is addictive. It's designed to increase your practical knowledge, skill, and speed, whether you are a novice user or have been using personal computers for years.

DOS Practice poses questions and presents exercises relating to all facets of DOS system operation, beginning with the easiest tasks and gradually increasing the level of difficulty as your skill improves. It keeps track of your progress and in different sessions occasionally repeats tasks, with an emphasis on the questions you answered incorrectly in the past.

Categories of tasks may be excluded if you like, and both minimum and maximum levels of difficulty may be set. The program also generates progress reports to show how well you are doing.

This disk also contains DOS Summary, a nifty program from Computer Knowledge (of DOS Tutor fame). DOS Summary is a hypertext tutorial and reference program that covers all DOS commands and drivers. The program can be used in tutorial mode for learning DOS commands in either alphabetical order or by command groupings.

DOS Summary can be operated in standalone mode at the DOS prompt using either menus or command mode. You might, for example, key in `dossum xcopy` and be instantly taken to an example-filled explanation of the command and its uses. Or you might just key in `dossum` to call up the program's main menu. DOS Summary can also be loaded as a hotkey-accessible TSR for instant help, even from within some other program.

DOS Summary puts the help function built into MS-DOS 5 to shame. And, while the hypertext-like help function offered with MS-DOS 6 includes many of the same features, many users will prefer DOS Summary's explanations and TSR/pop-up capabilities.

TYPING—PC-FASTYPE

PC-FASTYPE is one neat program. It's flexible, thoroughly professional, and fun to use. You will need a color graphics card (CGA), a VGA card that supports CGA mode (most do), a Hercules monographics card, or a clone. I took typing at night school. If personal computers had been invented at the time, and if I'd had this program, I could have stayed home and still become an excellent typist.

Other Special Applications

Security is a growing concern among computer users. Anymore, it's not enough to simply lock everything in your desk before you leave for the day. Anyone who knows how to use a computer can copy, print, and even alter your files should he or she gain access to your system. And then there's electronic mail. With e-mail, you must assume that if your message *can* be read it *will* be read by someone other than your correspondent.

Text files are also of interest because that is what most computer users spend most of their time creating. There are several programs to make manipulating—and searching through—text files easier.

ENCRYPTION—PC-CODE3/4 and The Confidant

It's a good idea to encrypt anything you want to keep private or secret. Without the proper program and password, an encrypted file is useless to almost anyone outside of the National Security Agency. Indeed, PC-CODE and The Confidant can so thoroughly encrypt a text or a binary file that the cipher experts employed by that agency would have a tough time decoding the result. But if you've got the key (password), you or your e-mail correspondent can do it in an instant.

TEXT SEARCH—AnyWord, LOOKFOR, and FGREP

AnyWord by Eric Balkan has the ability to parse any text file, build its own index of keywords, and allow you to search the file using sophisticated search logic. LOOKFOR by David Trafton works even faster. It lets you do AND, OR, wildcard, and proximity searches of text files for keywords with no prior indexing. You can then print (to disk or printer) relevant file excerpts. FGREP by Chris Dunford (author of CED) operates in a similar way, though it is more UNIX-like and not quite so user friendly.

TEXT TREATERS—Utilities, Indexing, and Style

This disk contains some 45 programs to manipulate a text file in virtually any way you can imagine, including Vernon Buerg's dynamite SORTF program for sorting the contents of a file seven ways from sundown. Also on the disk is CHOP3, the Sweeney Todd of text utilities. Tell it how many pieces you want and it does the rest. You can sort, expand/add tabs, eliminate white space, and clean up WordStar, PFS, and other text files containing machine language codes. The disk also contains a package by Peter Norton to create an index for a report, document, book, or whatever. Plus two programs that will run a "grade level" on the text you give it to assess the writing style and the grade level to which educators judge it most appropriate.

SECTION
9-4

GLOSSBRENNER'S
DOS QUARTERLY

As I said at the beginning of this part, getting the *right* information is crucial to becoming a power user. That means at least three things. It means having the information in hand. It means sifting the really important, useful nuggets from the vast quantity of chaff. And it means being able to find what you need, when you need it.

One cannot be a DOS user for very long without coming to grips with the information problem. What are Microsoft's plans for the future? What bugs have been discovered in DOS and what are the workarounds, if any? What was the name of that company that claims it can cut the cost of operating a laser printer in half? What are the latest and greatest PD and shareware utilities?

Computer magazines are great, but the tips they publish never go into enough detail. Power users often want to know more. Why does it work? How does it work? And how can I quickly find the tip I need when I need it?

It was to answer these and similar power user questions that *Gloss-brenner's DOS Quarterly* (*GDQ*) was created. Every quarter, we comb the leading computer magazines and newsletters for the best DOS-related tips, tricks, bug reports, workarounds, and other useful information. Publications include *Computer Shopper, Computer Language, Dr. Dobb's, Microsoft Systems Journal, PC/Computing, PC Magazine, PC World,* "Release 1.0," *Home Office Computing, InfoWorld, Today's Office,* and many more, including quite a few user group publications.

In my opinion, many of the tips and tricks included in computer magazines are far too terse to be truly useful. So, having identified an item of interest, I rewrite it—expanding, explaining, and incorporating additional information as necessary until I'm satisfied that anyone can understand and profit from the information.

As you might imagine, I also watch the world of PD and shareware software. (The latest and greatest DOS-enhancing utilities and other programs are included on the disk.) And, of course, I monitor Microsoft's latest official pronouncements, technical bulletins, and responses to user queries via the Microsoft KnowledgeBase online database.

Figure 9-4-1 Glossbrenner's DOS Quarterly Greeting Screen

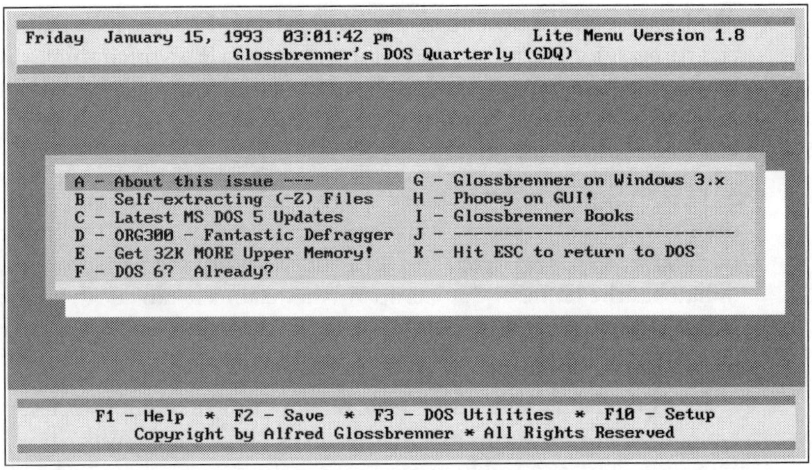

```
 Friday  January 15, 1993  03:01:42 pm              Lite Menu Version 1.8
                   Glossbrenner's DOS Quarterly (GDQ)




        A - About this issue ----       G - Glossbrenner on Windows 3.x
        B - Self-extracting (-Z) Files  H - Phooey on GUI!
        C - Latest MS DOS 5 Updates     I - Glossbrenner Books
        D - ORG300 - Fantastic Defragger J - ---------------------------
        E - Get 32K MORE Upper Memory!  K - Hit ESC to return to DOS
        F - DOS 6?  Already?




            F1 - Help  *  F2 - Save  *  F3 - DOS Utilities  *  F10 - Setup
            Copyright by Alfred Glossbrenner * All Rights Reserved
```

In short, *GDQ* keeps a practical eye on DOS. Published on disk four times a year, *GDQ* tells you what you need to know to easily become a more productive power user. It presents the *best* tips, tricks, and information about DOS and DOS-related subjects published in the preceding three months—plus the best DOS utilities. And it does so in a form that can easily be printed out and/or stored to disk for fast search and retrieval. *GDQ* puts the information you need at your fingertips. It also includes opinion, commentary, advice, and counsel.

If you are interested in becoming more comfortable and more proficient with your machine—and if you like the way subjects have been presented and explained in this book—*Glossbrenner's DOS Quarterly* may be just what you've been looking for. Published in January, April, July, and October, each issue covers the previous three months. The cost is $16 for four issues on 5.25-inch disk; $20 if you need 3.5-inch disks.

Quick Reference: Shareware Programs Discussed in Parts 1 through 8

Program Name	GBC Disk Name	Where discussed (Part # and Title)	
1TRY	Printer 1	7	Printing
ARC	Comm 3	8	Communicating
ASK	Utils 5	2	Making the Most of DOS
AUTOCON	Utils 9	1	Setting Up the System
BAT2EXEC	Utils 9	2	Making the Most of DOS
B&F	Core 10,11,12	4	Maximizing Memory
BIOSFIX	Utils 9	8	Communicating
CED	Core 1	1	Setting Up the System
		3	Turbocharged DOS
CHECKIRQ	Utils 9	8	Communicating
CHOP31	Text Treaters	3	Turbocharged DOS
CLEAN	Utils 8	5	Optimizing Your Hard Disk
CLEANUP	Utils 8	3	Turbocharged DOS
		5	Optimizing Your Hard Disk
COMFIX	Utils 9	8	Communicating
COPYIT	Utils 5	2	Making the Most of DOS
		3	Turbocharged DOS

(continued)

(continued)

Program Name	GBC Disk Name	Where discussed (Part # and Title)	
CT (CACHE TEST)	Utils 10	5	Optimizing Your Hard Disk
DIET	Utils 8	5	Optimizing Your Hard Disk
DISKID	Utils 8	3	Turbocharged DOS
DMP	Printer 1	3	Turbocharged DOS
		7	Printing
DPROTECT	Comm 3	3	Turbocharged DOS
DSZ	Comm 3	8	Communicating
EBL	Core 8	2	Making the Most of DOS
ELFRING FONTS	Laser 1	7	Printing
FAKEY	Utils 1	2	Making the Most of DOS
FANSI	Core 1,2	3	Turbocharged DOS
		6	Video/Keyboard Considerations
FF	Printer 1	7	Printing
FIFOFF	Utils 9	8	Communicating
FIFON	Utils 9	8	Communicating
FIFOSTAT	Utils 9	8	Communicating
FORMATQM	Utils 8	5	Optimizing Your Hard Disk
FREE	Utils 1	3	Turbocharged DOS
GRAB PLUS	Grab 1,2	7	Printing
GRAPHIC WORKSHOP	Graphics 6	8	Communicating
HYPERDISK	Utils 10	5	Optimizing Your Hard Disk
IMAGEPRINT	Printer 2	7	Printing
LHA (LHARC)	Comm 3,10	5	Optimizing Your Hard Disk
		8	Communicating

(continued)

(continued)

Program Name	GBC Disk Name	Where discussed (Part # and Title)	
LIST	Core 1	2	Making the Most of DOS
		3	Turbocharged DOS
		5	Optimizing Your Hard Disk
		8	Communicating
LOOKFOR	Text Search	3	Turbocharged DOS
		5	Optimizing Your Hard Disk
LQ	Printer 2	7	Printing
MAIL MACHINE	Mail Machine	7	Printing
MARK/RELEASE	Utils 2	1	Setting Up the System
		4	Maximizing Memory
MV	Utils 1	3	Turbocharged DOS
NEWKEY	Core 5	1	Setting Up the System
		3	Turbocharged DOS
		6	Video/Keyboard Considerations
NO	Utils 1	3	Turbocharged DOS
NUMBFILES	Utils 9	4	Maximizing Memory
NUMOFF	Core 1	1	Setting Up the System
ONBOOT	Utils 1	1	Setting Up the System
ONSIDE	Printer 4	7	Printing
ORG	Utils 8	5	Optimizing Your Hard Disk
OZBEXT	Comm 3	8	Communicating
PAK	Comm 3,10	8	Communicating
PC-FASTYPE	Typing	6	Video/Keyboard Considerations
PKZIP	Comm 3,10	5	Optimizing Your Hard Disk
		8	Communicating

(continued)

(continued)

Program Name	GBC Disk Name	Where discussed (Part # and Title)	
POPDOS	Utils 9	1	Setting Up the System
PROCOMM	Comm 1,2	8	Communicating
PRTSCR-LJ	Printer 1	3	Turbocharged DOS
QDR	Utils 1	3	Turbocharged DOS
		5	Optimizing Your Hard Disk
QFILER	Core 4	3	Turbocharged DOS
		5	Optimizing Your Hard Disk
		8	Communicating
QFONT	Laser 3	7	Printing
QUIKMENU	QuikMenu	3	Turbocharged DOS
REBEEP	Utils 1	2	Turbocharged DOS
REBOOT	Utils 1	1	Setting Up the System
RENDIR	Utils 1	3	Turbocharged DOS
SORTF	Text Treaters	3	Turbocharged DOS
STP	Laser 3	7	Printing
TAPCIS	Comm 7	8	Communicating
TSR DOWNLOAD	Laser 2	7	Printing
TUNE	Utils 1	2	Making the Most of DOS
UARTID	Utils 9	8	Communicating
UARTTOOLS	Utils 9	8	Communicating
UMBFILES	Utils 9	4	Maximizing Memory
WAIT/WAITUNTL	Utils 1	2	Making the Most of DOS
WHEREIS	Utils 1	3	Turbocharged DOS
XPATH	Utils 9	1	Setting Up the System

SECTION

9-5

DISK ORDER FORM

You can use the order form on the next page (or a photocopy) to order the Power DOS Toolkit, other Glossbrenner's Choice disks, and subscriptions to *Glossbrenner's DOS Quarterly*. We accept Visa and MasterCard, as well as checks or money orders made payable to Glossbrenner's Choice. (U.S. funds drawn on a U.S. bank or international money orders only, please.) Please allow one to two weeks for delivery. Mail your order to:

Glossbrenner's Choice
699 River Road
Yardley, PA 19067-1965

Glossbrenner's Choice Order Form for Readers of *Power DOS!*

Name _____

Address _____

City _____ State _____ ZIP _____

Phone _____

Payment [ ] Check or money order payable to Glossbrenner's Choice.
         [ ] Visa/MasterCard # _____ Exp __ /__

Signature _____

Mail to: Glossbrenner's Choice
         699 River Road
         Yardley, PA 19067-1965

Quantity   ORDER SUMMARY   Price

Power DOS Toolkit

Includes 10 disks from the Glossbrenner's Choice Collection which should
  be in *every* Power User's toolkit, at a 50% savings:

CORE 1 - FANSI, CED, LIST   UTILS 1 - Quick Shots
CORE 2 - FANSI Documentation UTILS 2 - Larger Programs I
CORE 4 - QFILER   UTILS 8 - Disk Maintenance Tools
CORE 5 - Newkey   UTILS 9 - System Configuration Tools
PRINTER 1 - Printer Utilities   UTILS 10 - HyperDisk Disk Cache

_____ 10-disk set in 5.25-inch format ($25)   _____
_____ 10-disk set in 3.5-inch format ($30)   _____

QuikMenu Special Offer

_____ 5.25-inch format ($2 per disk)   _____
_____ 3.5-inch format ($3 per disk)   _____

Individual Disks from Glossbrenner's Choice Collection

(Check off names of the disks you want on the back of this form.)

_____ 5.25-inch format ($5 per disk)   _____
_____ 3.5-inch format ($6 per disk)   _____

Subscription to Glossbrenner's DOS Quarterly

_____ Four issues, 5.25-inch format ($16)   _____
_____ Four issues, 3.5-inch format ($20)   _____

                                        TOTAL _____

Pennsylvania residents, please add 6% Sales Tax.   _____
Shipping Charge ($3.00 for shipment to U.S. addresses
  and $5.00 for shipment outside the U.S.)   _____

                  GRAND TOTAL ENCLOSED _____

Glossbrenner's Choice Disks

Please check the disks you want and record the total in the space provided on the reverse side of this form. Disks marked with an asterisk (*) may be ordered individually or as part of the Power DOS Toolkit.

The Core Collection:

_____	CORE 1*	FANSI Program, CED, and LIST
_____	CORE 2*	FANSI Documentation, PC-DeskTeam, and PC-Window
_____	CORE 4*	QFILER and Associates
_____	CORE 5*	Newkey
_____	CORE 8	Extended Batch Language-PLUS (EBL)
_____	CORE 10	Back & Forth Professional (B&F), 1 of 3
_____	CORE 11	Back & Forth Professional (B&F), 2 of 3
_____	CORE 12	Back & Forth Professional (B&F), 3 of 3

Utilities and System Tweakers:

_____	UTILS 1*	Quick Shots
_____	UTILS 2*	Larger Programs I
_____	UTILS 5	Larger Programs II
_____	UTILS 7	Laptop Solutions
_____	UTILS 8*	Disk Maintenance Tools
_____	UTILS 9*	System Configuration Tools
_____	UTILS 10*	HyperDisk Disk Cache

Printer Productivity:

_____	GRAB 1	Grab Plus Program Disk
_____	GRAB 2	Grab Plus Add-Ons
_____	LASER 1	Elfring Fonts, CHART, and KEYCHART
_____	LASER 2	TSR Download, Jet Pilot, Quicksoft Font Selector
_____	LASER 3	QFONT, Fontloader, STP (Save a Tree Printer)
_____	MAIL MACHINE	Mail Machine labeling/mailing program
_____	PRINTER 1*	Printer Utilities
_____	PRINTER 2	LQ and Image Print (dot matrix)
_____	PRINTER 4	On-Side (sideways printing for dot matrix)

Communications and Bulletin Boards:

_____	COMM 1	ProComm 2.4.3
_____	COMM 2	ProComm 2.4.3 Utilities
_____	COMM 3	Communicator's Toolchest
_____	COMM 7	TAPCIS
_____	COMM 10	Compression Programs (PKZIP, LHARC, PAK)
_____	MAXIHOST	Maxihost Bulletin Board System
_____	WILDCAT 1	Wildcat Bulletin Board System, 1 of 2
_____	WILDCAT 2	Wildcat Bulletin Board System, 2 of 2

Graphics:

_____	GRAPHICS 6	Graphic Workshop
_____	DTP	Desktop Paint
_____	DTP256	Desktop Paint for Super VGA

DOS and Computing Skills:

_____	ED 4	DOS Tutor
_____	ED 5	DOS Practice and DOS Summary
_____	TYPING 1	PC-Fastype

Other Special Applications:

_____	ENCRYPTION	PC-Code and The Confidant
_____	TEXT SEARCH	AnyWord, LOOKFOR, FGREP
_____	TEXT TREATERS	Utilities, Indexing, and Style

GLOSSBRENNER'S CHOICE GUARANTEE: If any disks disks you order from us prove to be defective, we will replace them free of charge. Simply mail the disk(s) to Glossbrenner's Choice, 699 River Road, Yardley, PA 19067.

INDEX

423